THE FUSE

VOL 3 · PERIHELION

WRITER · ANTONY JOHNSTON

ARTIST · JUSTIN GREENWOOD

COLORIST · SHARI CHANKHAMMA

LETTERER · RYAN FERRIER

image

fusecomic.com

FUSE CREATED BY JOHNSTON & GREENWOOD

IMAGE COMICS, INC.
Robert Kirkman – Chief Operating Officer
Erik Larsen – Chief Financial Officer
Todd McFarlane – President
Marc Silvestri – Chief Executive Officer
Jim Valentino – Vice-President

Eric Stephenson – Publisher
Corey Murphy – Director of Sales
Jeff Boison – Director of Publishing Planning & Book Trade Sales
Jeremy Sullivan – Director of Digital Sales
Kat Salazar – Director of PR & Marketing
Emily Miller – Director of Operations
Branwyn Bigglestone – Senior Accounts Manager
Sarah Mello – Accounts Manager
Drew Gill – Art Director
Jonathan Chan – Production Manager
Meredith Wallace – Print Manager
Briah Skelly – Publicity Assistant
Sasha Head – Sales & Marketing Production Designer
Randy Okamura – Digital Production Designer
David Brothers – Branding Manager
Ally Power – Content Manager
Addison Duke – Production Artist
Vincent Kukua – Production Artist
Tricia Ramos – Production Artist
Jeff Stang – Direct Market Sales Representative
Emilio Bautista – Digital Sales Associate
Leanna Caunter – Accounting Assistant
Chloe Ramos-Peterson – Administrative Assistant
IMAGECOMICS.COM

THE FUSE VOL 3: PERIHELION. First printing. May 2016.

ISBN: 978-1-63215-657-0. Contains material originally published in magazine form as THE FUSE #13-18.

Published by Image Comics, Inc. Office of publication: 2001 Center Street, 6th Floor, Berkeley, CA 94704.

THE FUSE™

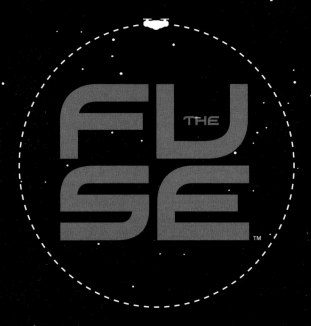

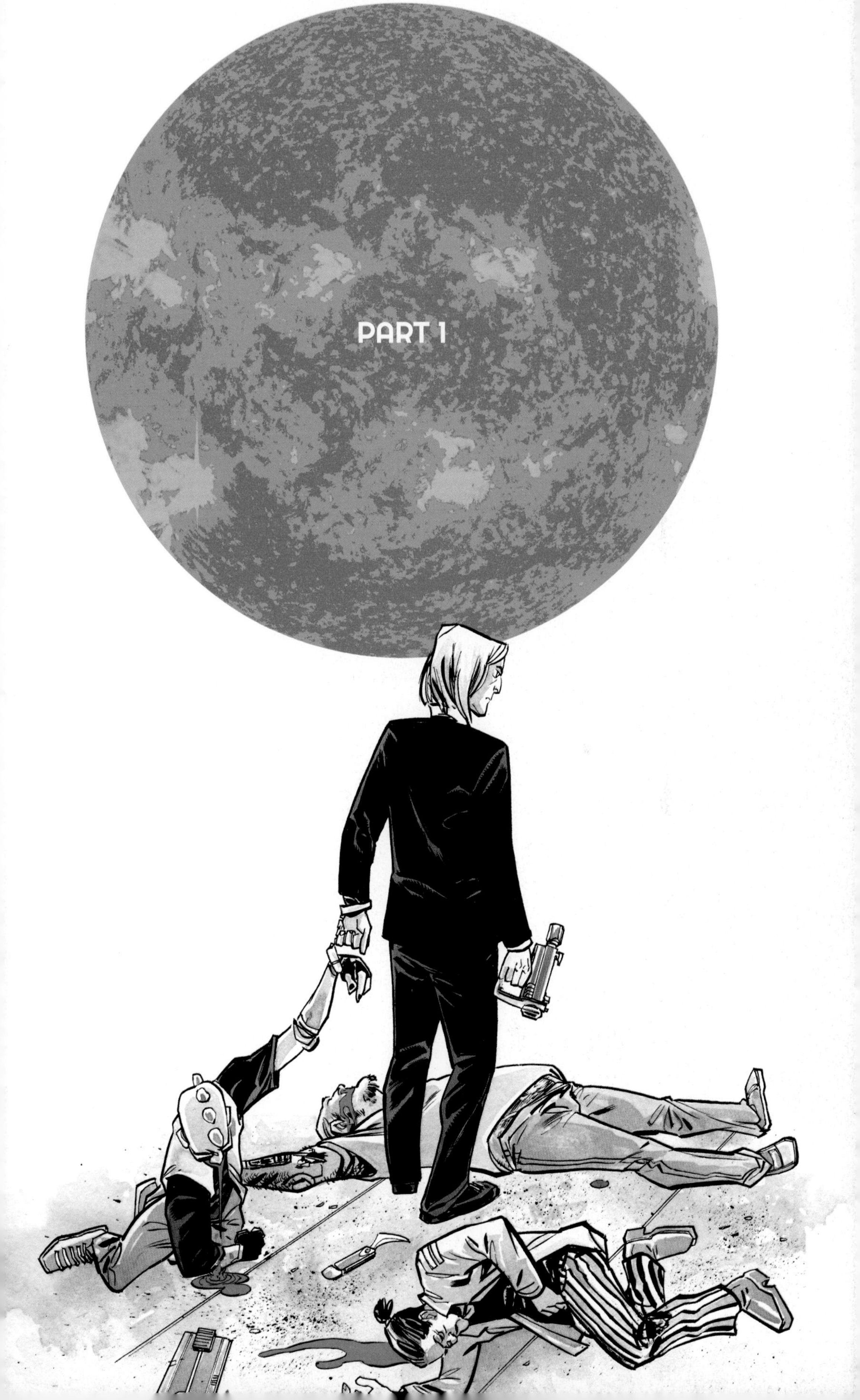
PART 1

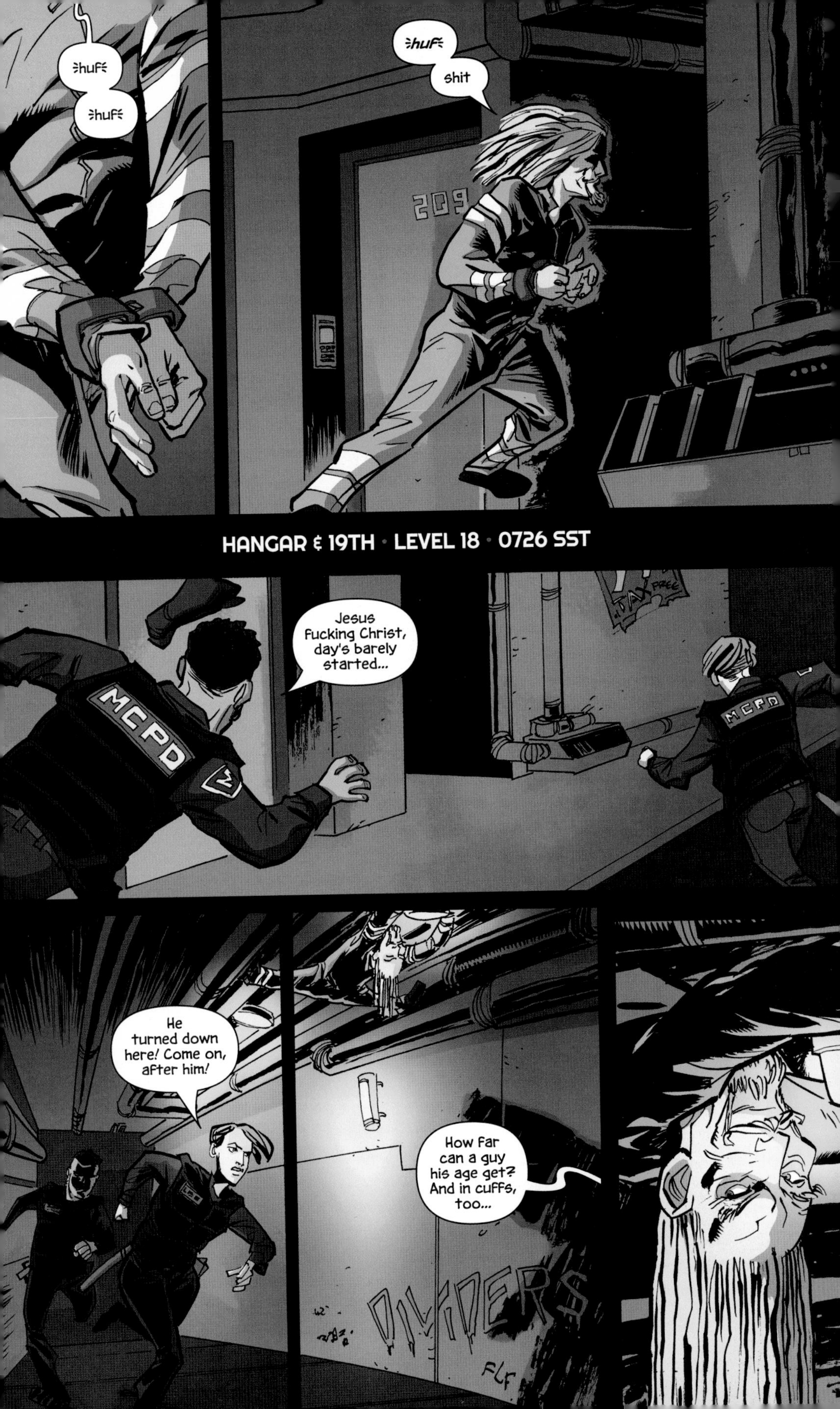

huf
huf
huf
shit
HANGAR & 19TH • LEVEL 18 • 0726 SST
Jesus Fucking Christ, day's barely started...
He turned down here! Come on, after him!
How far can a guy his age get? And in cuffs, too...
DIVIDERS

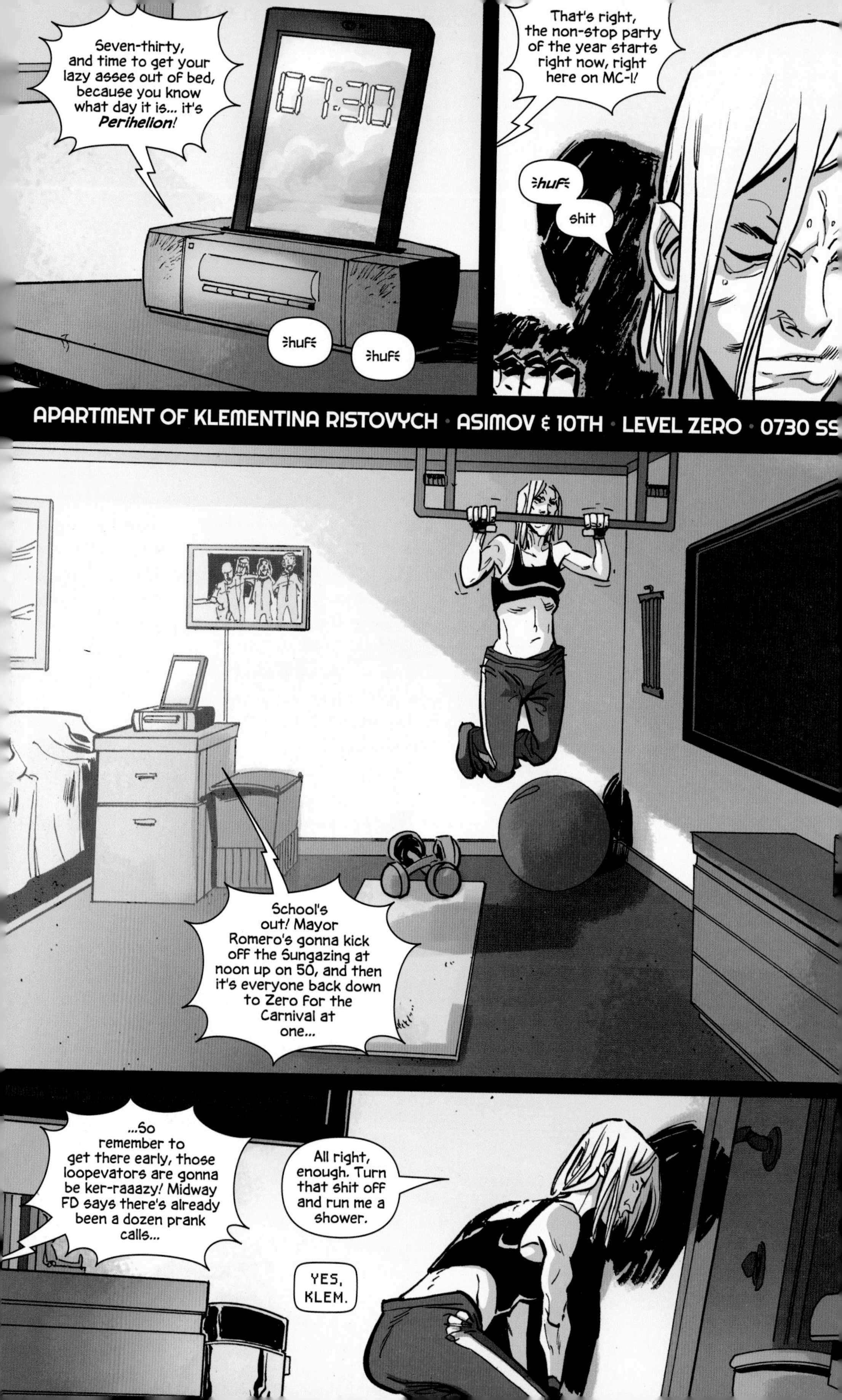

Seven-thirty, and time to get your lazy asses out of bed, because you know what day it is... it's *Perihelion*!
07:30
huf
huf
That's right, the non-stop party of the year starts right now, right here on MC-1!
huf
shit
APARTMENT OF KLEMENTINA RISTOVYCH • ASIMOV & 10TH • LEVEL ZERO • 0730 SS
School's out! Mayor Romero's gonna kick off the Sungazing at noon up on 50, and then it's everyone back down to Zero for the Carnival at one...
...So remember to get there early, those loopevators are gonna be ker-raaazy! Midway FD says there's already been a dozen prank calls...
All right, enough. Turn that shit off and run me a shower.
YES, KLEM.

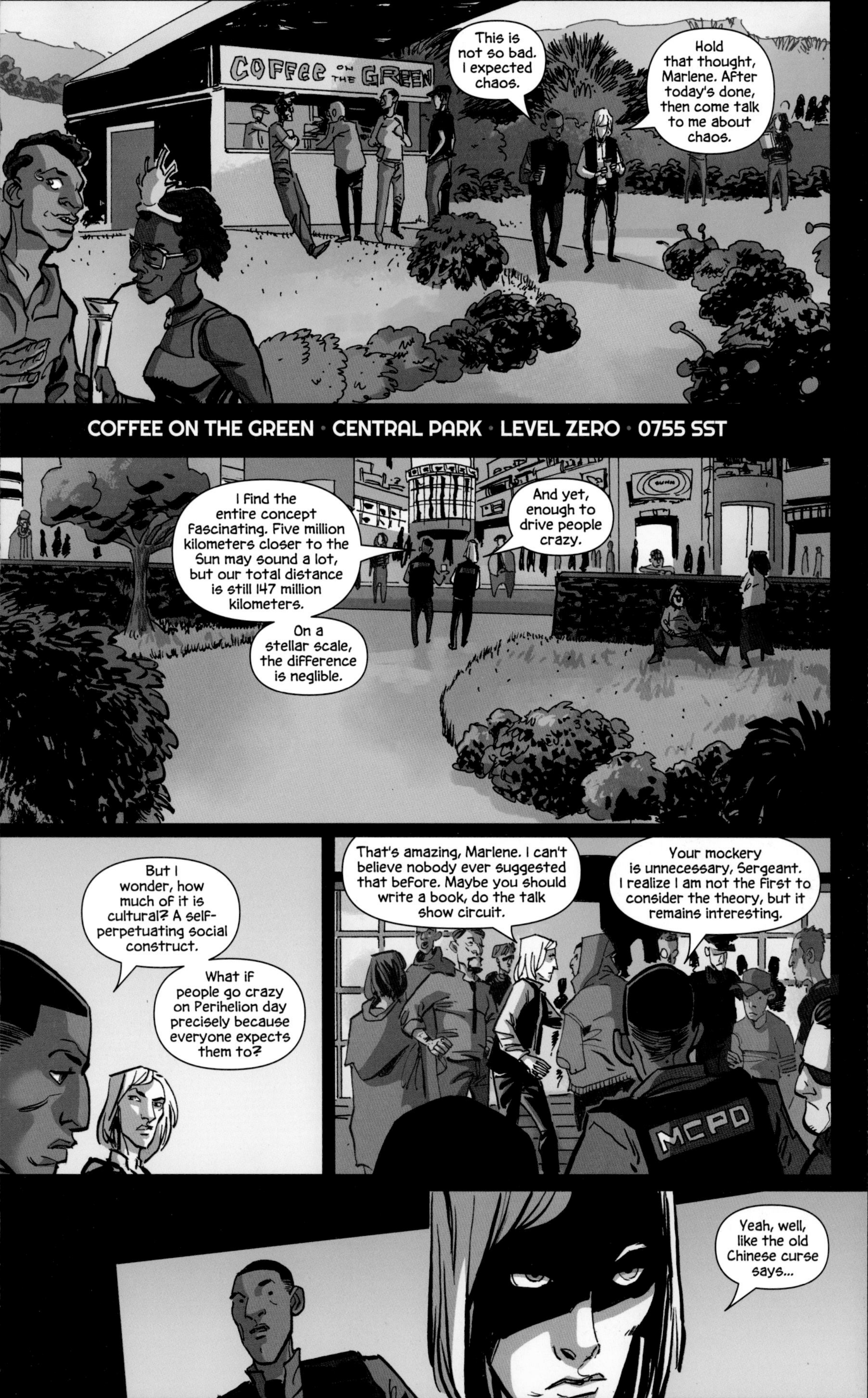
COFFEE ON THE GREEN
This is not so bad. I expected chaos.
Hold that thought, Marlene. After today's done, then come talk to me about chaos.
COFFEE ON THE GREEN • CENTRAL PARK • LEVEL ZERO • 0755 SST
I find the entire concept fascinating. Five million kilometers closer to the Sun may sound a lot, but our total distance is still 147 million kilometers.
On a stellar scale, the difference is neglible.
And yet, enough to drive people crazy.
But I wonder, how much of it is cultural? A self-perpetuating social construct.
What if people go crazy on Perihelion day precisely because everyone expects them to?
That's amazing, Marlene. I can't believe nobody ever suggested that before. Maybe you should write a book, do the talk show circuit.
Your mockery is unnecessary, Sergeant. I realize I am not the first to consider the theory, but it remains interesting.
MCPD
Yeah, well, like the old Chinese curse says...

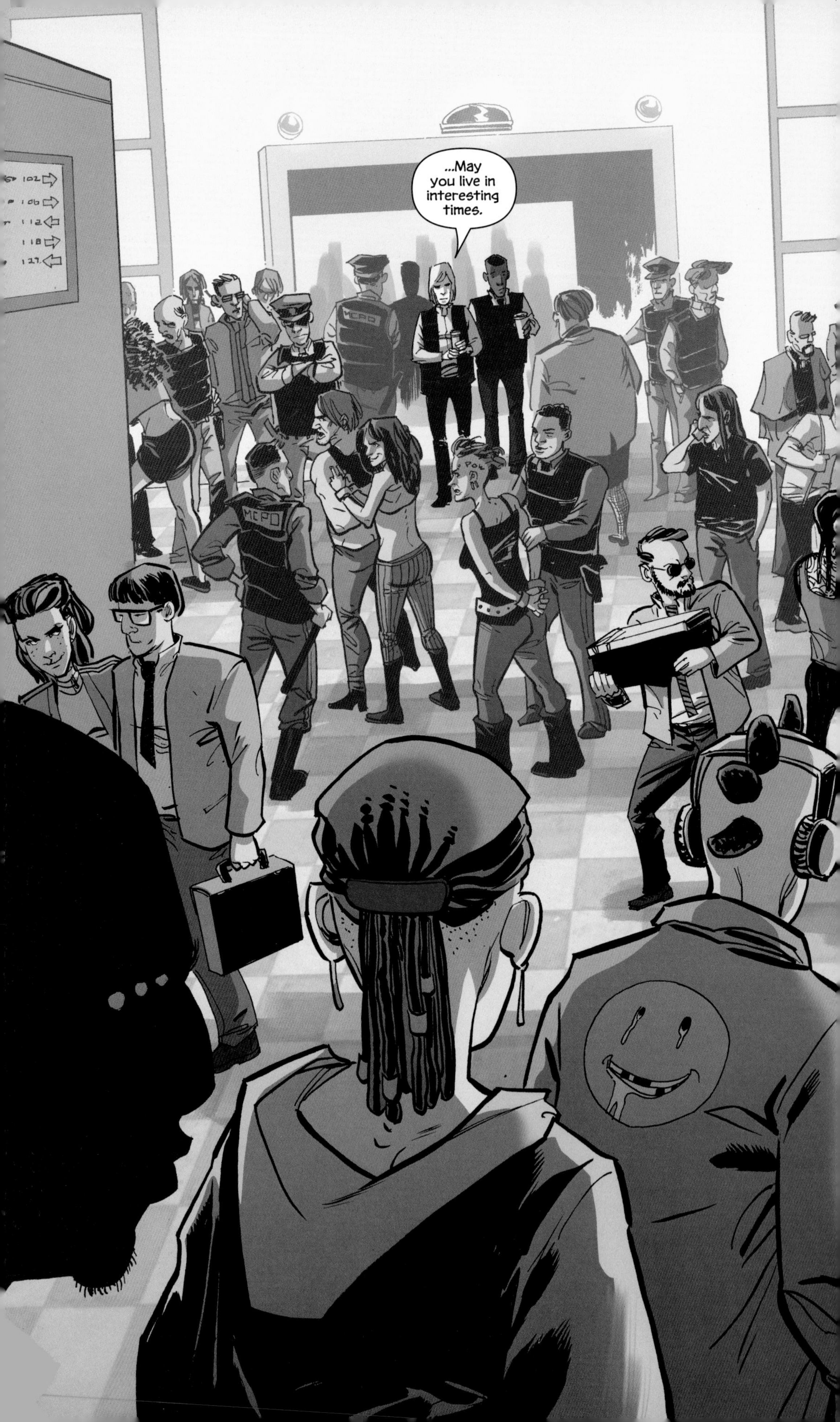

...May you live in interesting times.

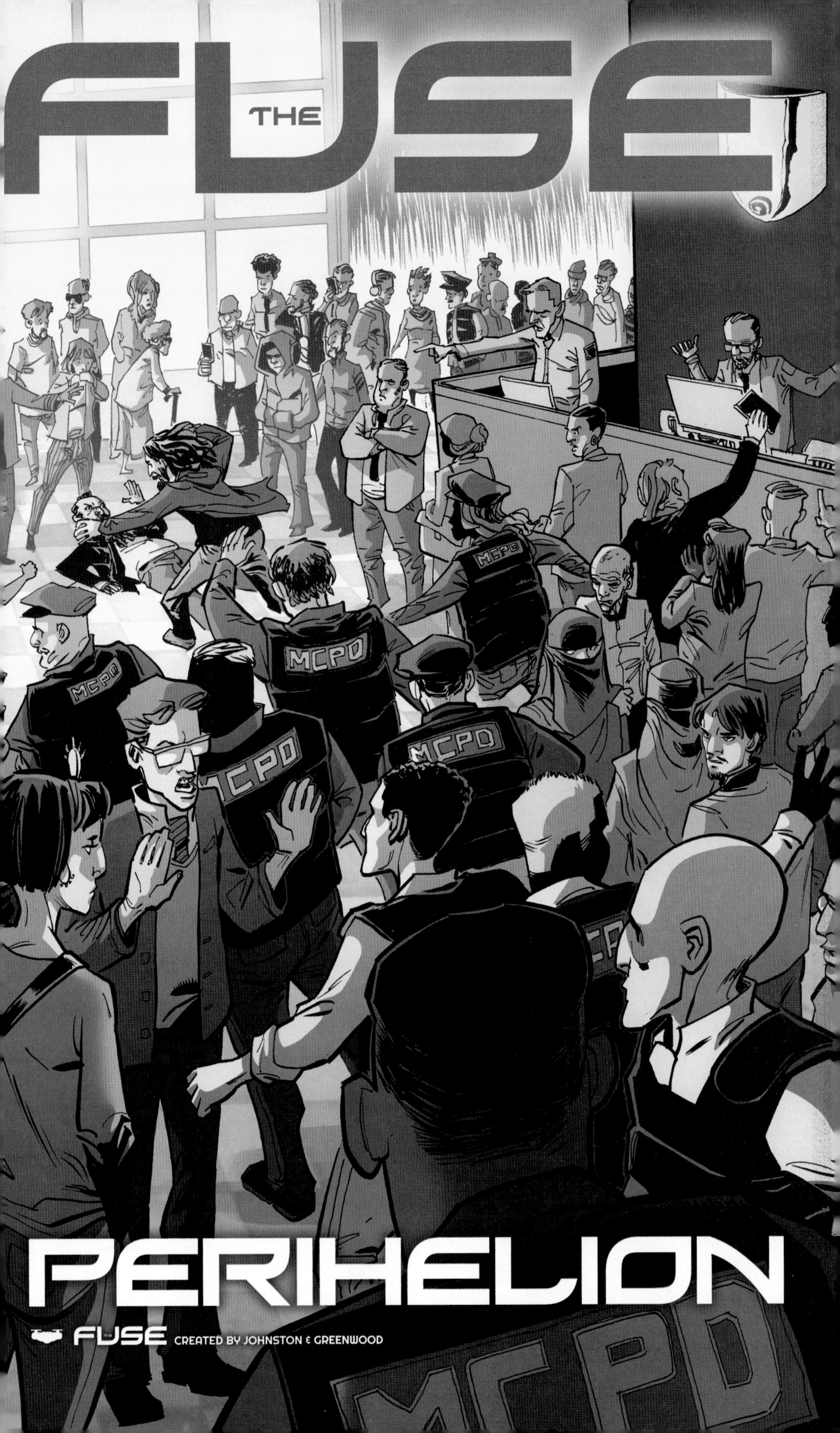
THE FUSE
MCPD
MCPD
MCPD
MCPD
MCPD
PERIHELION
FUSE CREATED BY JOHNSTON & GREENWOOD
MCPD

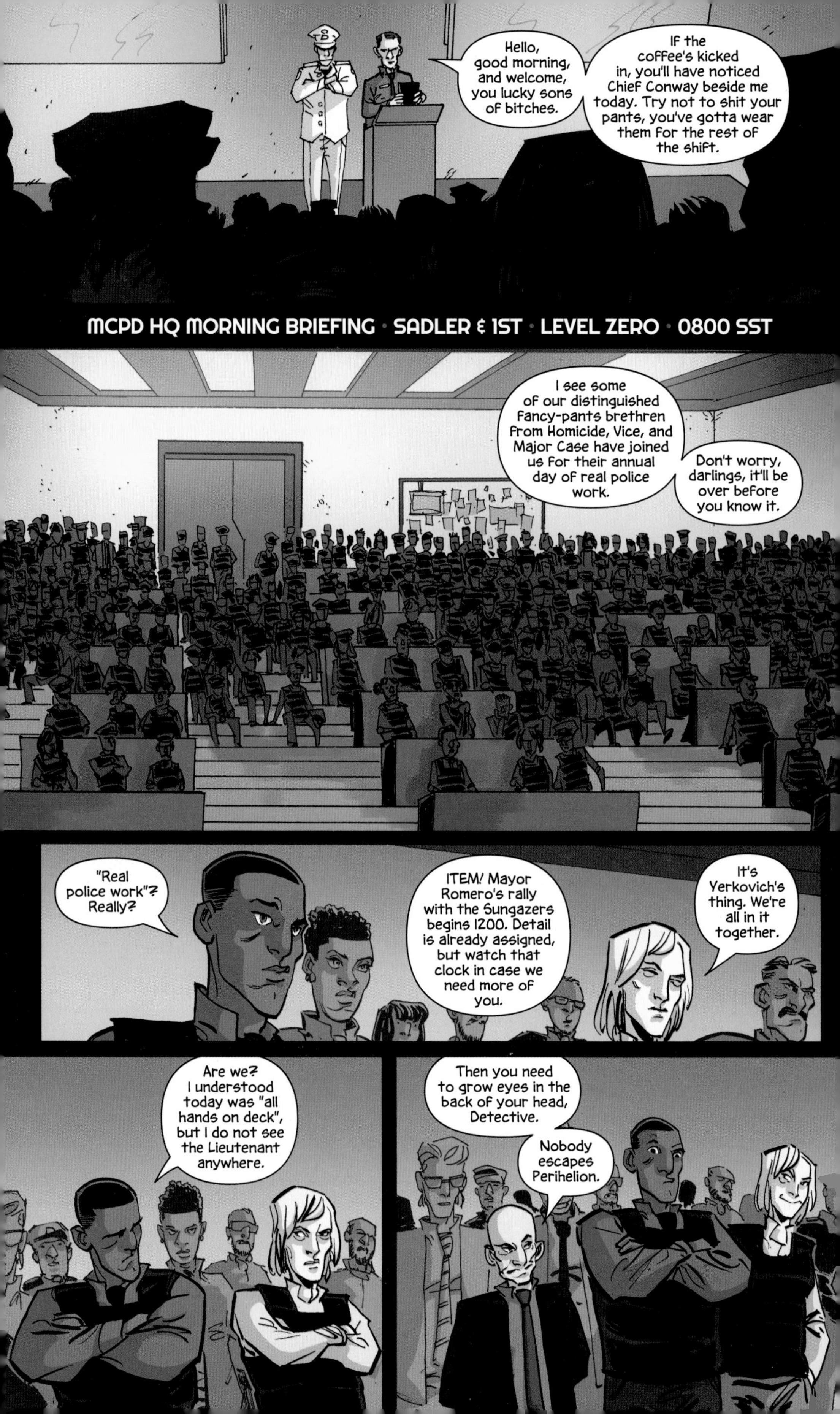
Hello, good morning, and welcome, you lucky sons of bitches.
If the coffee's kicked in, you'll have noticed Chief Conway beside me today. Try not to shit your pants, you've gotta wear them for the rest of the shift.
MCPD HQ MORNING BRIEFING · SADLER & 1ST · LEVEL ZERO · 0800 SST
I see some of our distinguished fancy-pants brethren from Homicide, Vice, and Major Case have joined us for their annual day of real police work.
Don't worry, darlings, it'll be over before you know it.
"Real police work"? Really?
ITEM! Mayor Romero's rally with the Sungazers begins 1200. Detail is already assigned, but watch that clock in case we need more of you.
It's Yerkovich's thing. We're all in it together.
Are we? I understood today was "all hands on deck", but I do not see the Lieutenant anywhere.
Then you need to grow eyes in the back of your head, Detective.
Nobody escapes Perihelion.

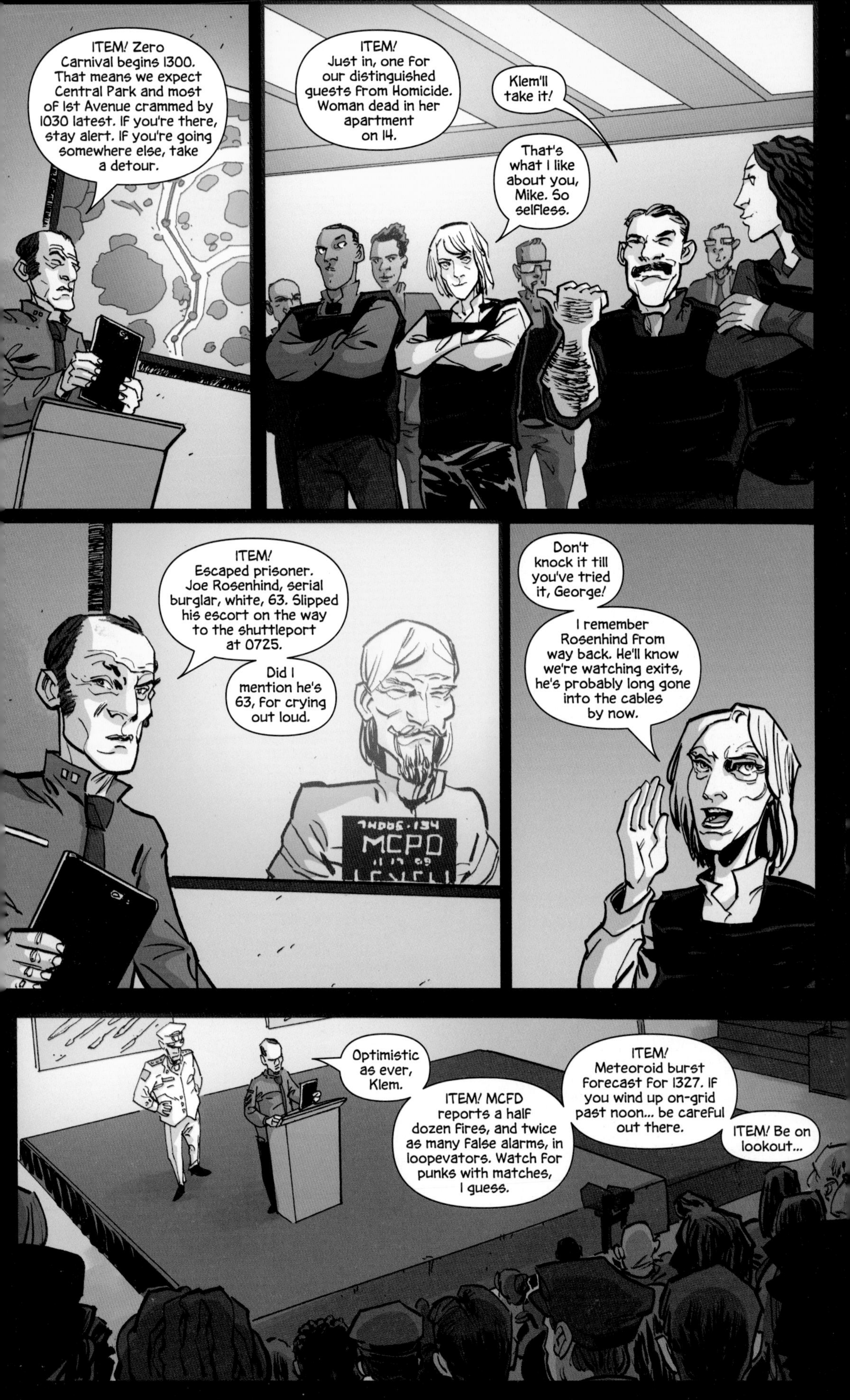
ITEM! Zero Carnival begins 1300. That means we expect Central Park and most of 1st Avenue crammed by 1030 latest. If you're there, stay alert. If you're going somewhere else, take a detour.
ITEM! Just in, one for our distinguished guests from Homicide. Woman dead in her apartment on 14.
Klem'll take it!
That's what I like about you, Mike. So selfless.
ITEM! Escaped prisoner. Joe Rosenhind, serial burglar, white, 63. Slipped his escort on the way to the shuttleport at 0725.
Did I mention he's 63, for crying out loud.
MCPO
Don't knock it till you've tried it, George!
I remember Rosenhind from way back. He'll know we're watching exits, he's probably long gone into the cables by now.
Optimistic as ever, Klem.
ITEM! MCFD reports a half dozen fires, and twice as many false alarms, in loopevators. Watch for punks with matches, I guess.
ITEM! Meteoroid burst forecast for 1327. If you wind up on-grid past noon... be careful out there.
ITEM! Be on lookout...

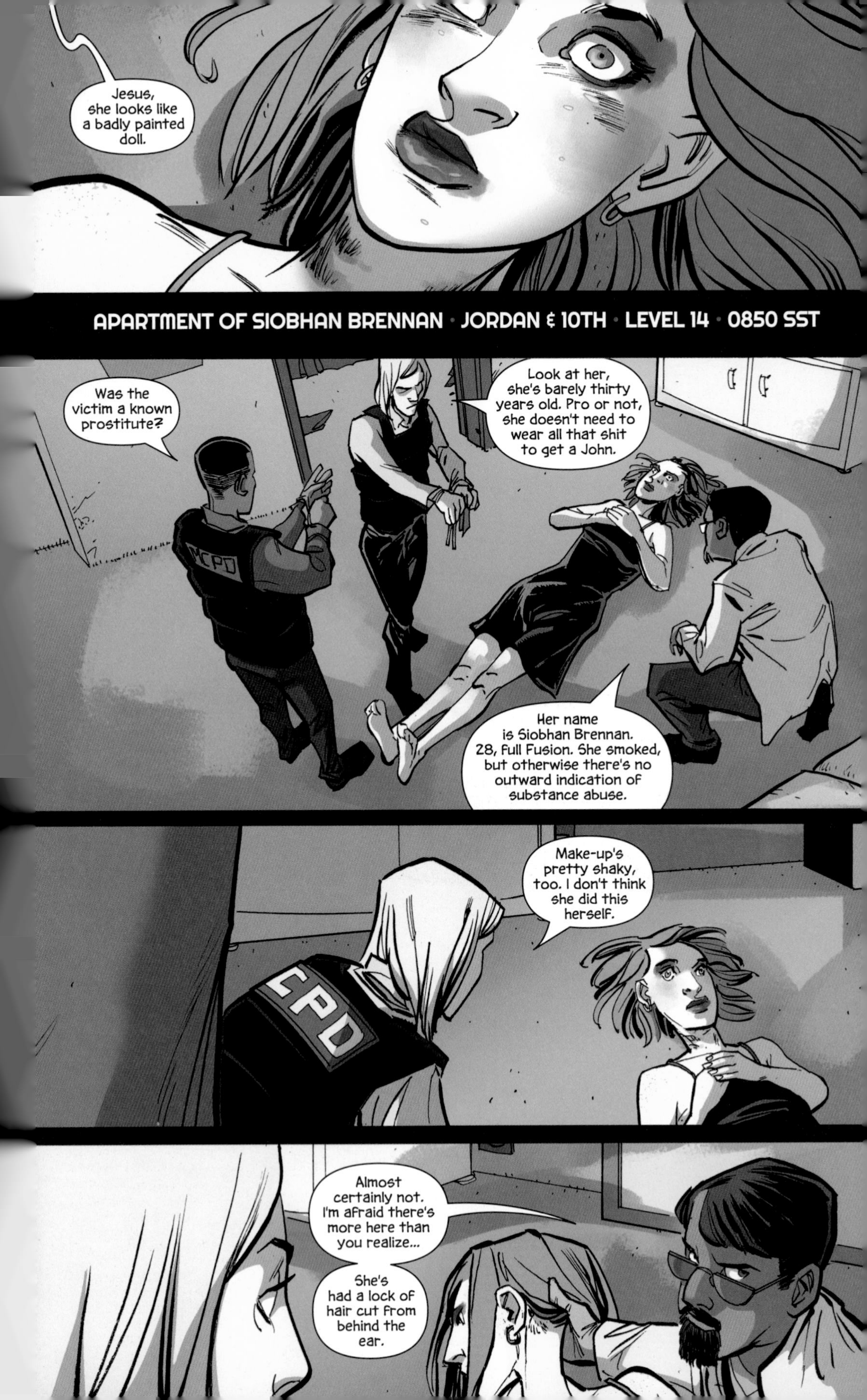
Jesus, she looks like a badly painted doll.
APARTMENT OF SIOBHAN BRENNAN · JORDAN & 10TH · LEVEL 14 · 0850 SST
Was the victim a known prostitute?
Look at her, she's barely thirty years old. Pro or not, she doesn't need to wear all that shit to get a John.
MCPD
Her name is Siobhan Brennan. 28, full Fusion. She smoked, but otherwise there's no outward indication of substance abuse.
Make-up's pretty shaky, too. I don't think she did this herself.
CPD
Almost certainly not. I'm afraid there's more here than you realize...
She's had a lock of hair cut from behind the ear.

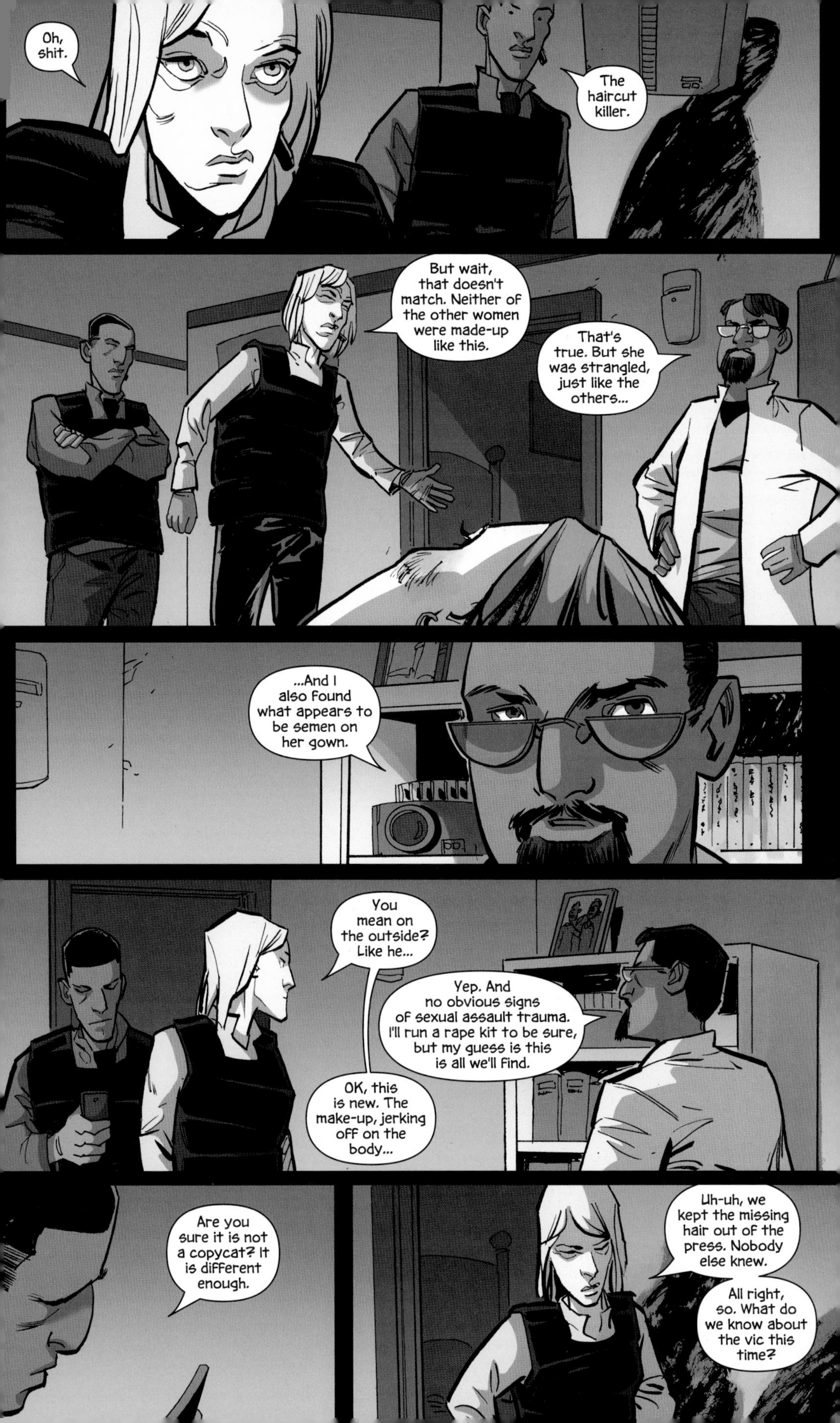
Oh, shit.
The haircut killer.
But wait, that doesn't match. Neither of the other women were made-up like this.
That's true. But she was strangled, just like the others...
...And I also found what appears to be semen on her gown.
You mean on the outside? Like he...
Yep. And no obvious signs of sexual assault trauma. I'll run a rape kit to be sure, but my guess is this is all we'll find.
OK, this is new. The make-up, jerking off on the body...
Are you sure it is not a copycat? It is different enough.
Uh-uh, we kept the missing hair out of the press. Nobody else knew.
All right, so. What do we know about the vic this time?

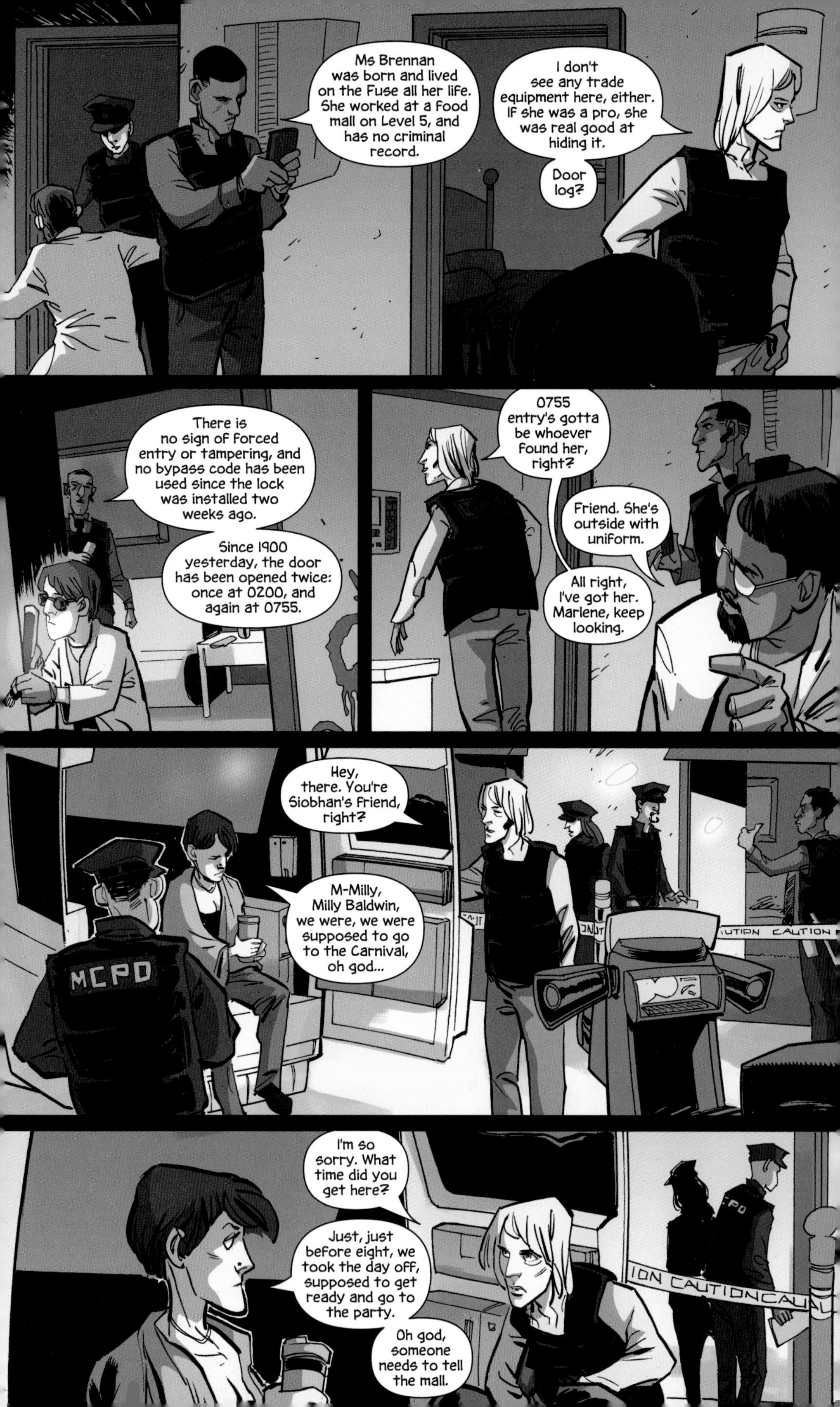
Ms Brennan was born and lived on the Fuse all her life. She worked at a food mall on Level 5, and has no criminal record.
I don't see any trade equipment here, either. If she was a pro, she was real good at hiding it.
Door log?
There is no sign of forced entry or tampering, and no bypass code has been used since the lock was installed two weeks ago.
Since 1900 yesterday, the door has been opened twice: once at 0200, and again at 0755.
0755 entry's gotta be whoever found her, right?
Friend. She's outside with uniform.
All right, I've got her. Marlene, keep looking.
Hey, there. You're Siobhan's friend, right?
M-Milly, Milly Baldwin, we were, we were supposed to go to the Carnival, oh god...
MCPD
CAUTION CAUTION
I'm so sorry. What time did you get here?
Just, just before eight, we took the day off, supposed to get ready and go to the party.
Oh god, someone needs to tell the mall.

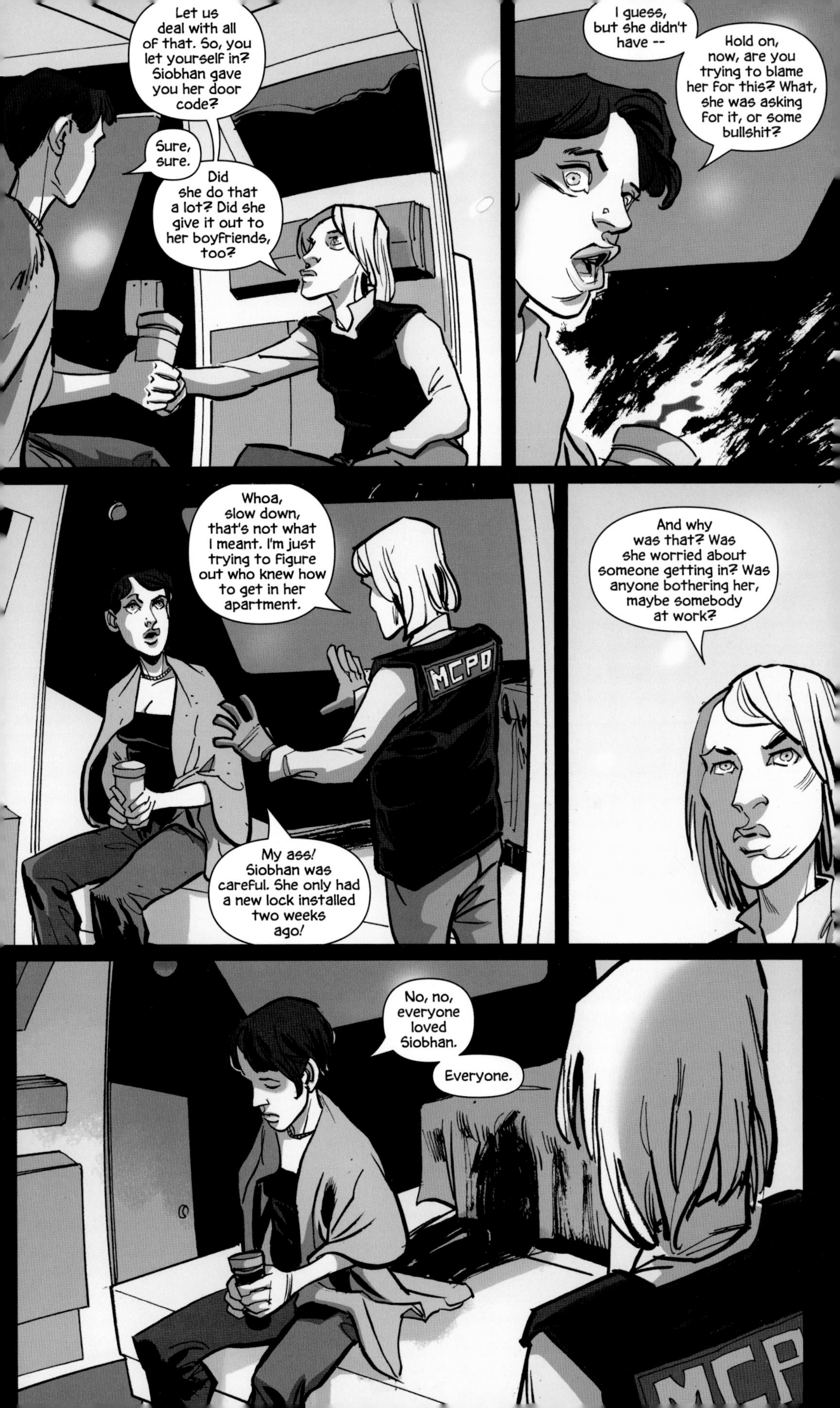
Let us deal with all of that. So, you let yourself in? Siobhan gave you her door code?
Sure, sure.
Did she do that a lot? Did she give it out to her boyfriends, too?
I guess, but she didn't have --
Hold on, now, are you trying to blame her for this? What, she was asking for it, or some bullshit?
Whoa, slow down, that's not what I meant. I'm just trying to figure out who knew how to get in her apartment.
My ass! Siobhan was careful. She only had a new lock installed two weeks ago!
MCPD
And why was that? Was she worried about someone getting in? Was anyone bothering her, maybe somebody at work?
No, no, everyone loved Siobhan.
Everyone.

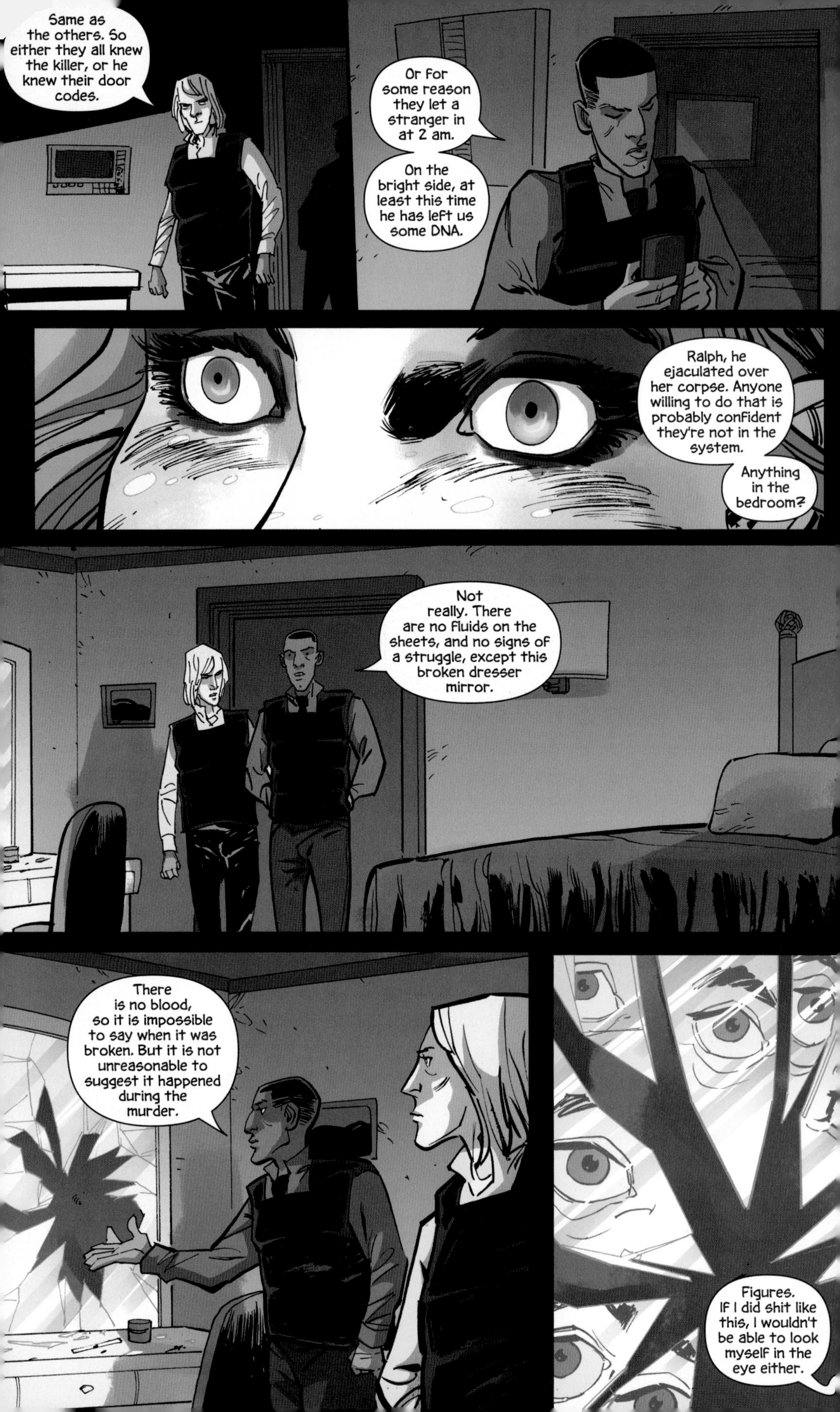
Same as the others. So either they all knew the killer, or he knew their door codes.
Or for some reason they let a stranger in at 2 am.
On the bright side, at least this time he has left us some DNA.
Ralph, he ejaculated over her corpse. Anyone willing to do that is probably confident they're not in the system.
Anything in the bedroom?
Not really. There are no fluids on the sheets, and no signs of a struggle, except this broken dresser mirror.
There is no blood, so it is impossible to say when it was broken. But it is not unreasonable to suggest it happened during the murder.
Figures. If I did shit like this, I wouldn't be able to look myself in the eye either.

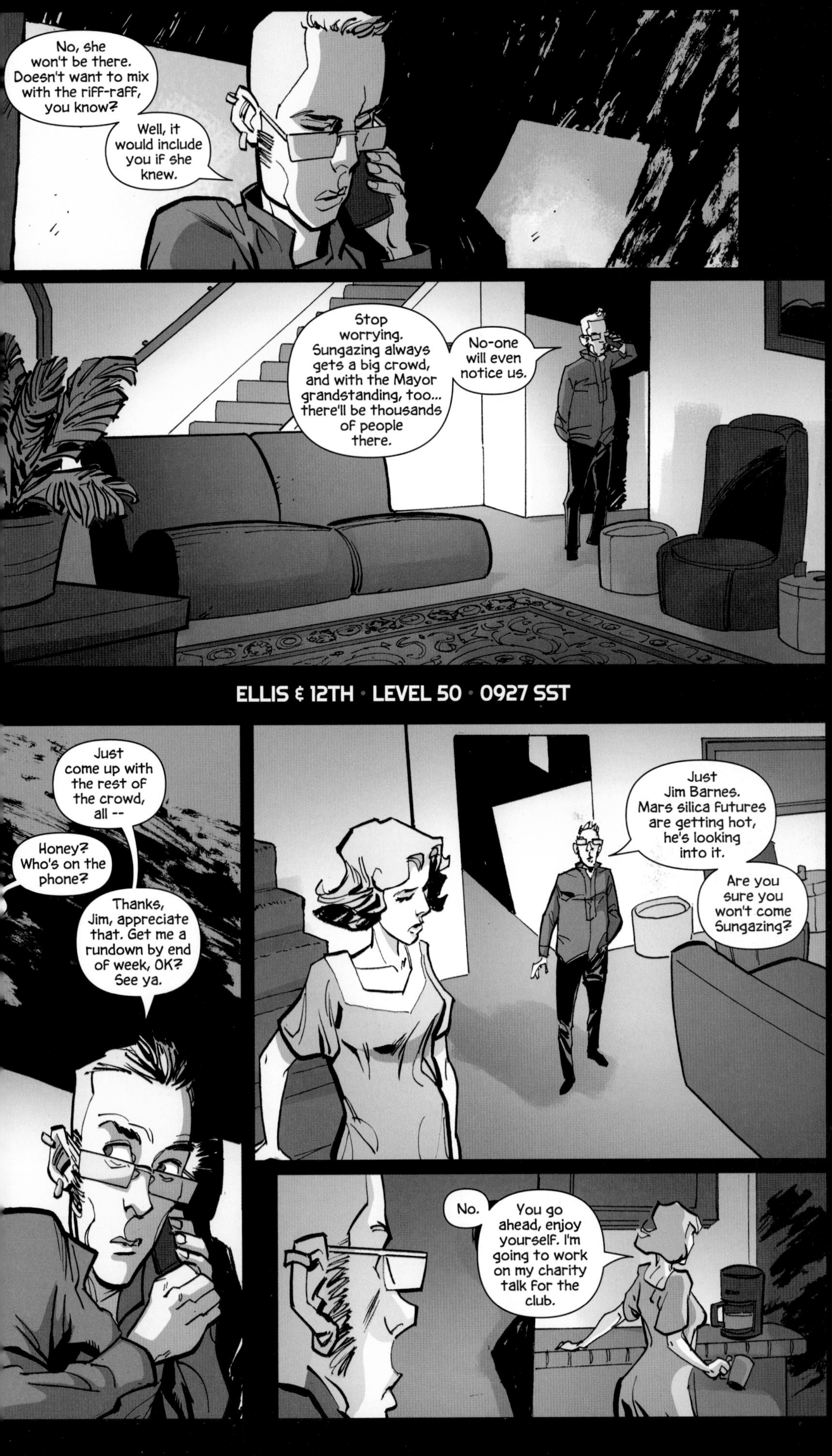
No, she won't be there. Doesn't want to mix with the riff-raff, you know?
Well, it would include you if she knew.
Stop worrying. Sungazing always gets a big crowd, and with the Mayor grandstanding, too... there'll be thousands of people there.
No-one will even notice us.
ELLIS & 12TH • LEVEL 50 • 0927 SST
Just come up with the rest of the crowd, all --
Honey? Who's on the phone?
Thanks, Jim, appreciate that. Get me a rundown by end of week, OK? See ya.
Just Jim Barnes. Mars silica futures are getting hot, he's looking into it.
Are you sure you won't come Sungazing?
No.
You go ahead, enjoy yourself. I'm going to work on my charity talk for the club.

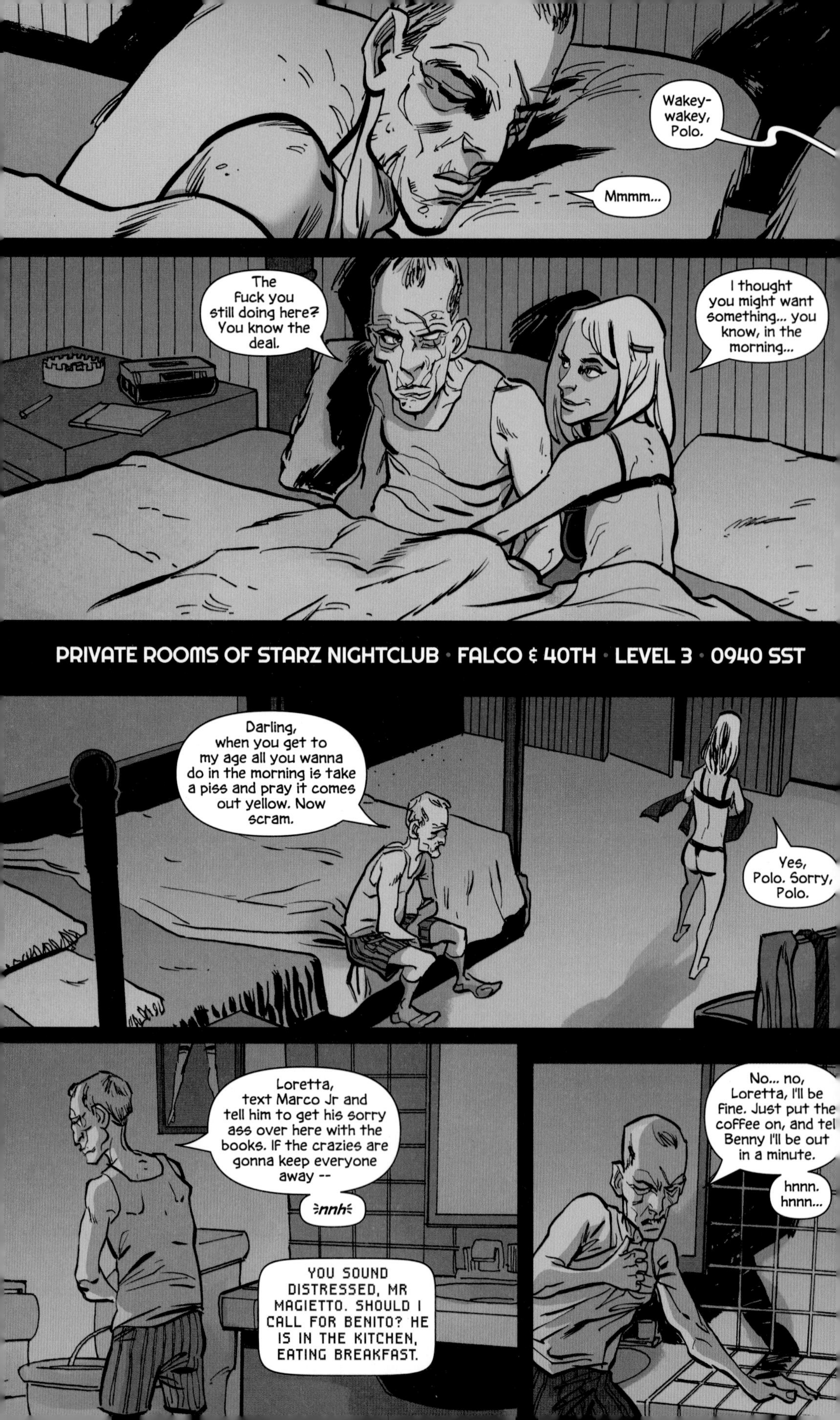
Wakey-wakey, Polo.
Mmmm...
The fuck you still doing here? You know the deal.
I thought you might want something... you know, in the morning...
PRIVATE ROOMS OF STARZ NIGHTCLUB · FALCO & 40TH · LEVEL 3 · 0940 SST
Darling, when you get to my age all you wanna do in the morning is take a piss and pray it comes out yellow. Now scram.
Yes, Polo. Sorry, Polo.
Loretta, text Marco Jr and tell him to get his sorry ass over here with the books. If the crazies are gonna keep everyone away --
nnh
YOU SOUND DISTRESSED, MR MAGIETTO. SHOULD I CALL FOR BENITO? HE IS IN THE KITCHEN, EATING BREAKFAST.
No... no, Loretta, I'll be fine. Just put the coffee on, and tel Benny I'll be out in a minute.
hnnn. hnnn...

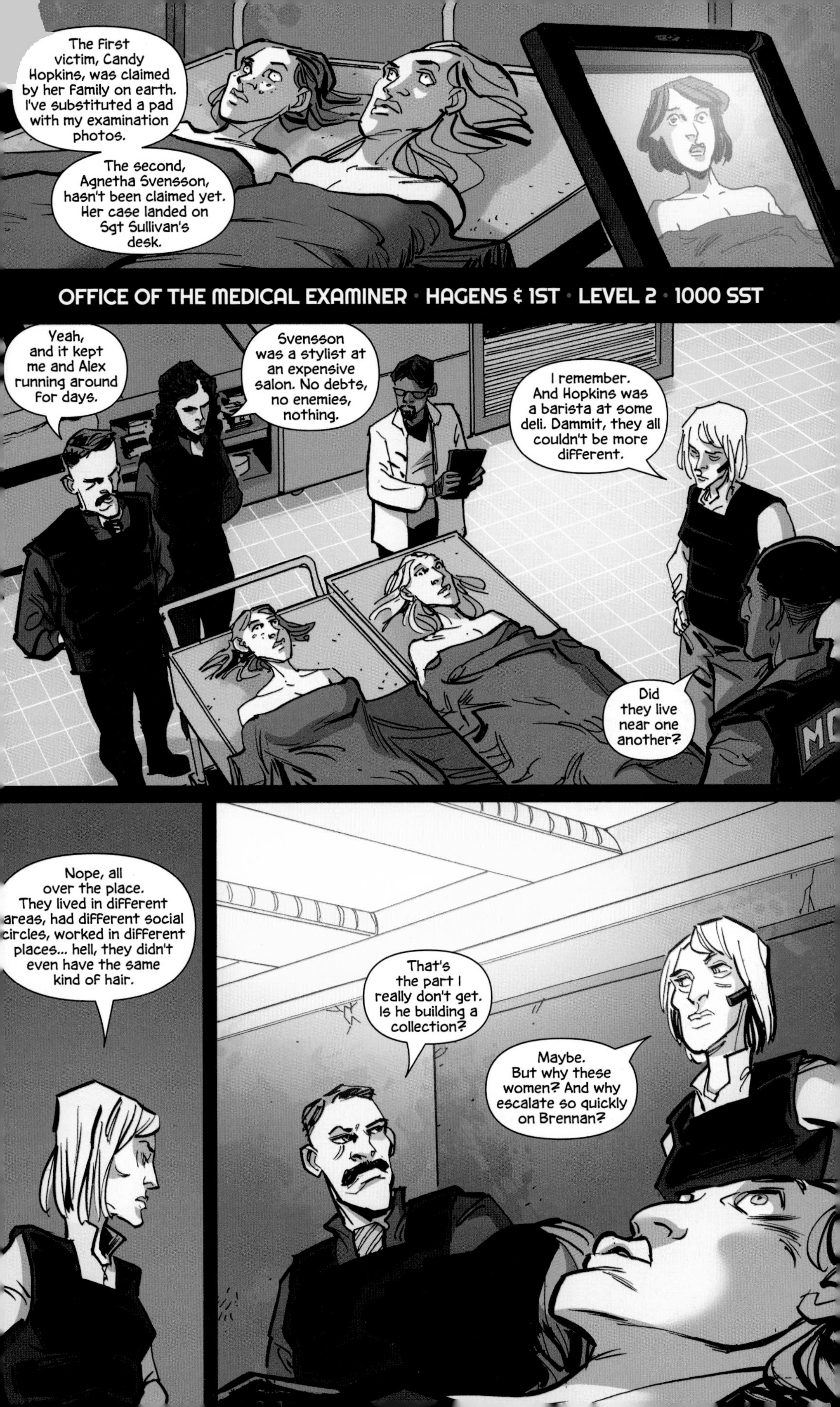

The first victim, Candy Hopkins, was claimed by her family on earth. I've substituted a pad with my examination photos.
The second, Agnetha Svensson, hasn't been claimed yet. Her case landed on Sgt Sullivan's desk.
OFFICE OF THE MEDICAL EXAMINER · HAGENS & 1ST · LEVEL 2 · 1000 SST
Yeah, and it kept me and Alex running around for days.
Svensson was a stylist at an expensive salon. No debts, no enemies, nothing.
I remember. And Hopkins was a barista at some deli. Dammit, they all couldn't be more different.
Did they live near one another?
Nope, all over the place. They lived in different areas, had different social circles, worked in different places... hell, they didn't even have the same kind of hair.
That's the part I really don't get. Is he building a collection?
Maybe. But why these women? And why escalate so quickly on Brennan?

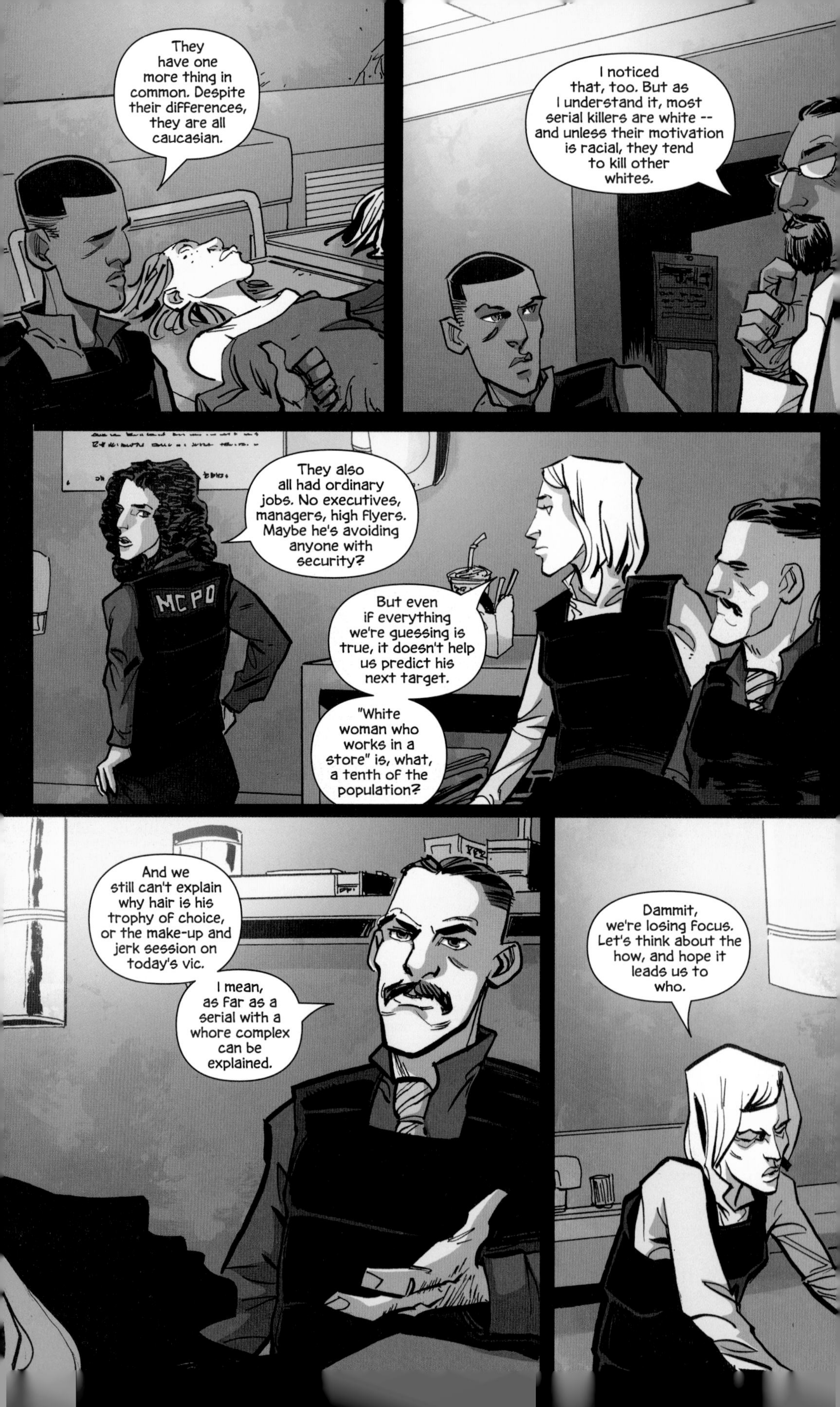
They have one more thing in common. Despite their differences, they are all caucasian.
I noticed that, too. But as I understand it, most serial killers are white -- and unless their motivation is racial, they tend to kill other whites.
They also all had ordinary jobs. No executives, managers, high flyers. Maybe he's avoiding anyone with security?
MCPD
But even if everything we're guessing is true, it doesn't help us predict his next target.
"White woman who works in a store" is, what, a tenth of the population?
And we still can't explain why hair is his trophy of choice, or the make-up and jerk session on today's vic.
I mean, as far as a serial with a whore complex can be explained.
Dammit, we're losing focus. Let's think about the how, and hope it leads us to who.

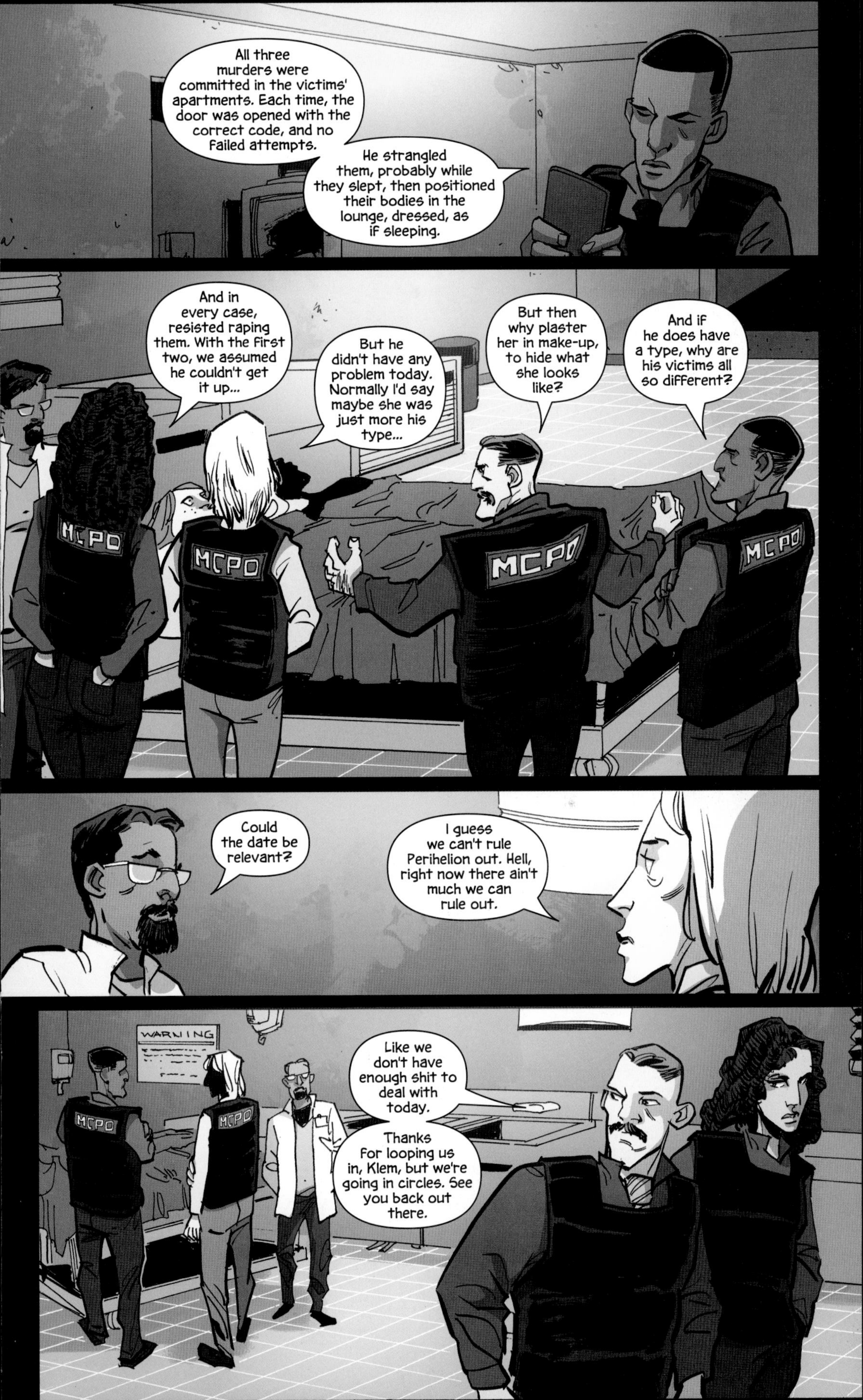
All three murders were committed in the victims' apartments. Each time, the door was opened with the correct code, and no failed attempts.
He strangled them, probably while they slept, then positioned their bodies in the lounge, dressed, as if sleeping.
And in every case, resisted raping them. With the first two, we assumed he couldn't get it up...
But he didn't have any problem today. Normally I'd say maybe she was just more his type...
But then why plaster her in make-up, to hide what she looks like?
And if he does have a type, why are his victims all so different?
MCPO
Could the date be relevant?
I guess we can't rule Perihelion out. Hell, right now there ain't much we can rule out.
WARNING
Like we don't have enough shit to deal with today.
Thanks for looping us in, Klem, but we're going in circles. See you back out there.

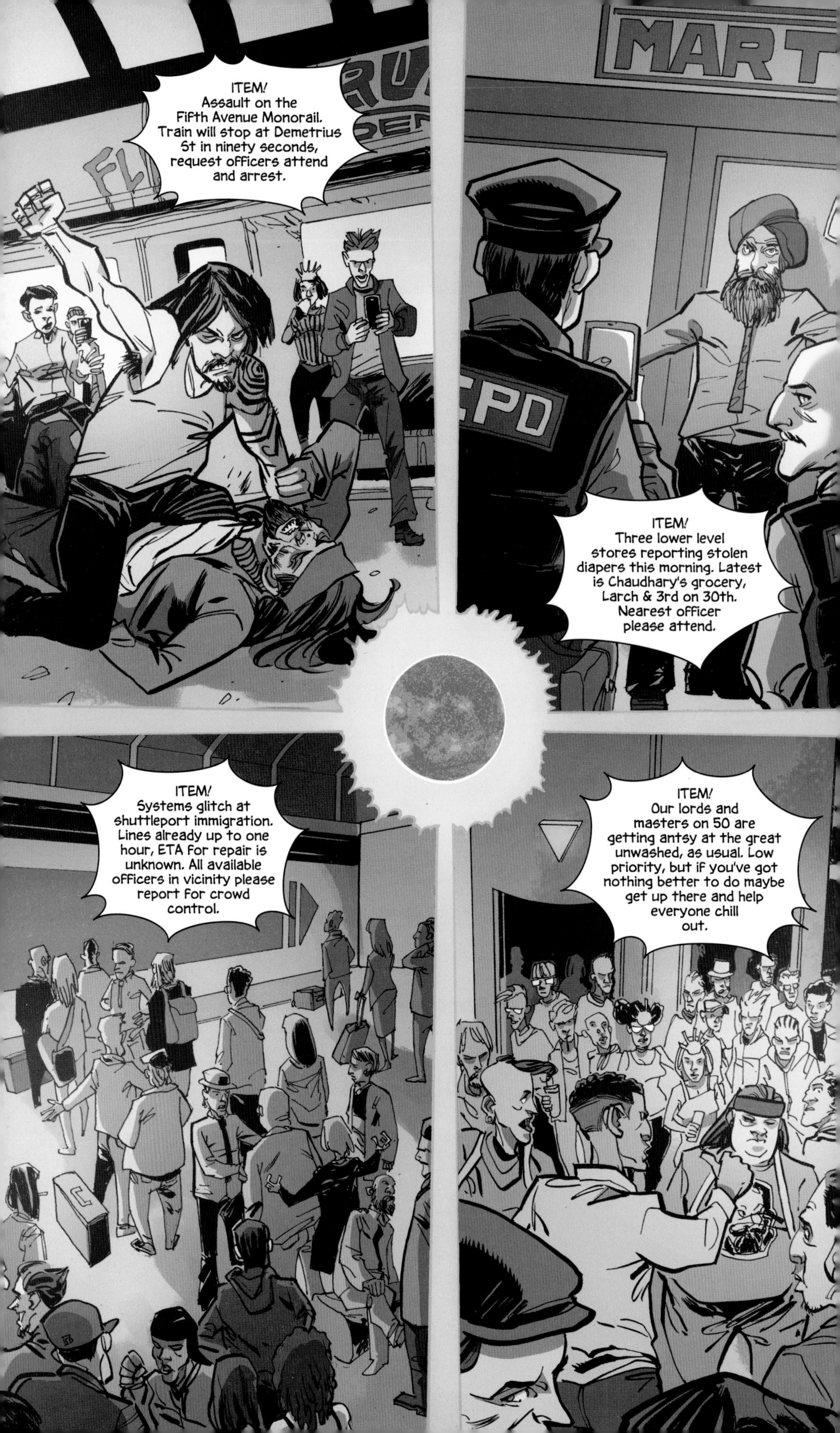
ITEM! Assault on the Fifth Avenue Monorail. Train will stop at Demetrius St in ninety seconds, request officers attend and arrest.
CPD
ITEM! Three lower level stores reporting stolen diapers this morning. Latest is Chaudhary's grocery, Larch & 3rd on 30th. Nearest officer please attend.
ITEM! Systems glitch at shuttleport immigration. Lines already up to one hour, ETA for repair is unknown. All available officers in vicinity please report for crowd control.
ITEM! Our lords and masters on 50 are getting antsy at the great unwashed, as usual. Low priority, but if you've got nothing better to do maybe get up there and help everyone chill out.

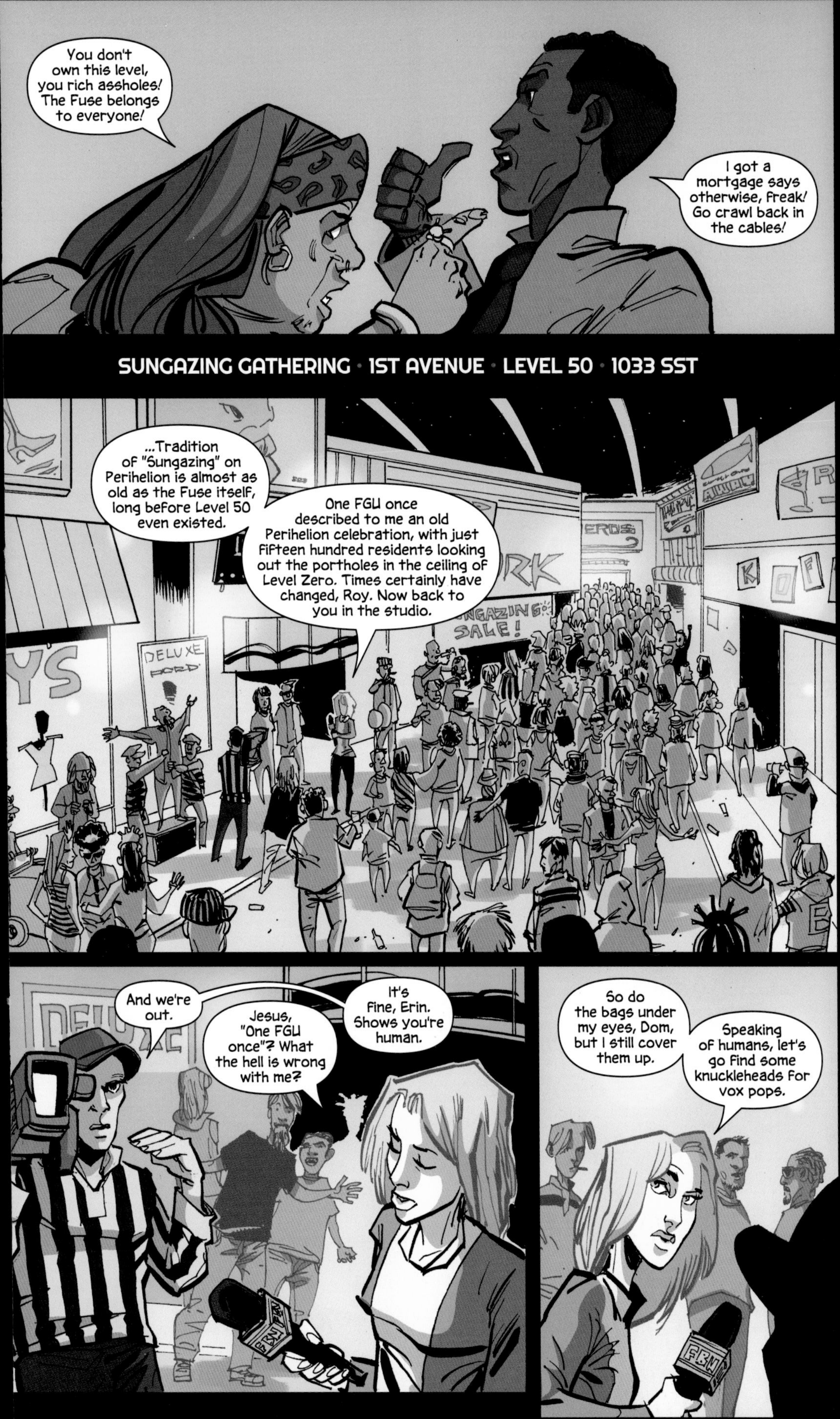
You don't own this level, you rich assholes! The Fuse belongs to everyone!
I got a mortgage says otherwise, freak! Go crawl back in the cables!
SUNGAZING GATHERING • 1ST AVENUE • LEVEL 50 • 1033 SST
...Tradition of "Sungazing" on Perihelion is almost as old as the Fuse itself, long before Level 50 even existed.
One FGU once described to me an old Perihelion celebration, with just fifteen hundred residents looking out the portholes in the ceiling of Level Zero. Times certainly have changed, Roy. Now back to you in the studio.
SUNGAZING SALE!
And we're out.
Jesus, "One FGU once"? What the hell is wrong with me?
It's fine, Erin. Shows you're human.
So do the bags under my eyes, Dom, but I still cover them up.
Speaking of humans, let's go find some knuckleheads for vox pops.

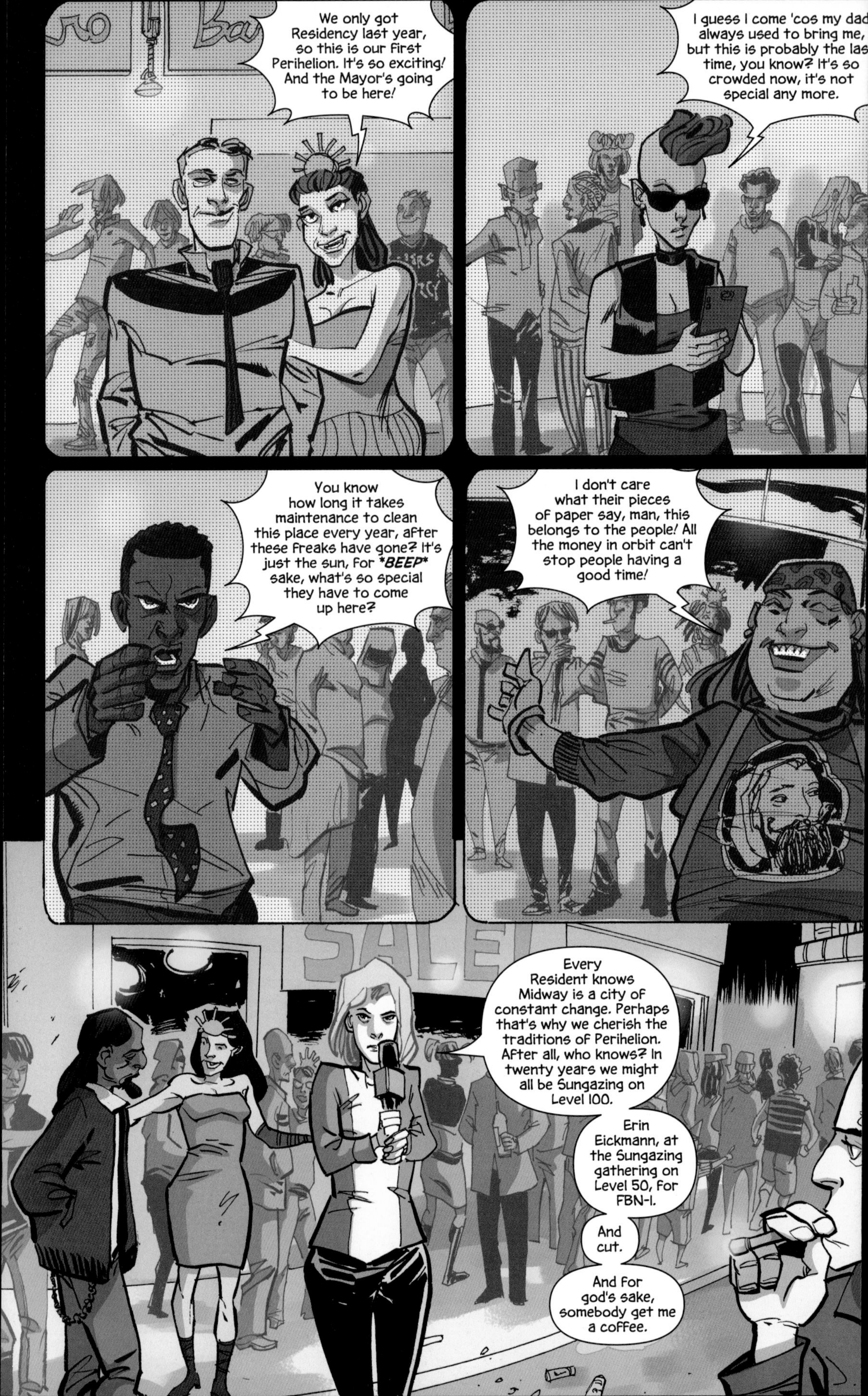
We only got Residency last year, so this is our first Perihelion. It's so exciting! And the Mayor's going to be here!
I guess I come 'cos my dad always used to bring me, but this is probably the las time, you know? It's so crowded now, it's not special any more.
You know how long it takes maintenance to clean this place every year, after these freaks have gone? It's just the sun, for *BEEP* sake, what's so special they have to come up here?
I don't care what their pieces of paper say, man, this belongs to the people! All the money in orbit can't stop people having a good time!
SALE
Every Resident knows Midway is a city of constant change. Perhaps that's why we cherish the traditions of Perihelion. After all, who knows? In twenty years we might all be Sungazing on Level 100.
Erin Eickmann, at the Sungazing gathering on Level 50, for FBN-1.
And cut.
And for god's sake, somebody get me a coffee.

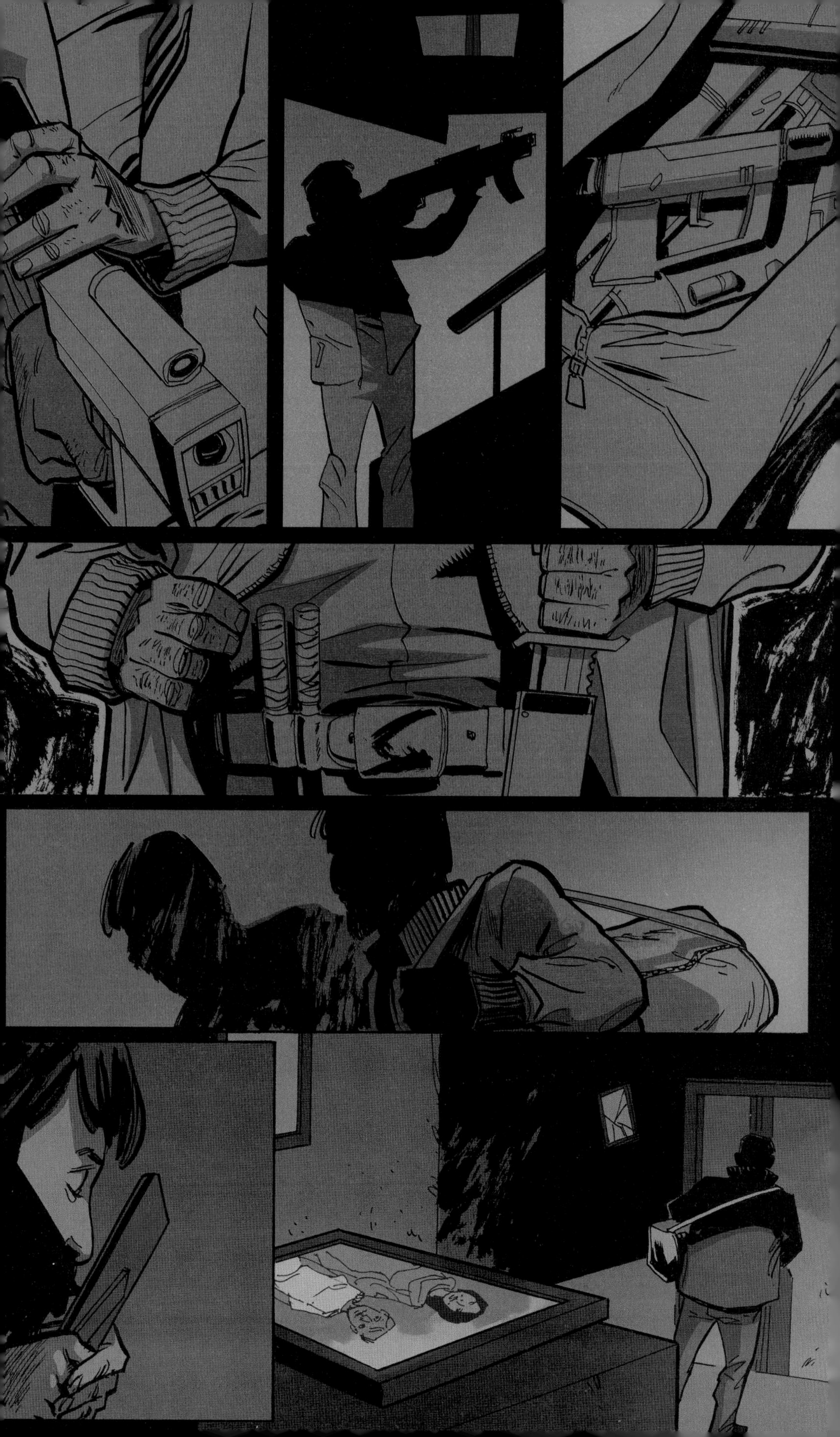

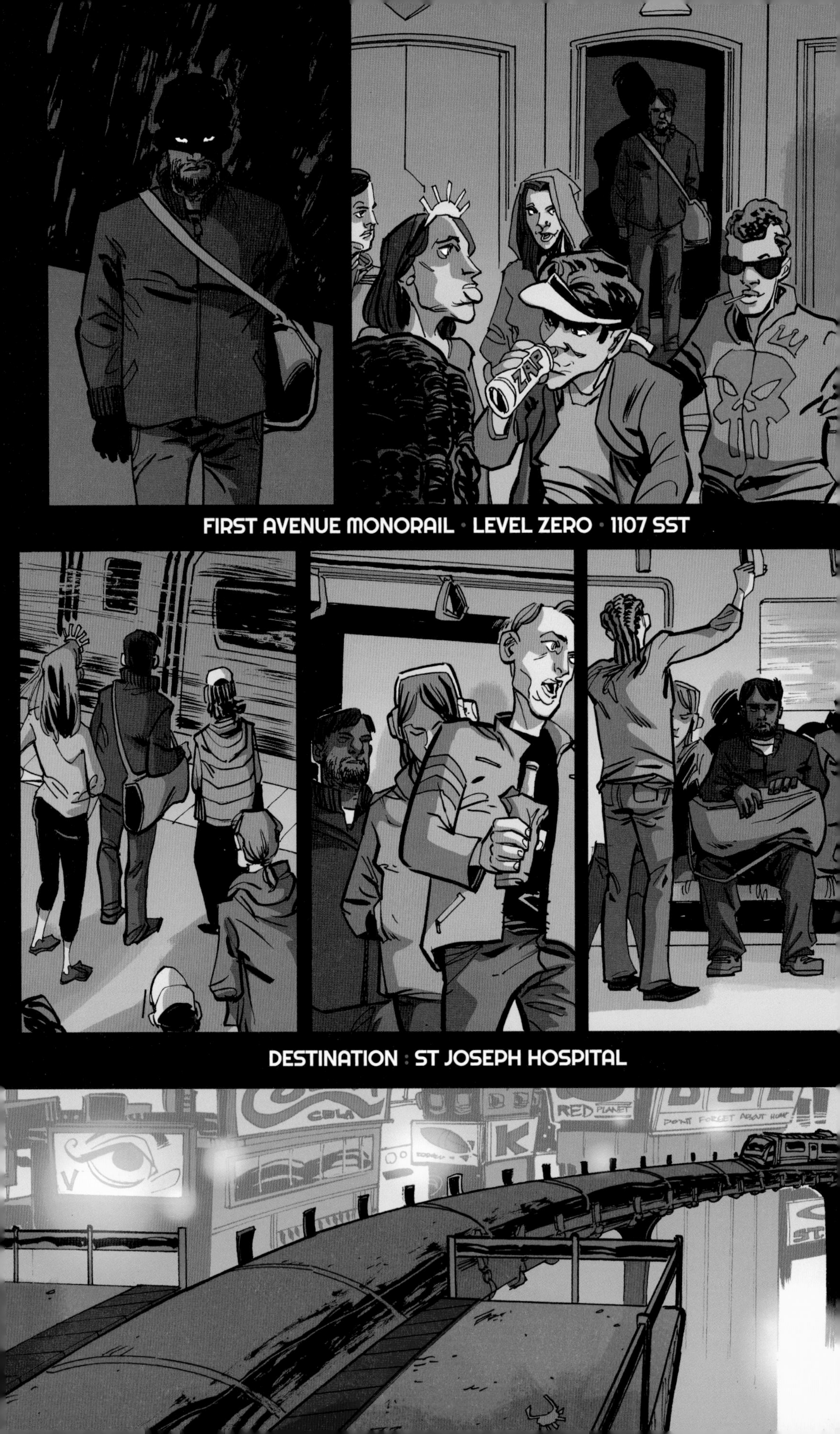
ZAP
FIRST AVENUE MONORAIL · LEVEL ZERO · 1107 SST
DESTINATION : ST JOSEPH HOSPITAL
RED PLANET

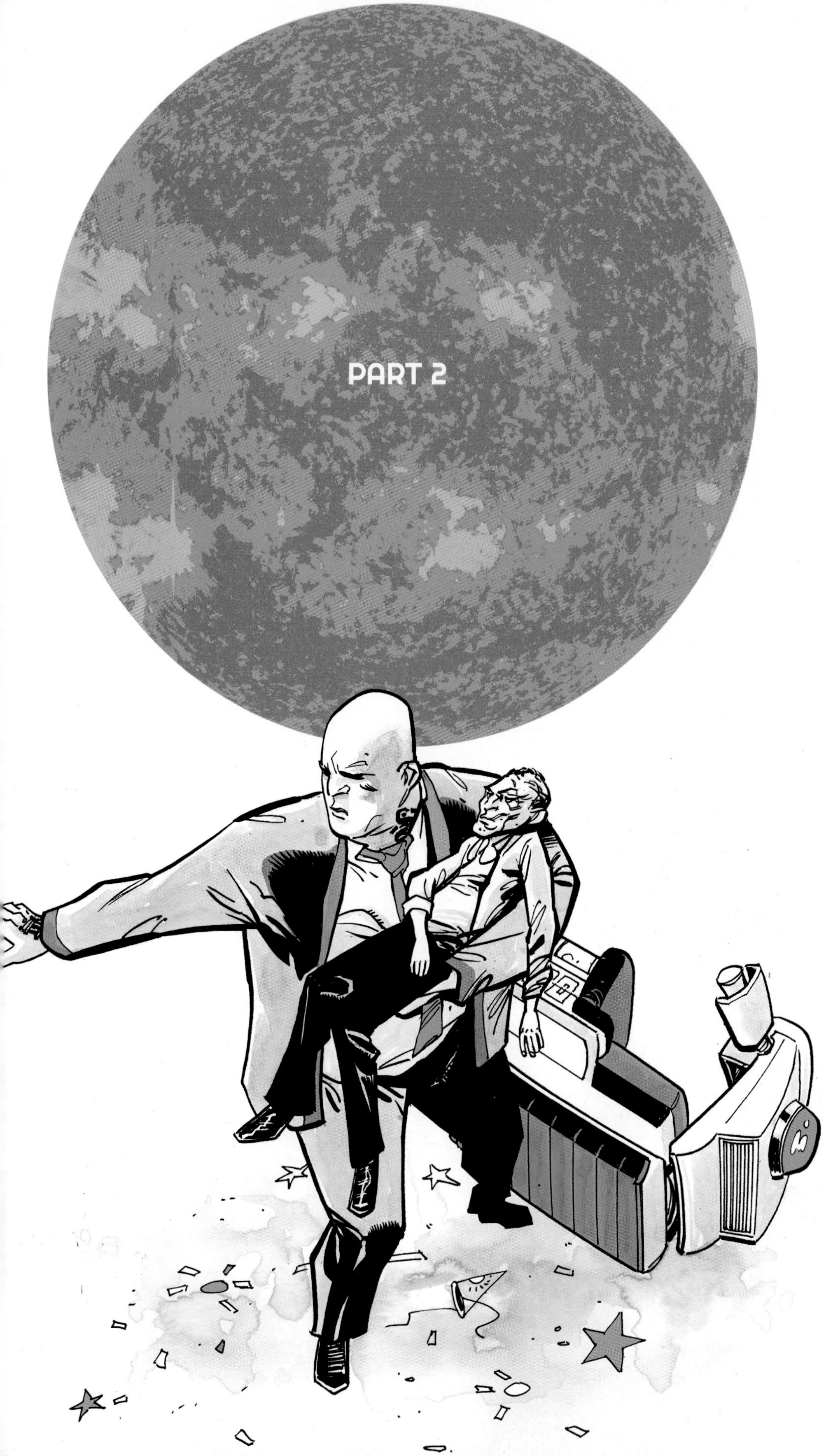
PART 2

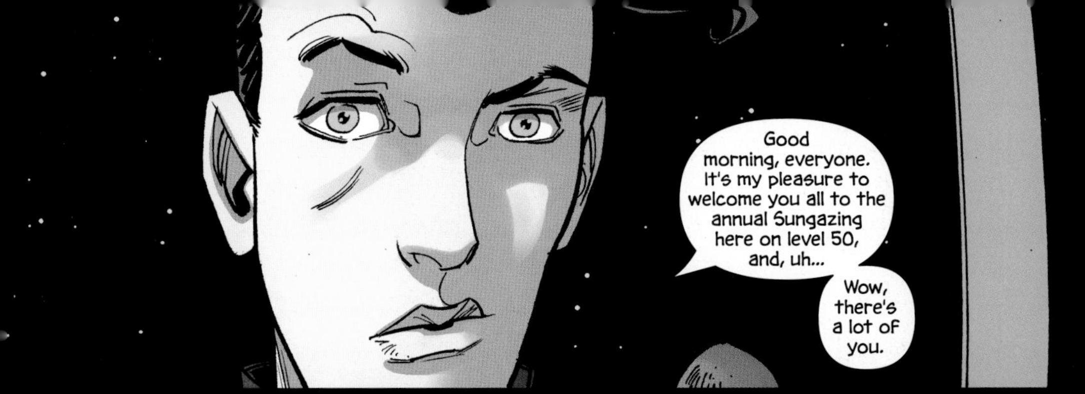
Good morning, everyone. It's my pleasure to welcome you all to the annual Sungazing here on level 50, and, uh...
Wow, there's a lot of you.

SUNGAZING GATHERING • 1ST AVENUE • LEVEL 50 • 1200 SST

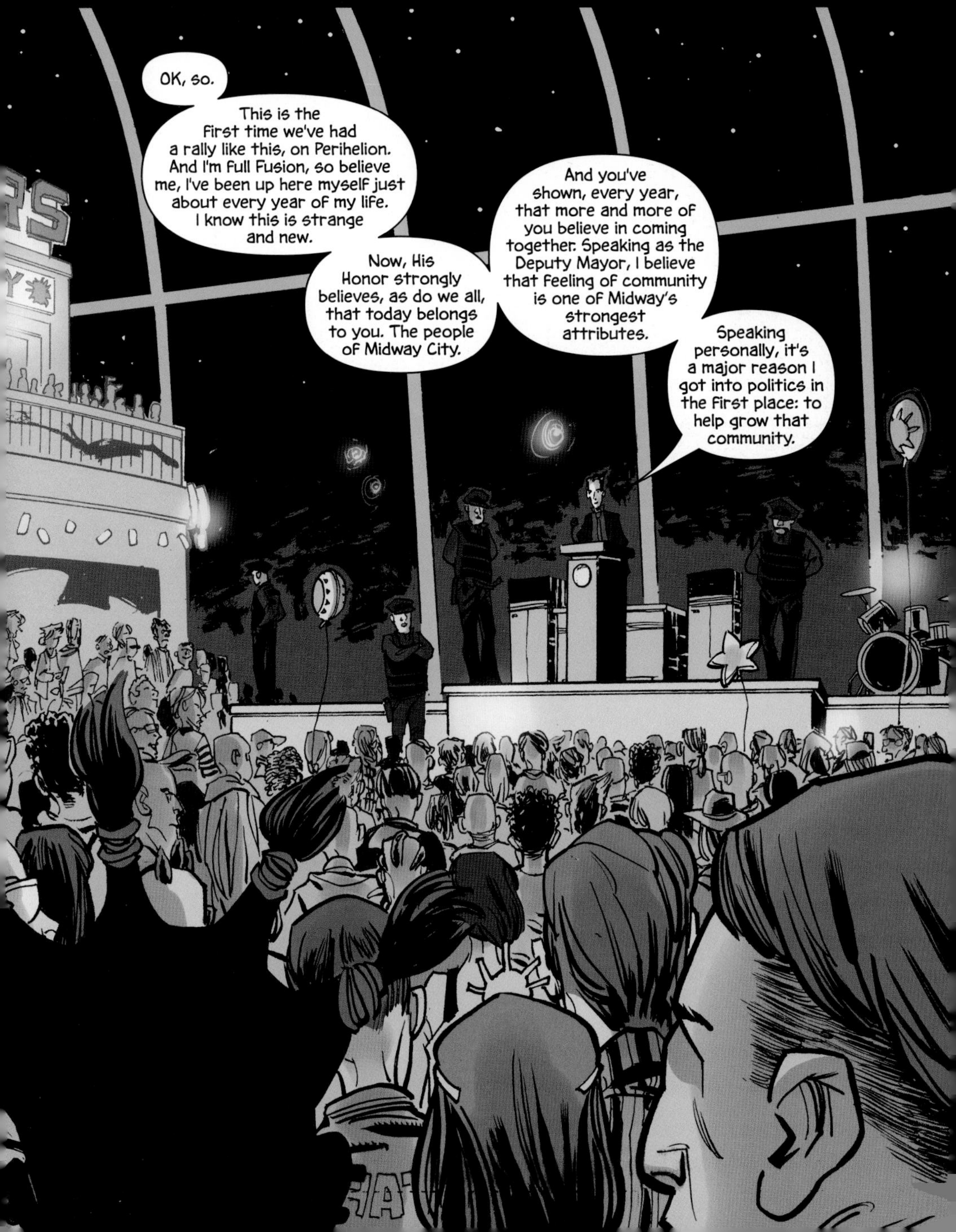
OK, so.
This is the first time we've had a rally like this, on Perihelion. And I'm full Fusion, so believe me, I've been up here myself just about every year of my life. I know this is strange and new.
Now, His Honor strongly believes, as do we all, that today belongs to you. The people of Midway City.
And you've shown, every year, that more and more of you believe in coming together. Speaking as the Deputy Mayor, I believe that feeling of community is one of Midway's strongest attributes.
Speaking personally, it's a major reason I got into politics in the first place: to help grow that community.

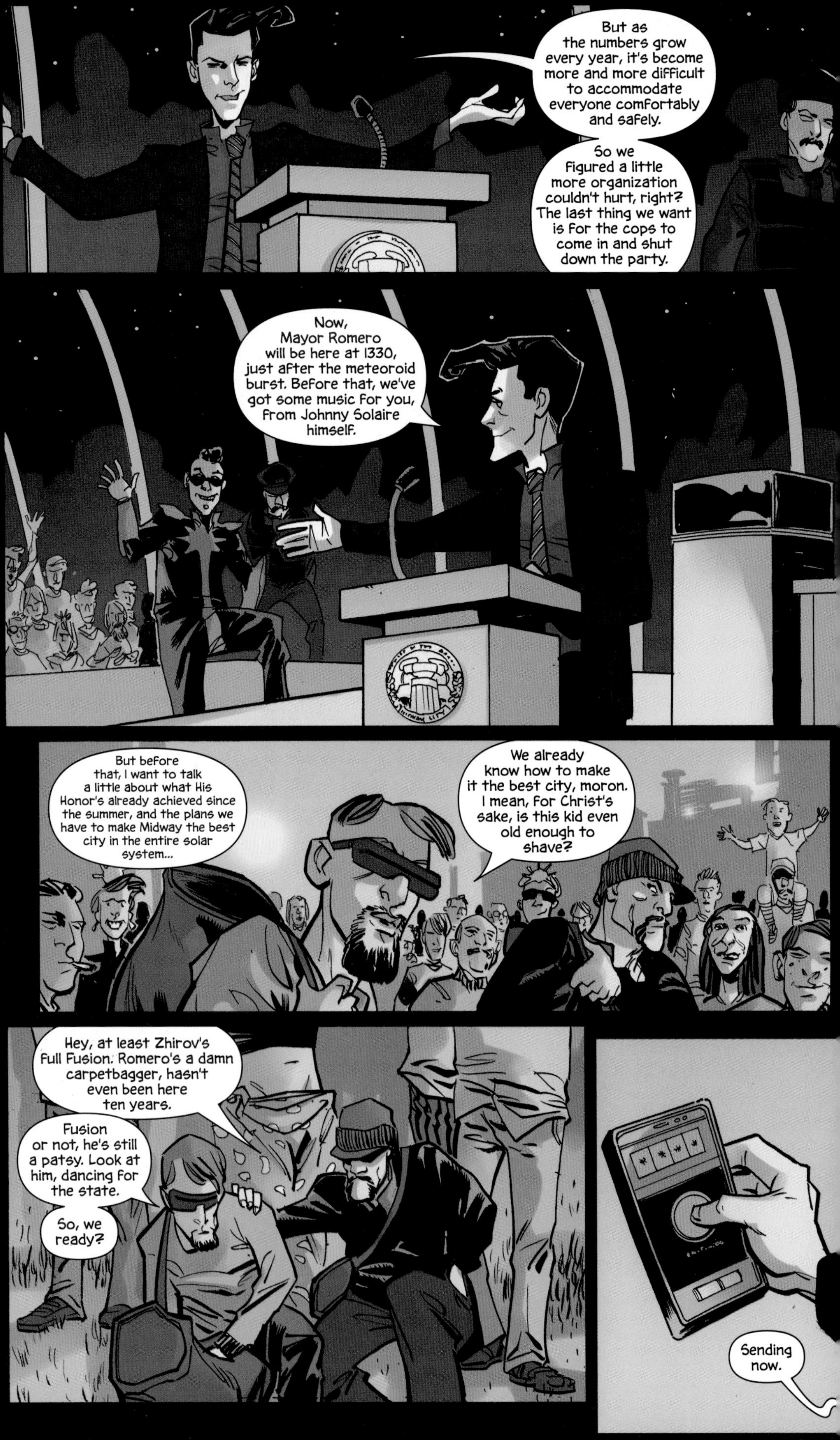
But as the numbers grow every year, it's become more and more difficult to accommodate everyone comfortably and safely.
So we figured a little more organization couldn't hurt, right? The last thing we want is for the cops to come in and shut down the party.
Now, Mayor Romero will be here at 1330, just after the meteoroid burst. Before that, we've got some music for you, from Johnny Solaire himself.
But before that, I want to talk a little about what His Honor's already achieved since the summer, and the plans we have to make Midway the best city in the entire solar system...
We already know how to make it the best city, moron. I mean, for Christ's sake, is this kid even old enough to shave?
Hey, at least Zhirov's Full Fusion. Romero's a damn carpetbagger, hasn't even been here ten years.
Fusion or not, he's still a patsy. Look at him, dancing for the state.
So, we ready?
Sending now.

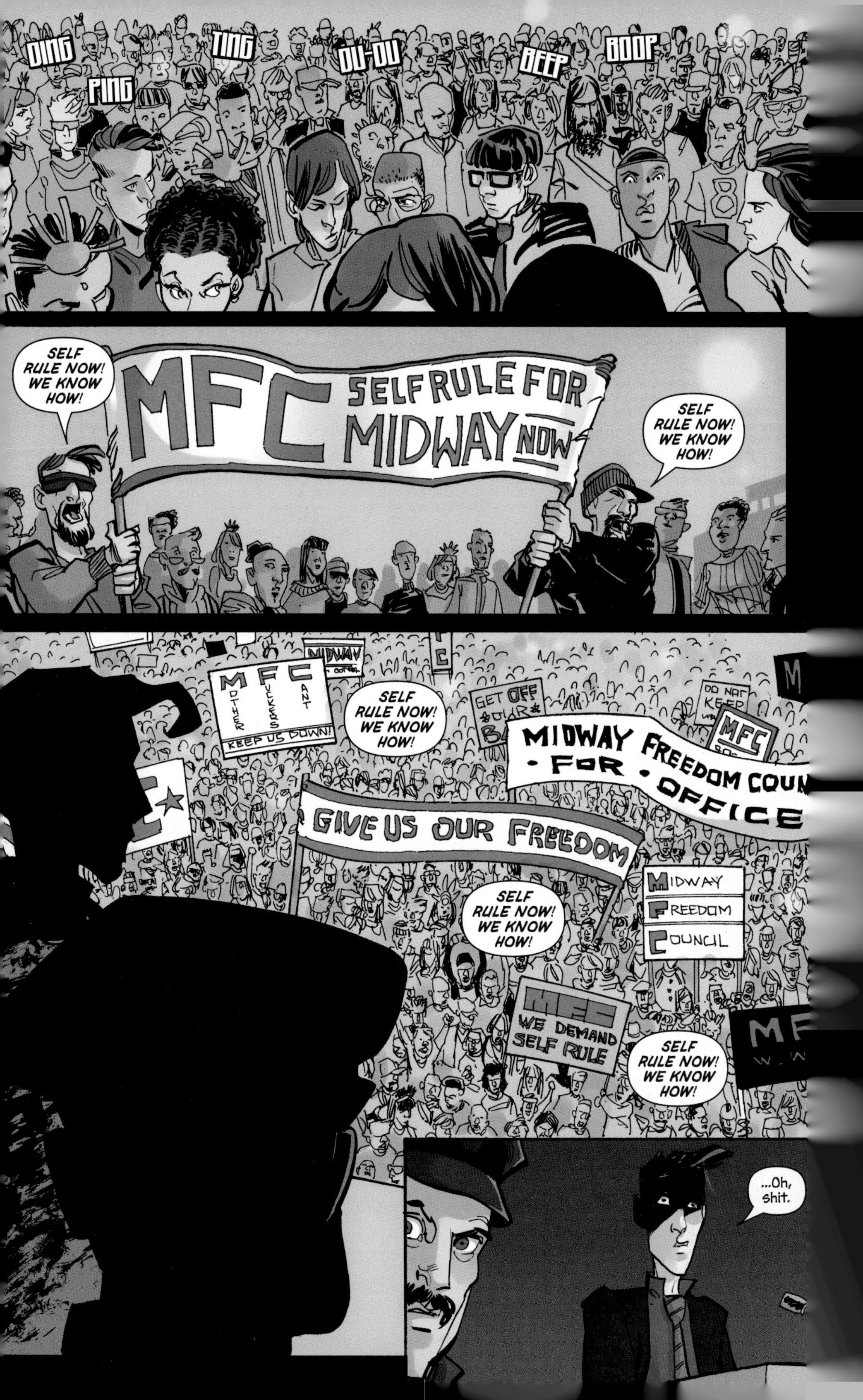
DING
PING
TING
DU-DU
BEEP
BOOP
SELF RULE NOW! WE KNOW HOW!
MFC SELF RULE FOR MIDWAY NOW
SELF RULE NOW! WE KNOW HOW!
MFC
MOTHER FUCKERS CANT
KEEP US DOWN!
SELF RULE NOW! WE KNOW HOW!
GET OFF OUR
DO NOT KEEP
MFC
MIDWAY FREEDOM COUN
FOR OFFICE
GIVE US OUR FREEDOM
MIDWAY FREEDOM COUNCIL
SELF RULE NOW! WE KNOW HOW!
MFC WE DEMAND SELF RULE
SELF RULE NOW! WE KNOW HOW!
...Oh, shit.

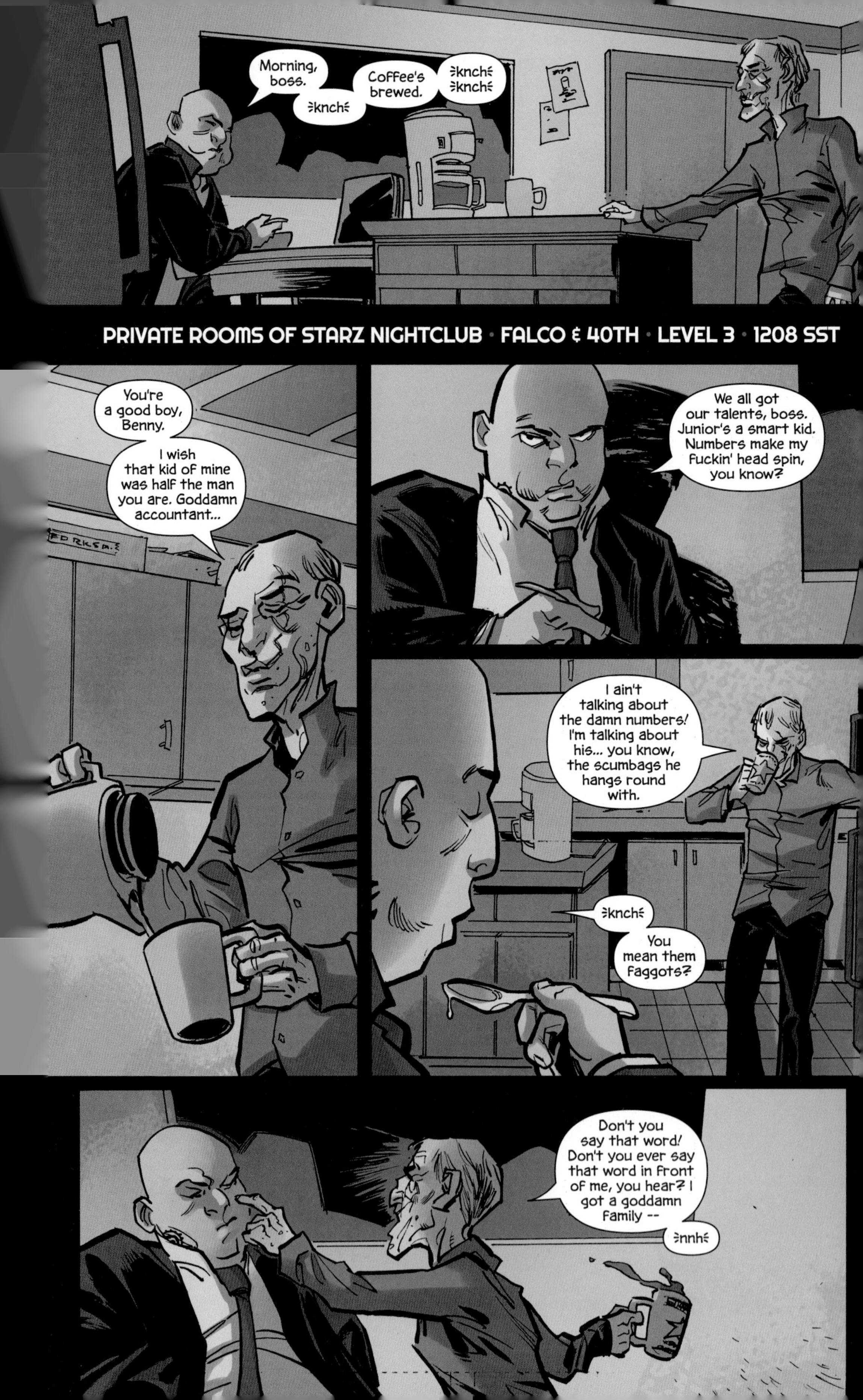
Morning, boss.
knch
Coffee's brewed.
knch knch
PRIVATE ROOMS OF STARZ NIGHTCLUB • FALCO & 40TH • LEVEL 3 • 1208 SST
You're a good boy, Benny.
I wish that kid of mine was half the man you are. Goddamn accountant...
We all got our talents, boss. Junior's a smart kid. Numbers make my fuckin' head spin, you know?
I ain't talking about the damn numbers! I'm talking about his... you know, the scumbags he hangs round with.
knch
You mean them faggots?
Don't you say that word! Don't you ever say that word in front of me, you hear? I got a goddamn family --
nnh

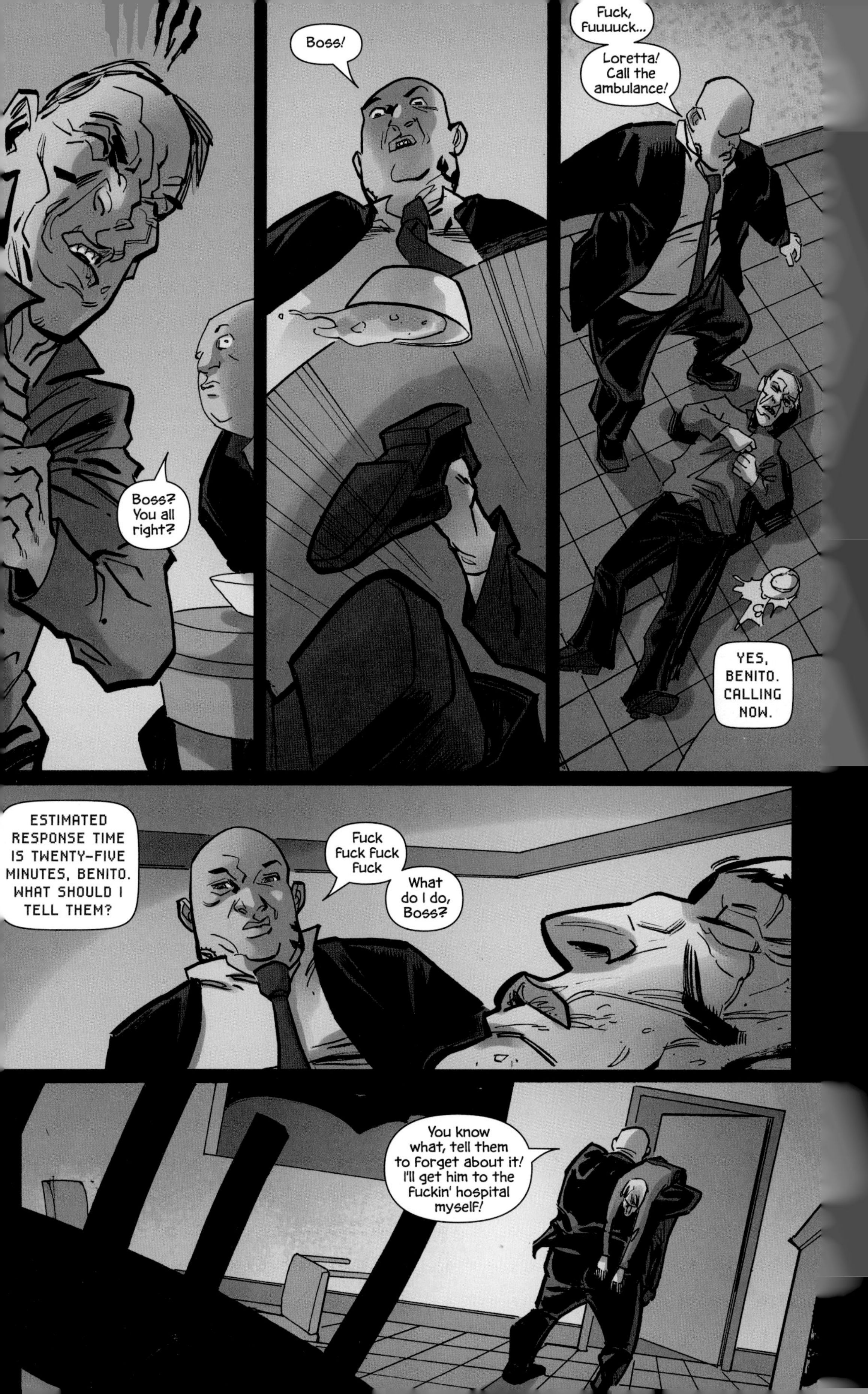
Boss? You all right?
Boss!
Fuck, Fuuuuck...
Loretta! Call the ambulance!
YES, BENITO. CALLING NOW.
ESTIMATED RESPONSE TIME IS TWENTY-FIVE MINUTES, BENITO. WHAT SHOULD I TELL THEM?
Fuck Fuck Fuck Fuck
What do I do, Boss?
You know what, tell them to forget about it! I'll get him to the fuckin' hospital myself!

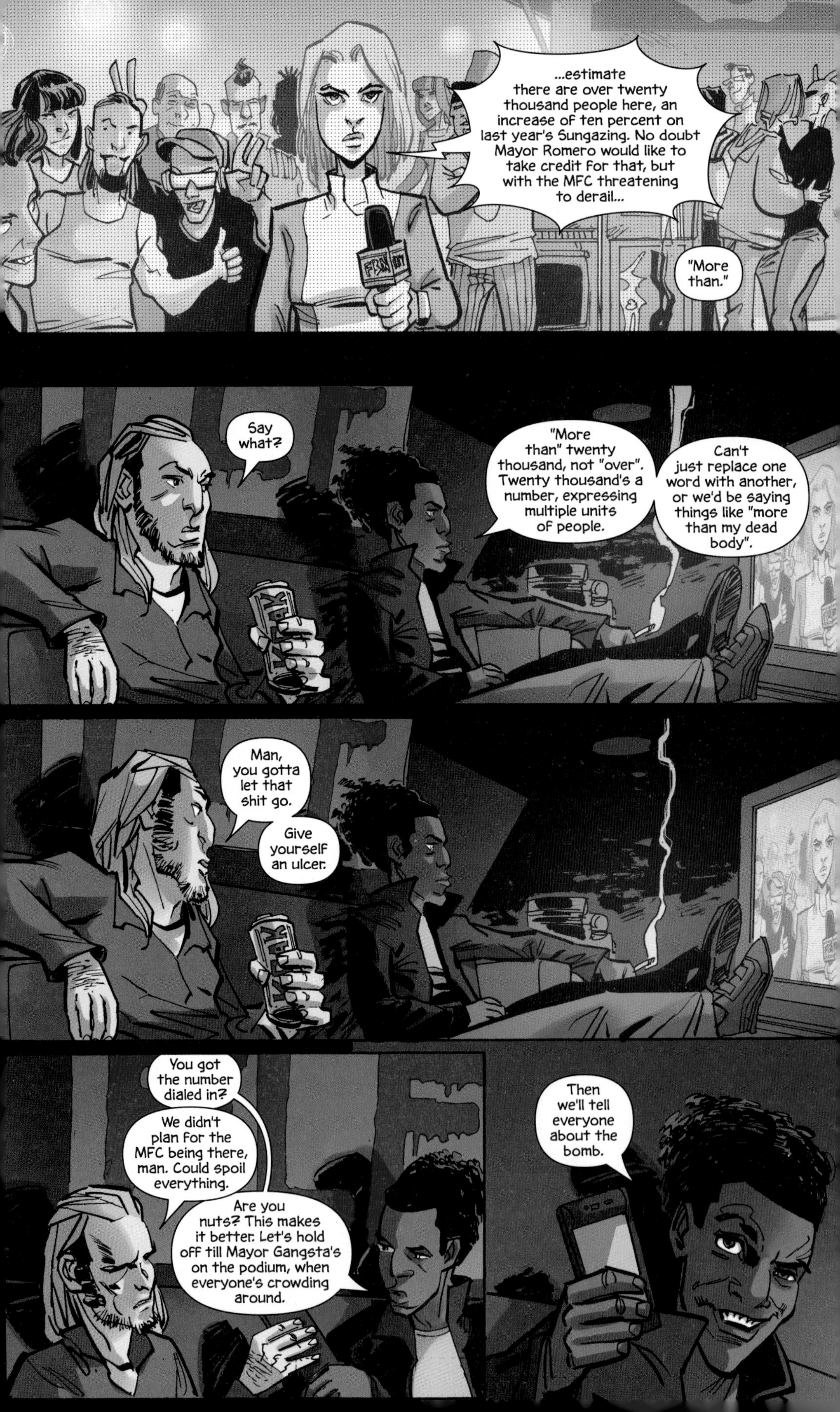
...estimate there are over twenty thousand people here, an increase of ten percent on last year's Sungazing. No doubt Mayor Romero would like to take credit for that, but with the MFC threatening to derail...
"More than."
Say what?
"More than" twenty thousand, not "over". Twenty thousand's a number, expressing multiple units of people.
Can't just replace one word with another, or we'd be saying things like "more than my dead body".
Man, you gotta let that shit go.
Give yourself an ulcer.
You got the number dialed in?
We didn't plan for the MFC being there, man. Could spoil everything.
Are you nuts? This makes it better. Let's hold off till Mayor Gangsta's on the podium, when everyone's crowding around.
Then we'll tell everyone about the bomb.

ADAMS & 2ND · LEVEL ZERO · 1225 SST

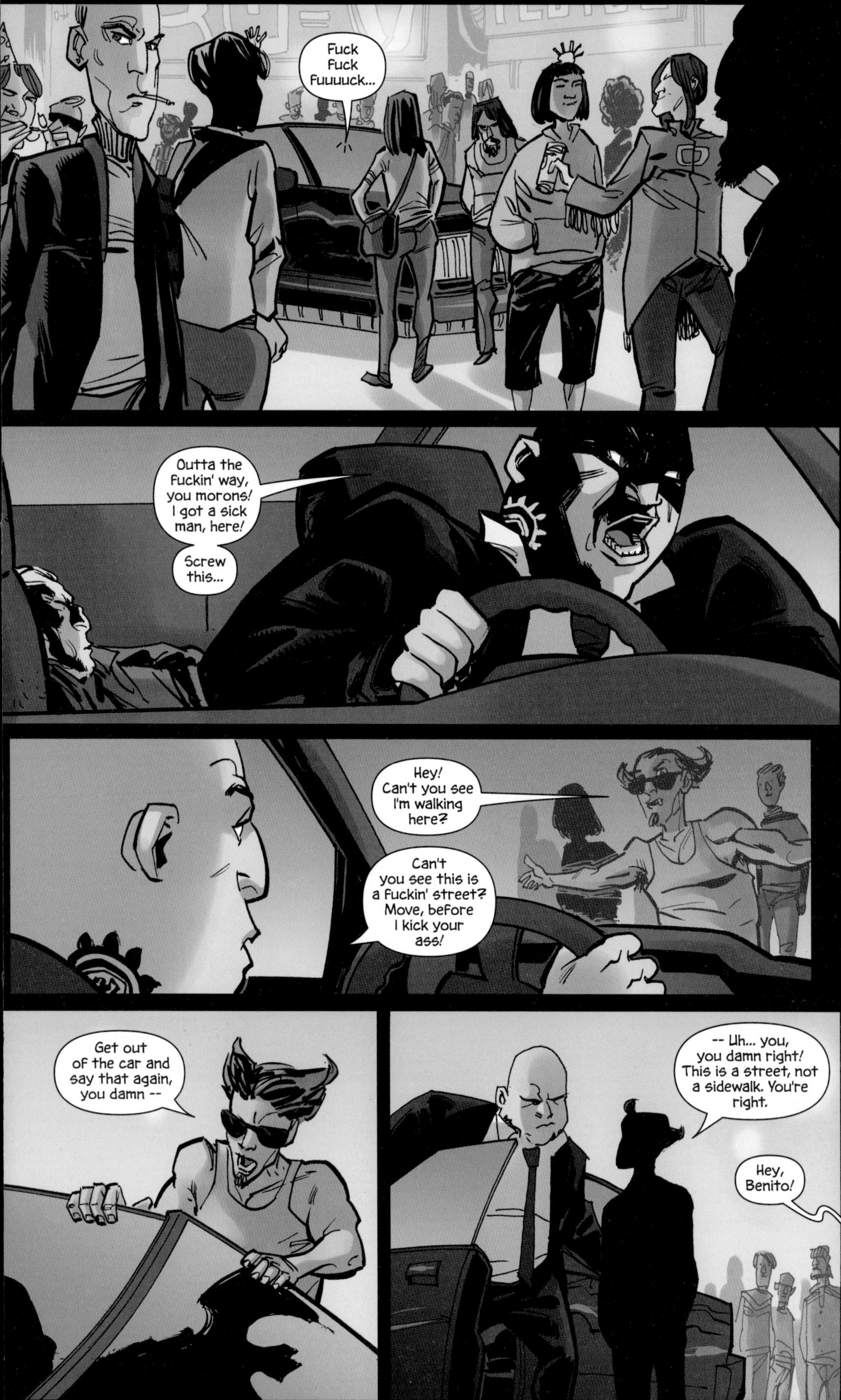

Fuck Fuck Fuuuuck...
Outta the fuckin' way, you morons! I got a sick man, here!
Screw this...
Hey! Can't you see I'm walking here?
Can't you see this is a fuckin' street? Move, before I kick your ass!
Get out of the car and say that again, you damn --
-- Uh... you, you damn right! This is a street, not a sidewalk. You're right.
Hey, Benito!

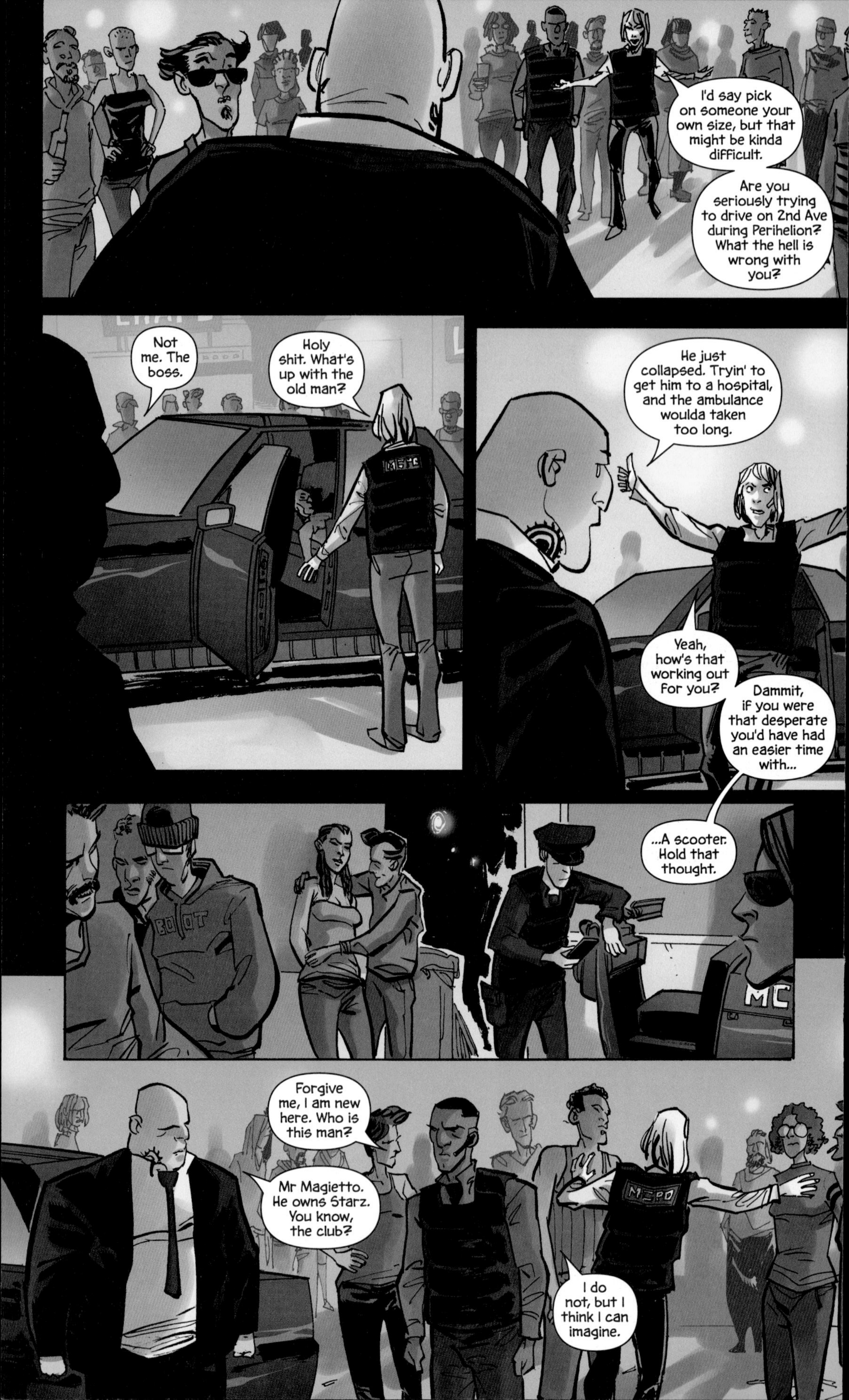
I'd say pick on someone your own size, but that might be kinda difficult.
Are you seriously trying to drive on 2nd Ave during Perihelion? What the hell is wrong with you?
Holy shit. What's up with the old man?
Not me. The boss.
He just collapsed. Tryin' to get him to a hospital, and the ambulance woulda taken too long.
Yeah, how's that working out for you?
Dammit, if you were that desperate you'd have had an easier time with...
...A scooter. Hold that thought.
Forgive me, I am new here. Who is this man?
Mr Magietto. He owns Starz. You know, the club?
I do not, but I think I can imagine.

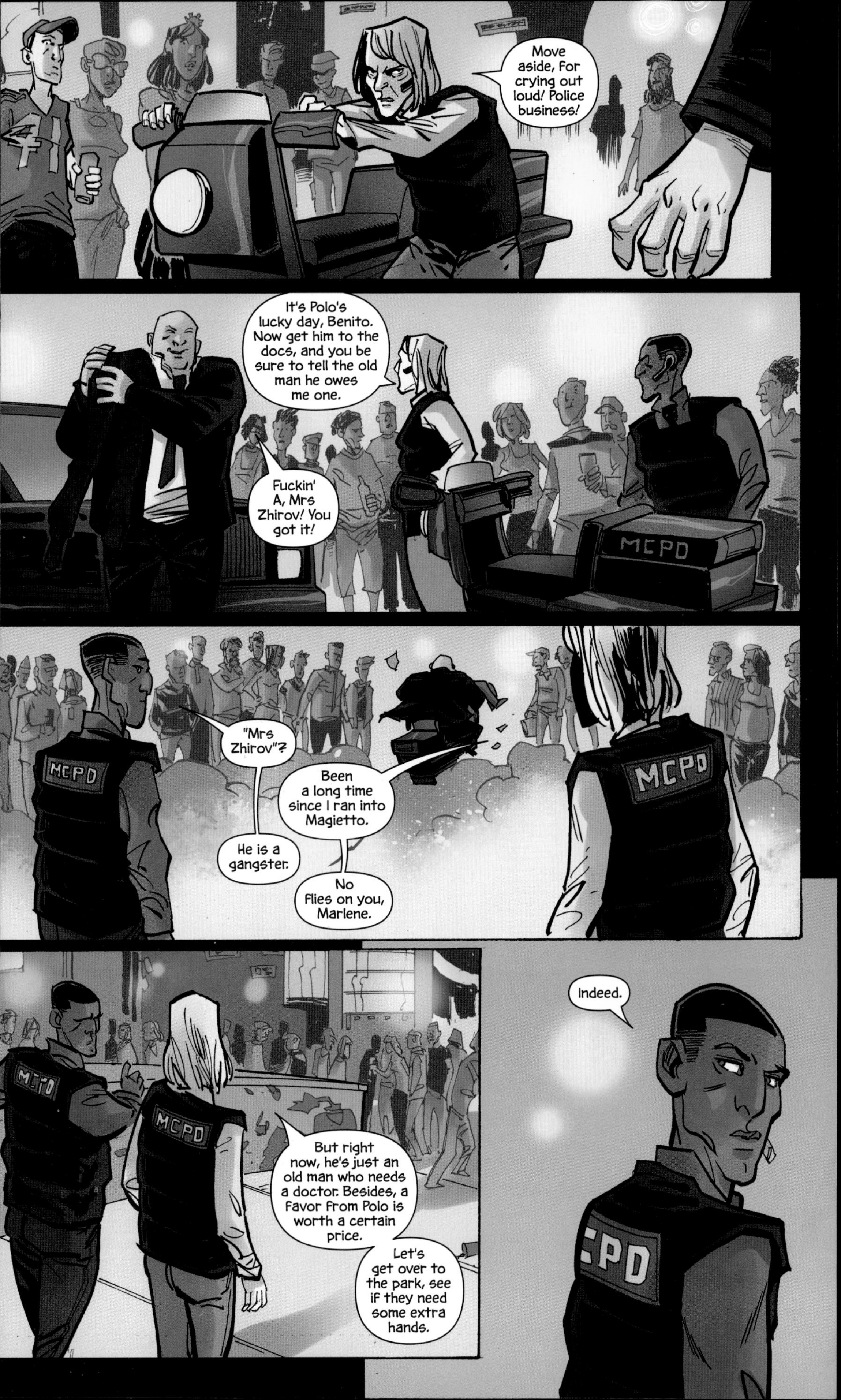
Move aside, For crying out loud! Police business!
It's Polo's lucky day, Benito. Now get him to the docs, and you be sure to tell the old man he owes me one.
Fuckin' A, Mrs Zhirov! You got it!
MCPD
"Mrs Zhirov"?
Been a long time since I ran into Magietto.
He is a gangster.
No Flies on you, Marlene.
MCPD
MCPD
Indeed.
MCPD
But right now, he's just an old man who needs a doctor. Besides, a favor from Polo is worth a certain price.
Let's get over to the park, see if they need some extra hands.

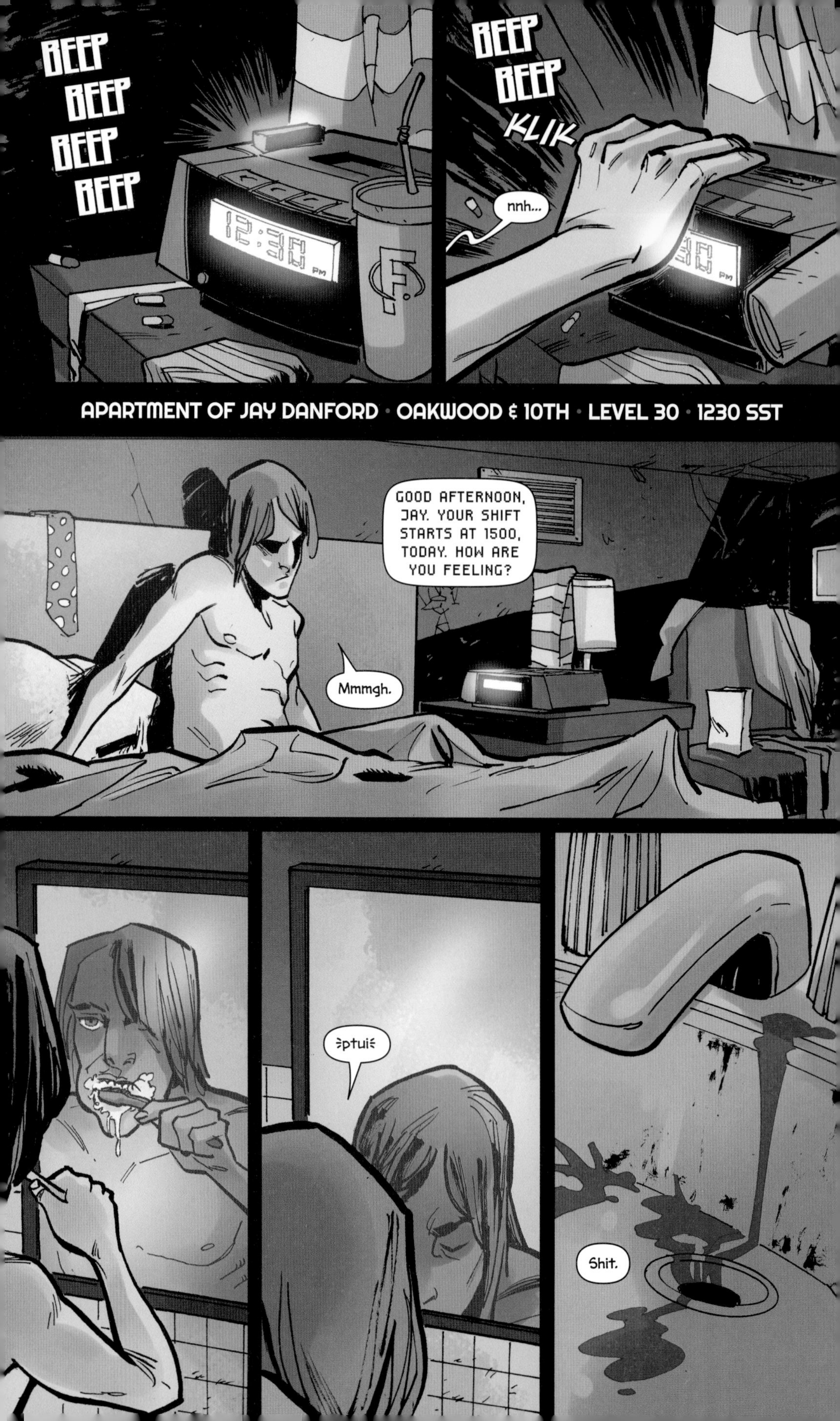
BEEP
BEEP
BEEP
BEEP
BEEP
BEEP
KLIK
nnh...
APARTMENT OF JAY DANFORD • OAKWOOD & 10TH • LEVEL 30 • 1230 SST
GOOD AFTERNOON, JAY. YOUR SHIFT STARTS AT 1500, TODAY. HOW ARE YOU FEELING?
Mmmgh.
ptui
Shit.

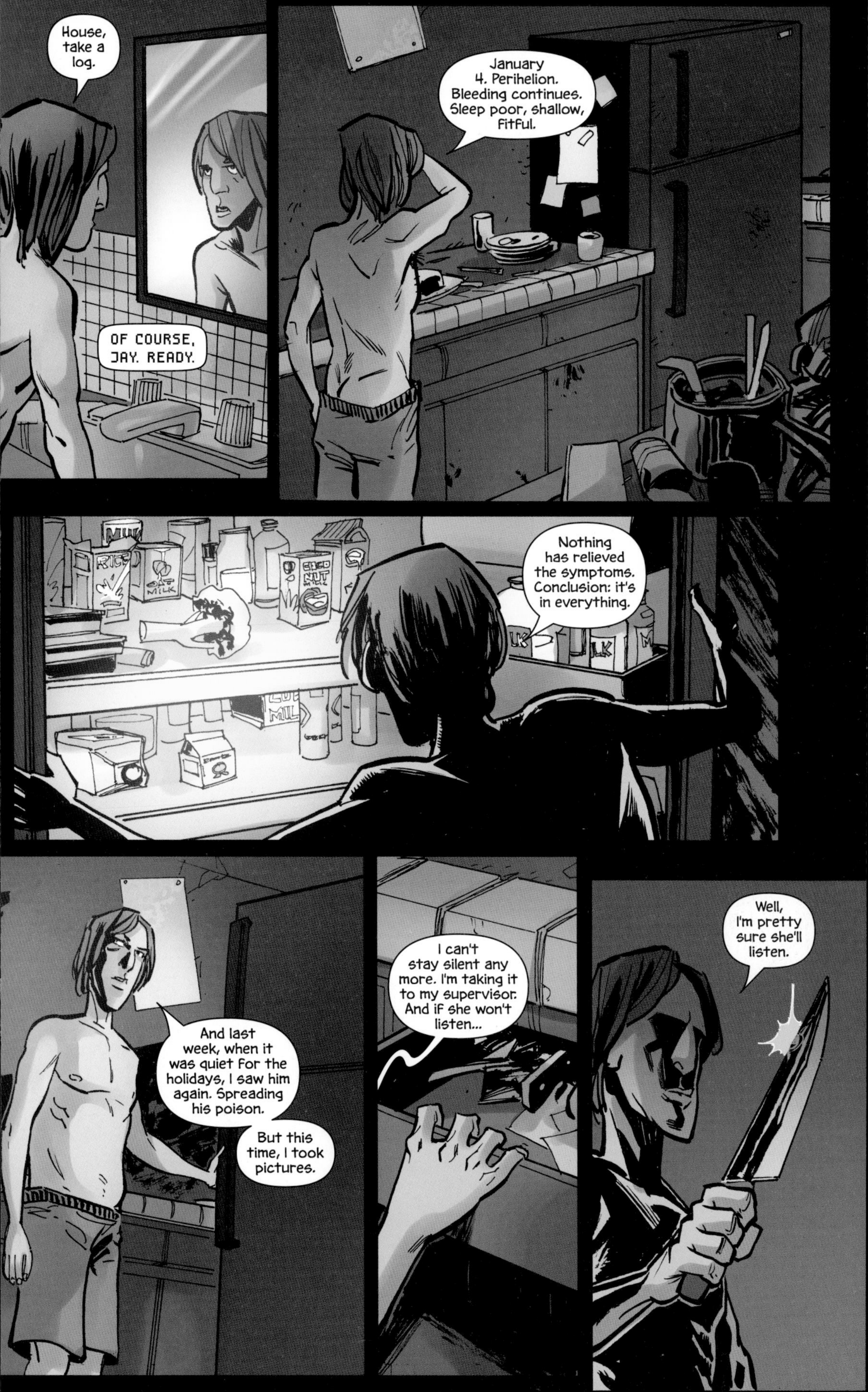

House, take a log.
OF COURSE, JAY. READY.
January 4. Perihelion. Bleeding continues. Sleep poor, shallow, fitful.
Nothing has relieved the symptoms. Conclusion: it's in everything.
And last week, when it was quiet for the holidays, I saw him again. Spreading his poison.
But this time, I took pictures.
I can't stay silent any more. I'm taking it to my supervisor. And if she won't listen...
Well, I'm pretty sure she'll listen.

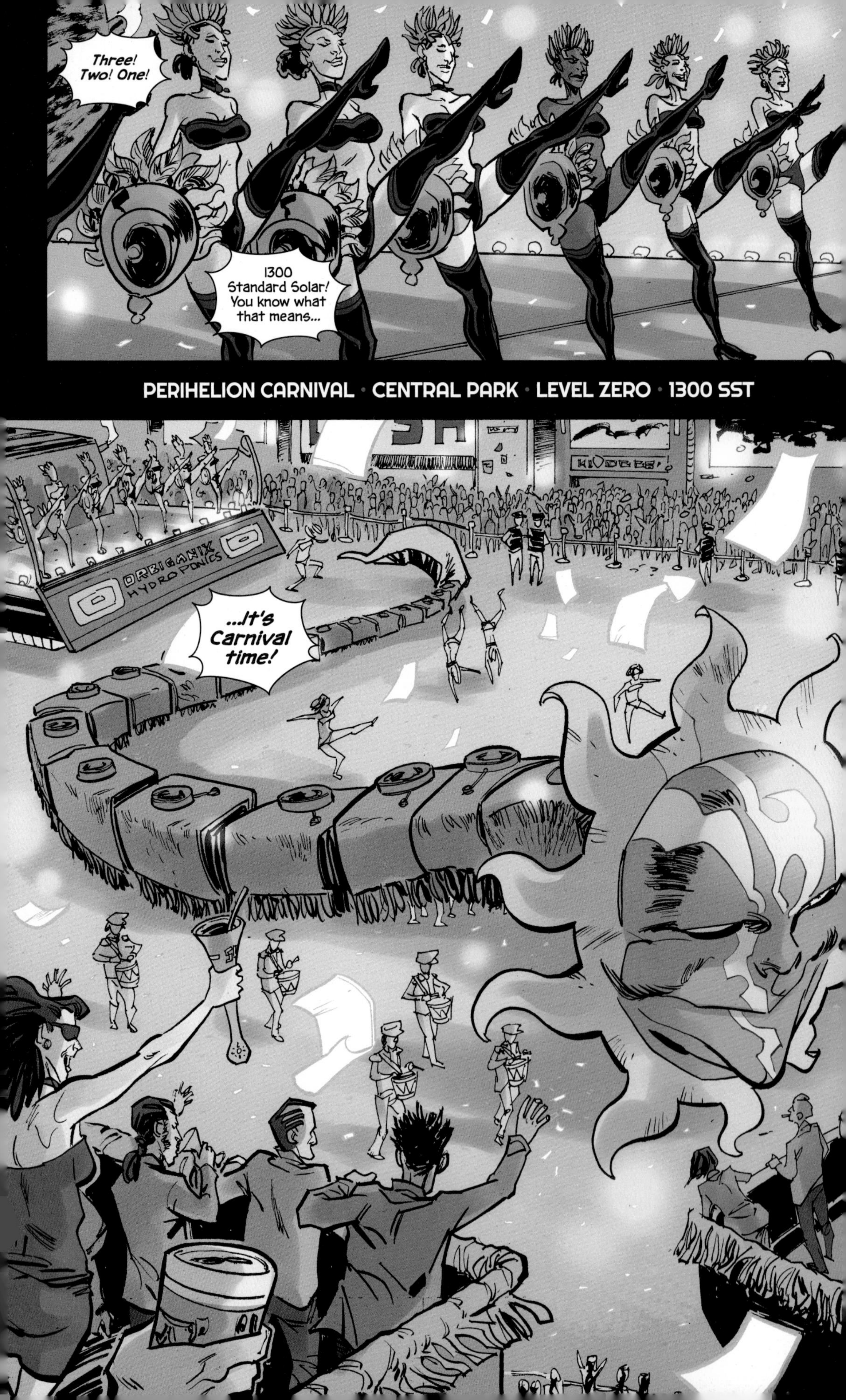
Three! Two! One!
1300 Standard Solar! You know what that means...
PERIHELION CARNIVAL • CENTRAL PARK • LEVEL ZERO • 1300 SST
ORBIGANIX HYDROPONICS
...It's Carnival time!

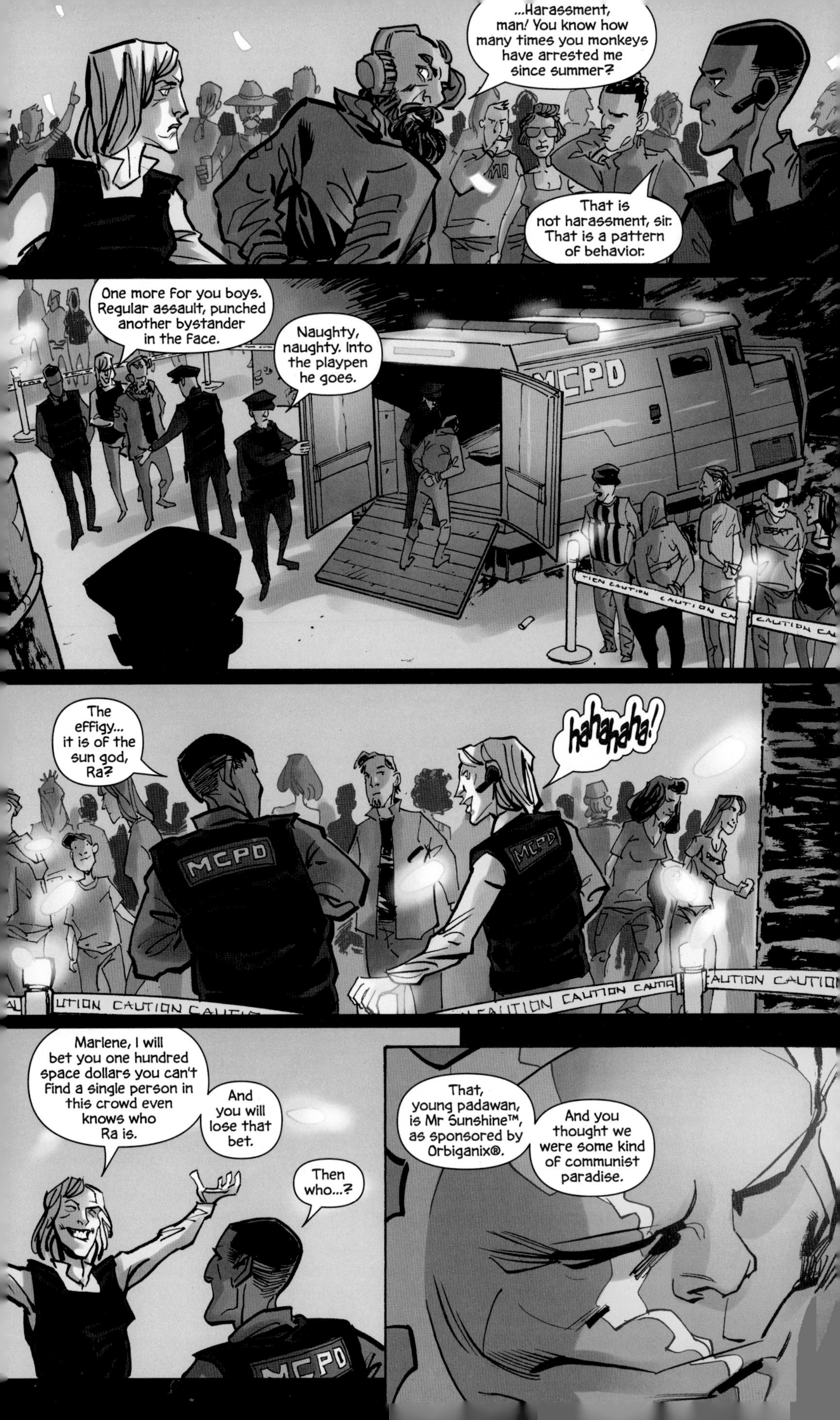
...Harassment, man! You know how many times you monkeys have arrested me since summer?
That is not harassment, sir. That is a pattern of behavior.
One more for you boys. Regular assault, punched another bystander in the face.
Naughty, naughty. Into the playpen he goes.
MCPD
CAUTION CAUTION CAUTION
The effigy... it is of the sun god, Ra?
hahahaha!
MCPD
MCPD
CAUTION CAUTION
Marlene, I will bet you one hundred space dollars you can't find a single person in this crowd even knows who Ra is.
And you will lose that bet.
Then who...?
MCPD
That, young padawan, is Mr Sunshine™, as sponsored by Orbiganix®.
And you thought we were some kind of communist paradise.

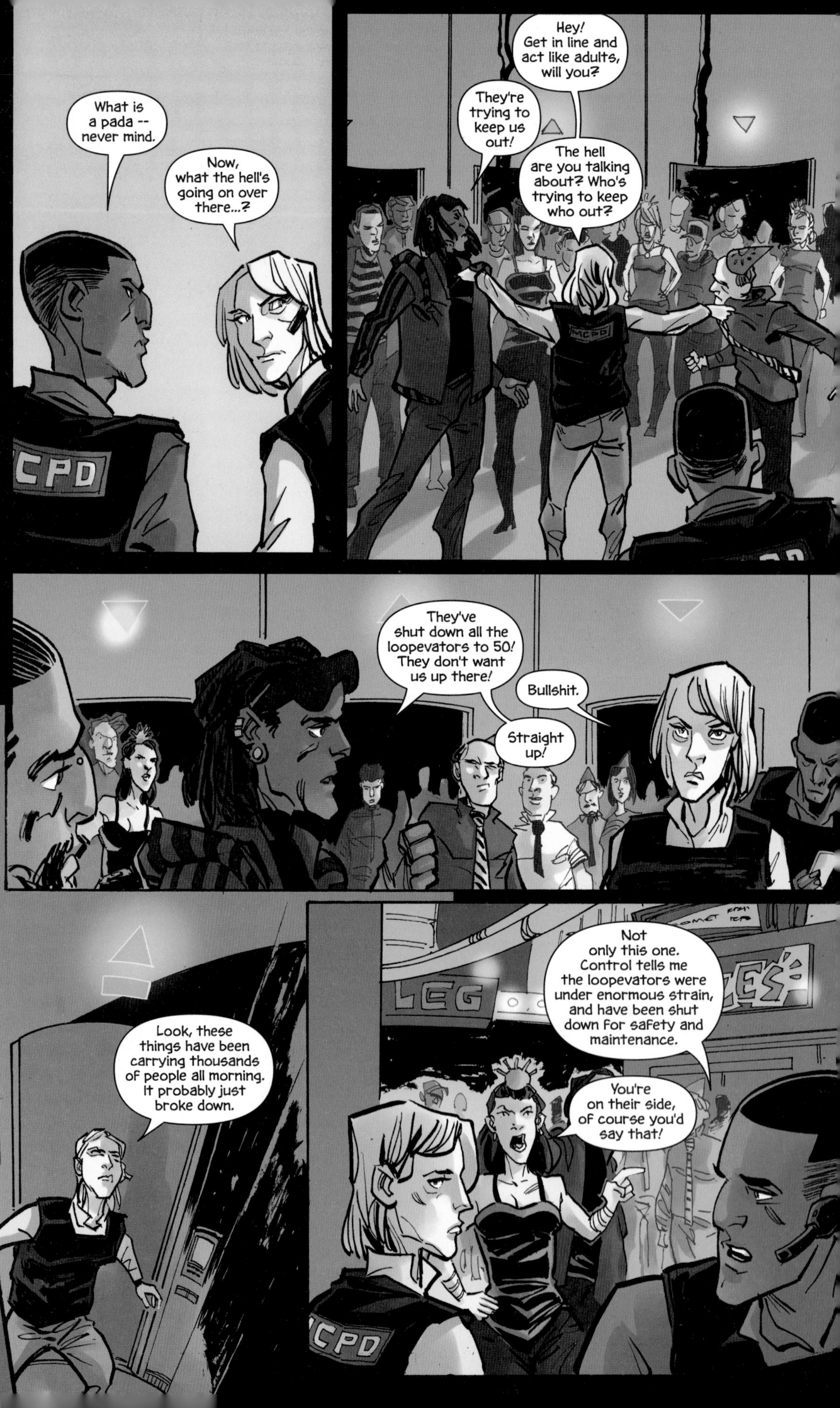
What is a pada -- never mind.
Now, what the hell's going on over there...?
Hey! Get in line and act like adults, will you?
They're trying to keep us out!
The hell are you talking about? Who's trying to keep who out?
MCPD
They've shut down all the loopevators to 50! They don't want us up there!
Bullshit.
Straight up!
Look, these things have been carrying thousands of people all morning. It probably just broke down.
Not only this one. Control tells me the loopevators were under enormous strain, and have been shut down for safety and maintenance.
You're on their side, of course you'd say that!
MCPD

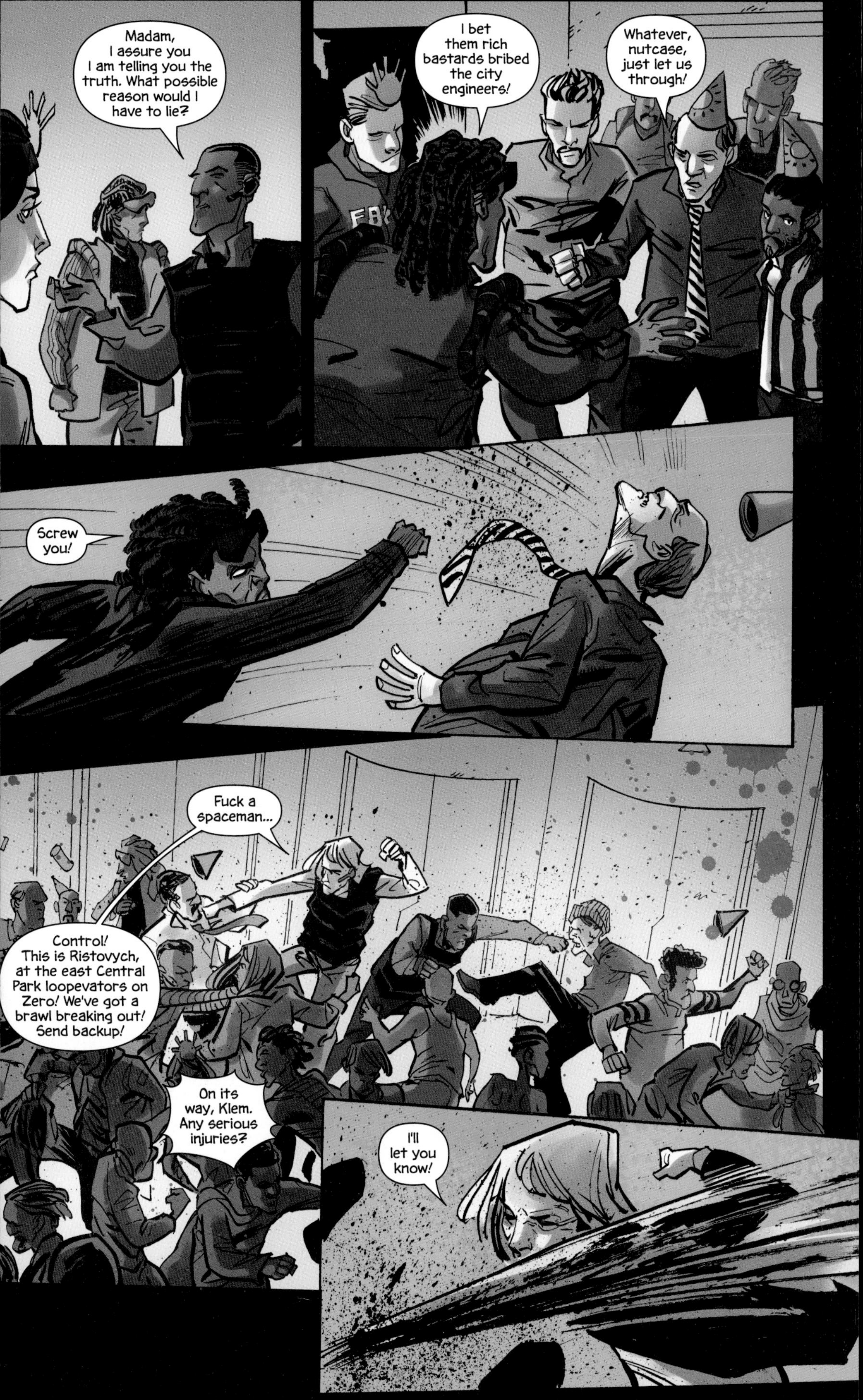

Madam, I assure you I am telling you the truth. What possible reason would I have to lie?
I bet them rich bastards bribed the city engineers!
Whatever, nutcase, just let us through!
FBK
Screw you!
Fuck a spaceman...
Control! This is Ristovych, at the east Central Park loopevators on Zero! We've got a brawl breaking out! Send backup!
On its way, Klem. Any serious injuries?
I'll let you know!

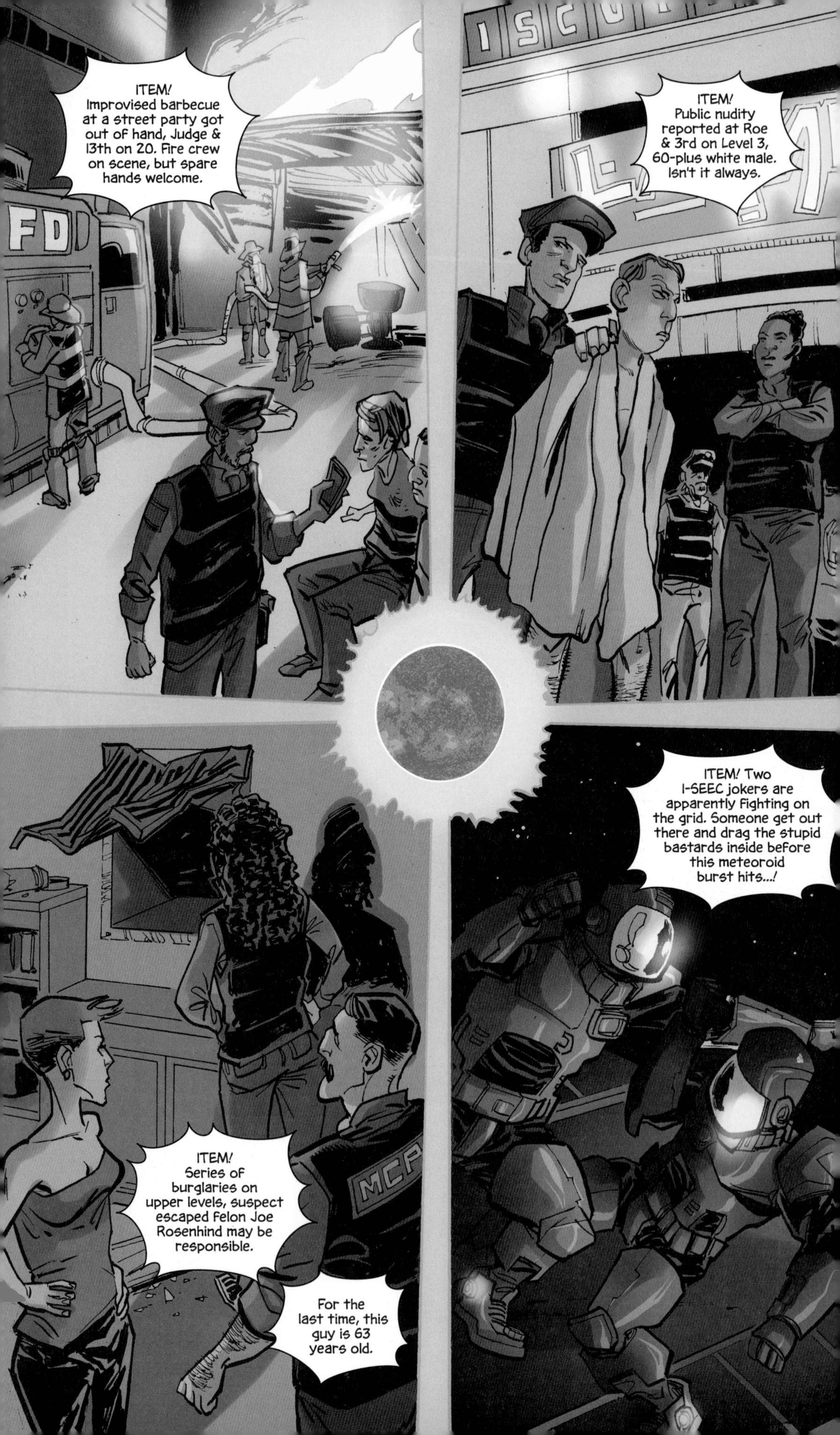
ITEM! Improvised barbecue at a street party got out of hand, Judge & 13th on 20. Fire crew on scene, but spare hands welcome.
FD
ITEM! Public nudity reported at Roe & 3rd on Level 3, 60-plus white male. Isn't it always.
ITEM! Series of burglaries on upper levels, suspect escaped felon Joe Rosenhind may be responsible.
For the last time, this guy is 63 years old.
ITEM! Two I-SEEC jokers are apparently fighting on the grid. Someone get out there and drag the stupid bastards inside before this meteoroid burst hits...!

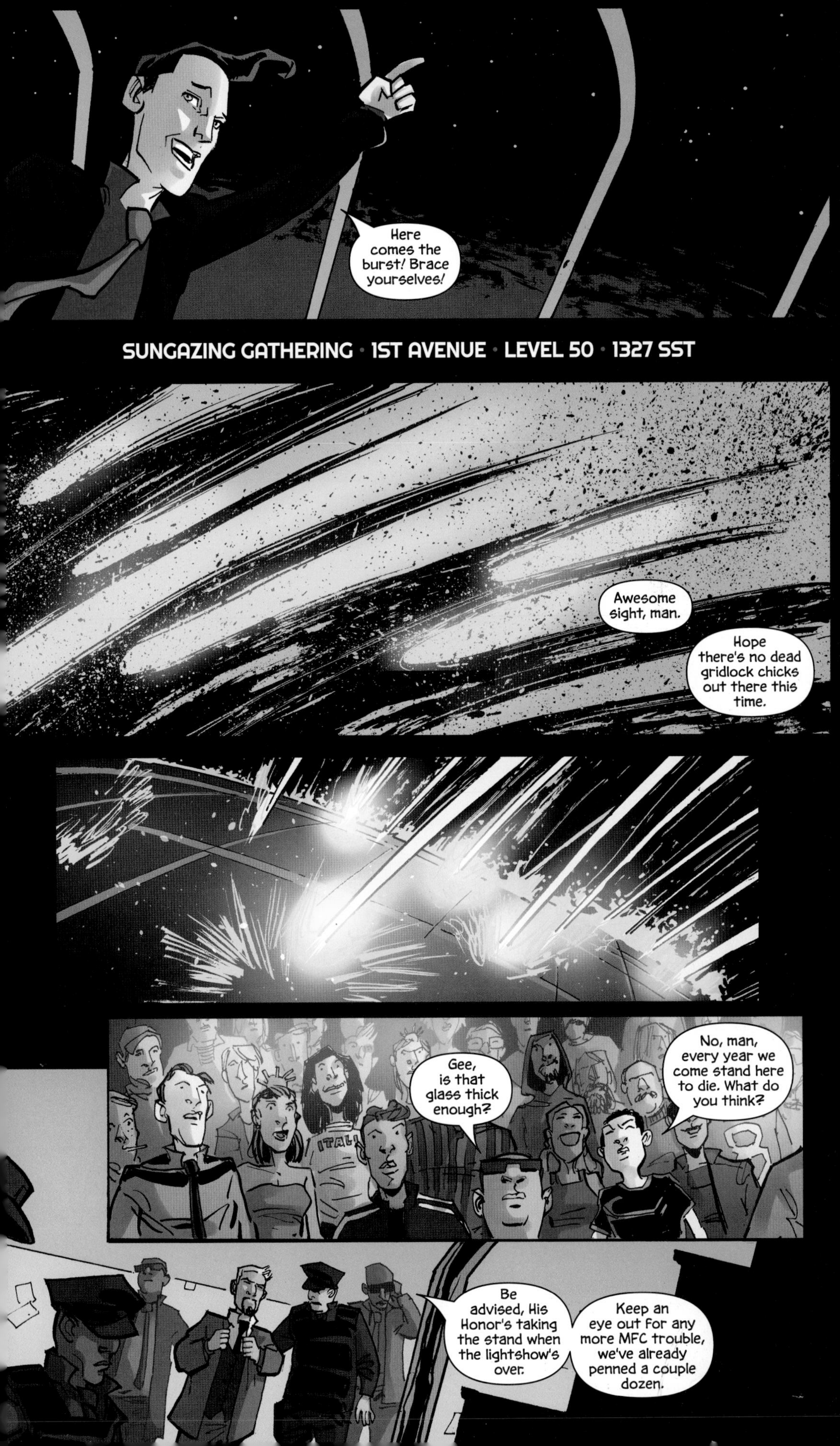
Here comes the burst! Brace yourselves!
SUNGAZING GATHERING • 1ST AVENUE • LEVEL 50 • 1327 SST
Awesome sight, man.
Hope there's no dead gridlock chicks out there this time.
Gee, is that glass thick enough?
No, man, every year we come stand here to die. What do you think?
Be advised, His Honor's taking the stand when the lightshow's over.
Keep an eye out for any more MFC trouble, we've already penned a couple dozen.

PERIHELION CARNIVAL • CENTRAL PARK • LEVEL ZERO • 1331 SST

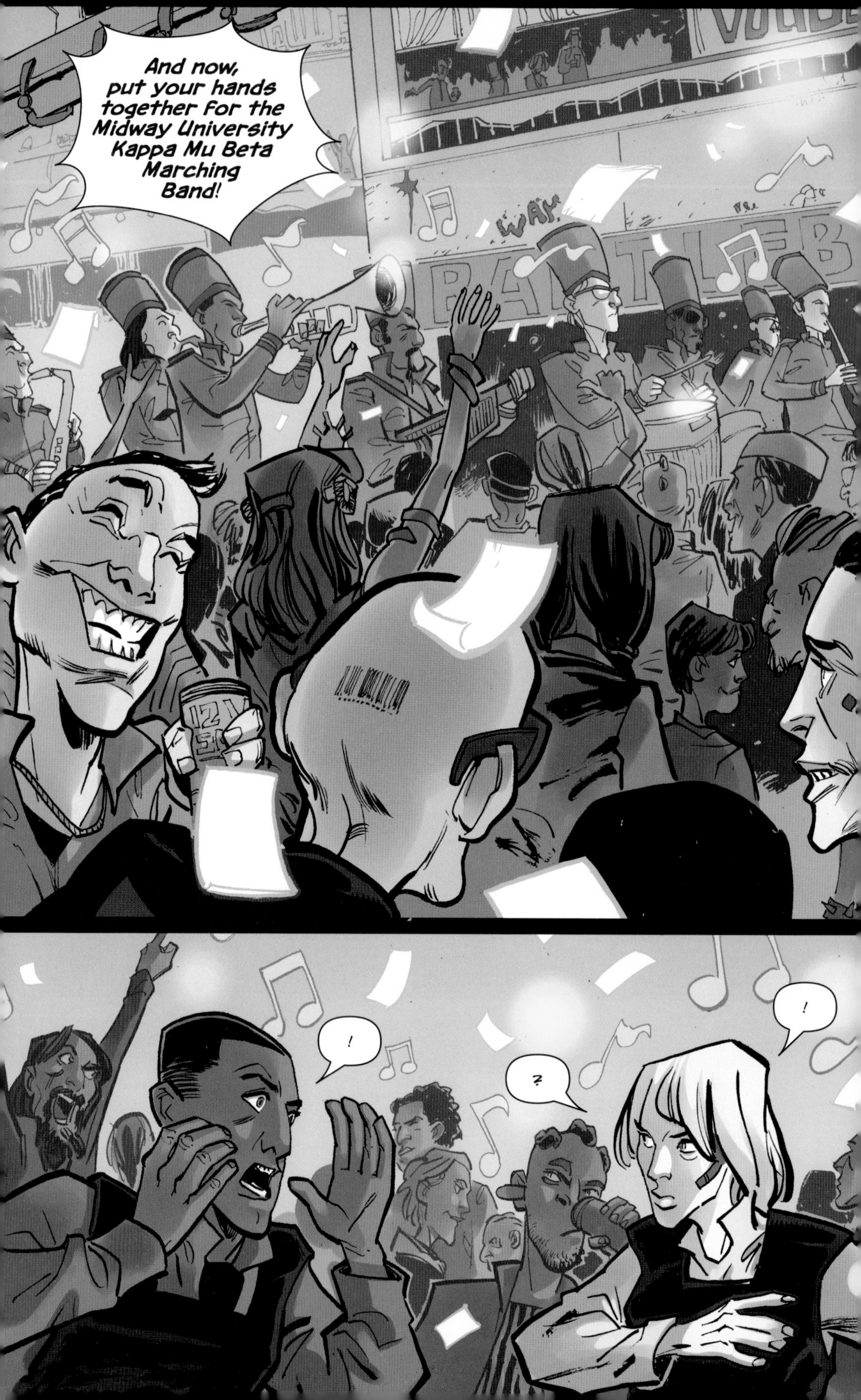
And now, put your hands together for the Midway University Kappa Mu Beta Marching Band!
WAY
!
?
!

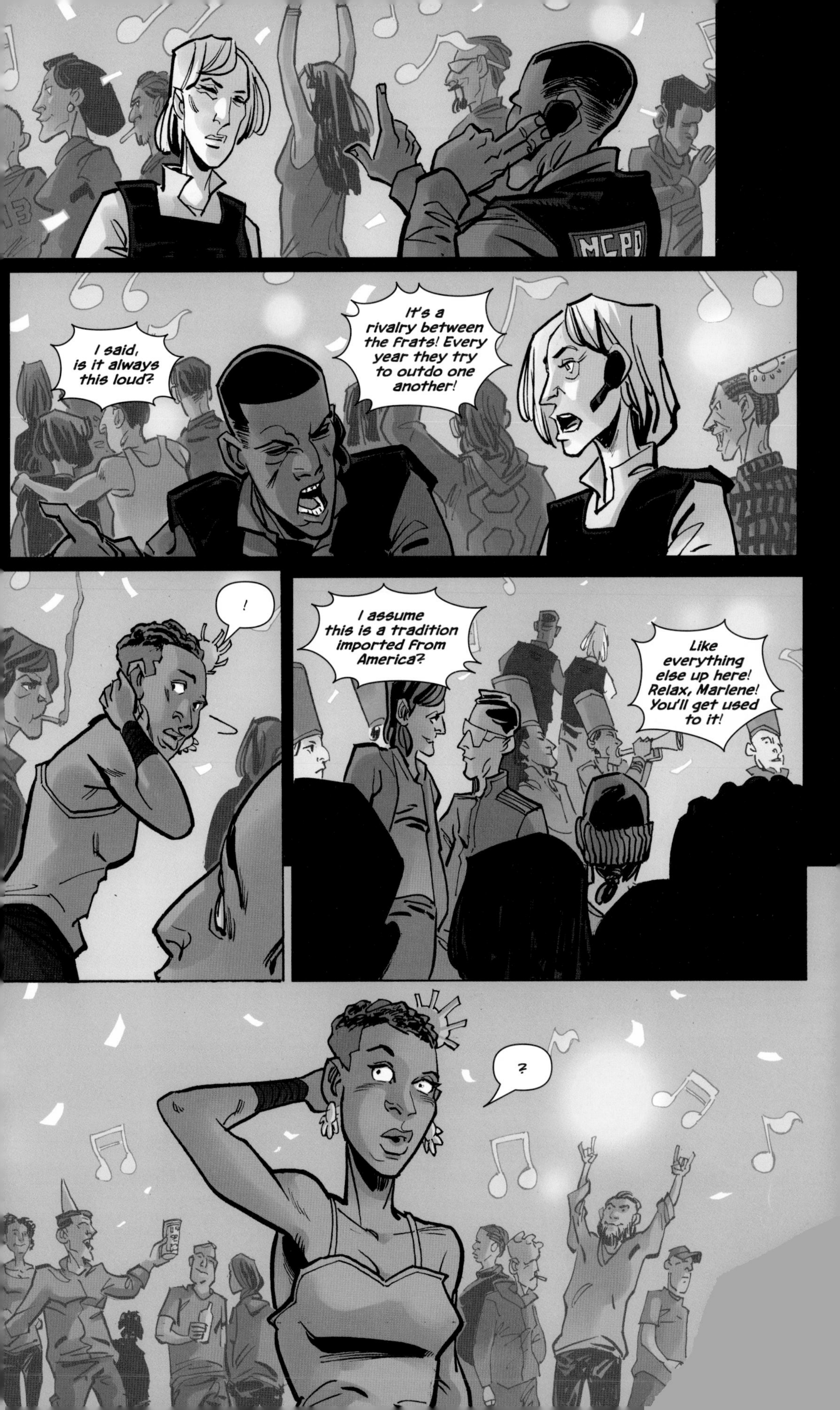
I said, is it always this loud?
It's a rivalry between the frats! Every year they try to outdo one another!
!
I assume this is a tradition imported from America?
Like everything else up here! Relax, Marlene! You'll get used to it!
?

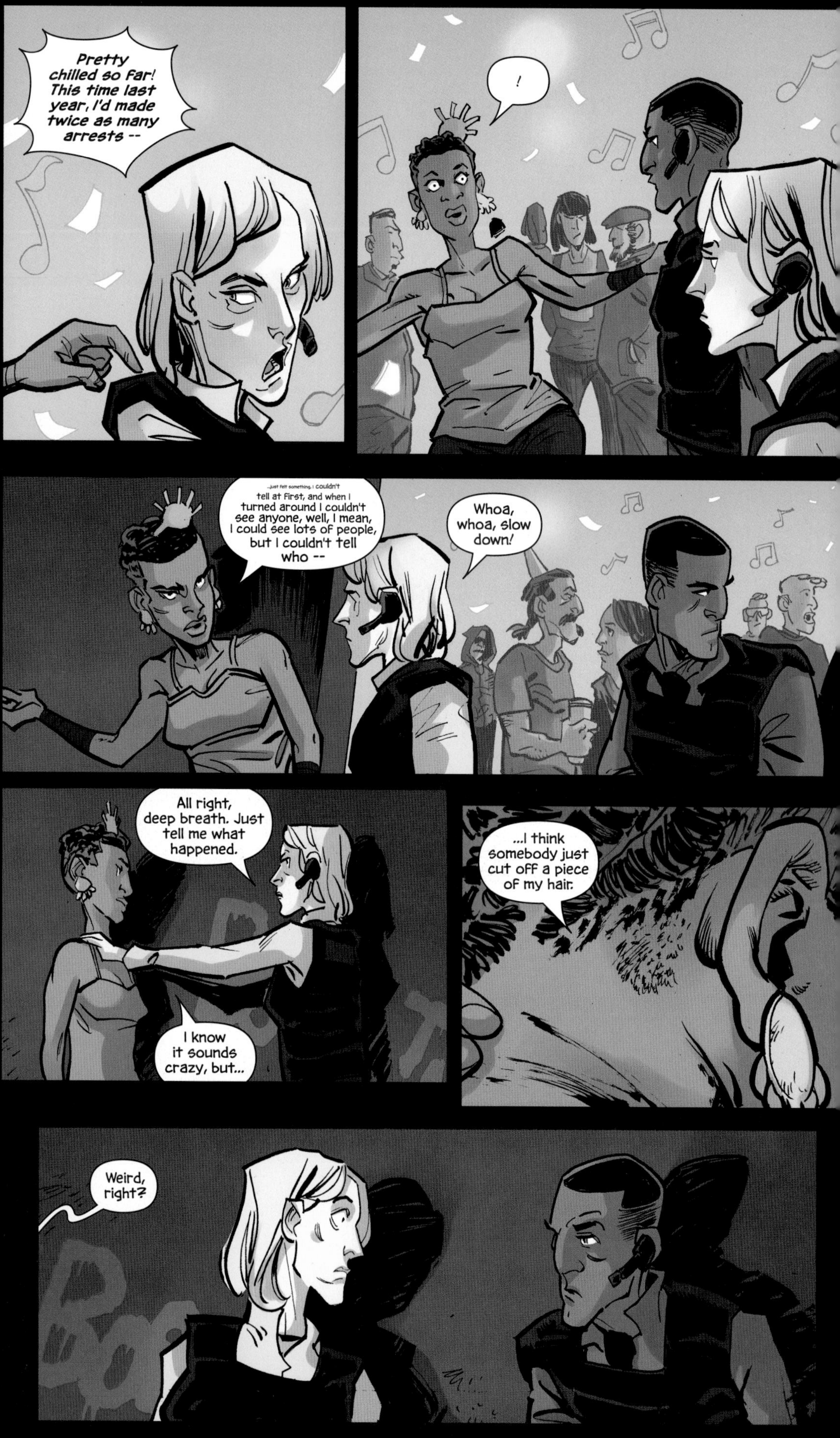
Pretty chilled so far! This time last year, I'd made twice as many arrests --
!
...just felt something. I couldn't tell at first, and when I turned around I couldn't see anyone, well, I mean, I could see lots of people, but I couldn't tell who --
Whoa, whoa, slow down!
All right, deep breath. Just tell me what happened.
I know it sounds crazy, but...
...I think somebody just cut off a piece of my hair.
Weird, right?

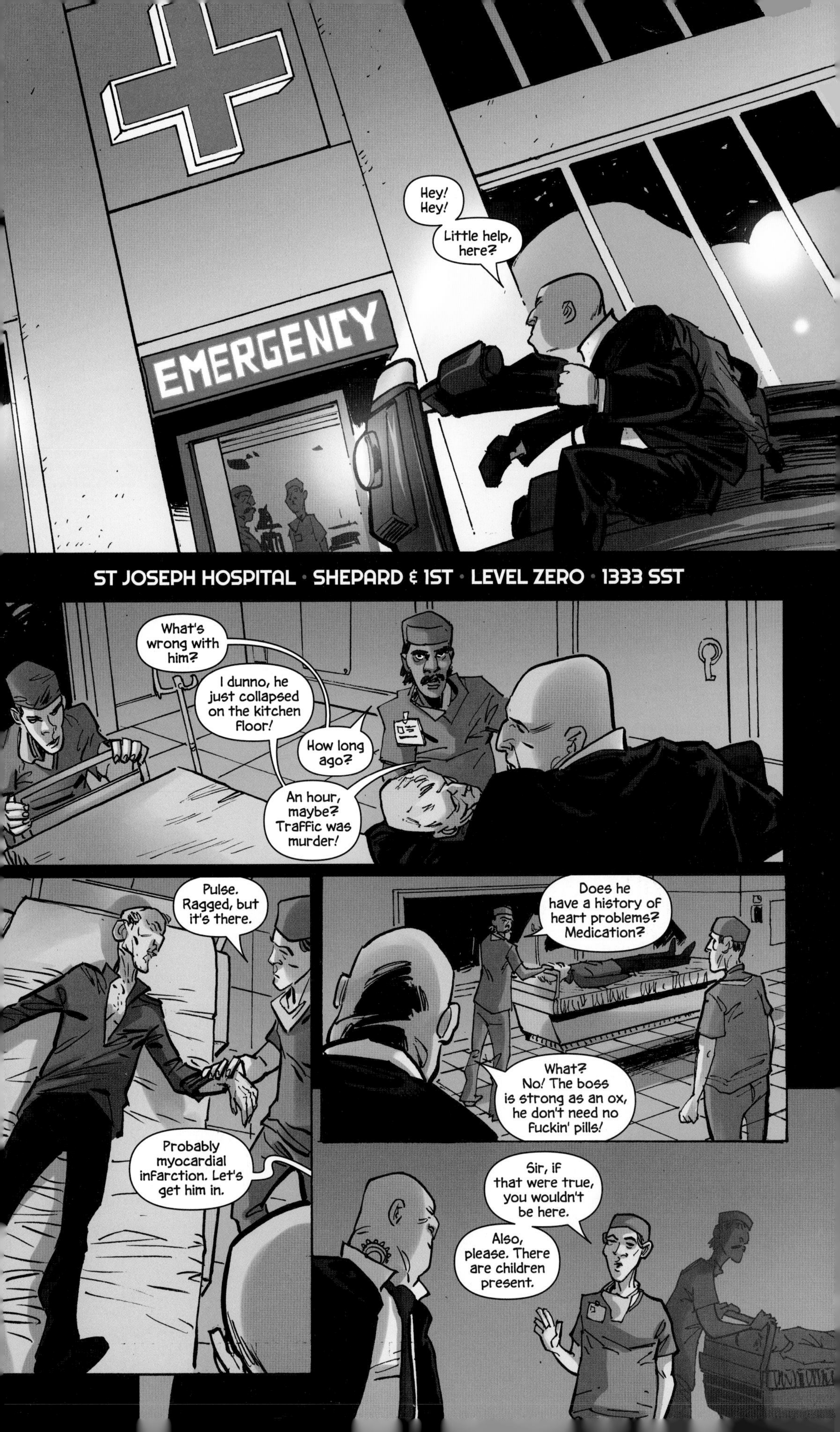

Hey! Hey!
Little help, here?
EMERGENCY
ST JOSEPH HOSPITAL • SHEPARD & 1ST • LEVEL ZERO • 1333 SST
What's wrong with him?
I dunno, he just collapsed on the kitchen floor!
How long ago?
An hour, maybe? Traffic was murder!
Pulse. Ragged, but it's there.
Probably myocardial infarction. Let's get him in.
Does he have a history of heart problems? Medication?
What? No! The boss is strong as an ox, he don't need no fuckin' pills!
Sir, if that were true, you wouldn't be here.
Also, please. There are children present.

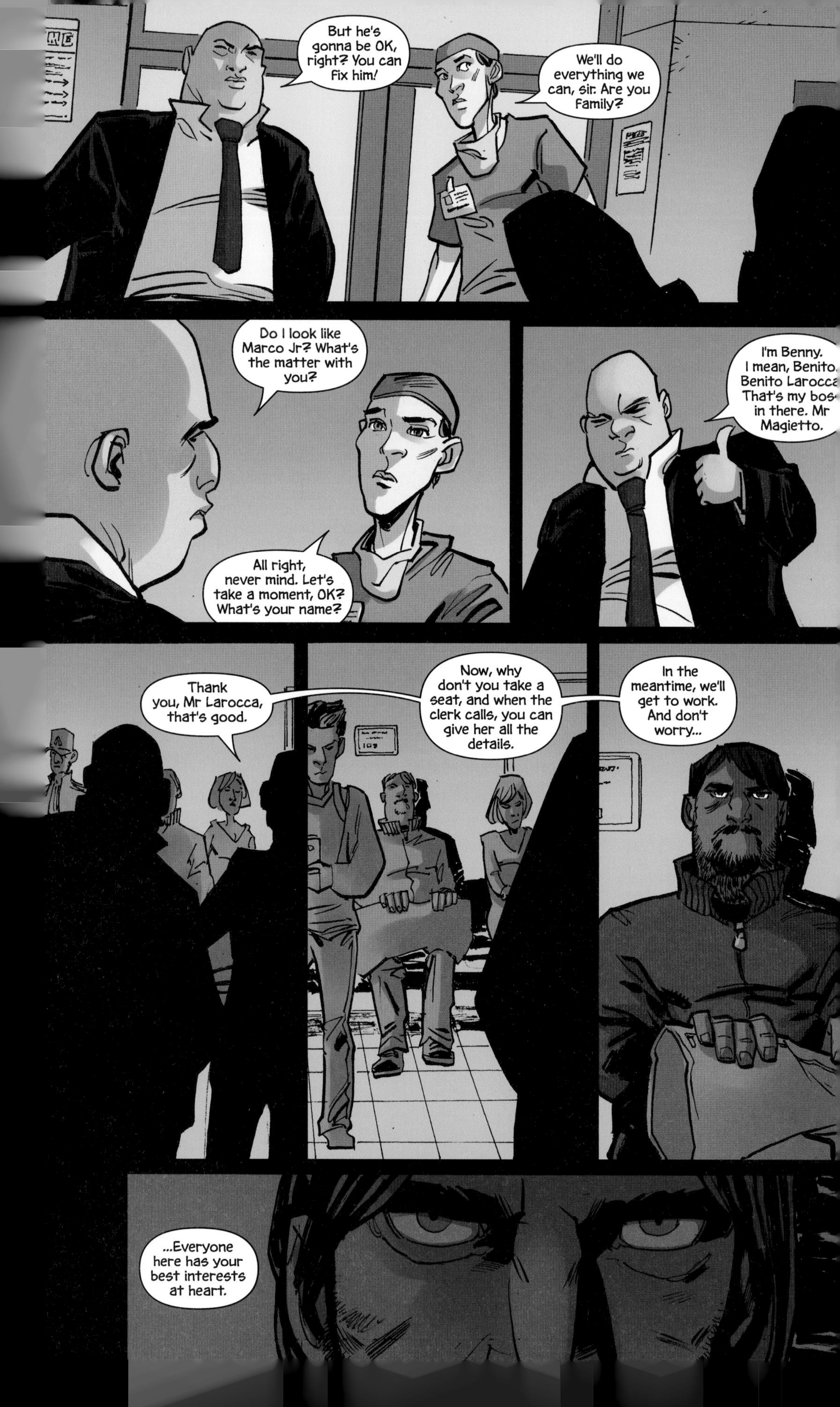
But he's gonna be OK, right? You can fix him!
We'll do everything we can, sir. Are you family?
Do I look like Marco Jr? What's the matter with you?
All right, never mind. Let's take a moment, OK? What's your name?
I'm Benny. I mean, Benito. Benito Larocca. That's my boss in there. Mr Magietto.
Thank you, Mr Larocca, that's good.
Now, why don't you take a seat, and when the clerk calls, you can give her all the details.
In the meantime, we'll get to work. And don't worry...
...Everyone here has your best interests at heart.

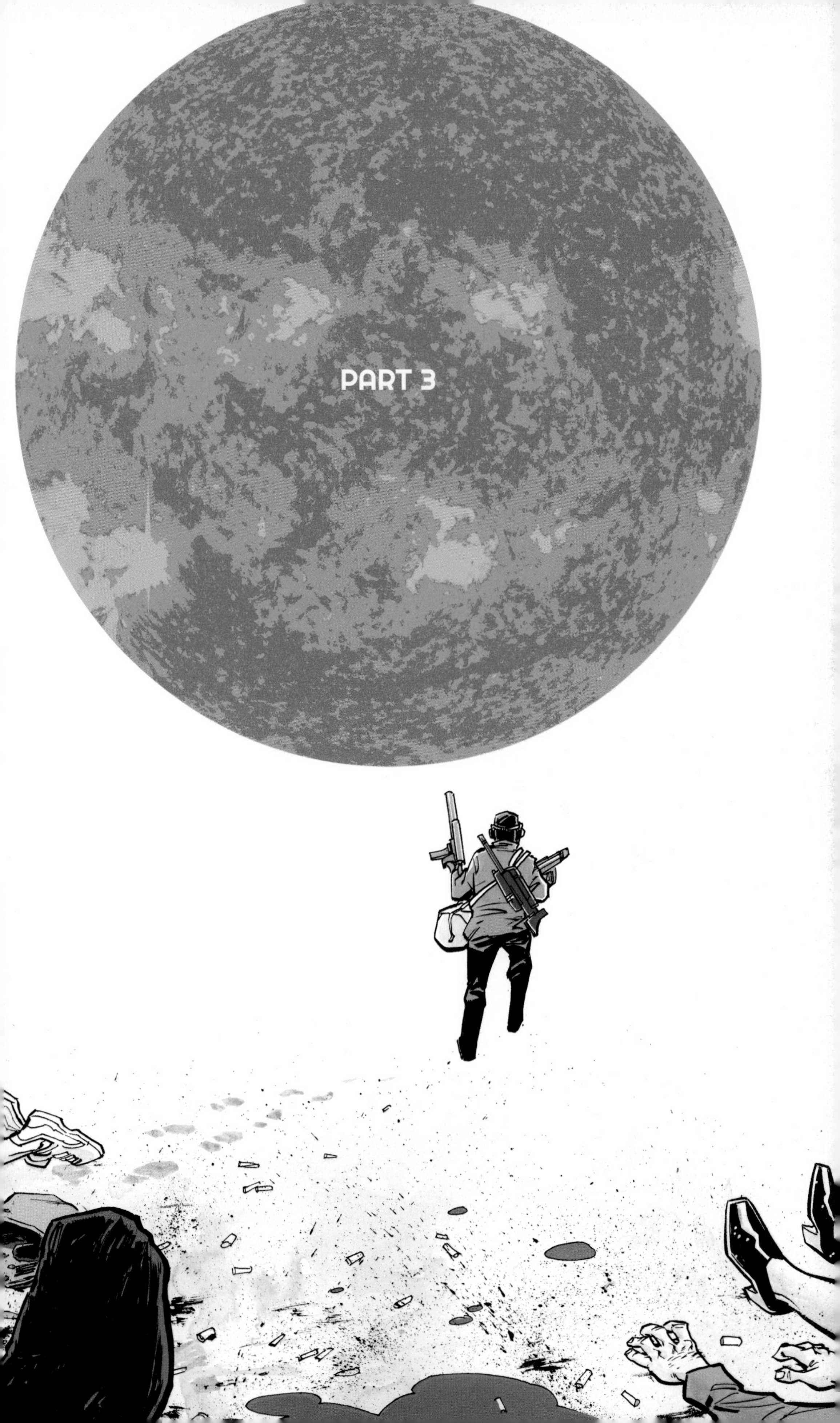
PART 3

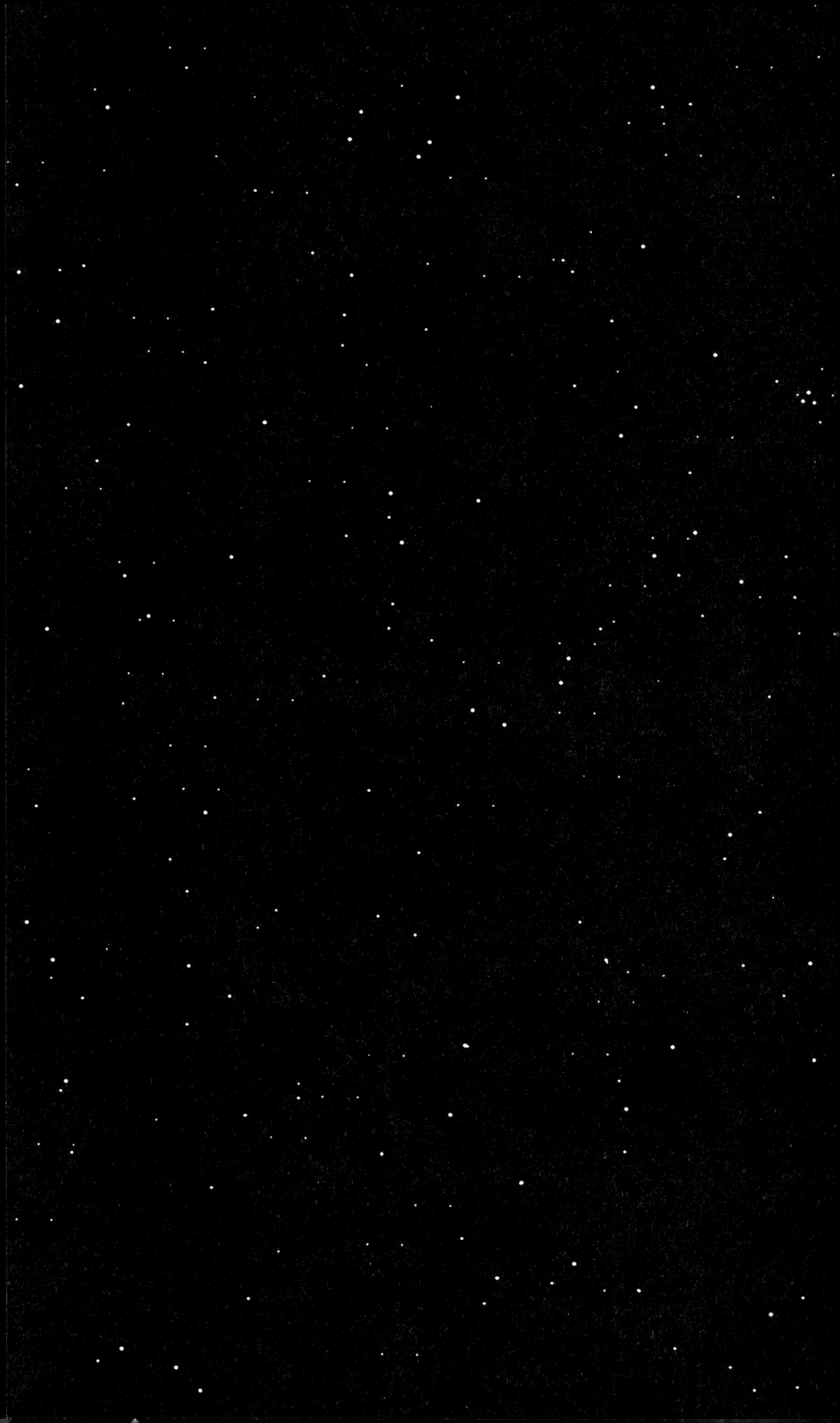

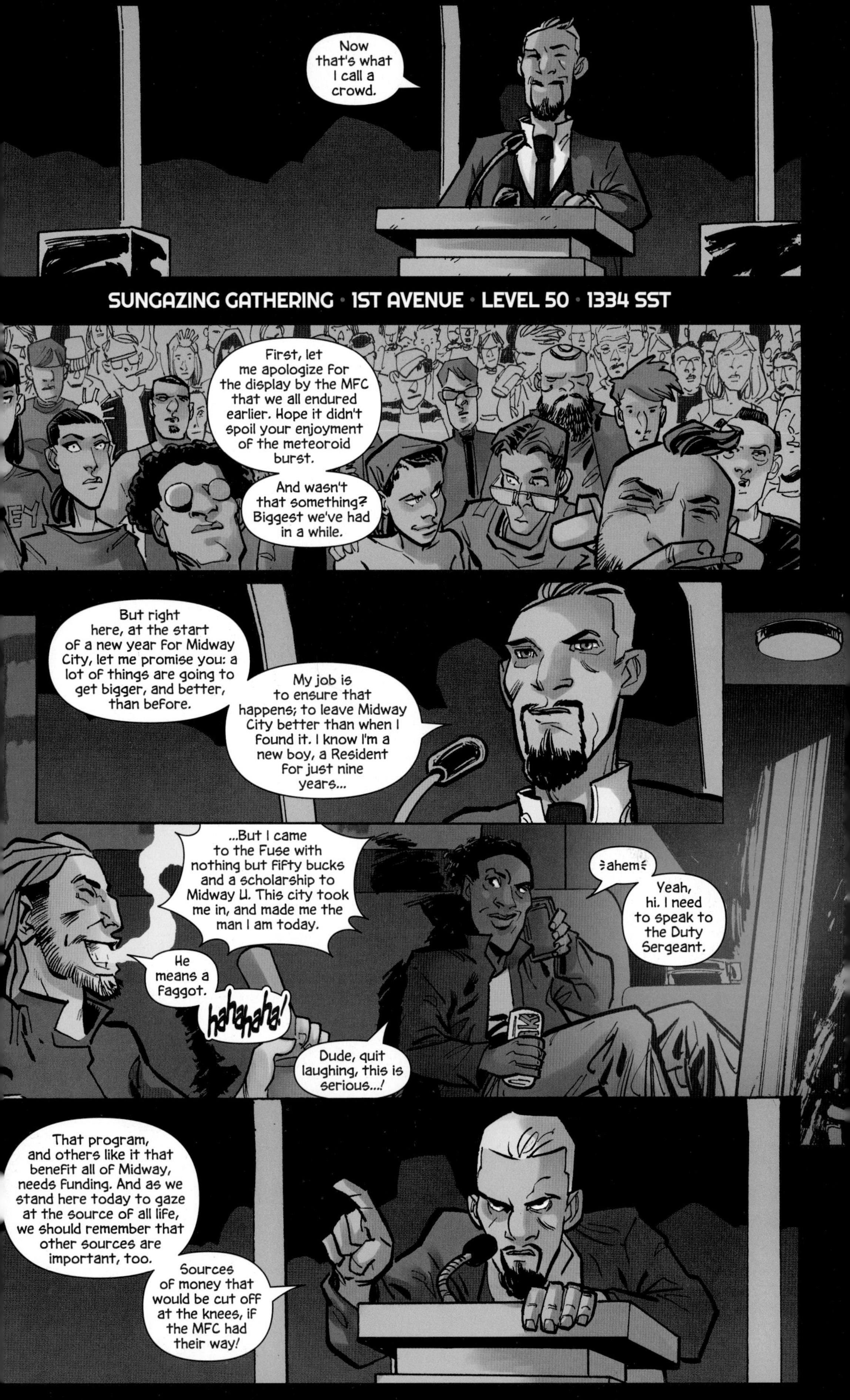
Now that's what I call a crowd.
SUNGAZING GATHERING • 1ST AVENUE • LEVEL 50 • 1334 SST
First, let me apologize for the display by the MFC that we all endured earlier. Hope it didn't spoil your enjoyment of the meteoroid burst.
And wasn't that something? Biggest we've had in a while.
But right here, at the start of a new year for Midway City, let me promise you: a lot of things are going to get bigger, and better, than before.
My job is to ensure that happens; to leave Midway City better than when I found it. I know I'm a new boy, a Resident for just nine years...
...But I came to the Fuse with nothing but fifty bucks and a scholarship to Midway U. This city took me in, and made me the man I am today.
He means a faggot.
hahahaha!
Dude, quit laughing, this is serious...!
ahem
Yeah, hi. I need to speak to the Duty Sergeant.
That program, and others like it that benefit all of Midway, needs funding. And as we stand here today to gaze at the source of all life, we should remember that other sources are important, too.
Sources of money that would be cut off at the knees, if the MFC had their way!

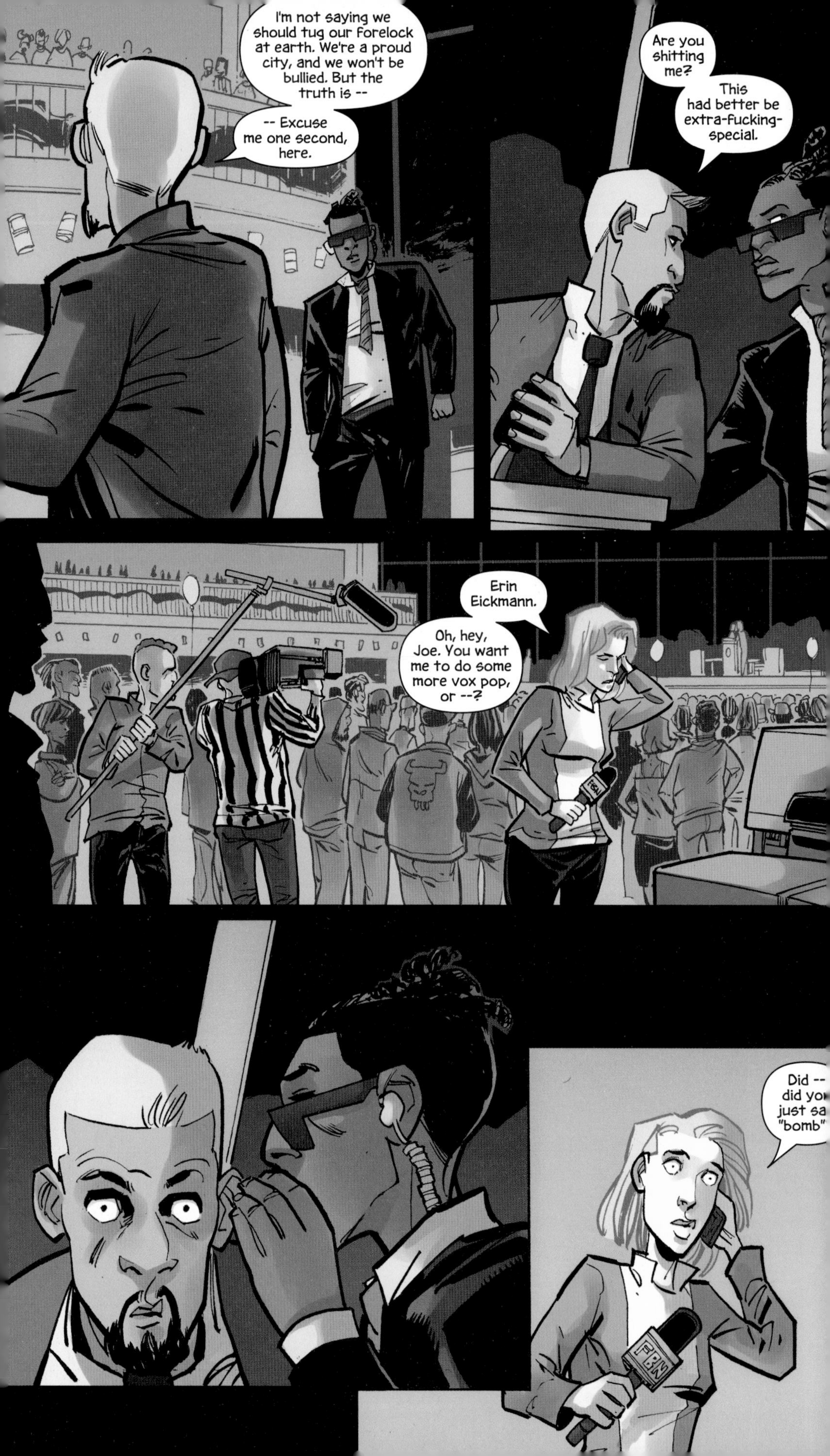
I'm not saying we should tug our forelock at earth. We're a proud city, and we won't be bullied. But the truth is --
-- Excuse me one second, here.
Are you shitting me?
This had better be extra-fucking-special.
Erin Eickmann.
Oh, hey, Joe. You want me to do some more vox pop, or --?
FBN
Did -- did yo just sa "bomb"
FBN

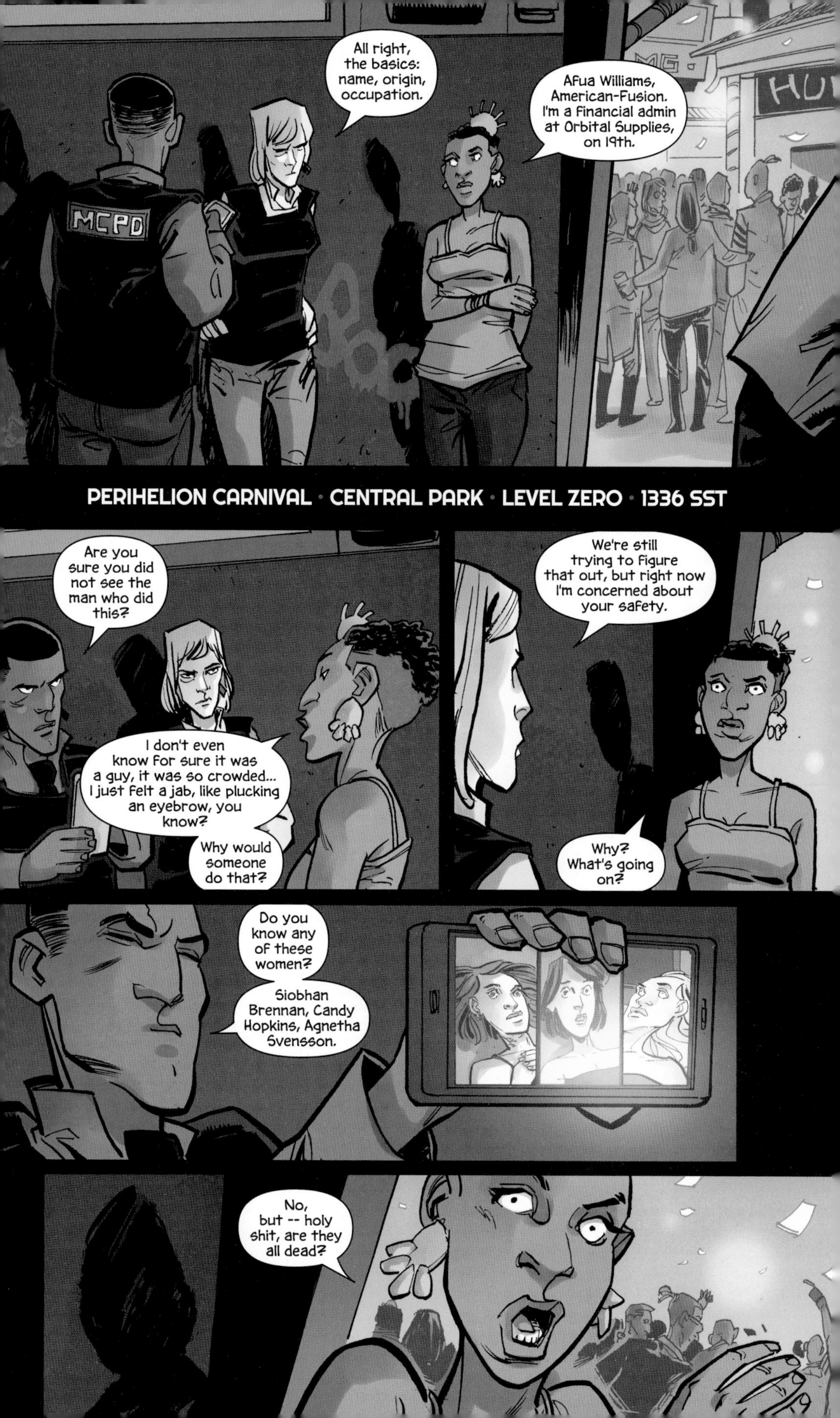
All right, the basics: name, origin, occupation.
Afua Williams, American-Fusion. I'm a financial admin at Orbital Supplies, on 19th.
MCPD
PERIHELION CARNIVAL · CENTRAL PARK · LEVEL ZERO · 1336 SST
Are you sure you did not see the man who did this?
I don't even know for sure it was a guy, it was so crowded... I just felt a jab, like plucking an eyebrow, you know?
Why would someone do that?
We're still trying to figure that out, but right now I'm concerned about your safety.
Why? What's going on?
Do you know any of these women?
Siobhan Brennan, Candy Hopkins, Agnetha Svensson.
No, but -- holy shit, are they all dead?

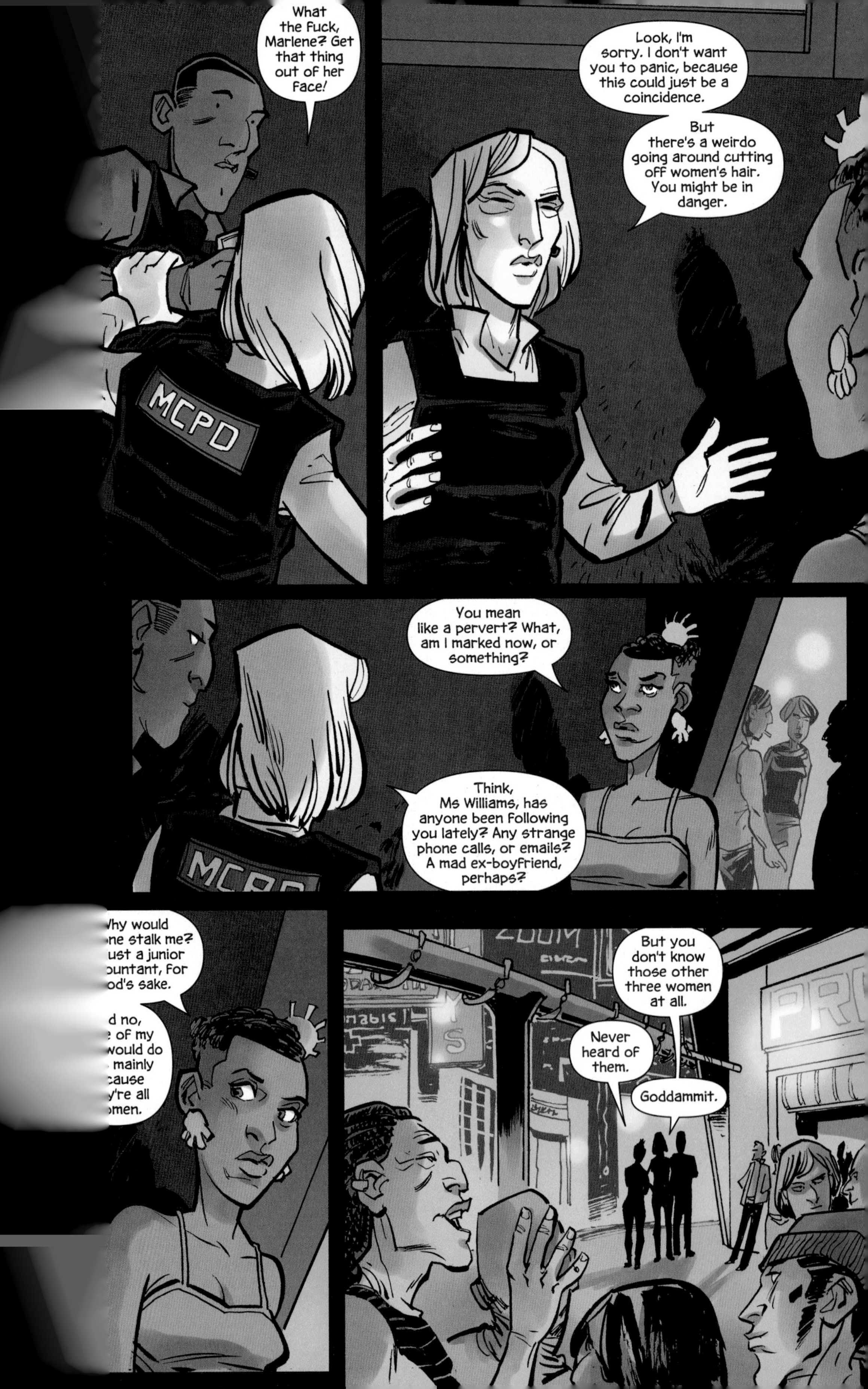
What the Fuck, Marlene? Get that thing out of her face!
MCPD
Look, I'm sorry. I don't want you to panic, because this could just be a coincidence.
But there's a weirdo going around cutting off women's hair. You might be in danger.
You mean like a pervert? What, am I marked now, or something?
Think, Ms Williams, has anyone been following you lately? Any strange phone calls, or emails? A mad ex-boyfriend, perhaps?
Why would
ne stalk me?
ust a junior
ountant, For
od's sake.
d no,
e of my
would do
mainly
cause
y're all
omen.
But you don't know those other three women at all.
Never heard of them.
Goddammit.

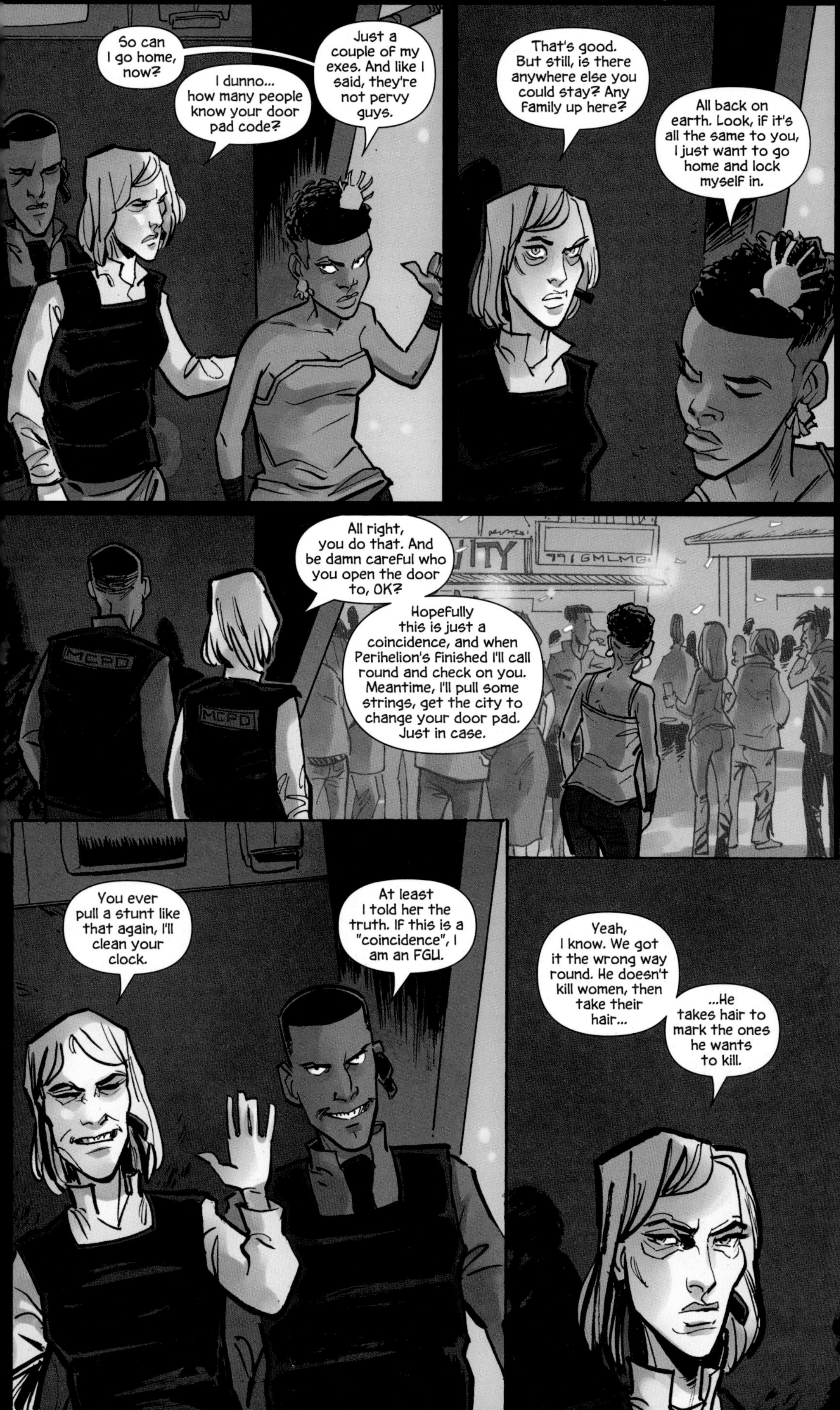
So can I go home, now?
I dunno... how many people know your door pad code?
Just a couple of my exes. And like I said, they're not pervy guys.
That's good. But still, is there anywhere else you could stay? Any family up here?
All back on earth. Look, if it's all the same to you, I just want to go home and lock myself in.
All right, you do that. And be damn careful who you open the door to, OK?
Hopefully this is just a coincidence, and when Perihelion's Finished I'll call round and check on you. Meantime, I'll pull some strings, get the city to change your door pad. Just in case.
You ever pull a stunt like that again, I'll clean your clock.
At least I told her the truth. If this is a "coincidence", I am an FGU.
Yeah, I know. We got it the wrong way round. He doesn't kill women, then take their hair...
...He takes hair to mark the ones he wants to kill.

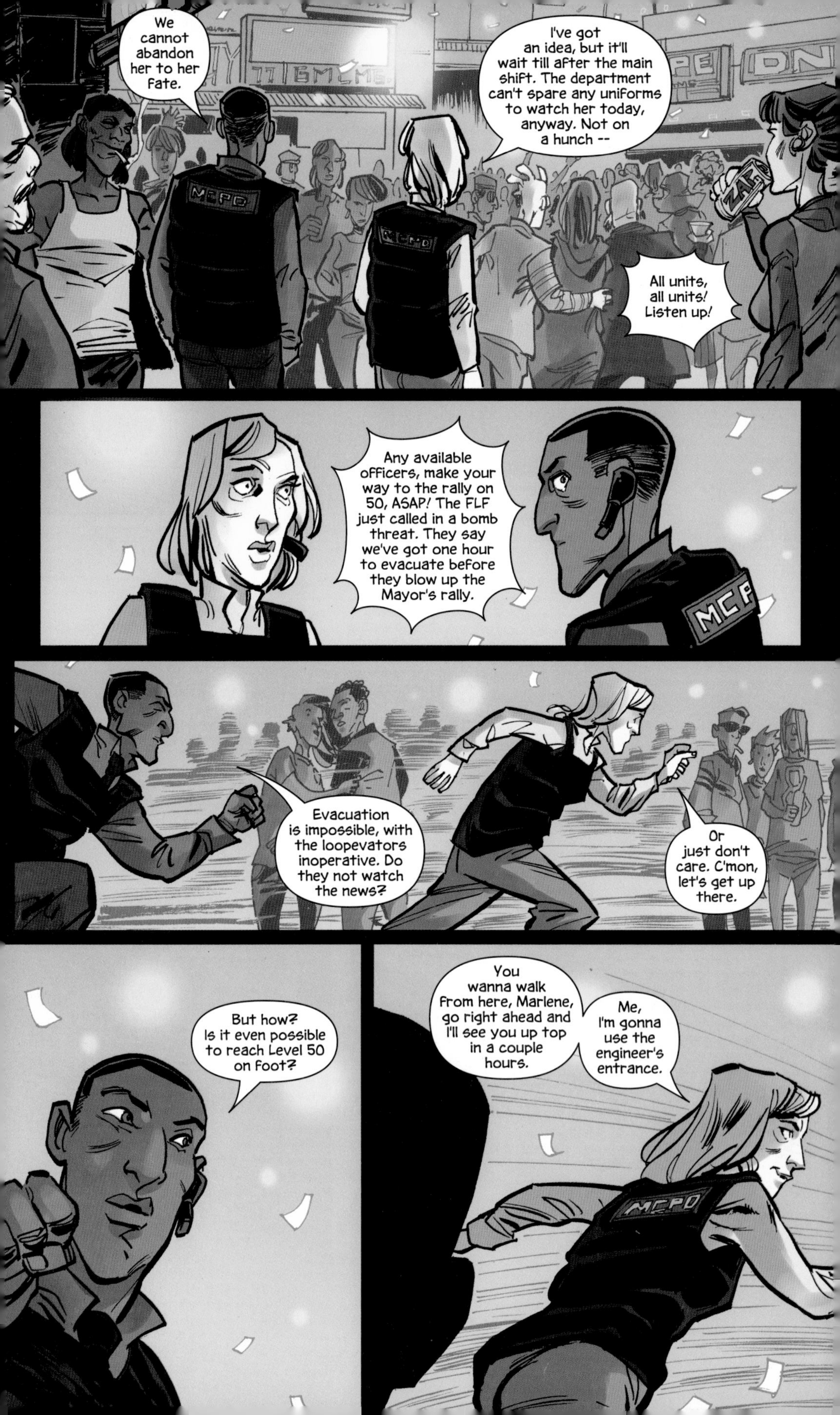
We cannot abandon her to her fate.
I've got an idea, but it'll wait till after the main shift. The department can't spare any uniforms to watch her today, anyway. Not on a hunch --
All units, all units! Listen up!
Any available officers, make your way to the rally on 50, ASAP! The FLF just called in a bomb threat. They say we've got one hour to evacuate before they blow up the Mayor's rally.
Evacuation is impossible, with the loopevators inoperative. Do they not watch the news?
Or just don't care. C'mon, let's get up there.
But how? Is it even possible to reach Level 50 on foot?
You wanna walk from here, Marlene, go right ahead and I'll see you up top in a couple hours.
Me, I'm gonna use the engineer's entrance.

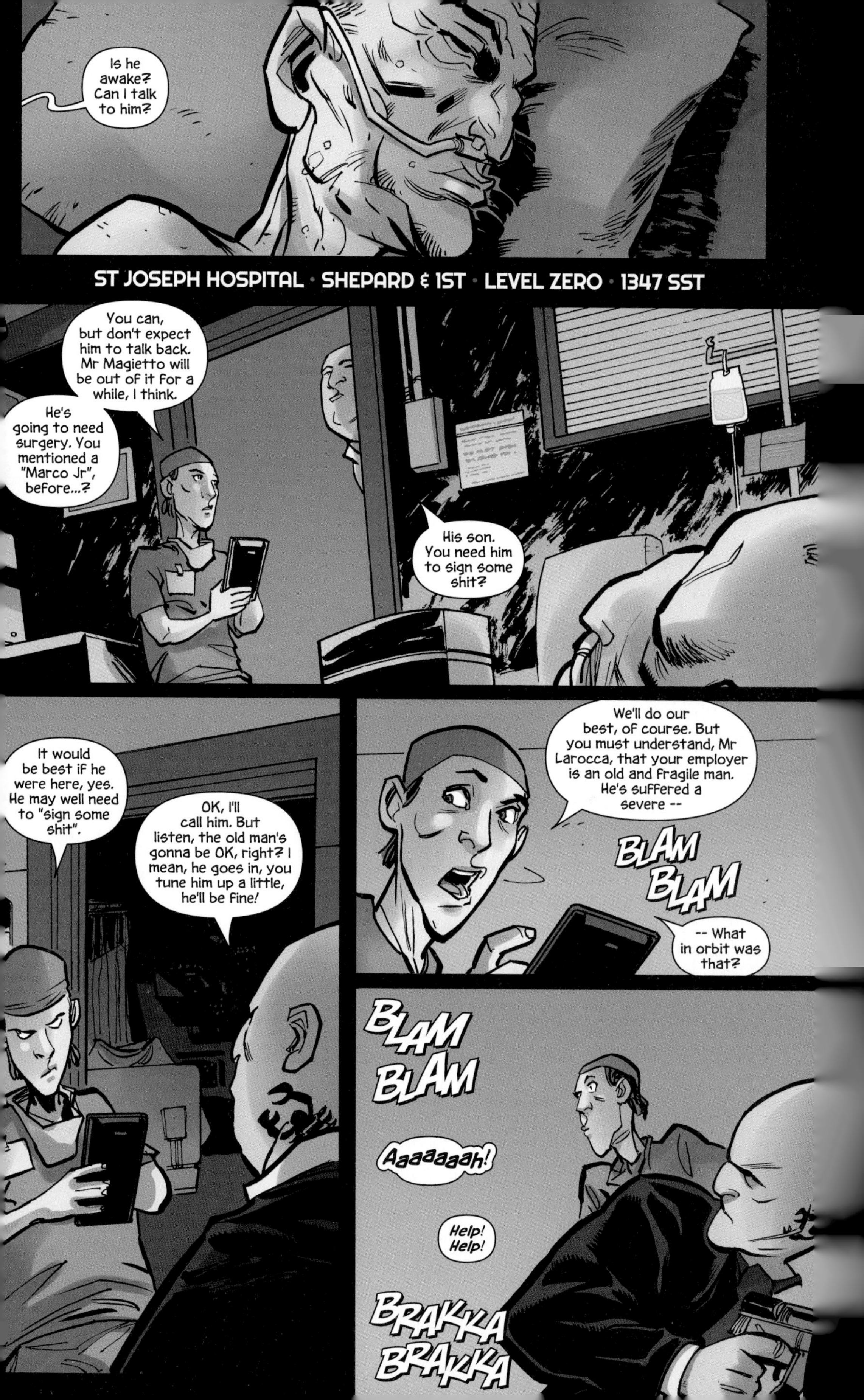
Is he awake? Can I talk to him?
ST JOSEPH HOSPITAL · SHEPARD & 1ST · LEVEL ZERO · 1347 SST
You can, but don't expect him to talk back. Mr Magietto will be out of it for a while, I think.
He's going to need surgery. You mentioned a "Marco Jr", before...?
His son. You need him to sign some shit?
It would be best if he were here, yes. He may well need to "sign some shit".
OK, I'll call him. But listen, the old man's gonna be OK, right? I mean, he goes in, you tune him up a little, he'll be fine!
We'll do our best, of course. But you must understand, Mr Larocca, that your employer is an old and fragile man. He's suffered a severe --
BLAM BLAM
-- What in orbit was that?
BLAM BLAM
Aaaaaaah!
Help! Help!
BRAKKA BRAKKA

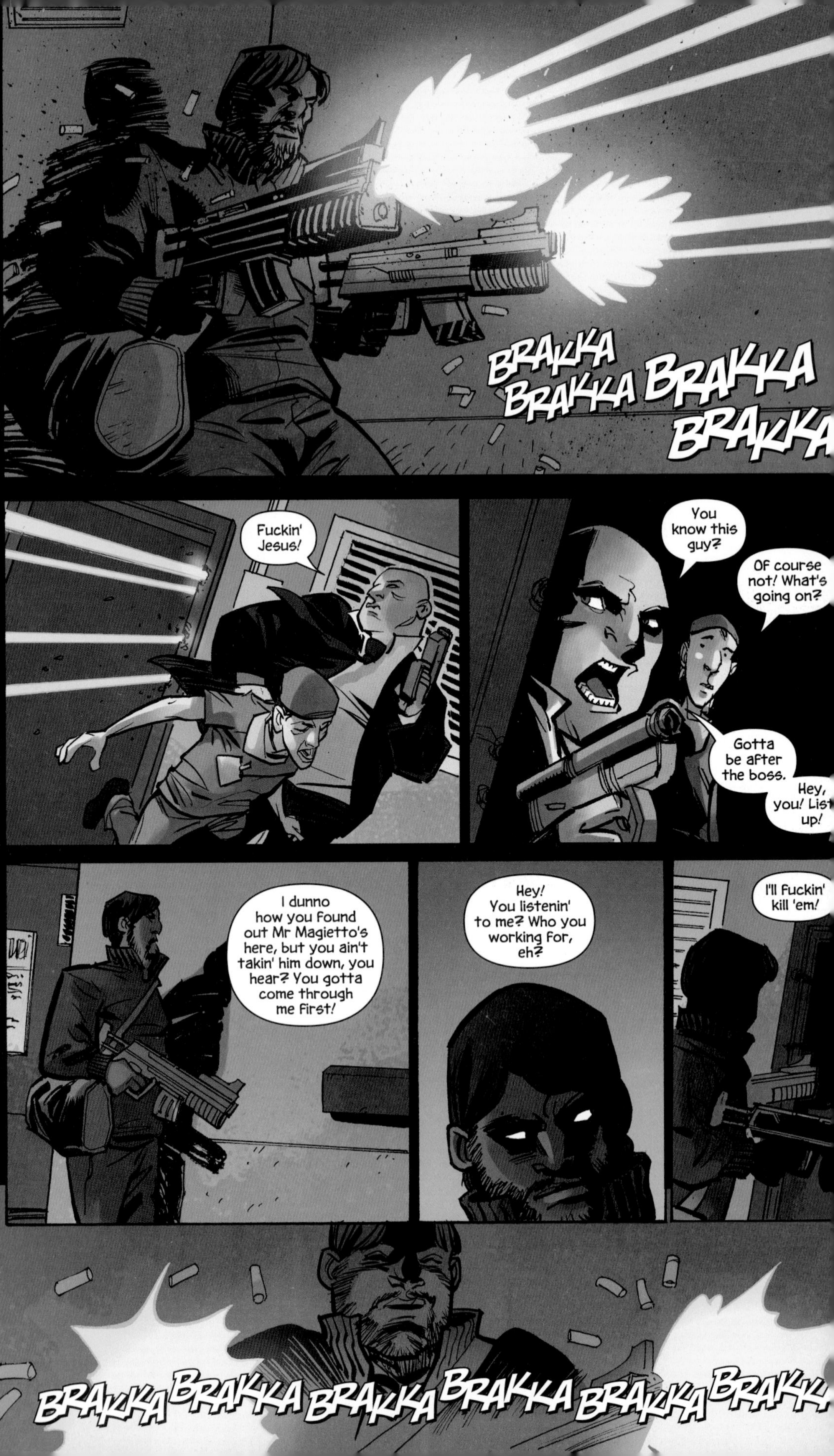
BRAKKA BRAKKA BRAKKA BRAKKA
Fuckin' Jesus!
You know this guy?
Of course not! What's going on?
Gotta be after the boss.
Hey, you! List up!
I dunno how you found out Mr Magietto's here, but you ain't takin' him down, you hear? You gotta come through me first!
Hey! You listenin' to me? Who you working for, eh?
I'll Fuckin' kill 'em!
BRAKKA BRAKKA BRAKKA BRAKKA BRAKKA BRAKK

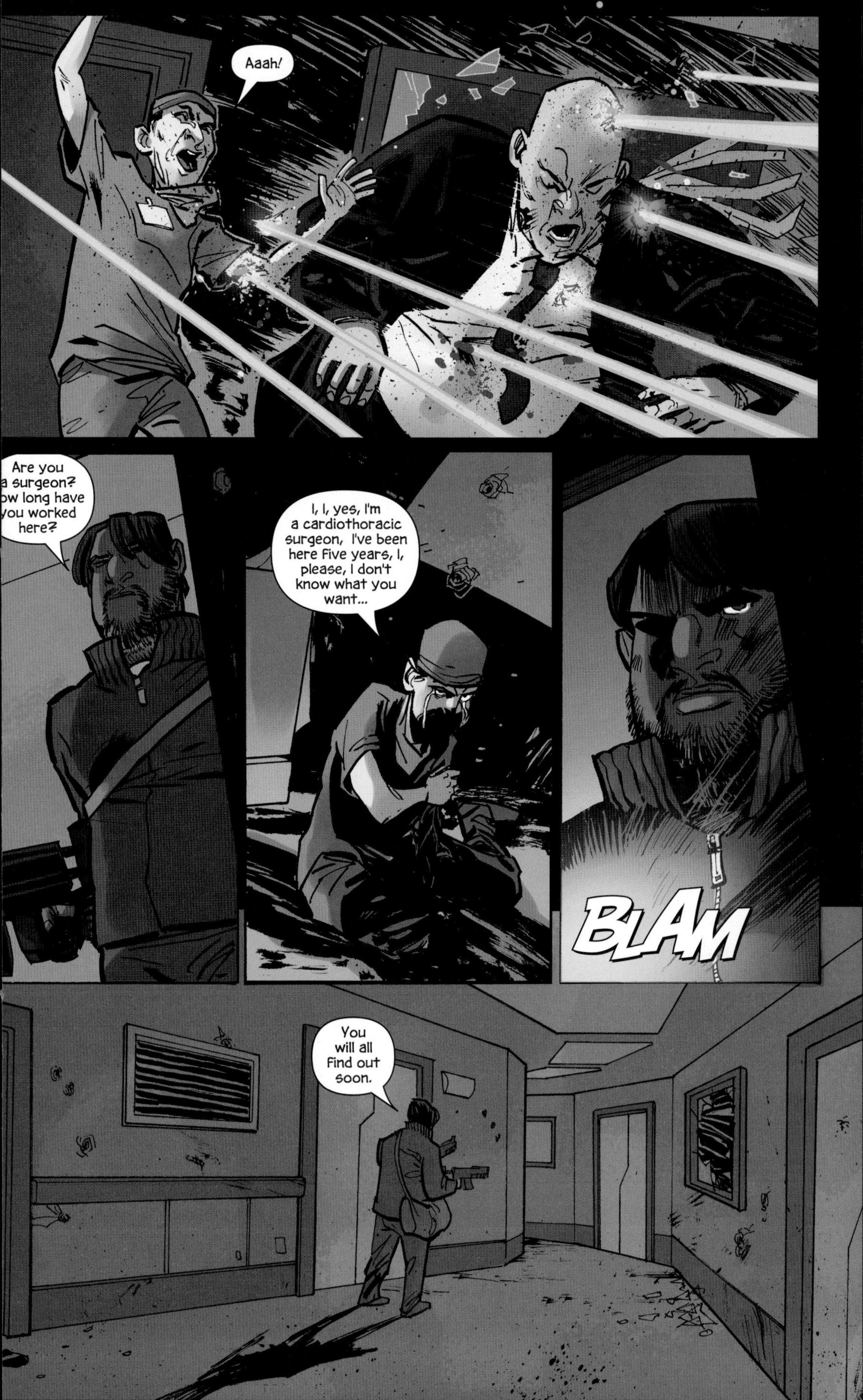
Aaah!
Are you a surgeon? ow long have you worked here?
I, I, yes, I'm a cardiothoracic surgeon, I've been here five years, I, please, I don't know what you want...
BLAM
You will all find out soon.

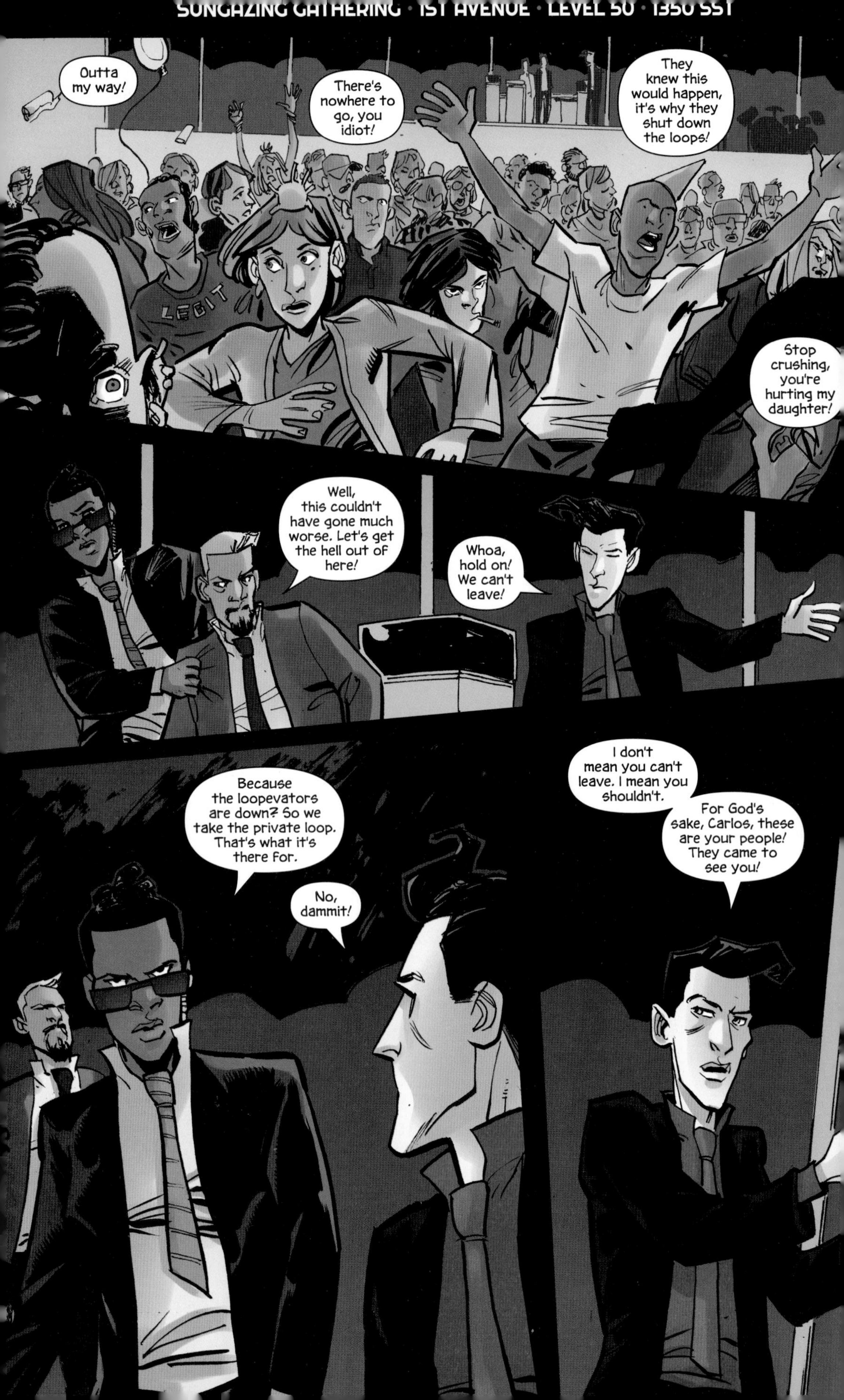
SUNGAZING GATHERING • 1ST AVENUE • LEVEL 50 • 1350 SST
Outta my way!
There's nowhere to go, you idiot!
They knew this would happen, it's why they shut down the loops!
LEGIT
Stop crushing, you're hurting my daughter!
Well, this couldn't have gone much worse. Let's get the hell out of here!
Whoa, hold on! We can't leave!
Because the loopevators are down? So we take the private loop. That's what it's there for.
No, dammit!
I don't mean you can't leave. I mean you shouldn't.
For God's sake, Carlos, these are your people! They came to see you!

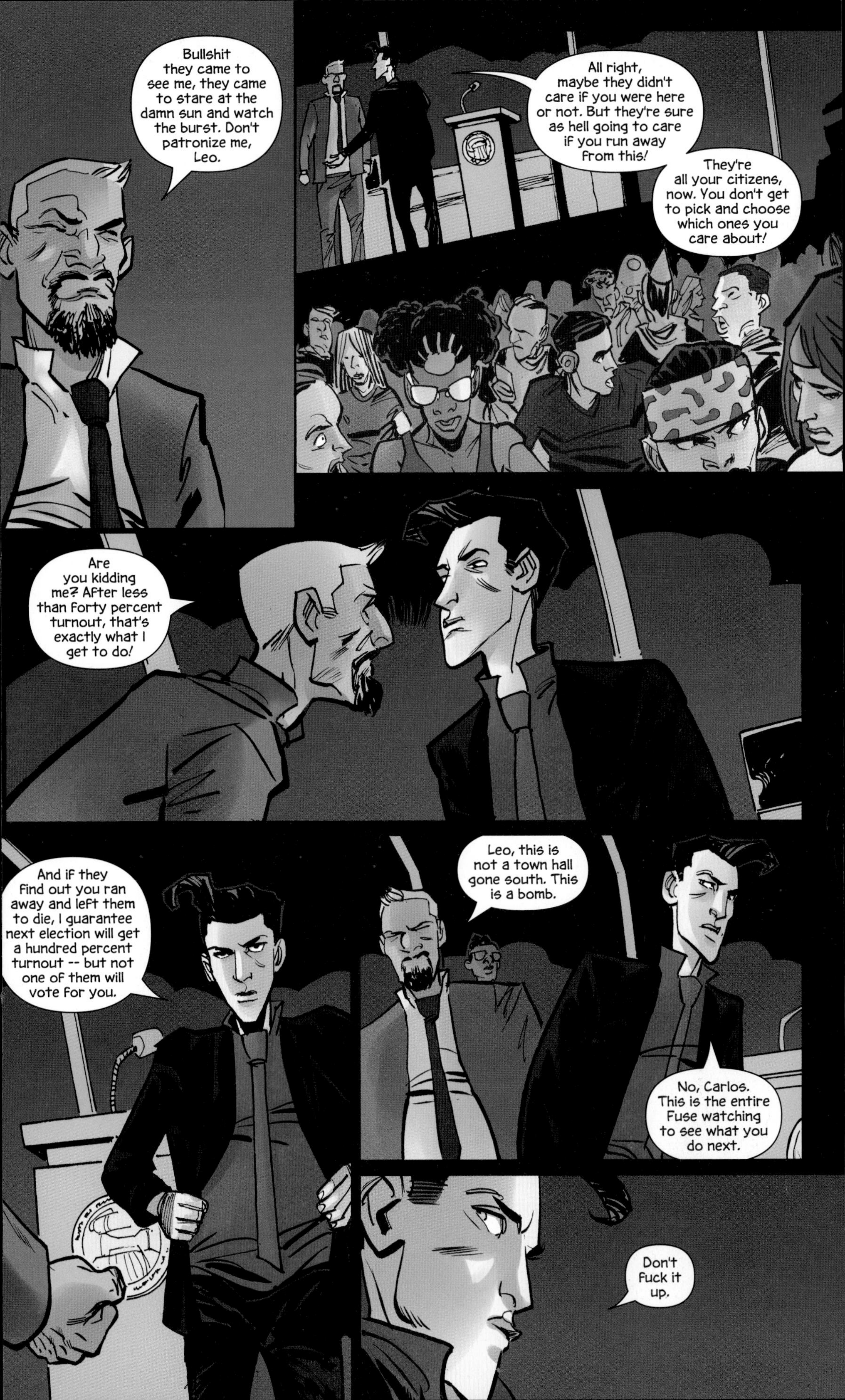
Bullshit they came to see me, they came to stare at the damn sun and watch the burst. Don't patronize me, Leo.
All right, maybe they didn't care if you were here or not. But they're sure as hell going to care if you run away from this!
They're all your citizens, now. You don't get to pick and choose which ones you care about!
Are you kidding me? After less than forty percent turnout, that's exactly what I get to do!
And if they find out you ran away and left them to die, I guarantee next election will get a hundred percent turnout -- but not one of them will vote for you.
Leo, this is not a town hall gone south. This is a bomb.
No, Carlos. This is the entire Fuse watching to see what you do next.
Don't fuck it up.

MAINTENANCE ELEVATOR · CLARKE & 3RD · LEVEL 50 · 1354 SST

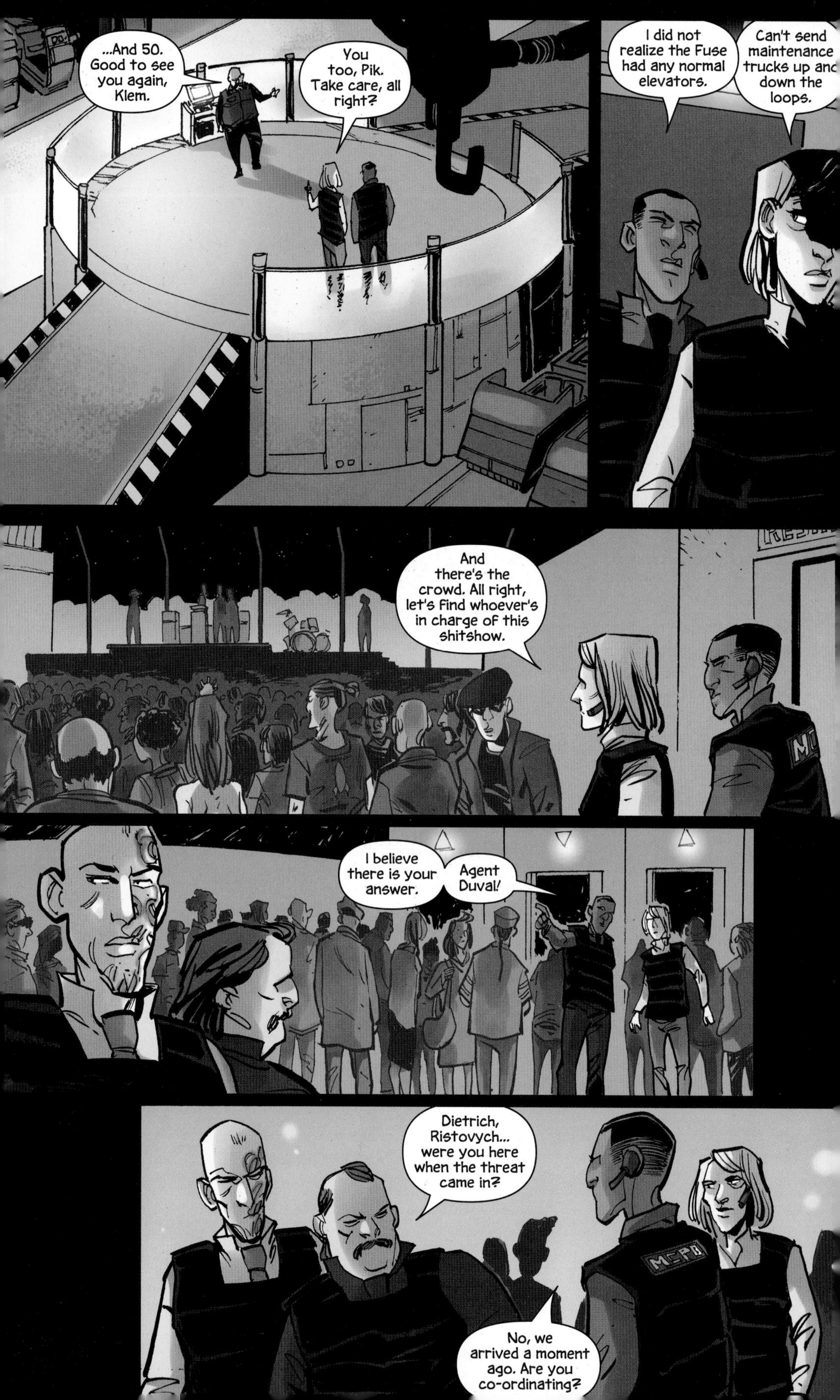
...And 50. Good to see you again, Klem.
You too, Pik. Take care, all right?
I did not realize the Fuse had any normal elevators.
Can't send maintenance trucks up and down the loops.
And there's the crowd. All right, let's find whoever's in charge of this shitshow.
I believe there is your answer.
Agent Duval!
Dietrich, Ristovych... were you here when the threat came in?
No, we arrived a moment ago. Are you co-ordinating?

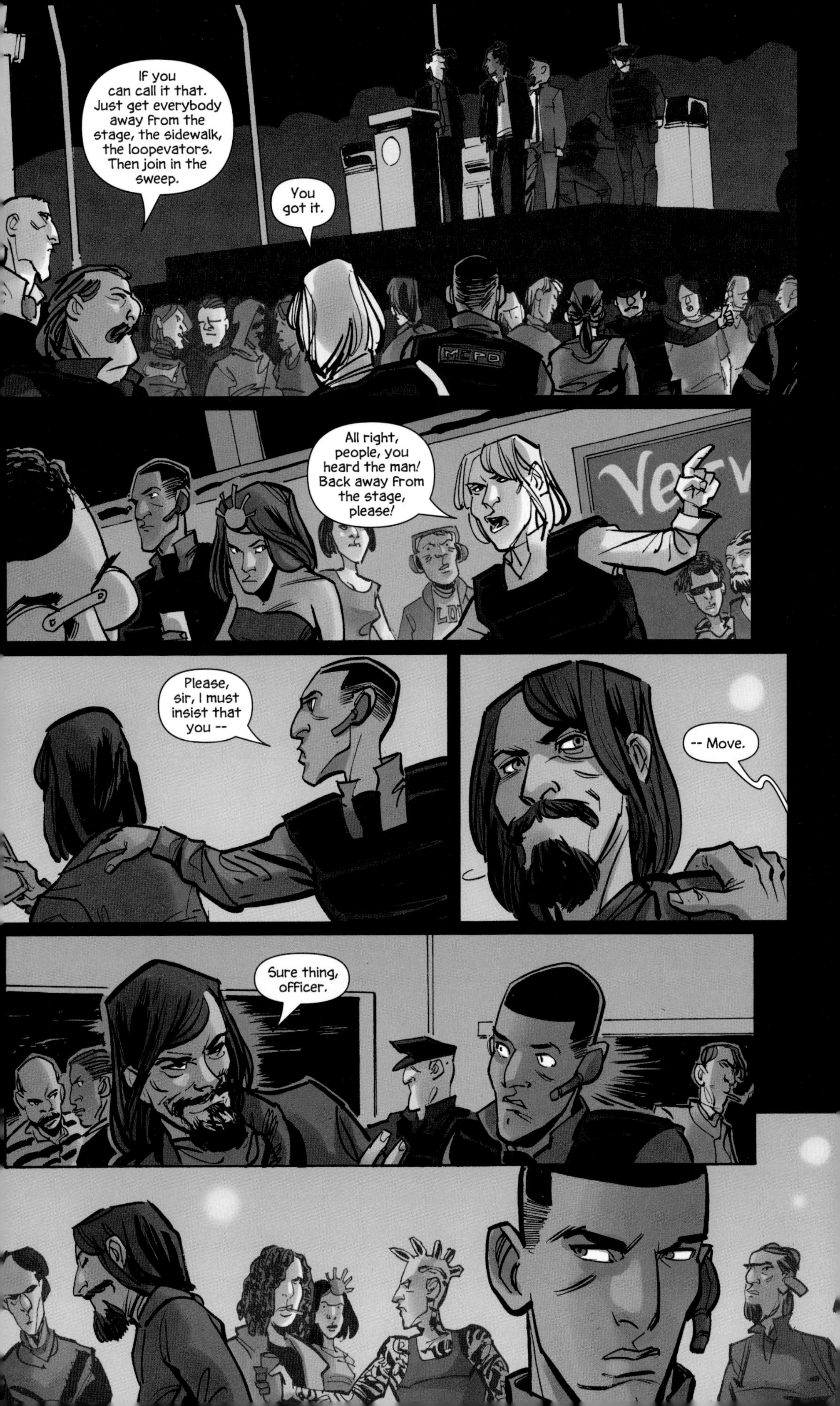
If you can call it that. Just get everybody away from the stage, the sidewalk, the loopevators. Then join in the sweep.
You got it.
M-PD
All right, people, you heard the man! Back away from the stage, please!
Please, sir, I must insist that you --
-- Move.
Sure thing, officer.

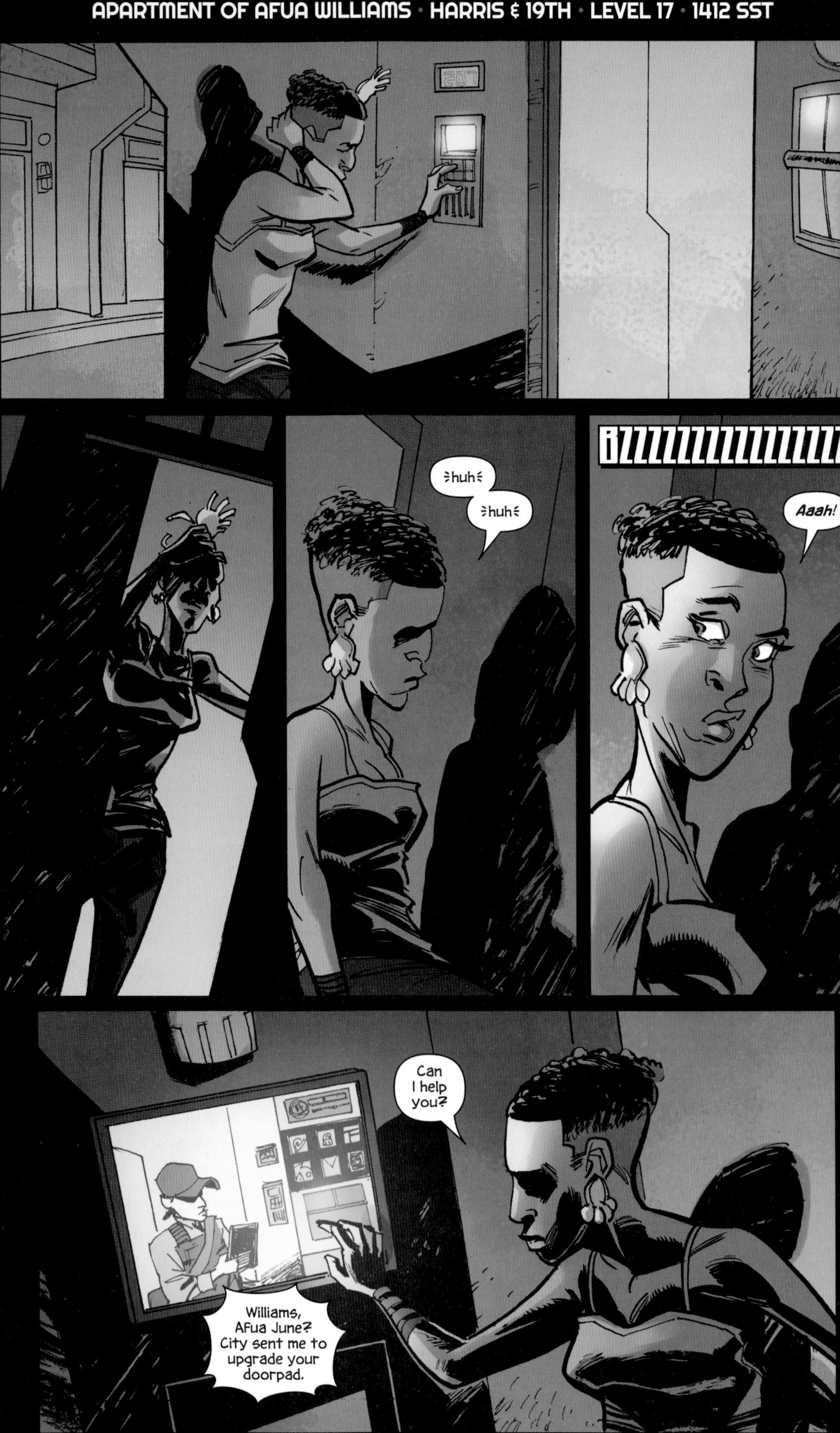
APARTMENT OF AFUA WILLIAMS · HARRIS & 19TH · LEVEL 17 · 1412 SST
huh
huh
BZZZZZZZZZZZZZZZZZ
Aaah!
Can I help you?
Williams, Afua June? City sent me to upgrade your doorpad.

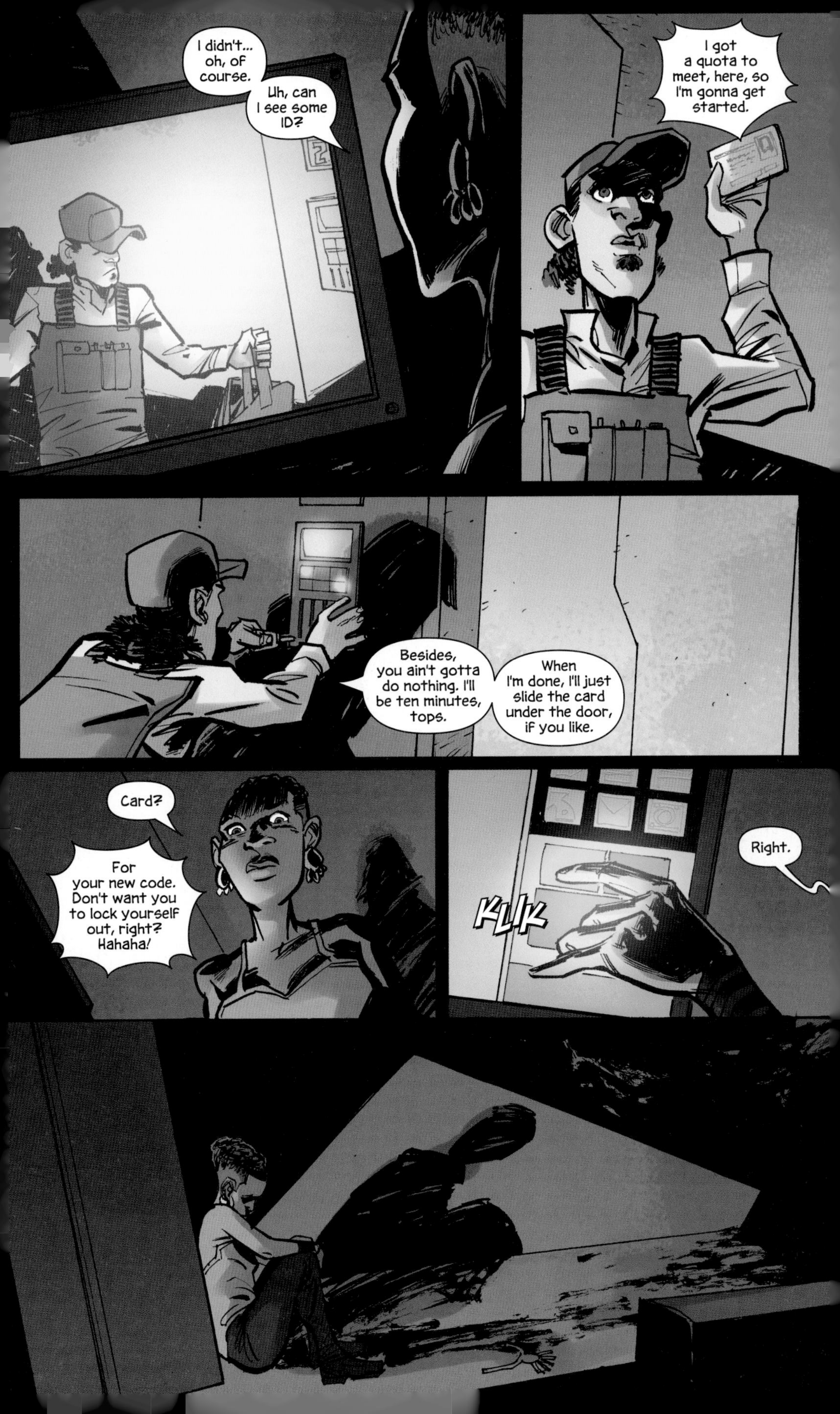
I didn't... oh, of course.
Uh, can I see some ID?
I got a quota to meet, here, so I'm gonna get started.
Besides, you ain't gotta do nothing. I'll be ten minutes, tops.
When I'm done, I'll just slide the card under the door, if you like.
Card?
For your new code. Don't want you to lock yourself out, right? Hahaha!
KLIK
Right.

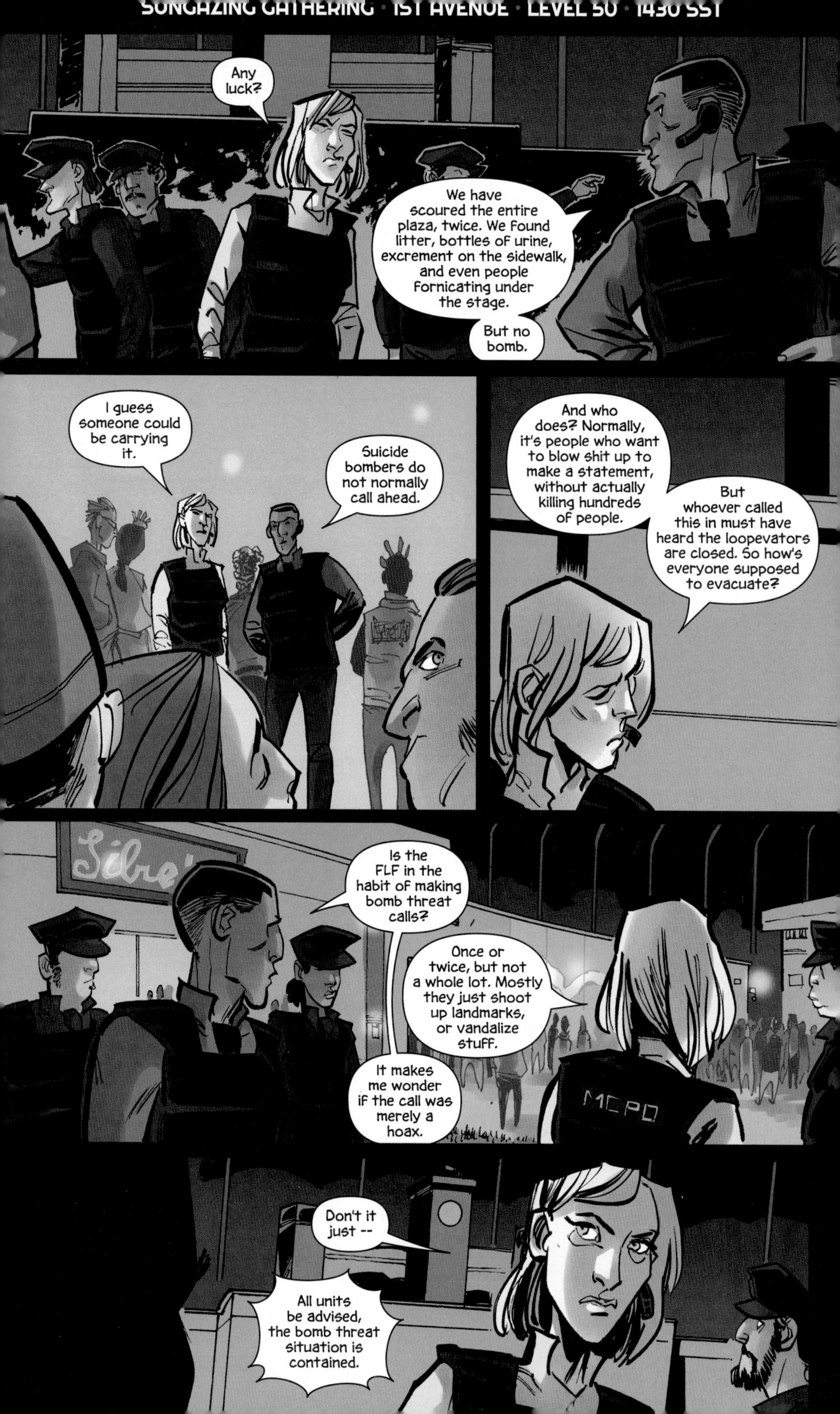
SUNGAZING GATHERING · 1ST AVENUE · LEVEL 50 · 1430 SST
Any luck?
We have scoured the entire plaza, twice. We found litter, bottles of urine, excrement on the sidewalk, and even people fornicating under the stage.
But no bomb.
I guess someone could be carrying it.
Suicide bombers do not normally call ahead.
And who does? Normally, it's people who want to blow shit up to make a statement, without actually killing hundreds of people.
But whoever called this in must have heard the loopevators are closed. So how's everyone supposed to evacuate?
Is the FLF in the habit of making bomb threat calls?
Once or twice, but not a whole lot. Mostly they just shoot up landmarks, or vandalize stuff.
It makes me wonder if the call was merely a hoax.
MCPD
Don't it just --
All units be advised, the bomb threat situation is contained.

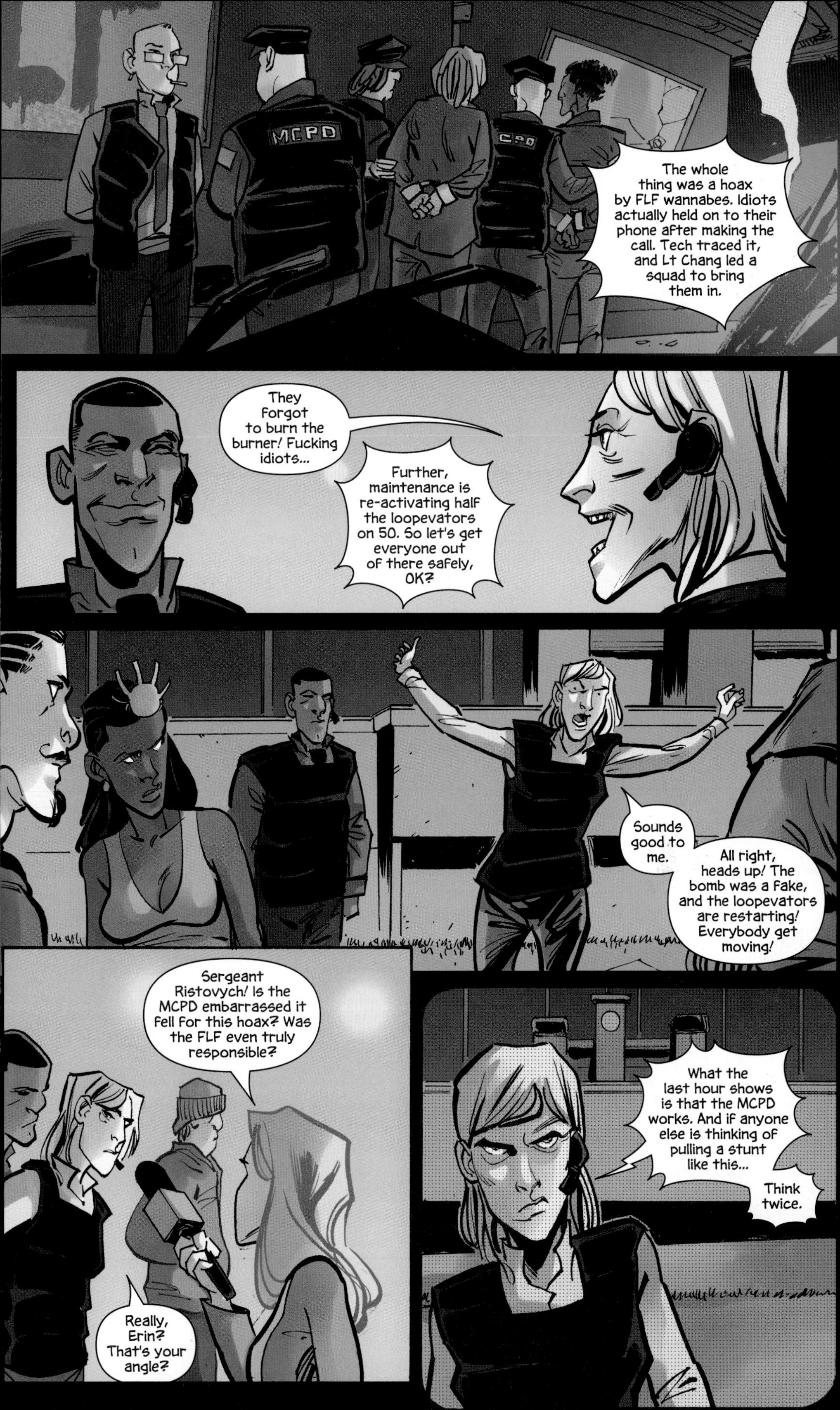
MCPD
C.P.D
The whole thing was a hoax by FLF wannabes. Idiots actually held on to their phone after making the call. Tech traced it, and Lt Chang led a squad to bring them in.
They forgot to burn the burner! Fucking idiots...
Further, maintenance is re-activating half the loopevators on 50. So let's get everyone out of there safely, OK?
Sounds good to me.
All right, heads up! The bomb was a fake, and the loopevators are restarting! Everybody get moving!
Sergeant Ristovych! Is the MCPD embarrassed it fell for this hoax? Was the FLF even truly responsible?
Really, Erin? That's your angle?
What the last hour shows is that the MCPD works. And if anyone else is thinking of pulling a stunt like this...
Think twice.

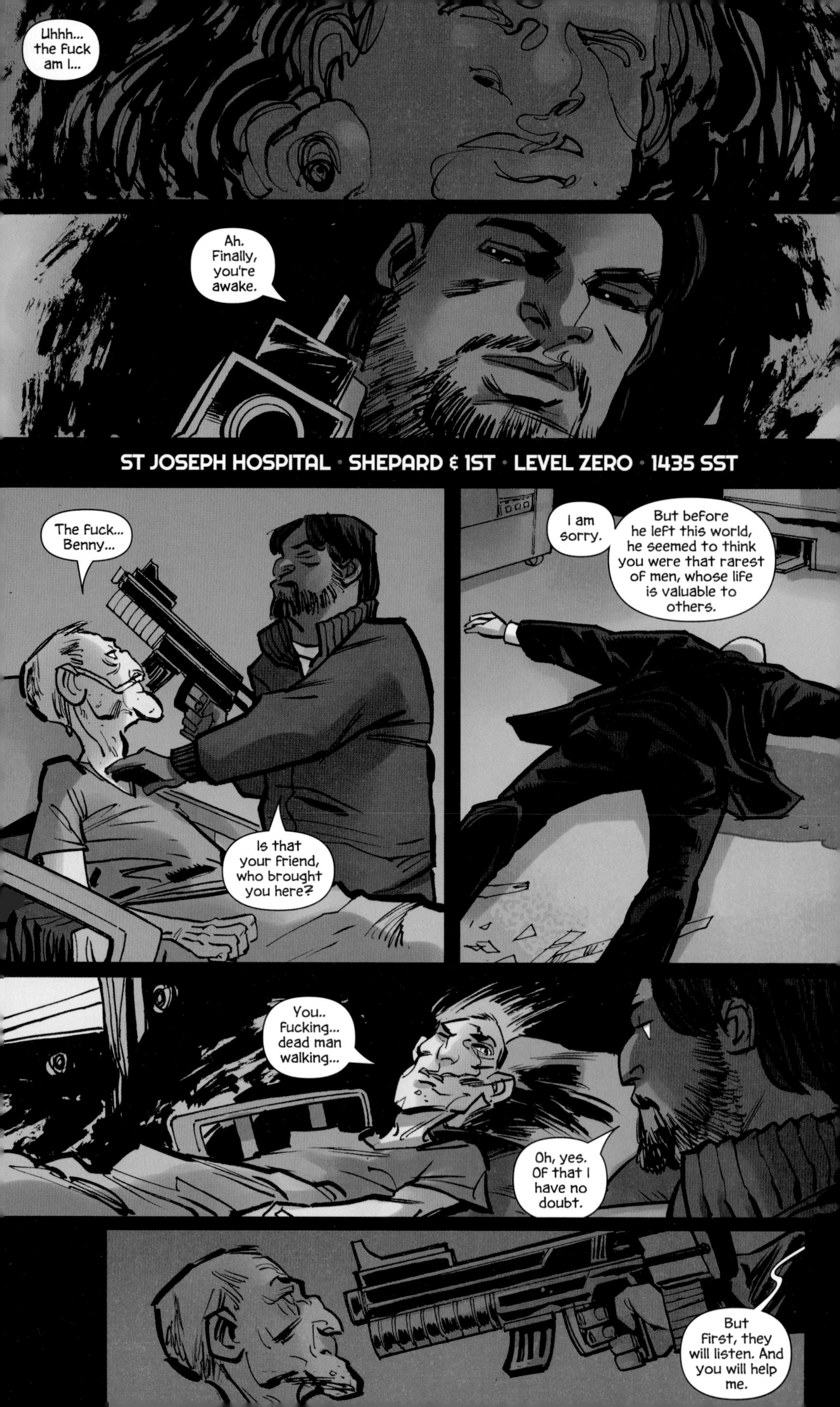

Uhhh... the fuck am I...
Ah. Finally, you're awake.
ST JOSEPH HOSPITAL · SHEPARD & 1ST · LEVEL ZERO · 1435 SST
The fuck... Benny...
Is that your friend, who brought you here?
I am sorry.
But before he left this world, he seemed to think you were that rarest of men, whose life is valuable to others.
You.. fucking... dead man walking...
Oh, yes. Of that I have no doubt.
But first, they will listen. And you will help me.

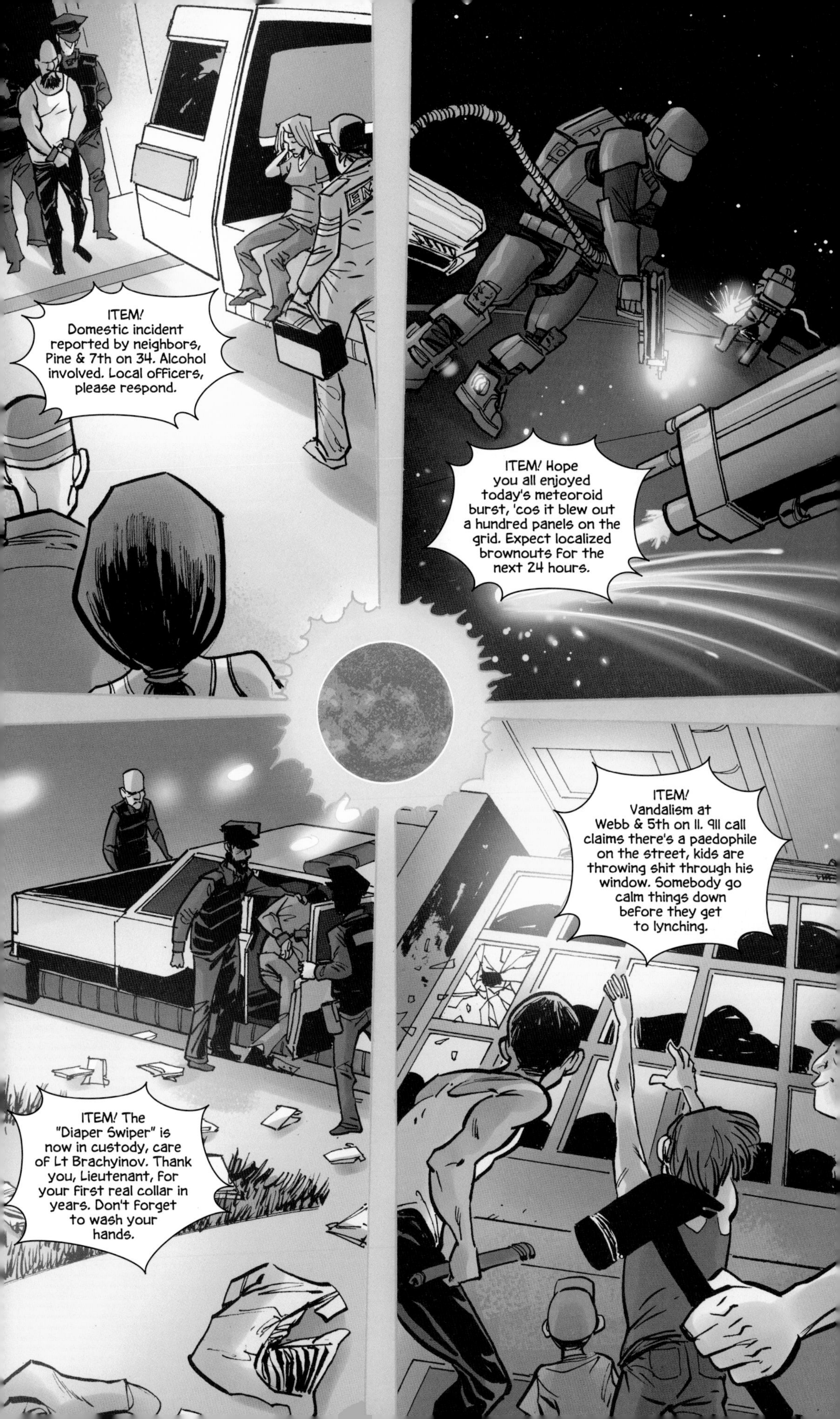
ITEM! Domestic incident reported by neighbors, Pine & 7th on 34. Alcohol involved. Local officers, please respond.
ITEM! Hope you all enjoyed today's meteoroid burst, 'cos it blew out a hundred panels on the grid. Expect localized brownouts for the next 24 hours.
ITEM! The "Diaper Swiper" is now in custody, care of Lt Brachyinov. Thank you, Lieutenant, for your first real collar in years. Don't forget to wash your hands.
ITEM! Vandalism at Webb & 5th on 11. 911 call claims there's a paedophile on the street, kids are throwing shit through his window. Somebody go calm things down before they get to lynching.

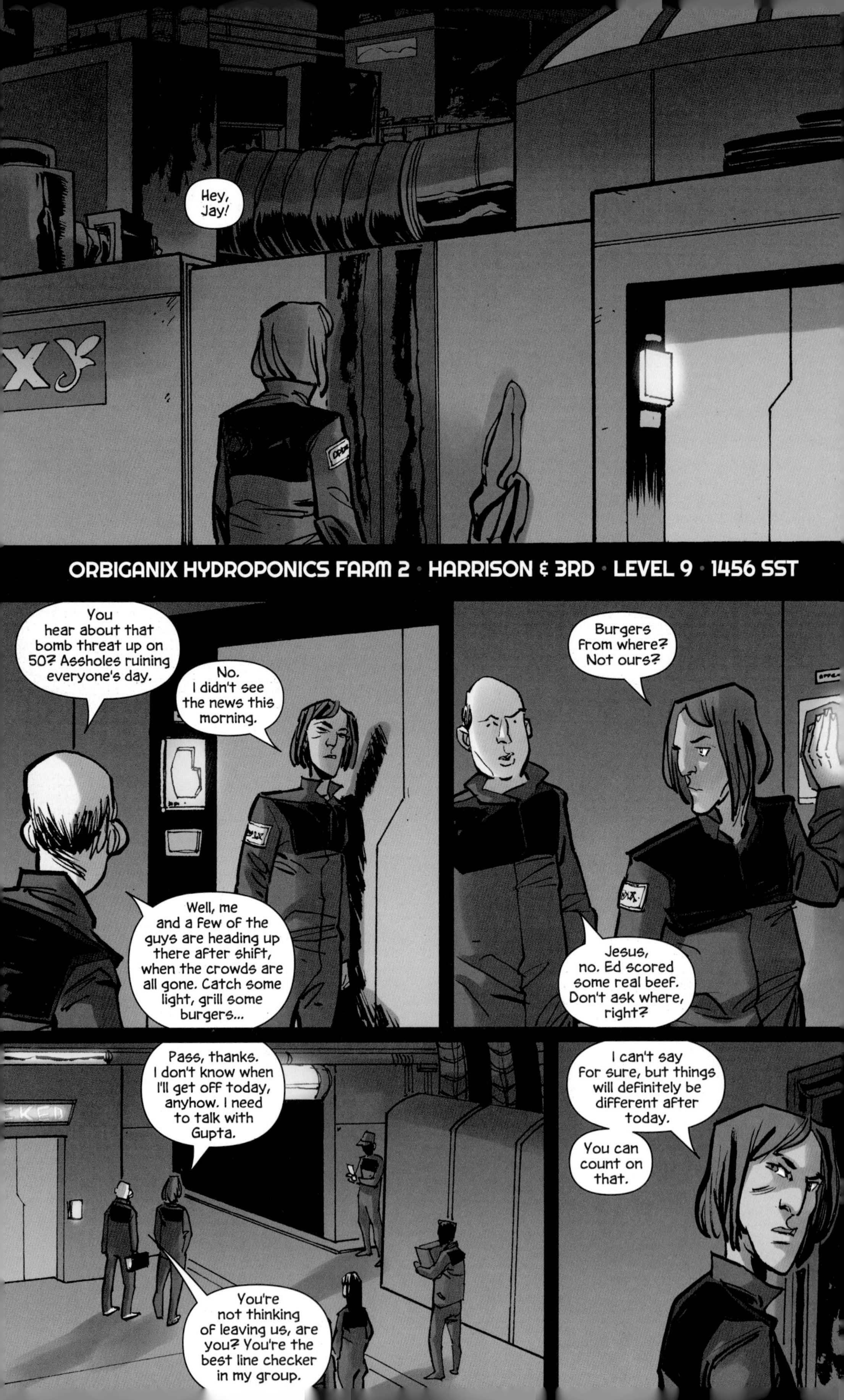
Hey, Jay!
ORBIGANIX HYDROPONICS FARM 2 • HARRISON & 3RD • LEVEL 9 • 1456 SST
You hear about that bomb threat up on 50? Assholes ruining everyone's day.
No. I didn't see the news this morning.
Well, me and a few of the guys are heading up there after shift, when the crowds are all gone. Catch some light, grill some burgers...
Burgers from where? Not ours?
Jesus, no. Ed scored some real beef. Don't ask where, right?
Pass, thanks. I don't know when I'll get off today, anyhow. I need to talk with Gupta.
You're not thinking of leaving us, are you? You're the best line checker in my group.
I can't say for sure, but things will definitely be different after today.
You can count on that.

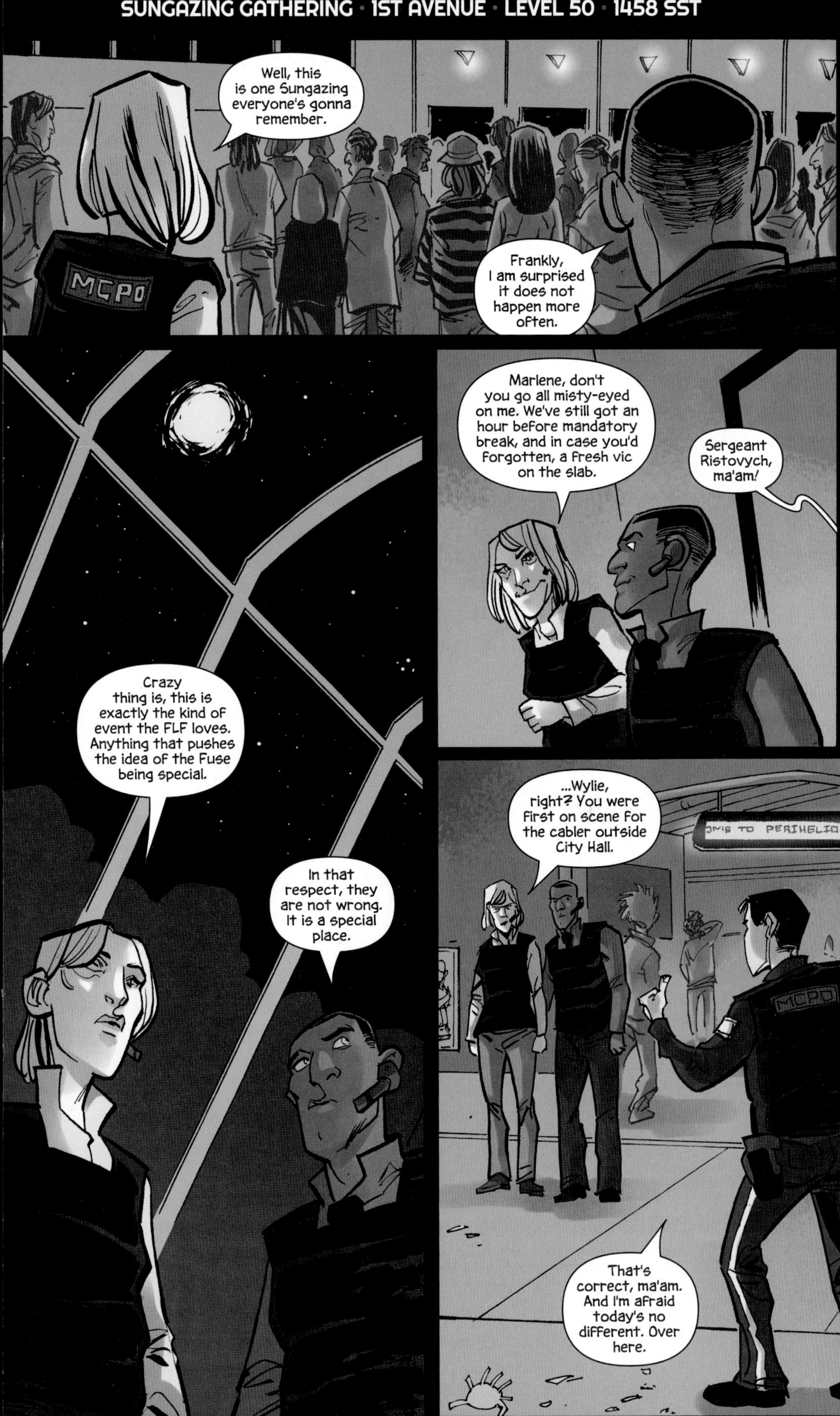
SUNGAZING GATHERING · 1ST AVENUE · LEVEL 50 · 1458 SST
Well, this is one Sungazing everyone's gonna remember.
Frankly, I am surprised it does not happen more often.
Crazy thing is, this is exactly the kind of event the FLF loves. Anything that pushes the idea of the Fuse being special.
In that respect, they are not wrong. It is a special place.
Marlene, don't you go all misty-eyed on me. We've still got an hour before mandatory break, and in case you'd forgotten, a fresh vic on the slab.
Sergeant Ristovych, ma'am!
...Wylie, right? You were first on scene for the cabler outside City Hall.
That's correct, ma'am. And I'm afraid today's no different. Over here.
MCPO

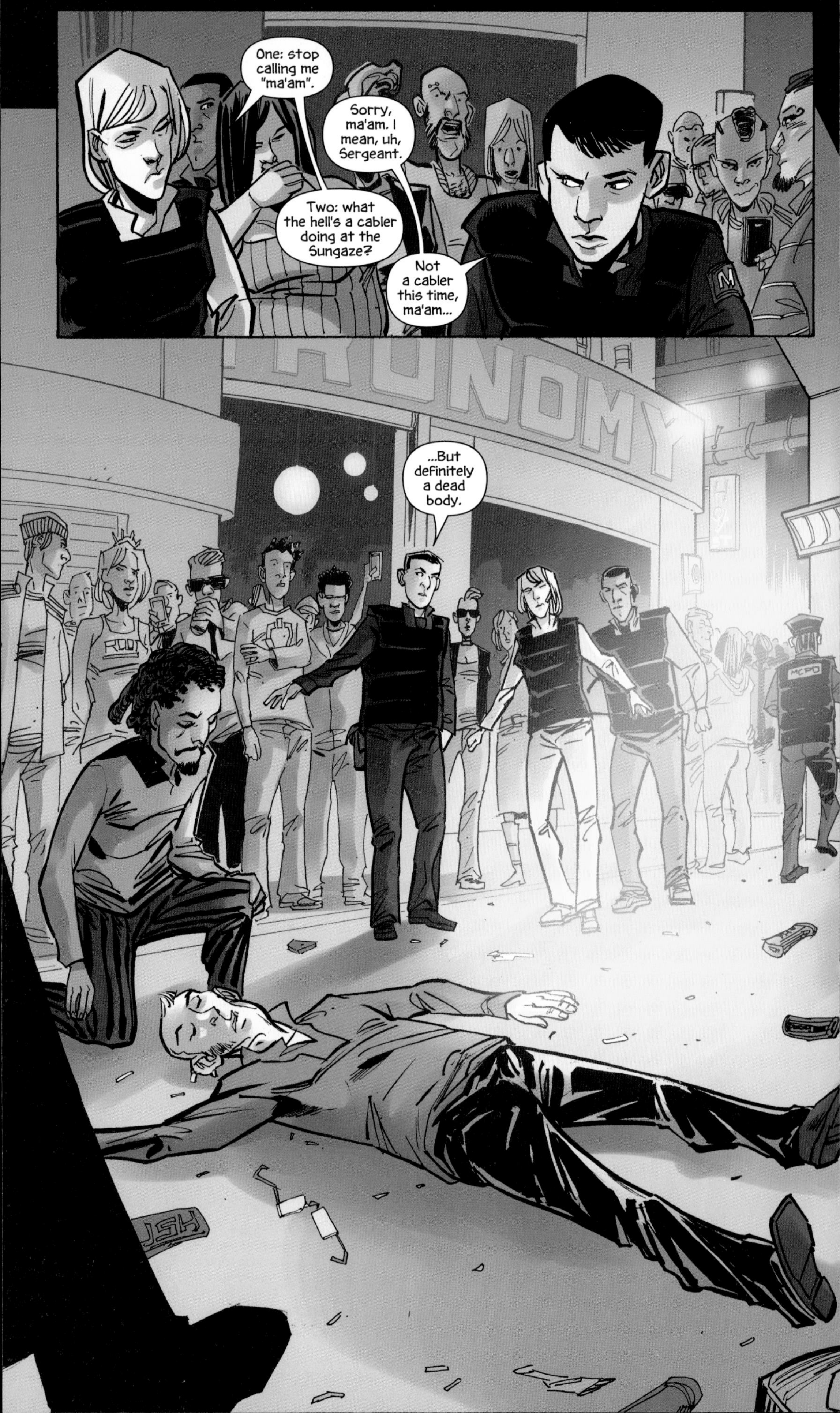
One: stop calling me "ma'am".
Sorry, ma'am. I mean, uh, Sergeant.
Two: what the hell's a cabler doing at the Sungaze?
Not a cabler this time, ma'am...
...But definitely a dead body.

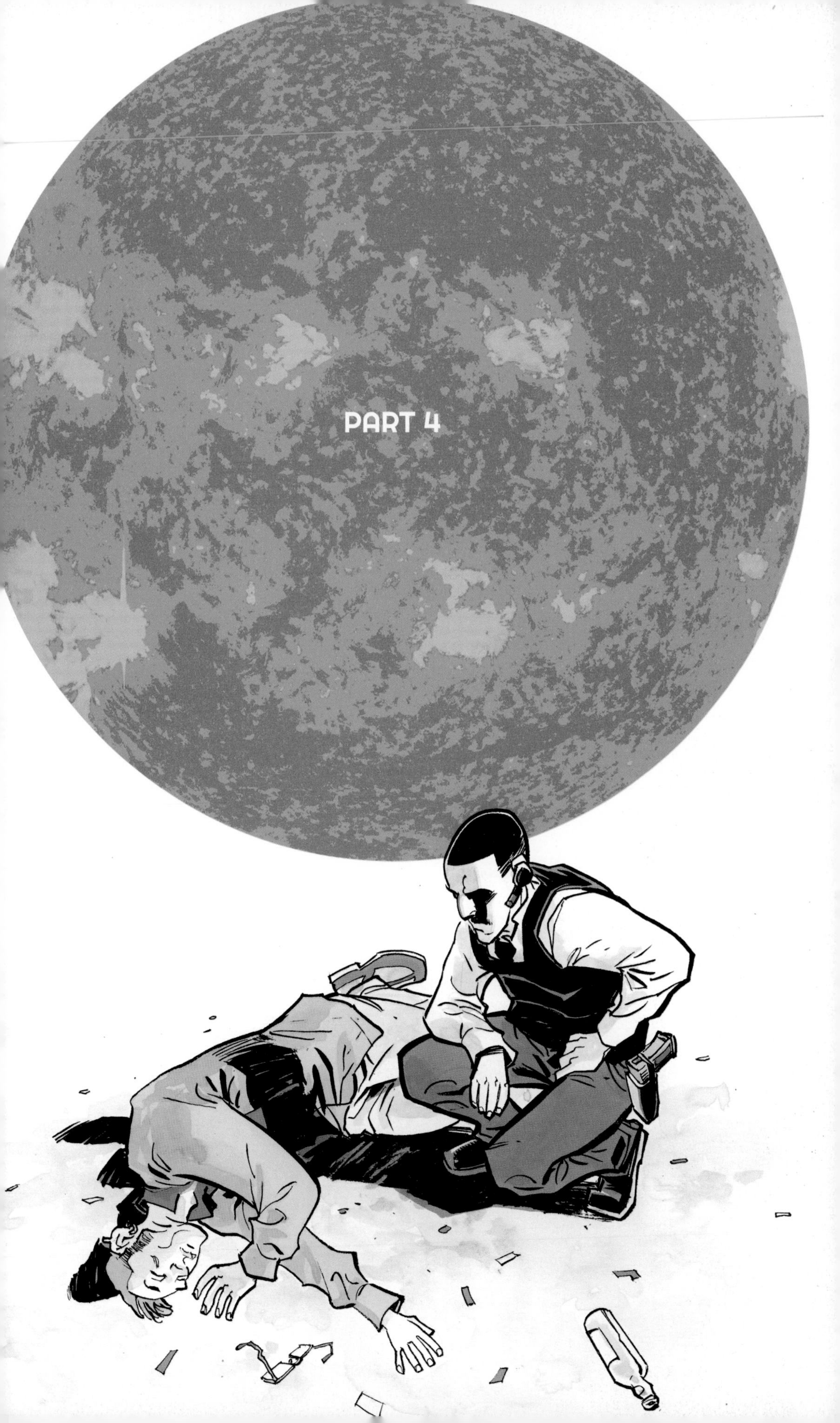
PART 4

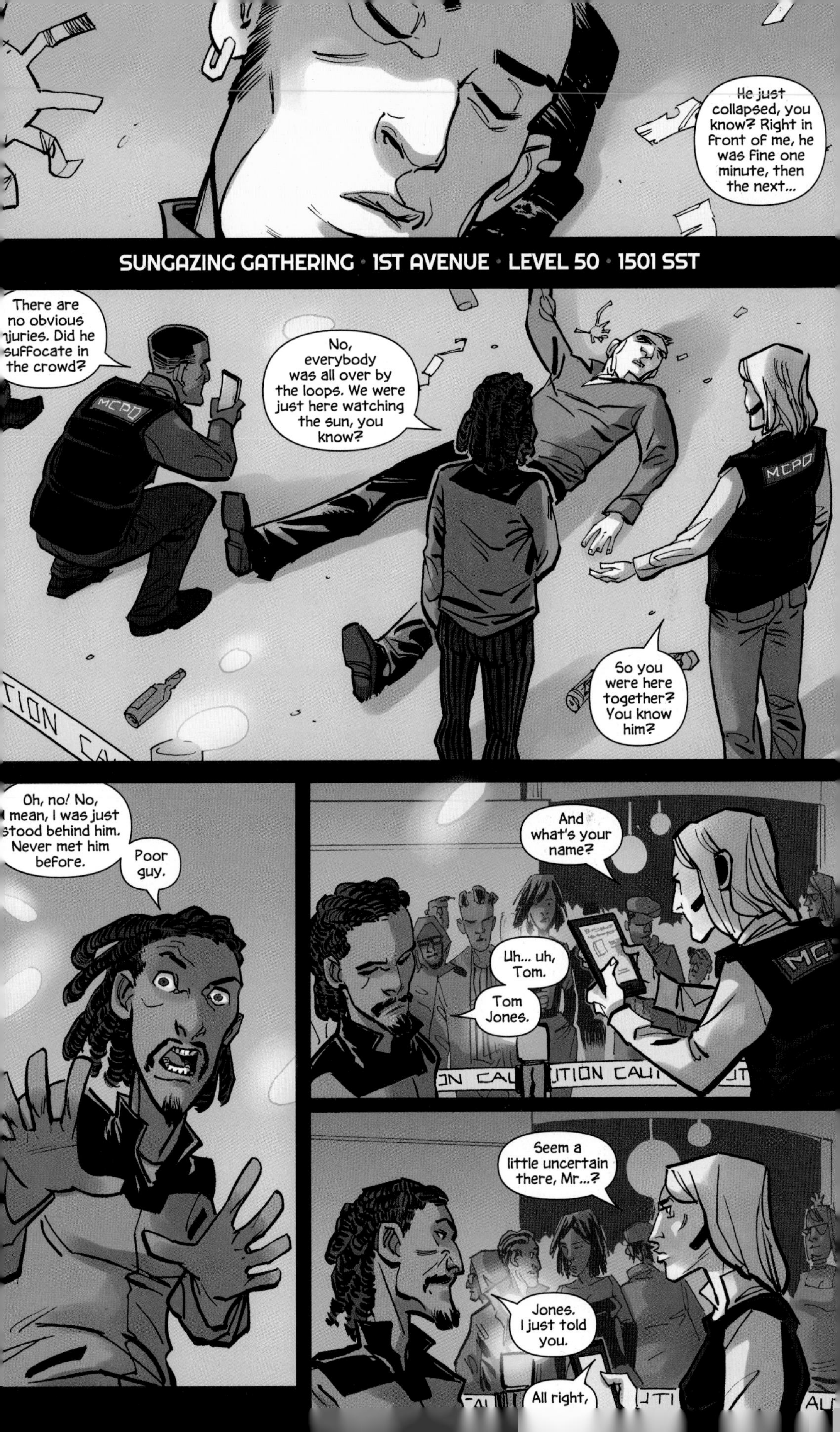
He just collapsed, you know? Right in front of me, he was fine one minute, then the next...
SUNGAZING GATHERING · 1ST AVENUE · LEVEL 50 · 1501 SST
There are no obvious injuries. Did he suffocate in the crowd?
No, everybody was all over by the loops. We were just here watching the sun, you know?
MCPD
MCPD
So you were here together? You know him?
Oh, no! No, I mean, I was just stood behind him. Never met him before.
Poor guy.
And what's your name?
Uh... uh, Tom.
Tom Jones.
Seem a little uncertain there, Mr...?
Jones. I just told you.
All right,

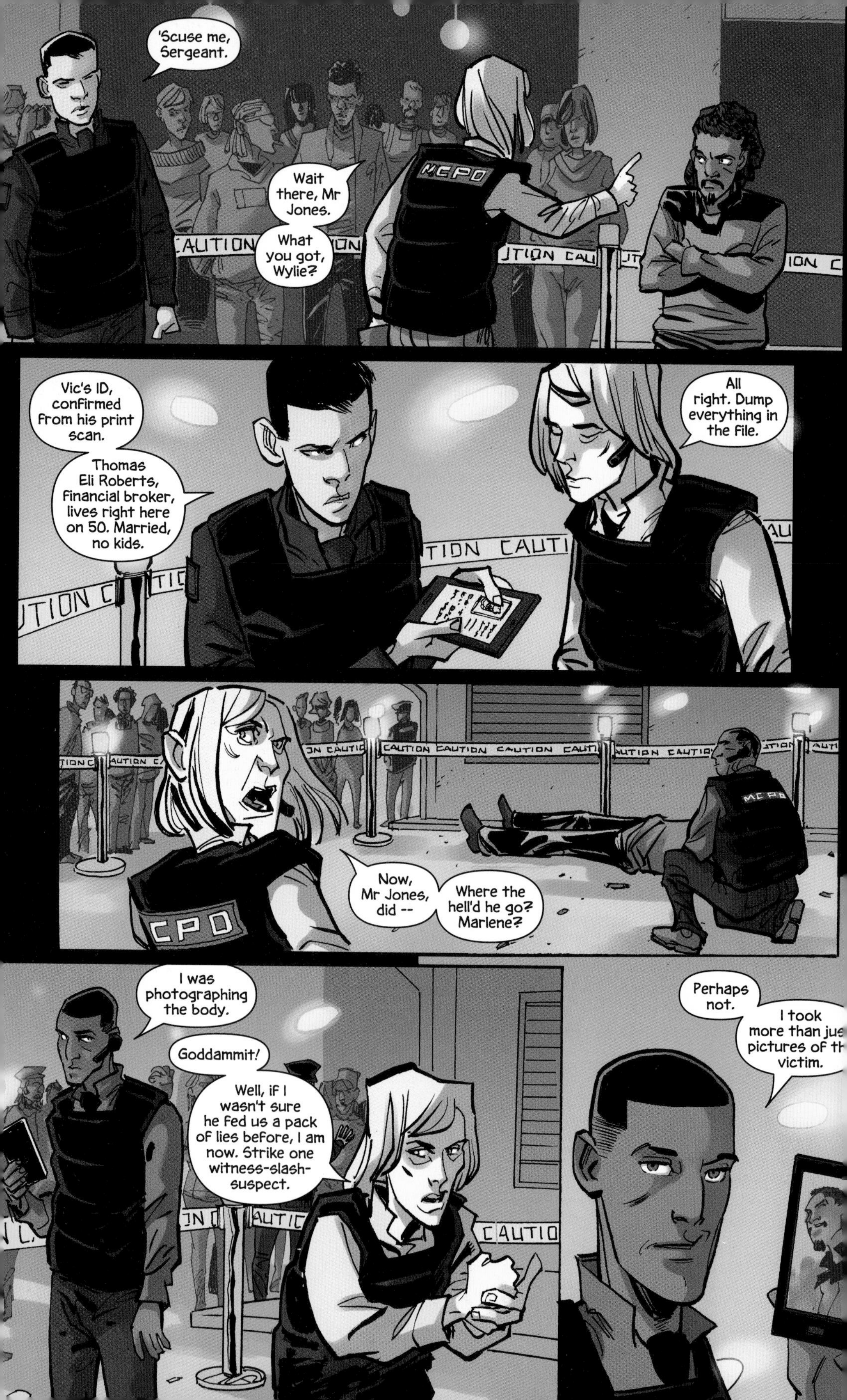

'Scuse me, Sergeant.
Wait there, Mr Jones.
What you got, Wylie?
CAUTION
Vic's ID, confirmed from his print scan.
Thomas Eli Roberts, financial broker, lives right here on 50. Married, no kids.
All right. Dump everything in the file.
MCPD
Now, Mr Jones, did --
Where the hell'd he go? Marlene?
I was photographing the body.
Goddammit!
Well, if I wasn't sure he fed us a pack of lies before, I am now. Strike one witness-slash-suspect.
Perhaps not.
I took more than jus pictures of th victim.

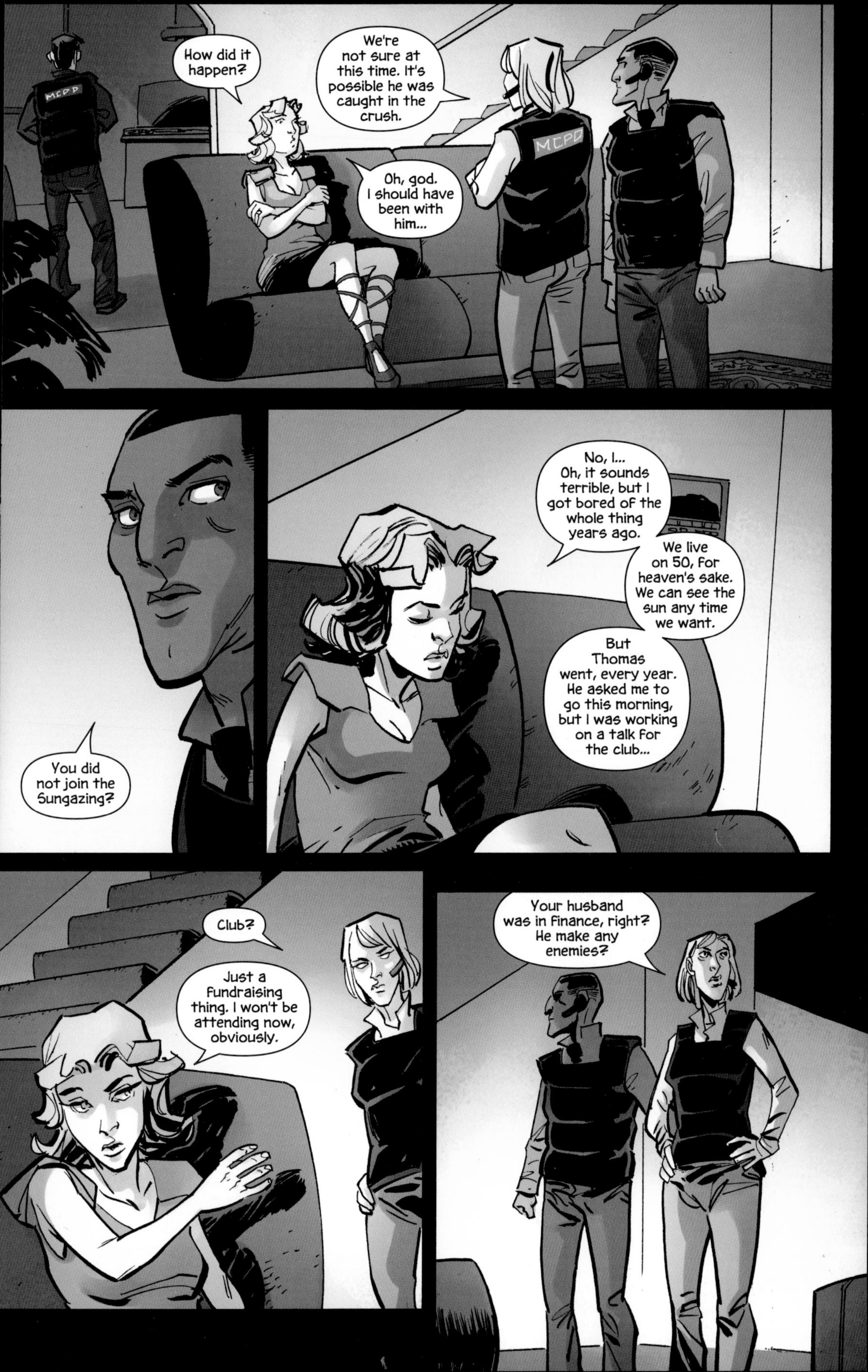
How did it happen?
We're not sure at this time. It's possible he was caught in the crush.
Oh, god. I should have been with him...
You did not join the Sungazing?
No, I... Oh, it sounds terrible, but I got bored of the whole thing years ago.
We live on 50, for heaven's sake. We can see the sun any time we want.
But Thomas went, every year. He asked me to go this morning, but I was working on a talk for the club...
Club?
Just a fundraising thing. I won't be attending now, obviously.
Your husband was in finance, right? He make any enemies?

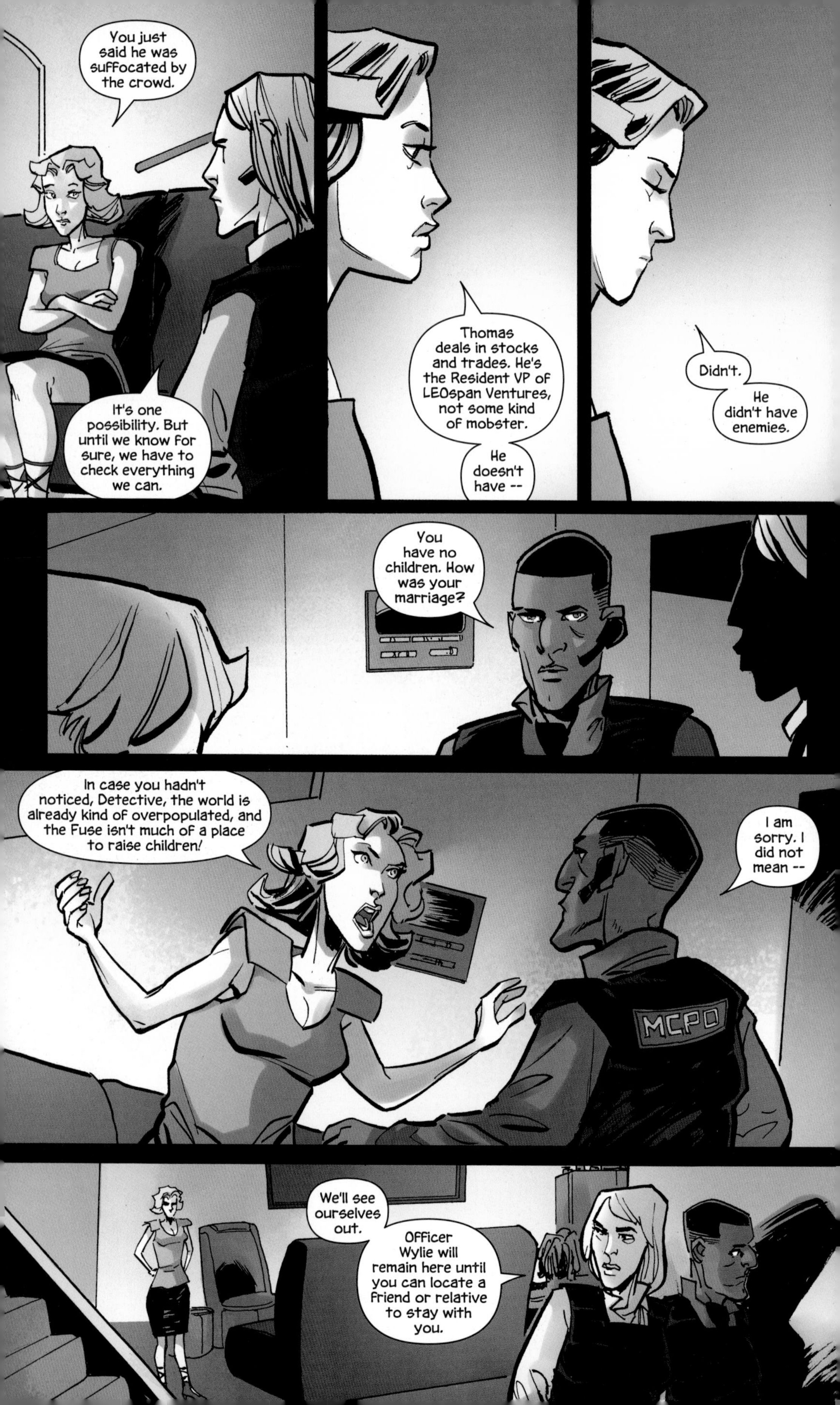

You just said he was suffocated by the crowd.
It's one possibility. But until we know for sure, we have to check everything we can.
Thomas deals in stocks and trades. He's the Resident VP of LEOspan Ventures, not some kind of mobster.
He doesn't have --
Didn't.
He didn't have enemies.
You have no children. How was your marriage?
In case you hadn't noticed, Detective, the world is already kind of overpopulated, and the Fuse isn't much of a place to raise children!
I am sorry. I did not mean --
MCPO
We'll see ourselves out.
Officer Wylie will remain here until you can locate a friend or relative to stay with you.

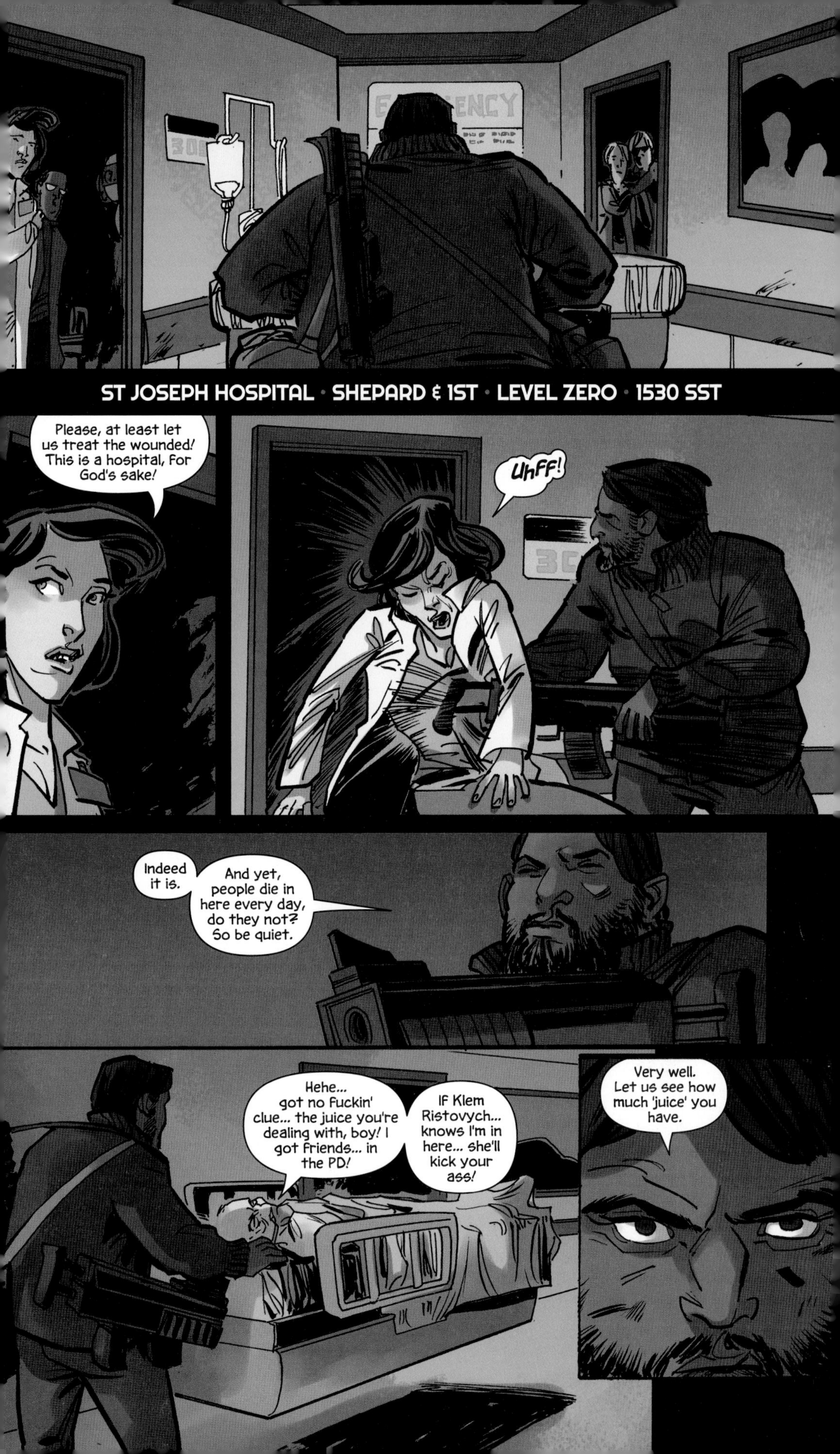
ST JOSEPH HOSPITAL · SHEPARD & 1ST · LEVEL ZERO · 1530 SST
Please, at least let us treat the wounded! This is a hospital, for God's sake!
UHFF!
Indeed it is.
And yet, people die in here every day, do they not? So be quiet.
Hehe... got no fuckin' clue... the juice you're dealing with, boy! I got friends... in the PD!
If Klem Ristovych... knows I'm in here... she'll kick your ass!
Very well. Let us see how much 'juice' you have.

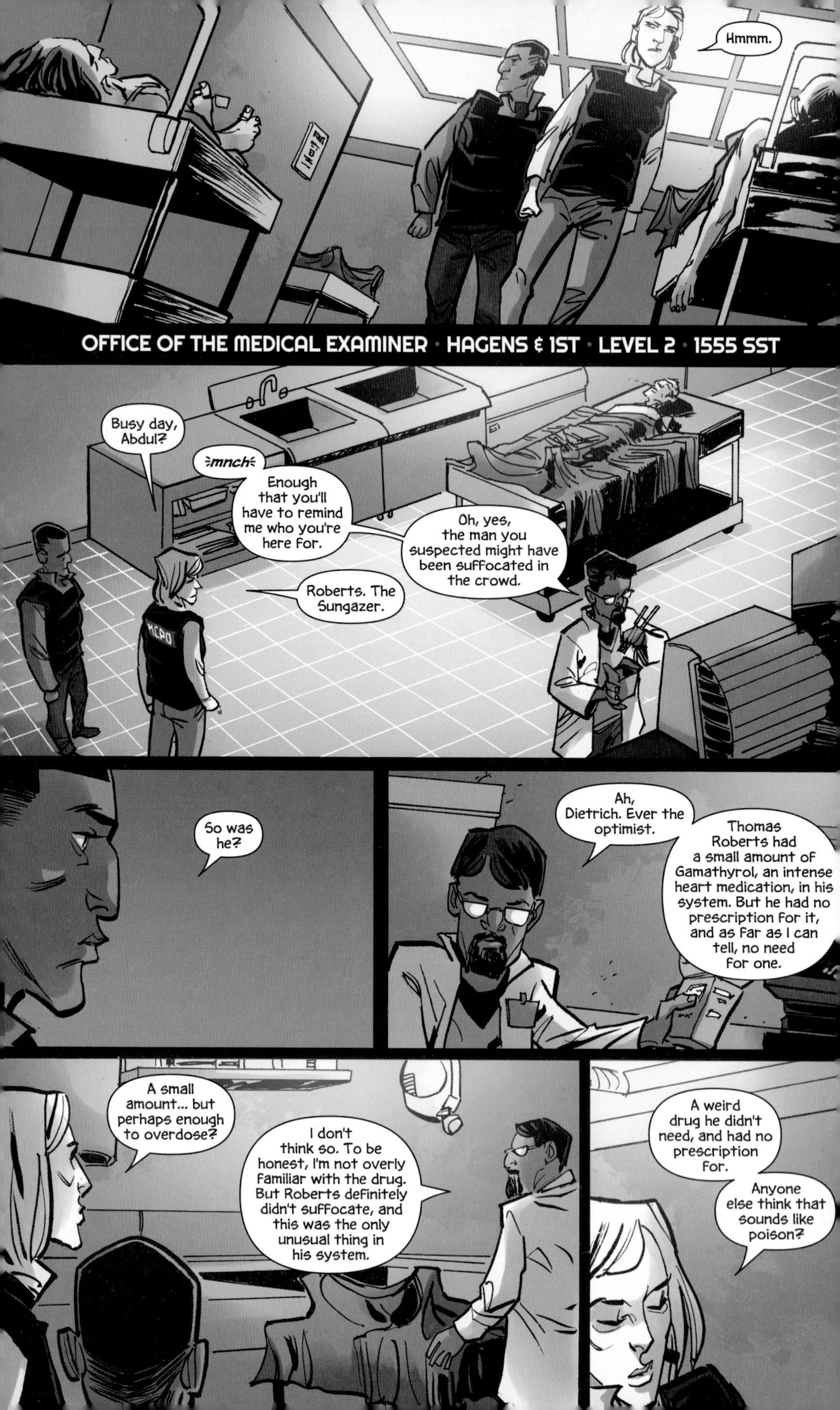
Hmmm.
OFFICE OF THE MEDICAL EXAMINER · HAGENS & 1ST · LEVEL 2 · 1555 SST
Busy day, Abdul?
mnch
Enough that you'll have to remind me who you're here for.
Roberts. The Sungazer.
Oh, yes, the man you suspected might have been suffocated in the crowd.
MCPD
So was he?
Ah, Dietrich. Ever the optimist.
Thomas Roberts had a small amount of Gamathyrol, an intense heart medication, in his system. But he had no prescription for it, and as far as I can tell, no need for one.
A small amount... but perhaps enough to overdose?
I don't think so. To be honest, I'm not overly familiar with the drug. But Roberts definitely didn't suffocate, and this was the only unusual thing in his system.
A weird drug he didn't need, and had no prescription for.
Anyone else think that sounds like poison?

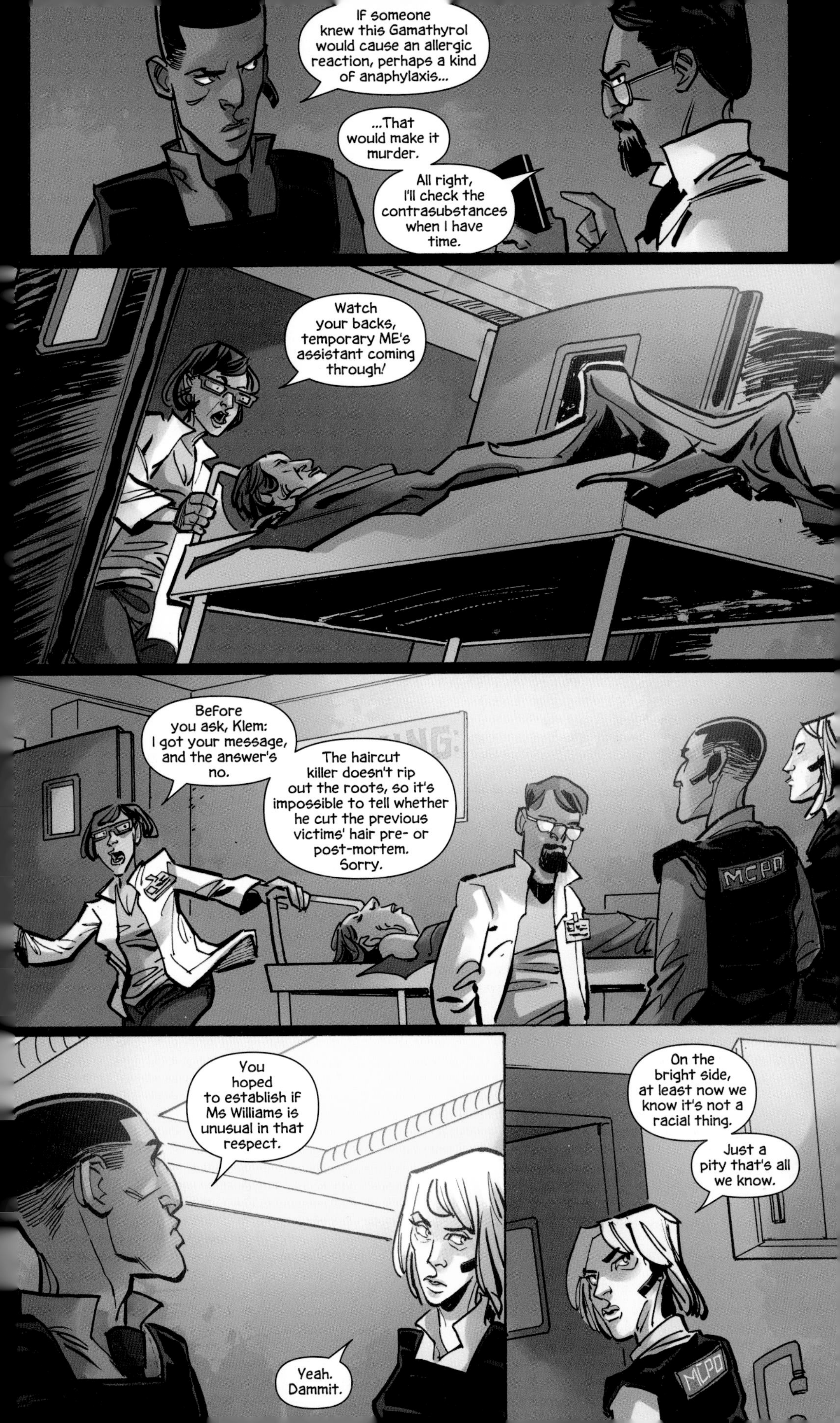
If someone knew this Gamathyrol would cause an allergic reaction, perhaps a kind of anaphylaxis...
...That would make it murder.
All right, I'll check the contrasubstances when I have time.
Watch your backs, temporary ME's assistant coming through!
Before you ask, Klem: I got your message, and the answer's no.
The haircut killer doesn't rip out the roots, so it's impossible to tell whether he cut the previous victims' hair pre- or post-mortem. Sorry.
MCPD
You hoped to establish if Ms Williams is unusual in that respect.
Yeah. Dammit.
On the bright side, at least now we know it's not a racial thing.
Just a pity that's all we know.
MCPD

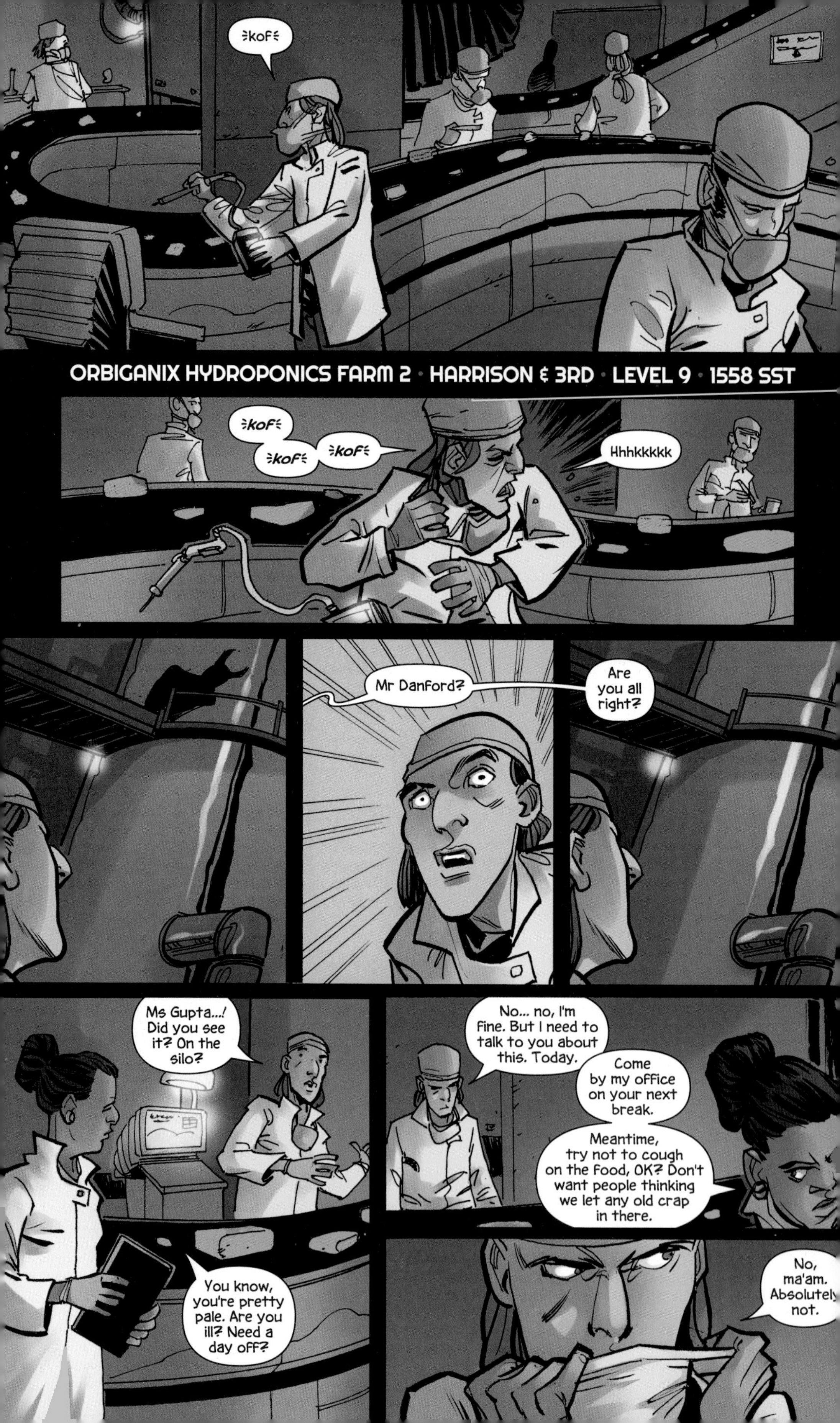
kof
ORBIGANIX HYDROPONICS FARM 2 · HARRISON & 3RD · LEVEL 9 · 1558 SST
kof
kof
kof
Hhhkkkkk
Mr Danford?
Are you all right?
Ms Gupta...! Did you see it? On the silo?
You know, you're pretty pale. Are you ill? Need a day off?
No... no, I'm fine. But I need to talk to you about this. Today.
Come by my office on your next break.
Meantime, try not to cough on the food, OK? Don't want people thinking we let any old crap in there.
No, ma'am. Absolutely not.

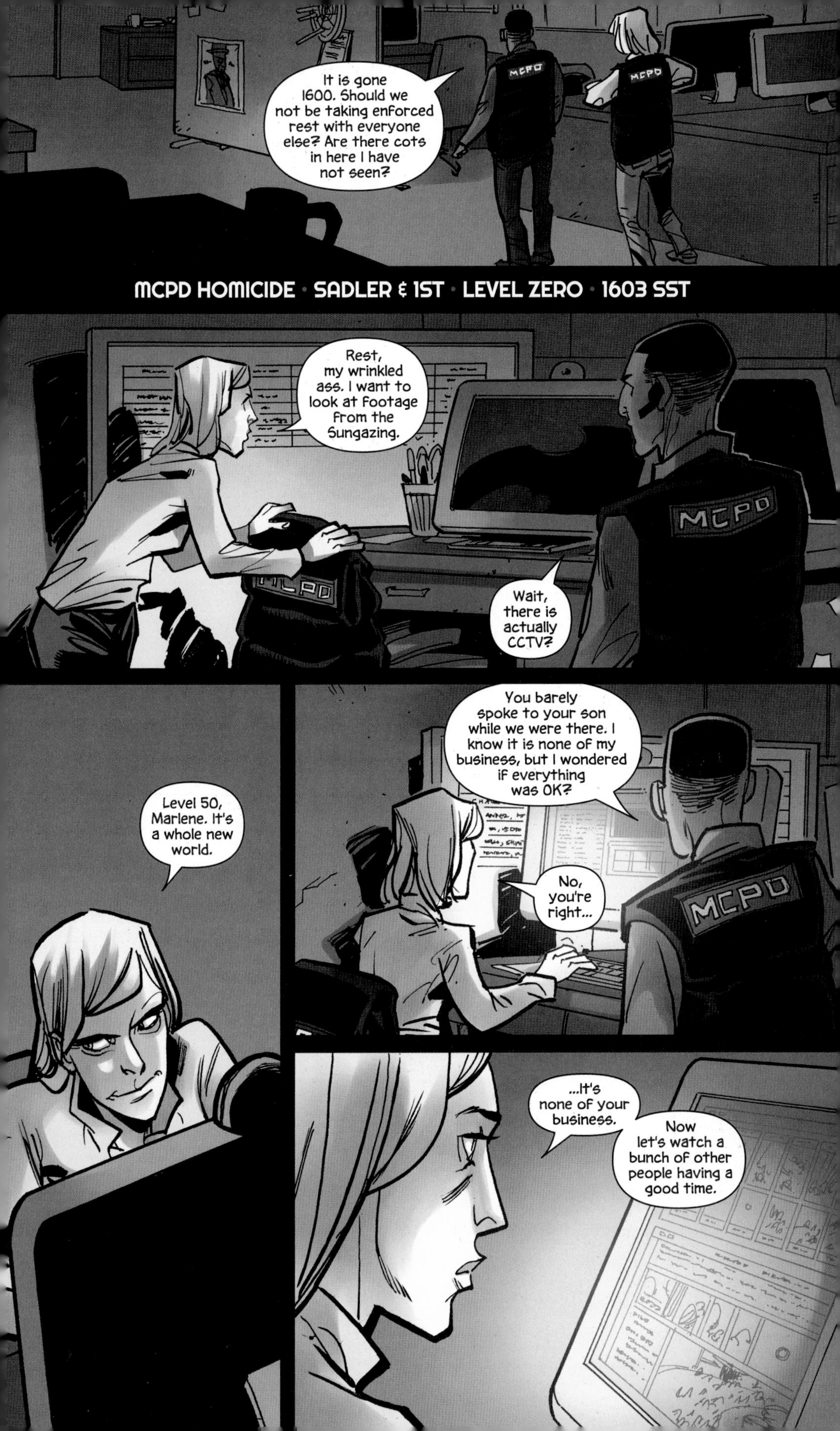
It is gone 1600. Should we not be taking enforced rest with everyone else? Are there cots in here I have not seen?
MCPD HOMICIDE • SADLER & 1ST • LEVEL ZERO • 1603 SST
Rest, my wrinkled ass. I want to look at footage from the Sungazing.
Wait, there is actually CCTV?
Level 50, Marlene. It's a whole new world.
You barely spoke to your son while we were there. I know it is none of my business, but I wondered if everything was OK?
No, you're right...
...It's none of your business.
Now let's watch a bunch of other people having a good time.

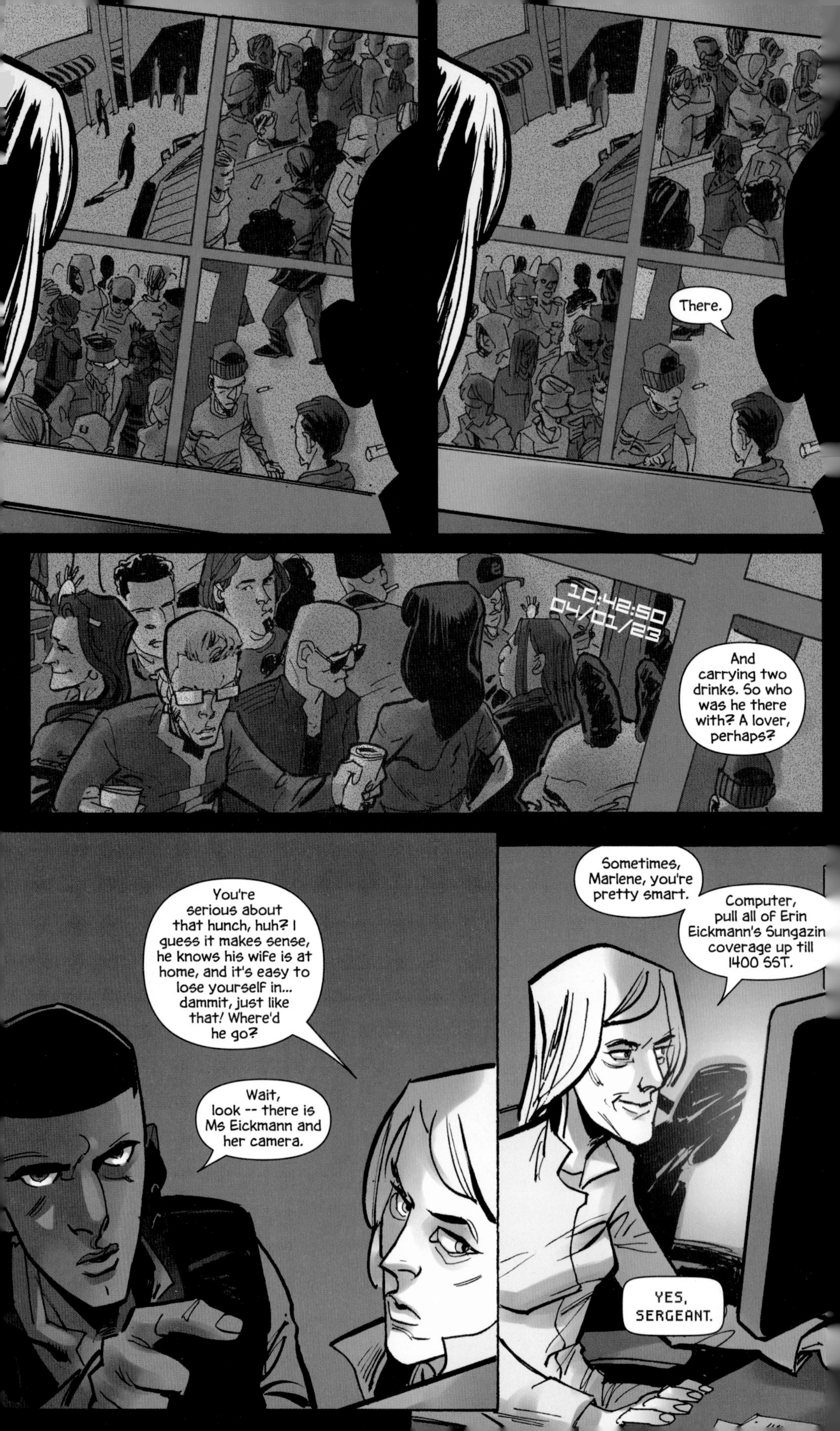
There.
10:42:50 04/01/23
And carrying two drinks. So who was he there with? A lover, perhaps?
You're serious about that hunch, huh? I guess it makes sense, he knows his wife is at home, and it's easy to lose yourself in... dammit, just like that! Where'd he go?
Wait, look -- there is Ms Eickmann and her camera.
Sometimes, Marlene, you're pretty smart.
Computer, pull all of Erin Eickmann's Sungazin coverage up till 1400 SST.
YES, SERGEANT.

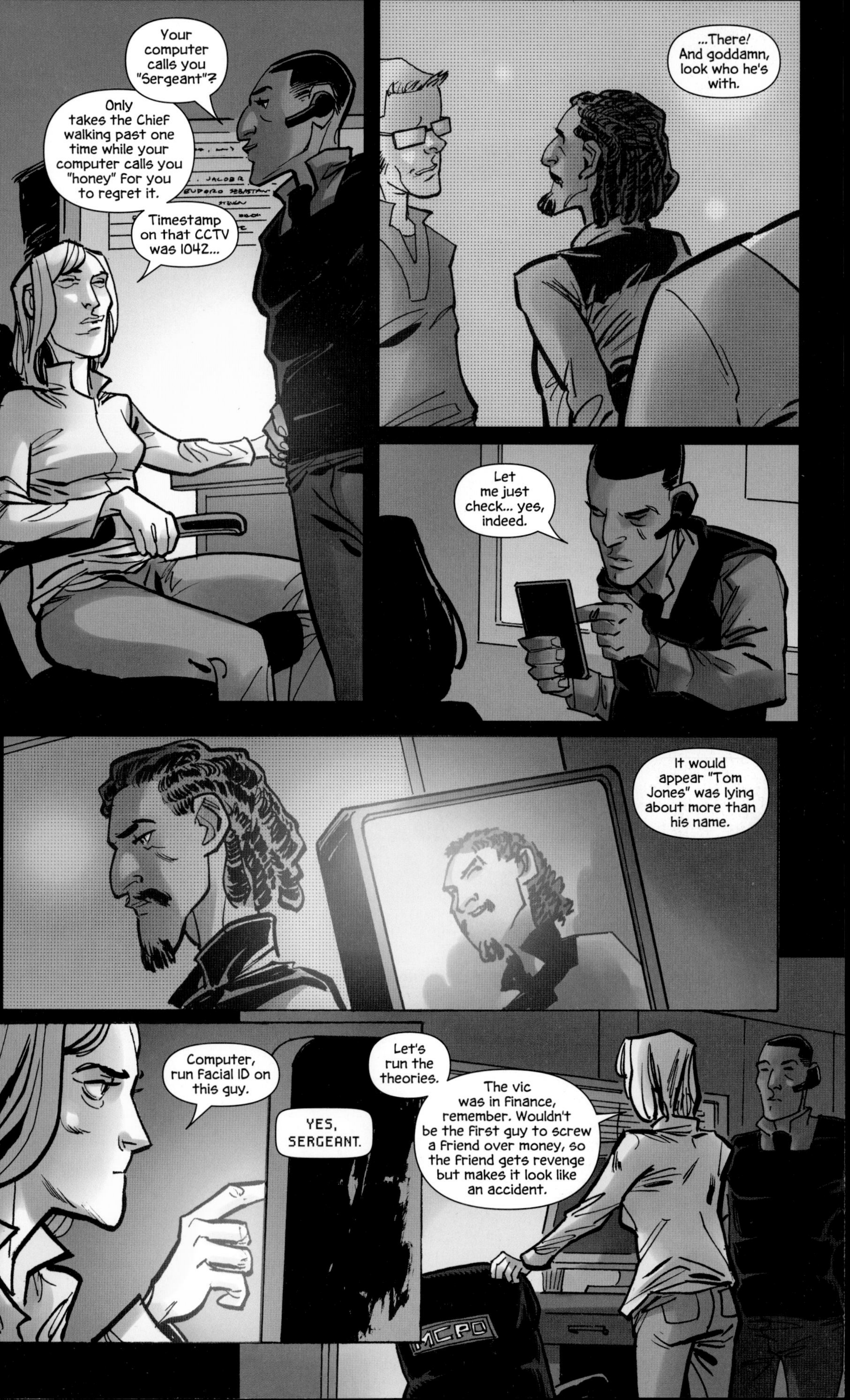

Your computer calls you "Sergeant"?
Only takes the Chief walking past one time while your computer calls you "honey" for you to regret it.
Timestamp on that CCTV was 1042...
...There! And goddamn, look who he's with.
Let me just check... yes, indeed.
It would appear "Tom Jones" was lying about more than his name.
Computer, run Facial ID on this guy.
YES, SERGEANT.
Let's run the theories.
The vic was in finance, remember. Wouldn't be the first guy to screw a friend over money, so the friend gets revenge but makes it look like an accident.
MCPO

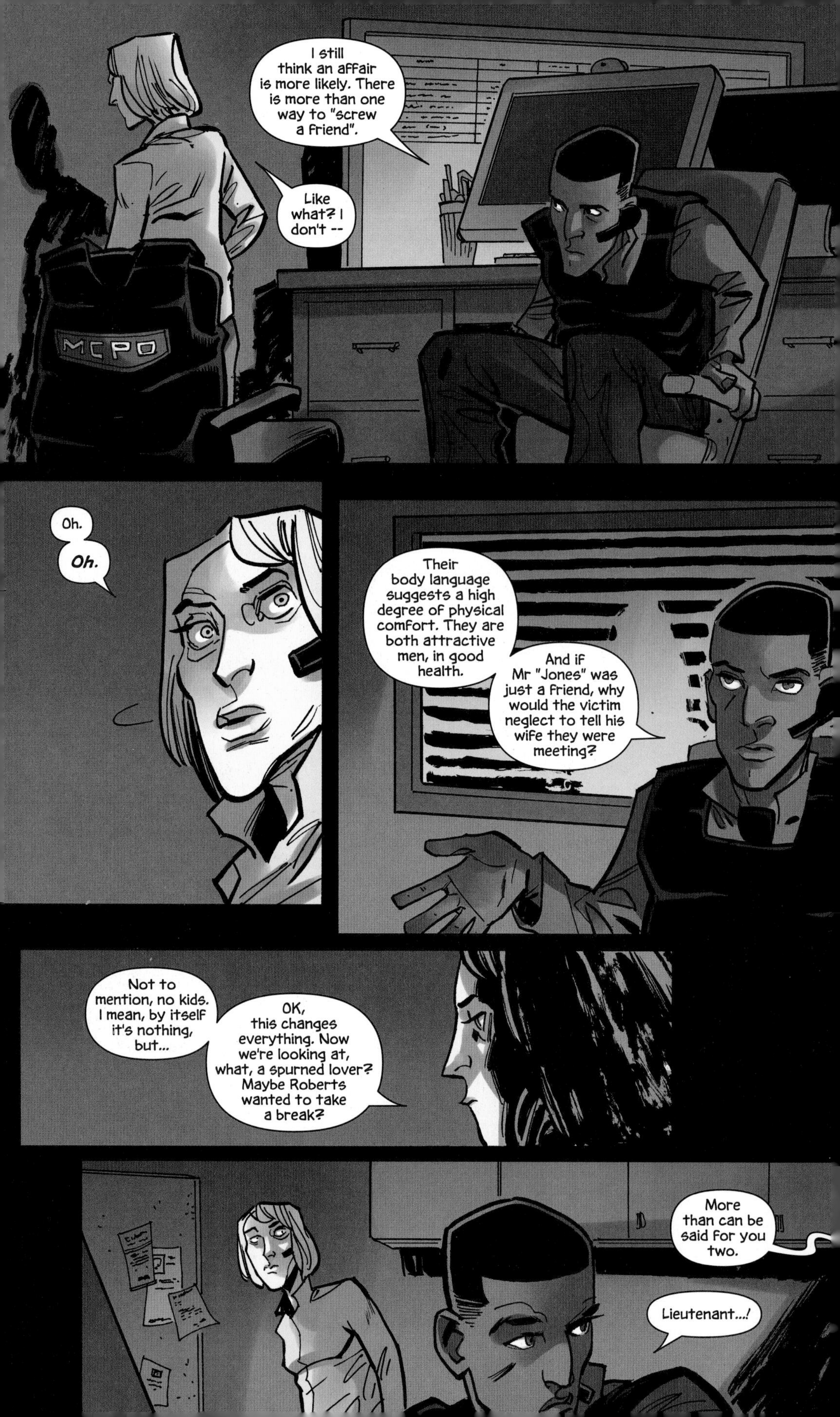
I still think an affair is more likely. There is more than one way to "screw a friend".
Like what? I don't --
MCPO
Oh.
Oh.
Their body language suggests a high degree of physical comfort. They are both attractive men, in good health.
And if Mr "Jones" was just a friend, why would the victim neglect to tell his wife they were meeting?
Not to mention, no kids. I mean, by itself it's nothing, but...
OK, this changes everything. Now we're looking at, what, a spurned lover? Maybe Roberts wanted to take a break?
More than can be said for you two.
Lieutenant...!

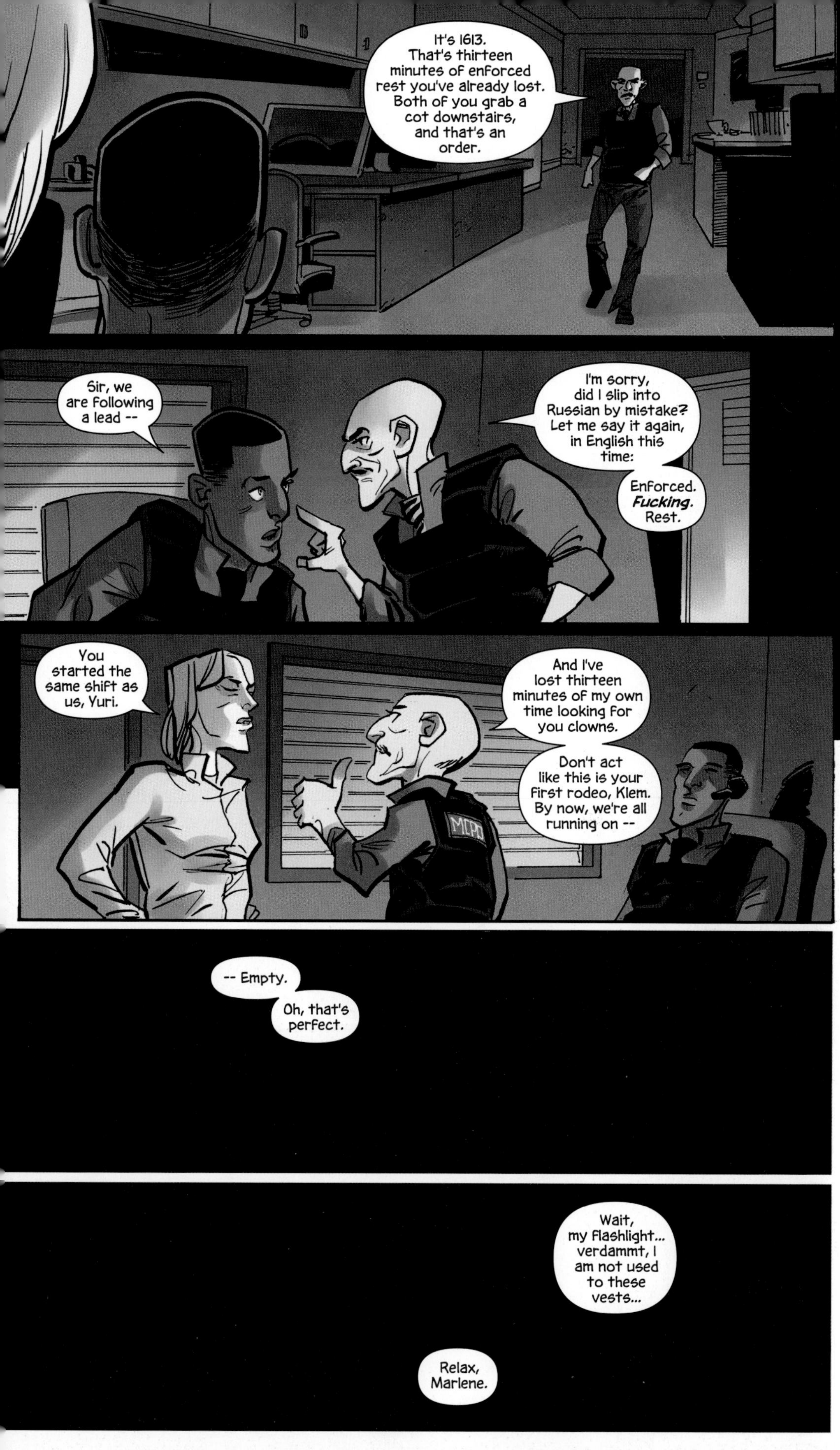

It's 1613. That's thirteen minutes of enforced rest you've already lost. Both of you grab a cot downstairs, and that's an order.
Sir, we are following a lead --
I'm sorry, did I slip into Russian by mistake? Let me say it again, in English this time:
Enforced. ***Fucking.*** Rest.
You started the same shift as us, Yuri.
And I've lost thirteen minutes of my own time looking for you clowns.
Don't act like this is your first rodeo, Klem. By now, we're all running on --
MCPD
-- Empty.
Oh, that's perfect.
Wait, my flashlight... verdammt, I am not used to these vests...
Relax, Marlene.

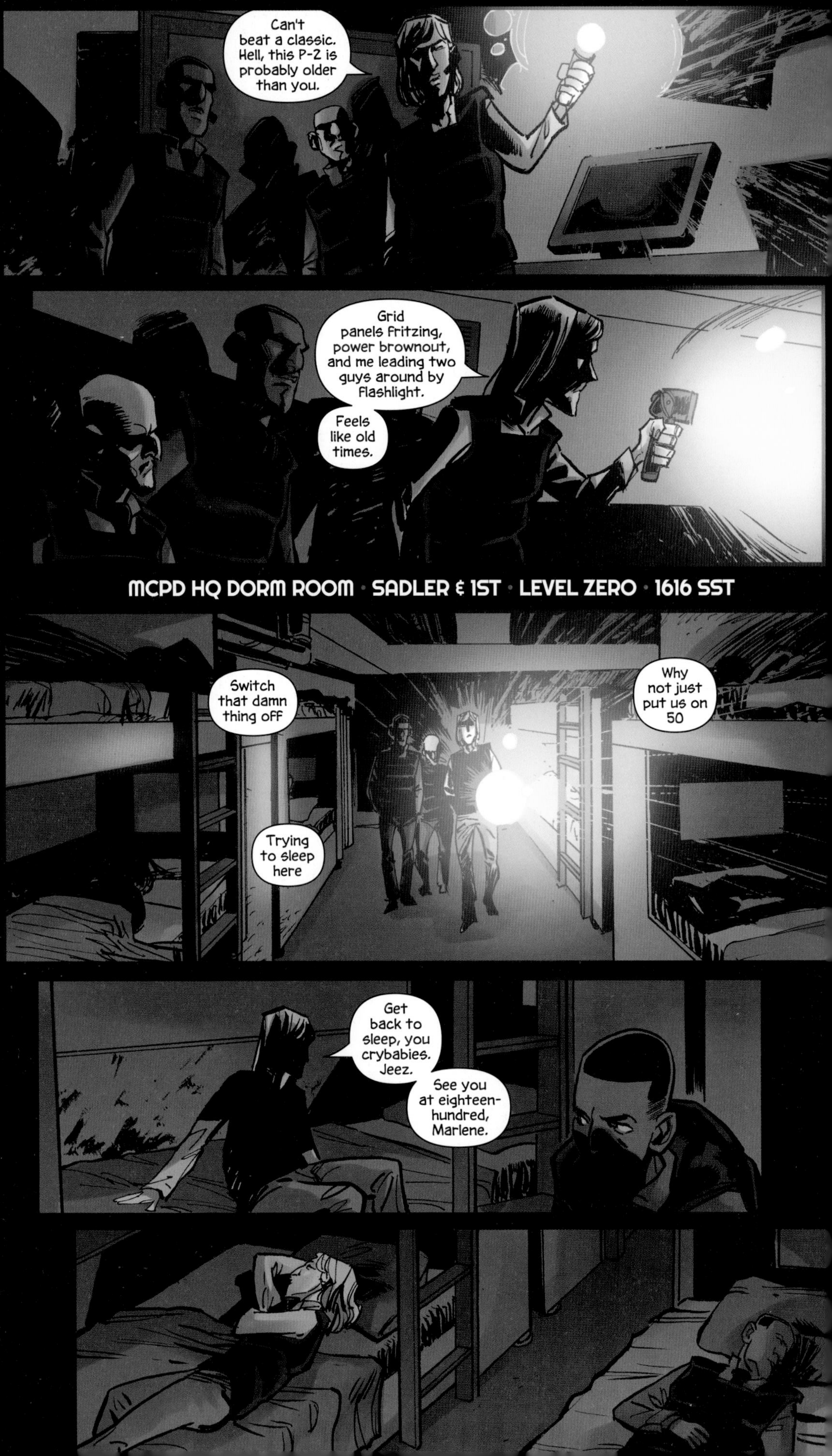
Can't beat a classic. Hell, this P-2 is probably older than you.
Grid panels fritzing, power brownout, and me leading two guys around by flashlight.
Feels like old times.
MCPD HQ DORM ROOM • SADLER & 1ST • LEVEL ZERO • 1616 SST
Switch that damn thing off
Why not just put us on 50
Trying to sleep here
Get back to sleep, you crybabies. Jeez.
See you at eighteen-hundred, Marlene.

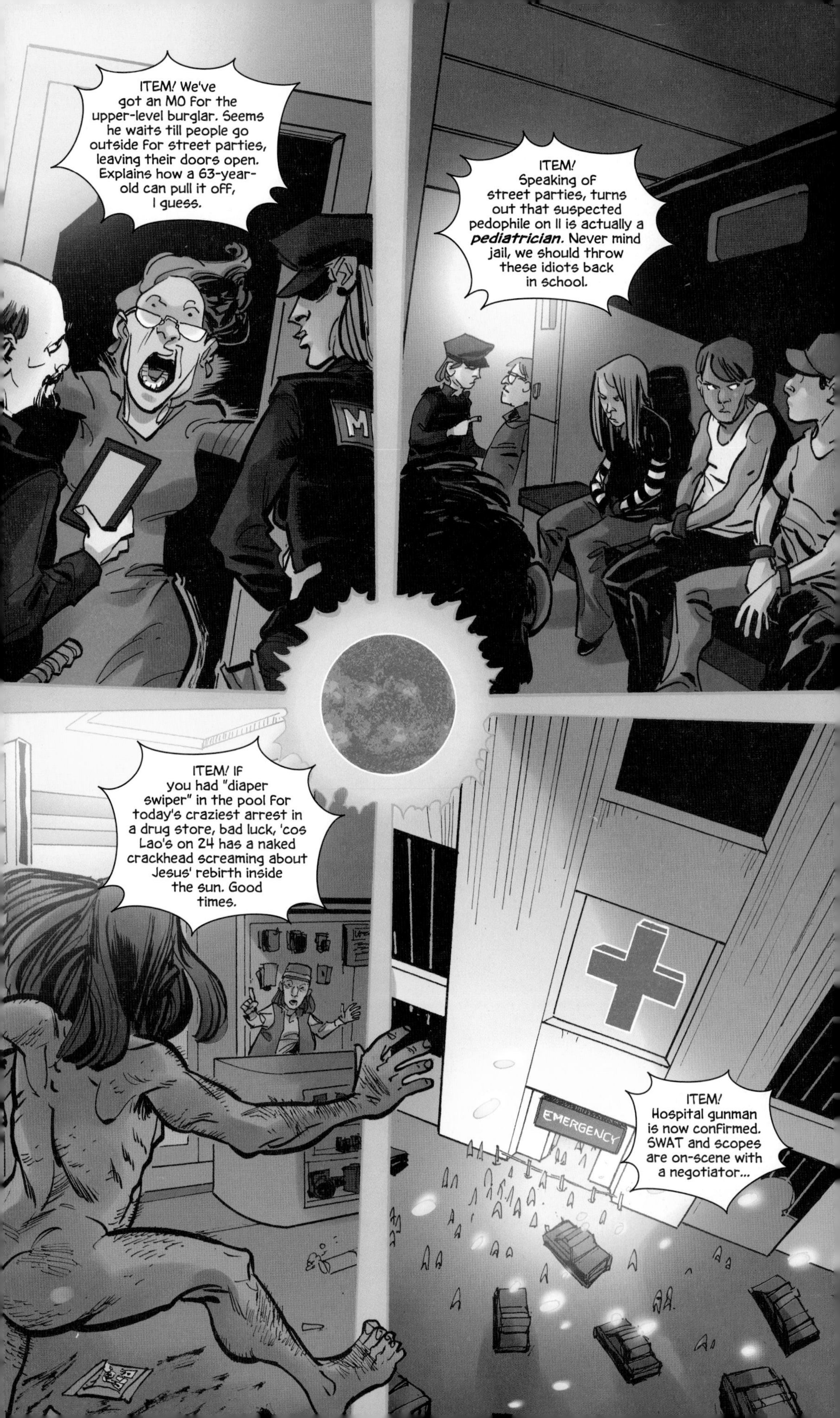
ITEM! We've got an MO for the upper-level burglar. Seems he waits till people go outside for street parties, leaving their doors open. Explains how a 63-year-old can pull it off, I guess.
M
ITEM! Speaking of street parties, turns out that suspected pedophile on 11 is actually a *pediatrician*. Never mind jail, we should throw these idiots back in school.
ITEM! If you had "diaper swiper" in the pool for today's craziest arrest in a drug store, bad luck, 'cos Lao's on 24 has a naked crackhead screaming about Jesus' rebirth inside the sun. Good times.
EMERGENCY
ITEM! Hospital gunman is now confirmed. SWAT and scopes are on-scene with a negotiator...

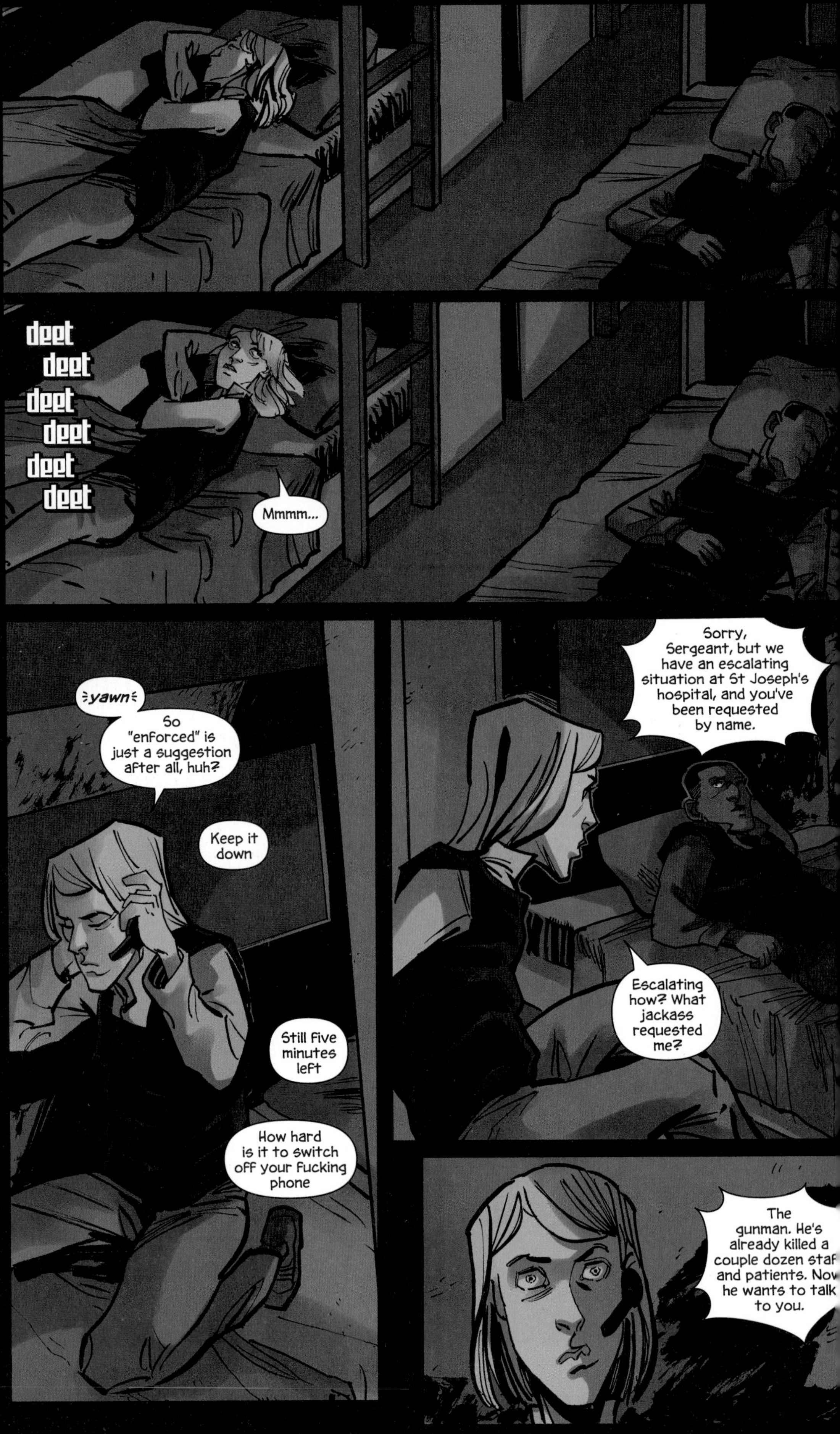
deet deet deet deet deet deet
Mmmm...
yawn
So "enforced" is just a suggestion after all, huh?
Keep it down
Still five minutes left
How hard is it to switch off your fucking phone
Sorry, Sergeant, but we have an escalating situation at St Joseph's hospital, and you've been requested by name.
Escalating how? What jackass requested me?
The gunman. He's already killed a couple dozen staf and patients. Nov he wants to talk to you.

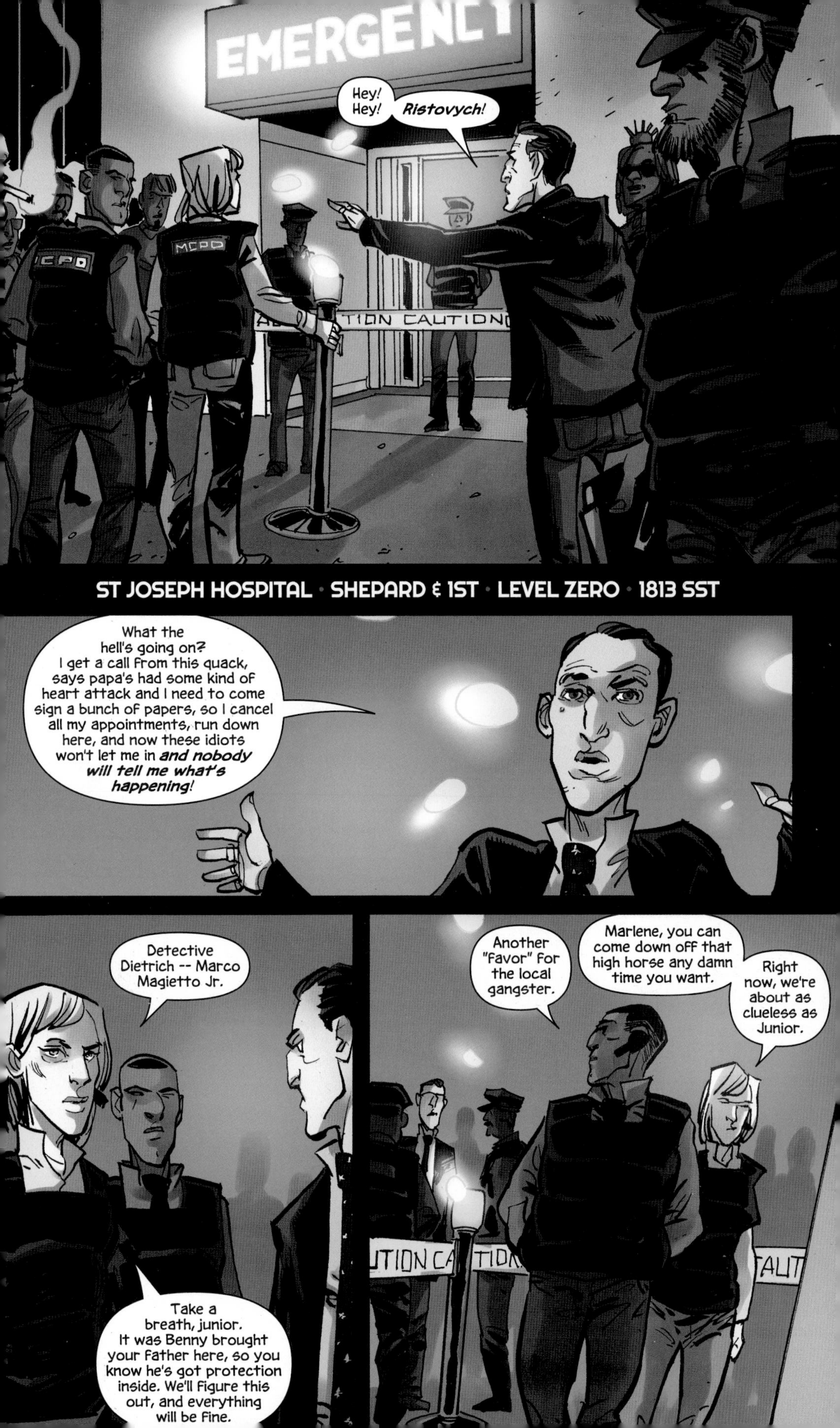
Hey! Hey! Ristovych!
ST JOSEPH HOSPITAL · SHEPARD & 1ST · LEVEL ZERO · 1813 SST
What the hell's going on? I get a call from this quack, says papa's had some kind of heart attack and I need to come sign a bunch of papers, so I cancel all my appointments, run down here, and now these idiots won't let me in and nobody will tell me what's happening!
Detective Dietrich -- Marco Magietto Jr.
Take a breath, junior. It was Benny brought your father here, so you know he's got protection inside. We'll figure this out, and everything will be fine.
Another "favor" for the local gangster.
Marlene, you can come down off that high horse any damn time you want.
Right now, we're about as clueless as Junior.

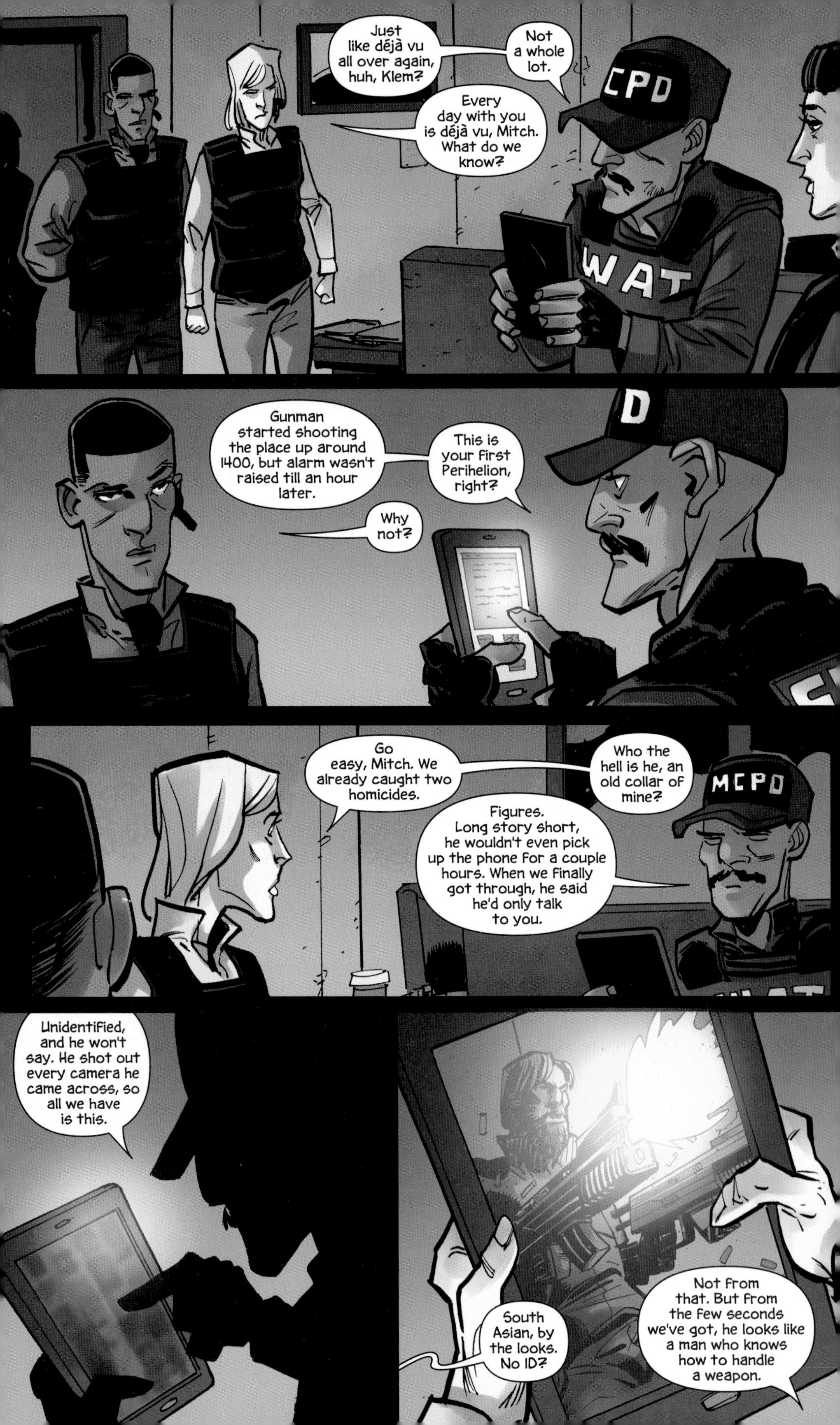
Just like déjà vu all over again, huh, Klem?
Not a whole lot.
Every day with you is déjà vu, Mitch. What do we know?
CPD
WAT
Gunman started shooting the place up around 1400, but alarm wasn't raised till an hour later.
This is your first Perihelion, right?
Why not?
Go easy, Mitch. We already caught two homicides.
Who the hell is he, an old collar of mine?
Figures. Long story short, he wouldn't even pick up the phone for a couple hours. When we finally got through, he said he'd only talk to you.
MCPD
Unidentified, and he won't say. He shot out every camera he came across, so all we have is this.
South Asian, by the looks. No ID?
Not from that. But from the few seconds we've got, he looks like a man who knows how to handle a weapon.

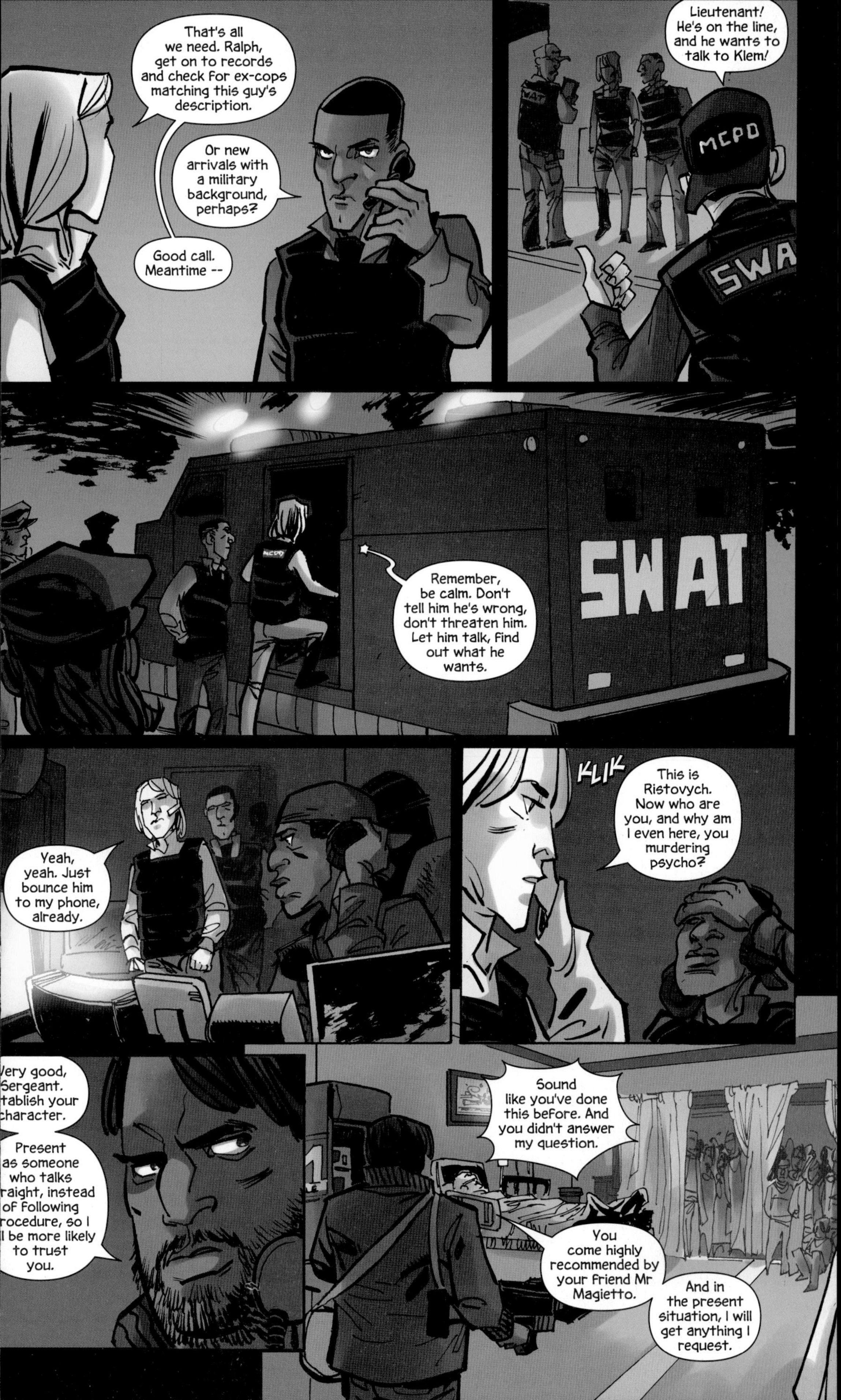
That's all we need. Ralph, get on to records and check for ex-cops matching this guy's description.
Or new arrivals with a military background, perhaps?
Good call. Meantime --
Lieutenant! He's on the line, and he wants to talk to Klem!
MCPD
SWAT
SWAT
Remember, be calm. Don't tell him he's wrong, don't threaten him. Let him talk, find out what he wants.
Yeah, yeah. Just bounce him to my phone, already.
KLIK
This is Ristovych. Now who are you, and why am I even here, you murdering psycho?
ery good, Sergeant. tablish your character.
Present as someone who talks raight, instead of following rocedure, so I l be more likely to trust you.
Sound like you've done this before. And you didn't answer my question.
You come highly recommended by your friend Mr Magietto.
And in the present situation, I will get anything I request.

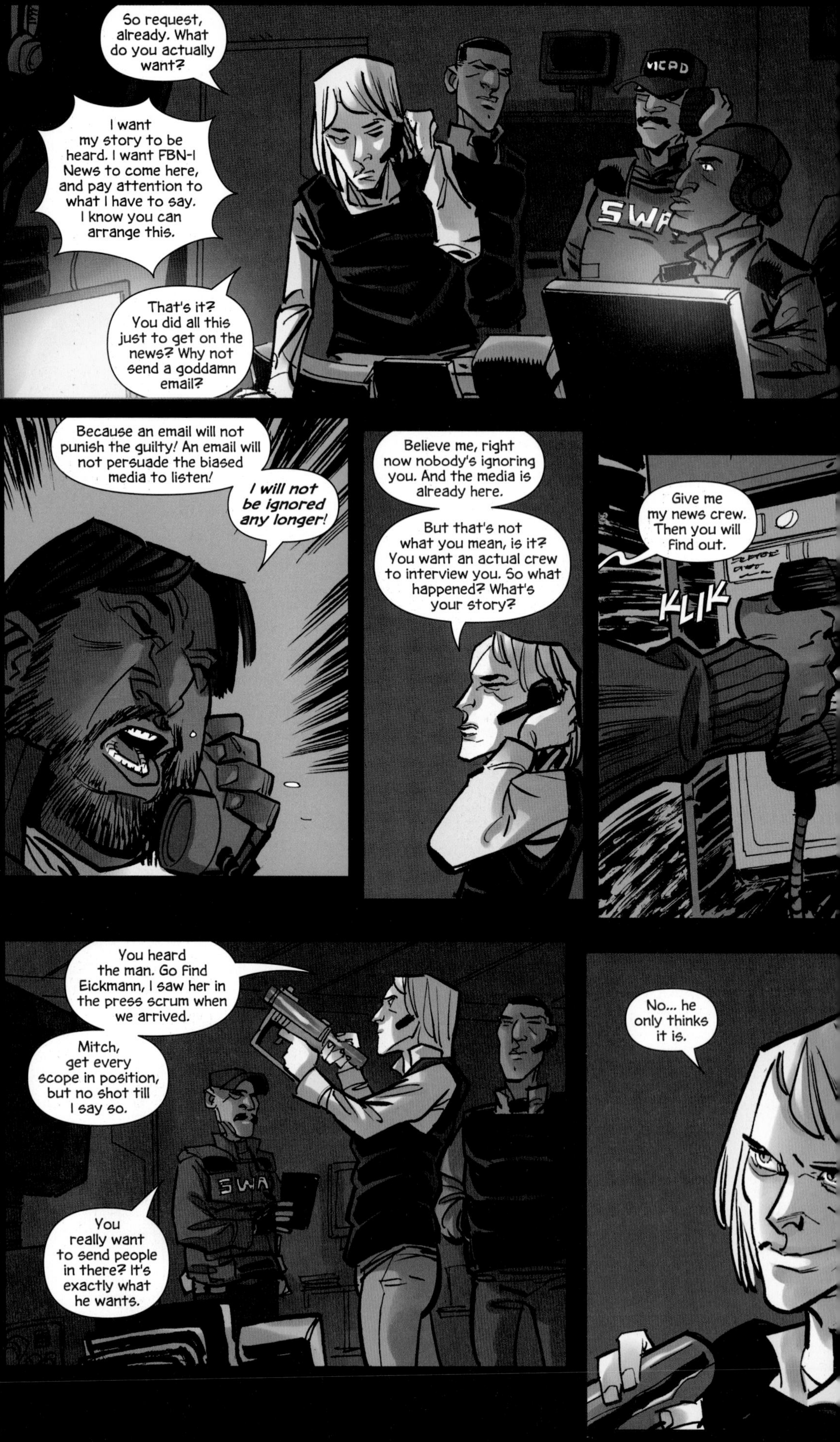

So request, already. What do you actually want?
I want my story to be heard. I want FBN-I News to come here, and pay attention to what I have to say. I know you can arrange this.
That's it? You did all this just to get on the news? Why not send a goddamn email?
Because an email will not punish the guilty! An email will not persuade the biased media to listen!
I will not be ignored any longer!
Believe me, right now nobody's ignoring you. And the media is already here.
But that's not what you mean, is it? You want an actual crew to interview you. So what happened? What's your story?
Give me my news crew. Then you will find out.
KLIK
You heard the man. Go find Eickmann, I saw her in the press scrum when we arrived.
Mitch, get every scope in position, but no shot till I say so.
You really want to send people in there? It's exactly what he wants.
No... he only thinks it is.

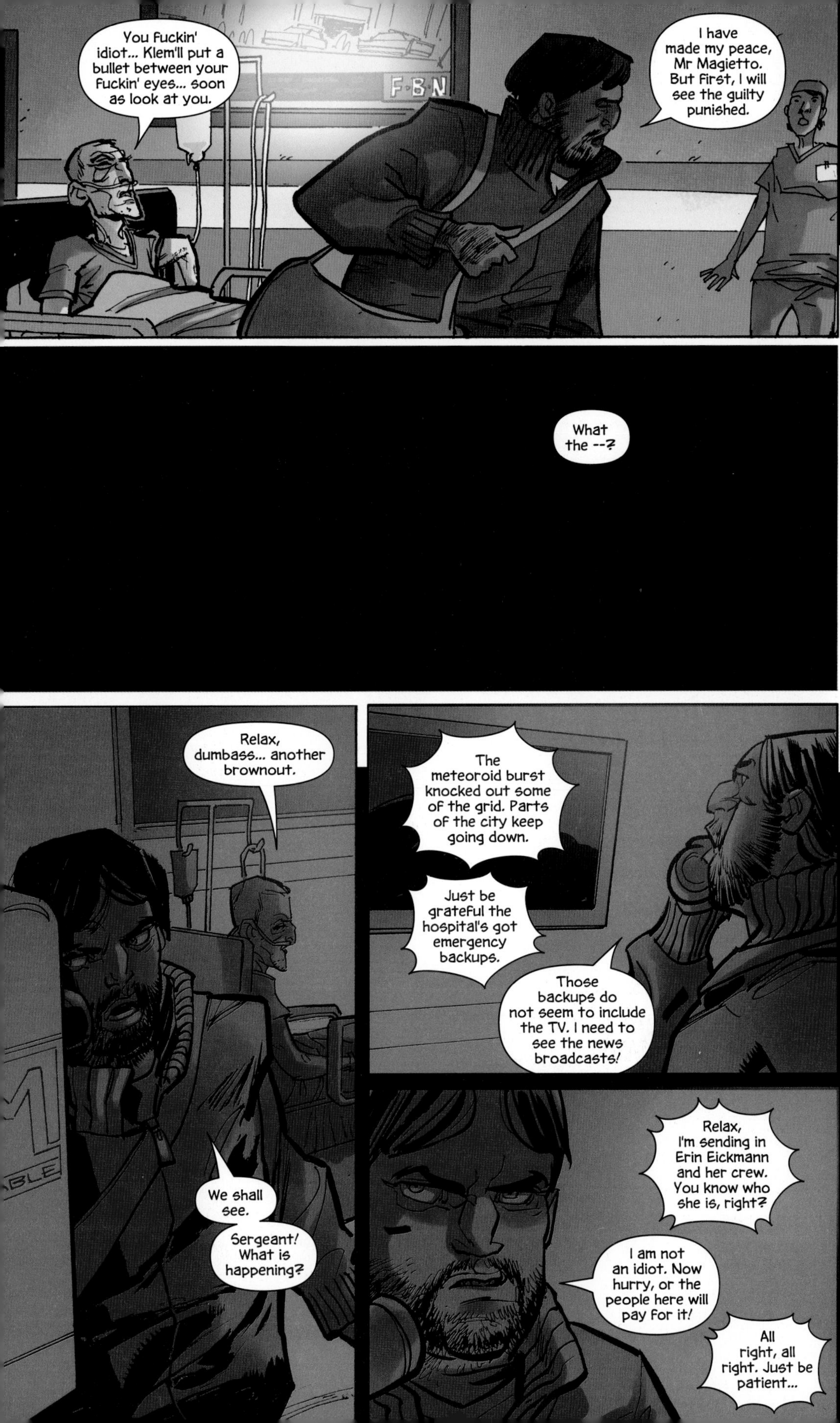
You fuckin' idiot... Klem'll put a bullet between your fuckin' eyes... soon as look at you.
F B N
I have made my peace, Mr Magietto. But first, I will see the guilty punished.
What the --?
Relax, dumbass... another brownout.
We shall see.
Sergeant! What is happening?
The meteoroid burst knocked out some of the grid. Parts of the city keep going down.
Just be grateful the hospital's got emergency backups.
Those backups do not seem to include the TV. I need to see the news broadcasts!
Relax, I'm sending in Erin Eickmann and her crew. You know who she is, right?
I am not an idiot. Now hurry, or the people here will pay for it!
All right, all right. Just be patient...

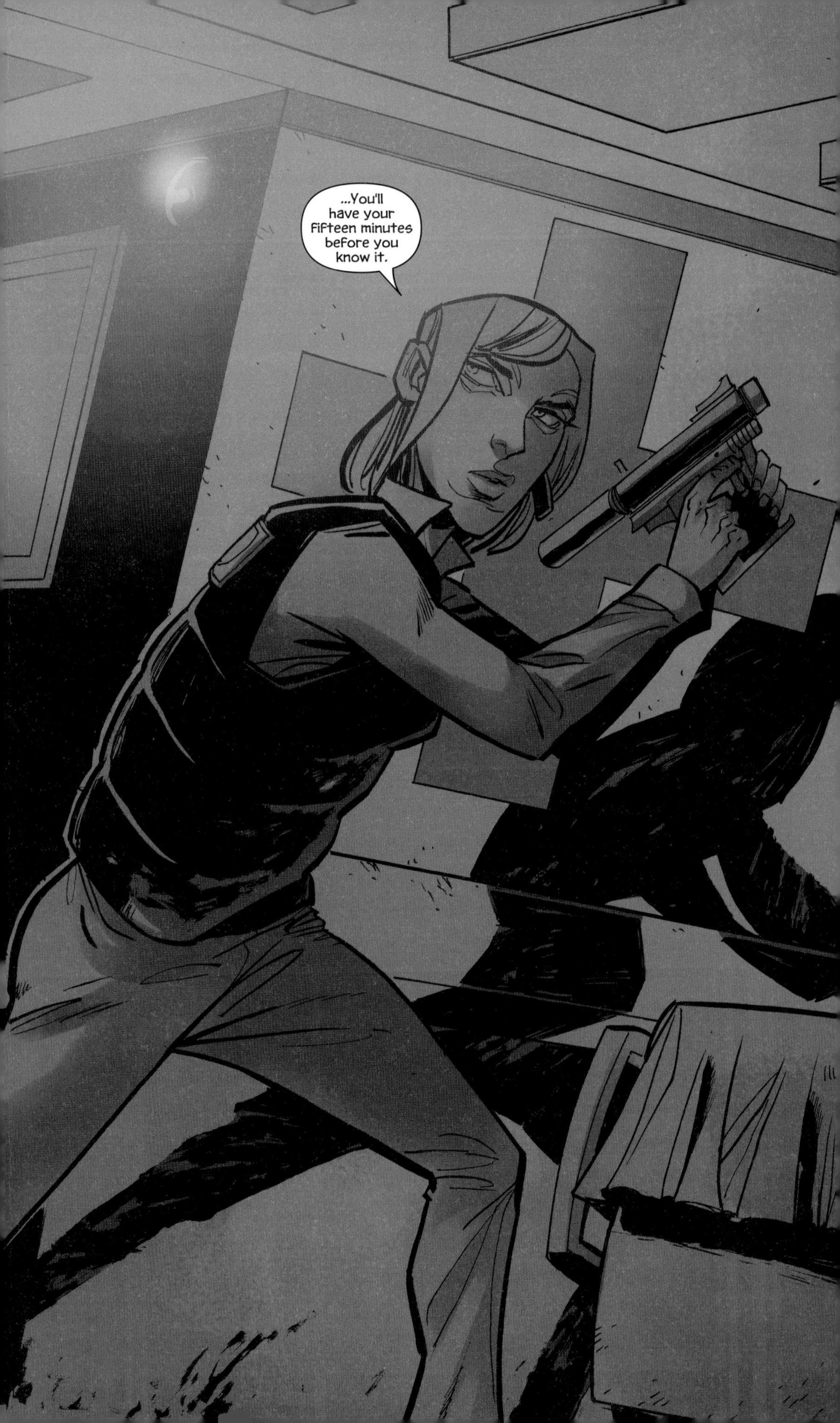
...You'll have your fifteen minutes before you know it.

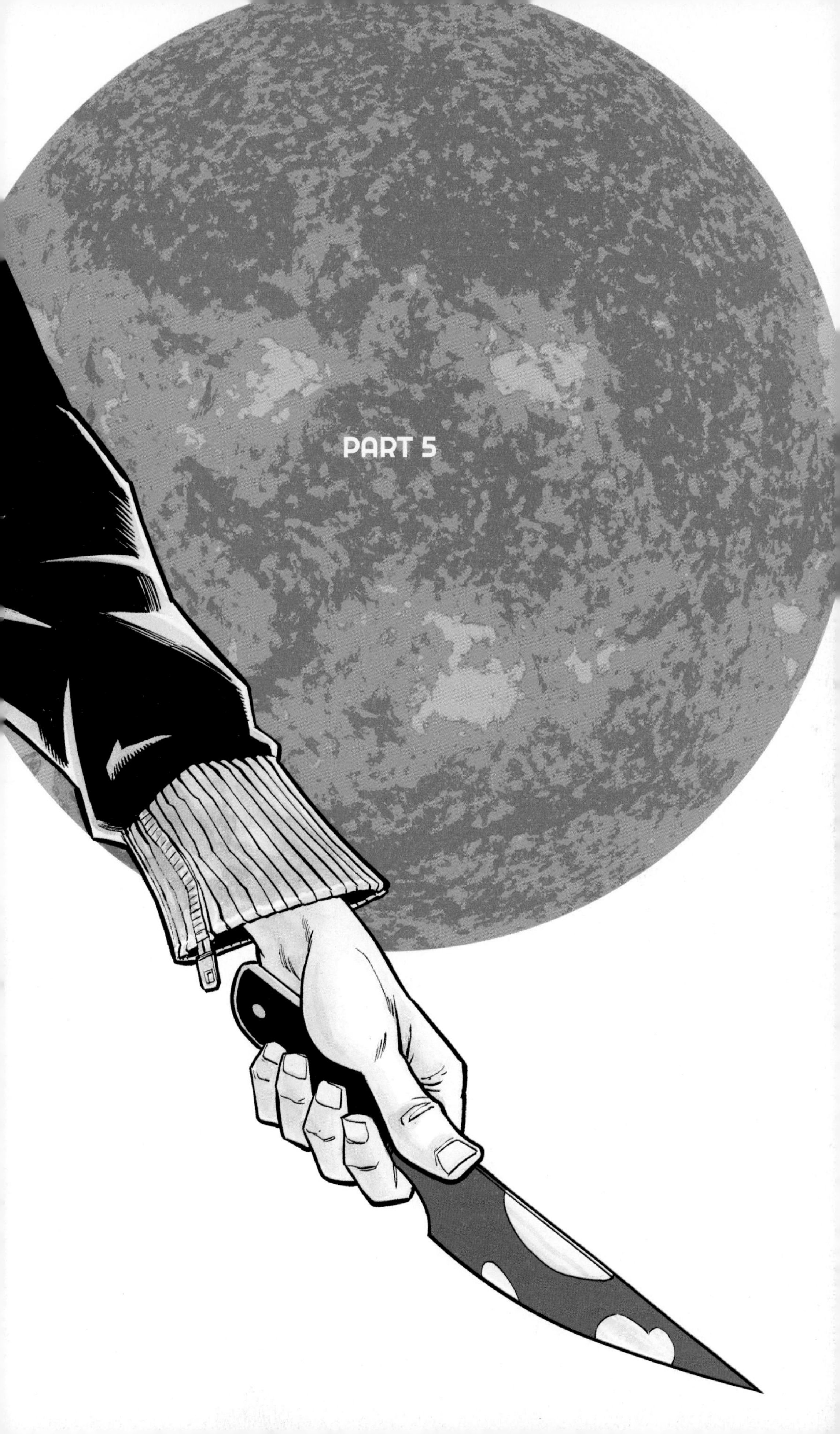
PART 5

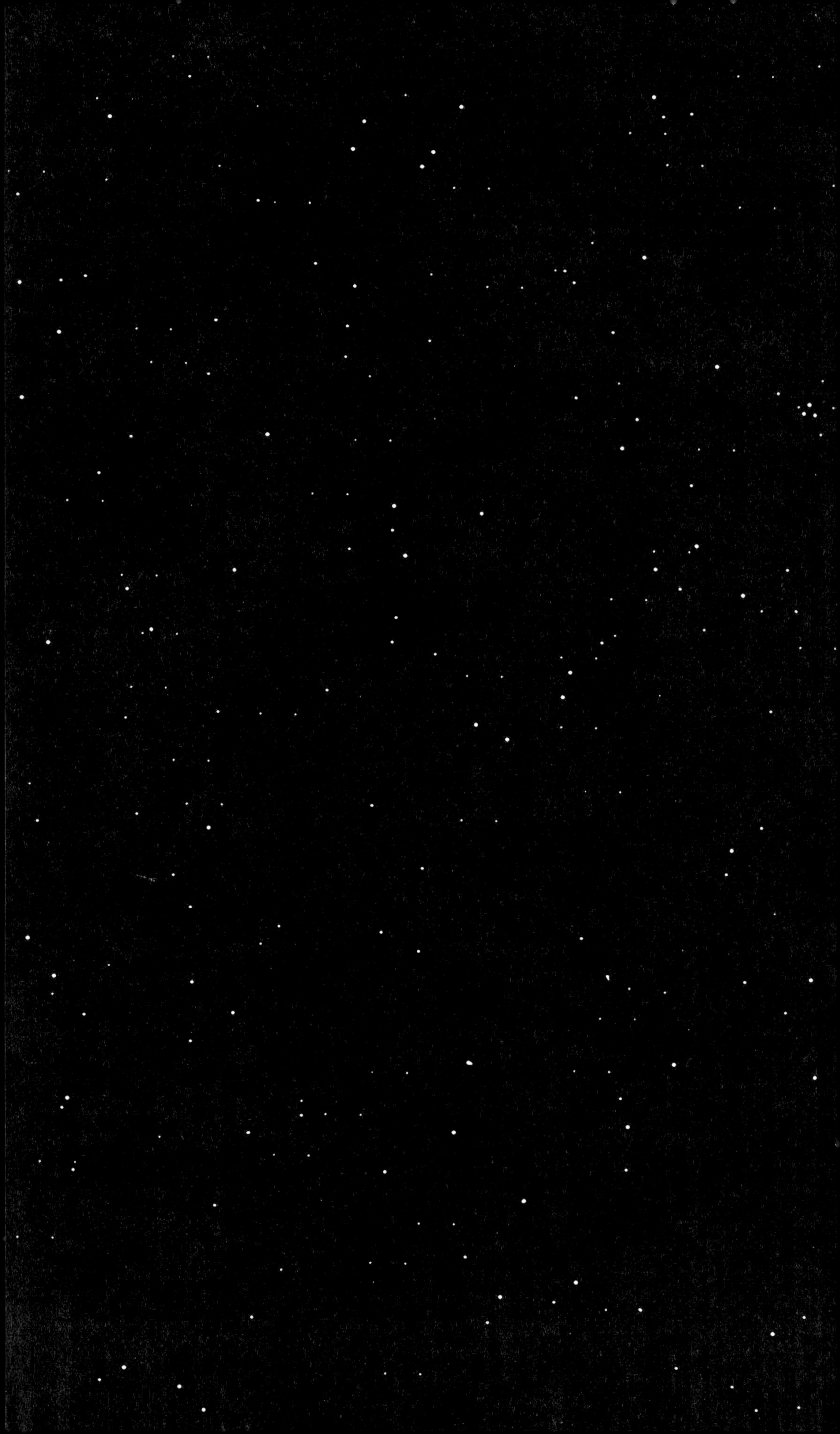

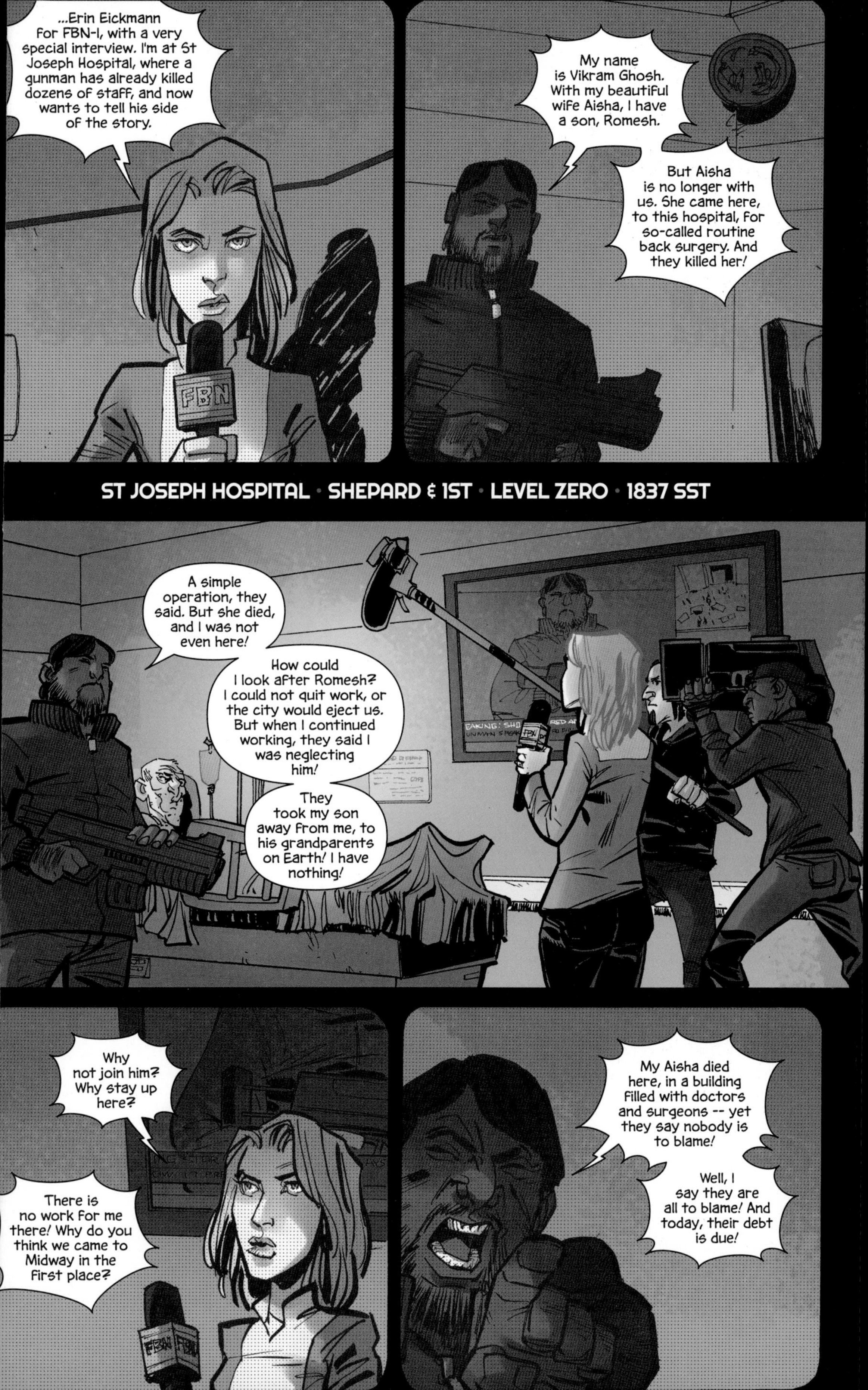
...Erin Eickmann for FBN-1, with a very special interview. I'm at St Joseph Hospital, where a gunman has already killed dozens of staff, and now wants to tell his side of the story.
FBN
My name is Vikram Ghosh. With my beautiful wife Aisha, I have a son, Romesh.
But Aisha is no longer with us. She came here, to this hospital, for so-called routine back surgery. And they killed her!
ST JOSEPH HOSPITAL • SHEPARD & 1ST • LEVEL ZERO • 1837 SST
A simple operation, they said. But she died, and I was not even here!
How could I look after Romesh? I could not quit work, or the city would eject us. But when I continued working, they said I was neglecting him!
They took my son away from me, to his grandparents on Earth! I have nothing!
Why not join him? Why stay up here?
There is no work for me there! Why do you think we came to Midway in the first place?
FBN
My Aisha died here, in a building filled with doctors and surgeons -- yet they say nobody is to blame!
Well, I say they are all to blame! And today, their debt is due!

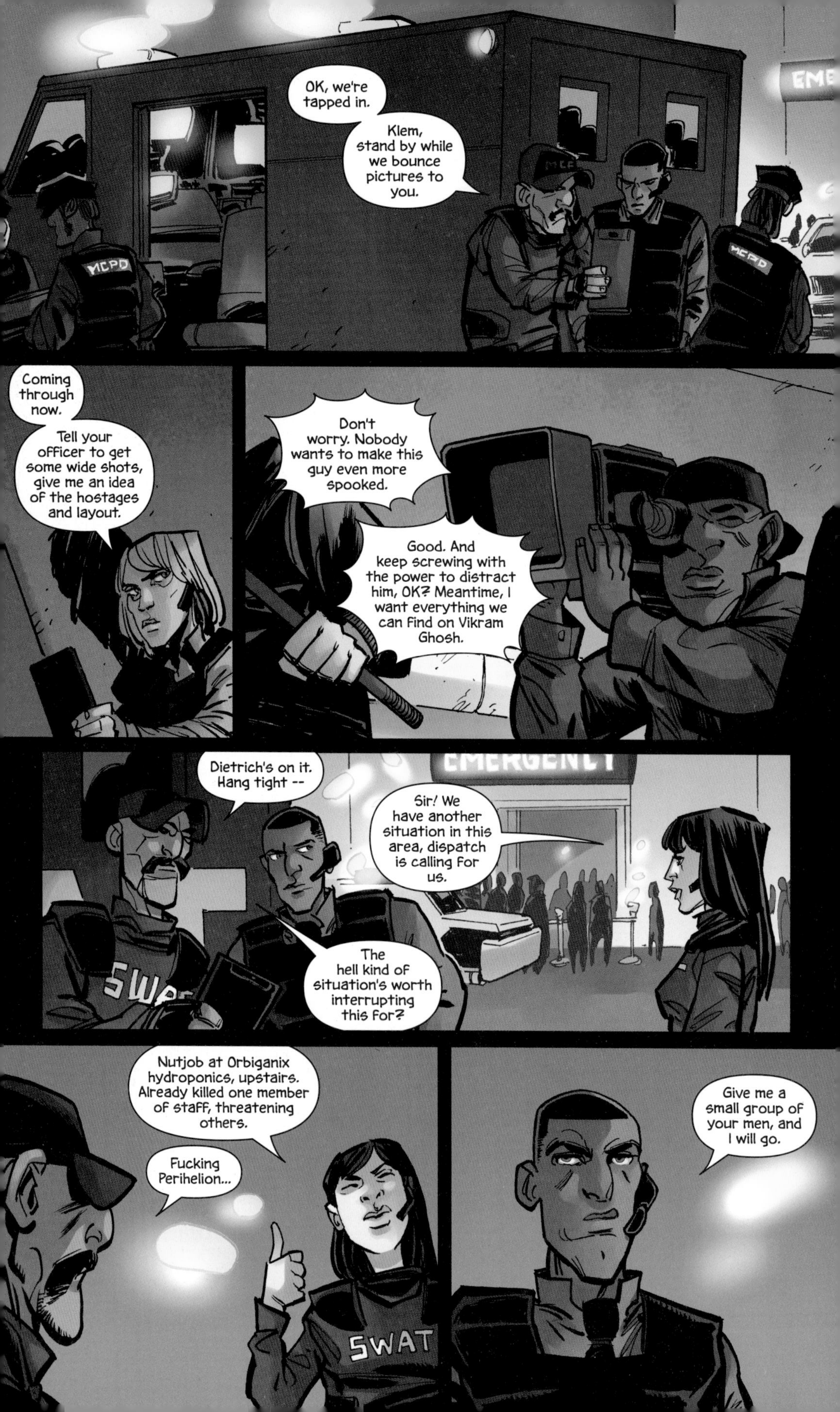
EME
OK, we're tapped in.
Klem, stand by while we bounce pictures to you.
MCPD
MCPD
Coming through now.
Tell your officer to get some wide shots, give me an idea of the hostages and layout.
Don't worry. Nobody wants to make this guy even more spooked.
Good. And keep screwing with the power to distract him, OK? Meantime, I want everything we can find on Vikram Ghosh.
EMERGENCY
Dietrich's on it. Hang tight --
Sir! We have another situation in this area, dispatch is calling for us.
The hell kind of situation's worth interrupting this for?
Nutjob at Orbiganix hydroponics, upstairs. Already killed one member of staff, threatening others.
Fucking Perihelion...
SWAT
Give me a small group of your men, and I will go.

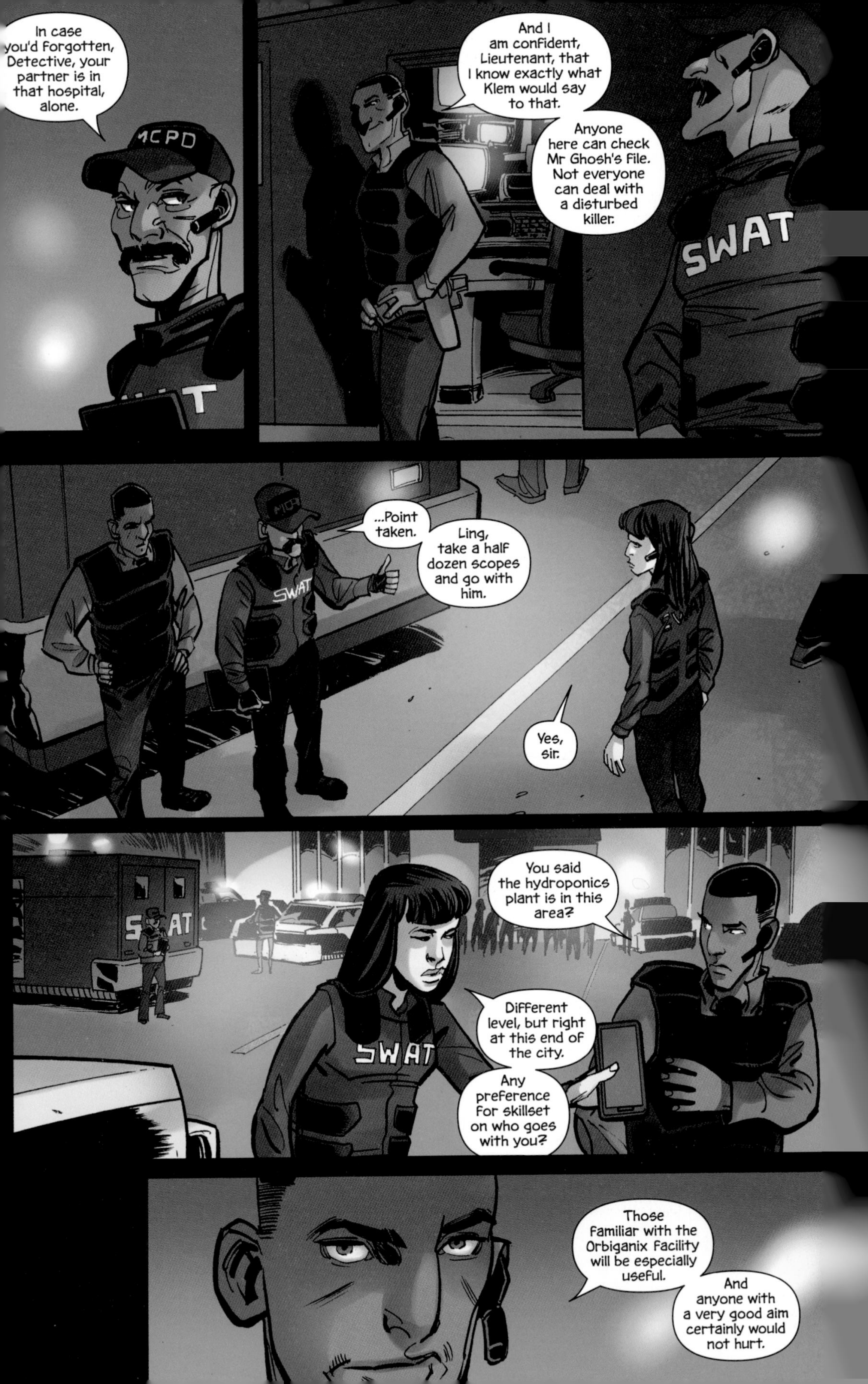
In case you'd Forgotten, Detective, your partner is in that hospital, alone.
And I am confident, Lieutenant, that I know exactly what Klem would say to that.
Anyone here can check Mr Ghosh's File. Not everyone can deal with a disturbed killer.
MCPD
SWAT
...Point taken.
Ling, take a half dozen scopes and go with him.
Yes, sir.
SWAT
You said the hydroponics plant is in this area?
Different level, but right at this end of the city.
Any preference for skillset on who goes with you?
Those familiar with the Orbiganix Facility will be especially useful.
And anyone with a very good aim certainly would not hurt.

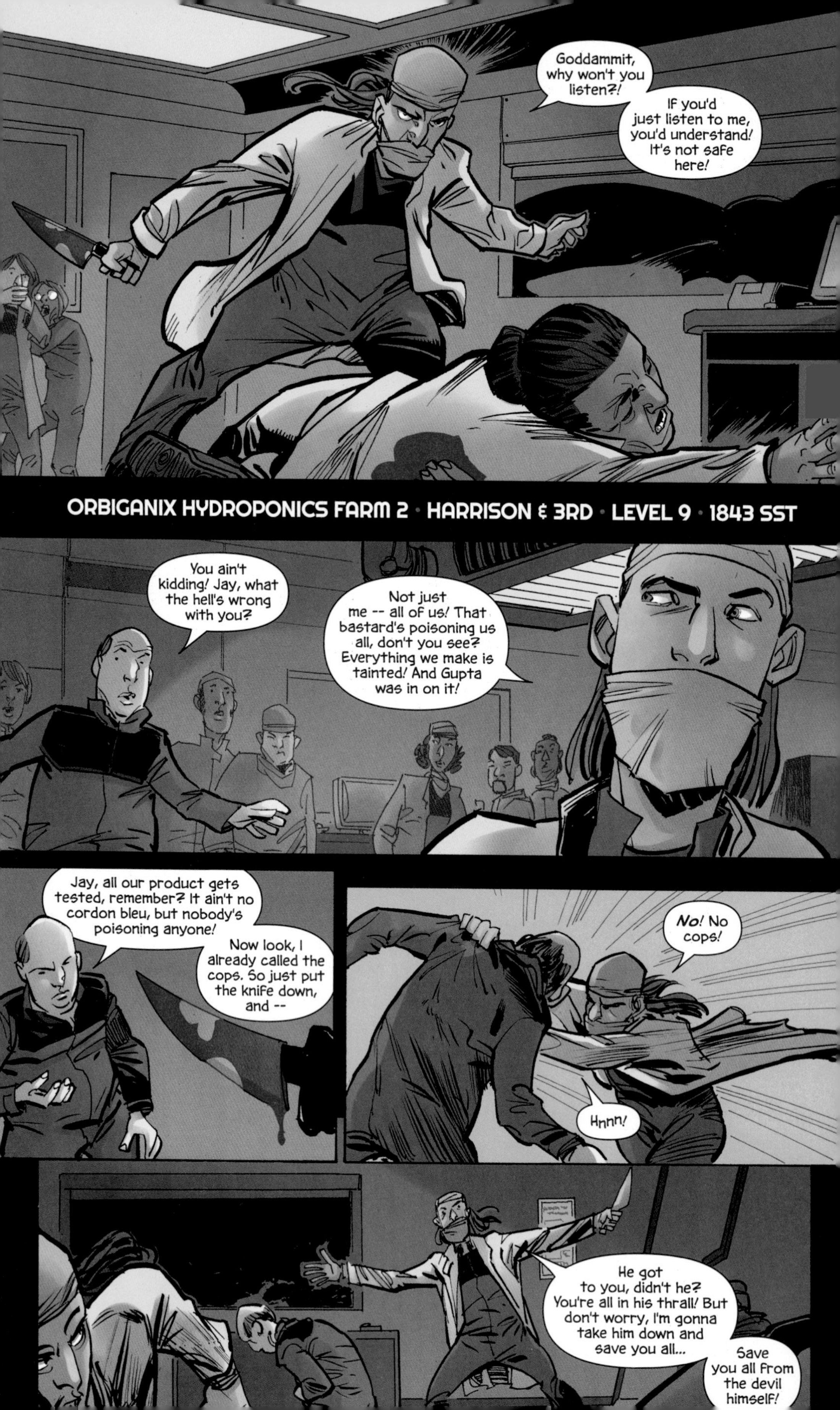
Goddammit, why won't you listen?!
If you'd just listen to me, you'd understand! It's not safe here!
ORBIGANIX HYDROPONICS FARM 2 • HARRISON & 3RD • LEVEL 9 • 1843 SST
You ain't kidding! Jay, what the hell's wrong with you?
Not just me -- all of us! That bastard's poisoning us all, don't you see? Everything we make is tainted! And Gupta was in on it!
Jay, all our product gets tested, remember? It ain't no cordon bleu, but nobody's poisoning anyone!
Now look, I already called the cops. So just put the knife down, and --
No! No cops!
Hnnn!
He got to you, didn't he? You're all in his thrall! But don't worry, I'm gonna take him down and save you all...
Save you all from the devil himself!

ST JOSEPH HOSPITAL · SHEPARD & 1ST · LEVEL ZERO · 1848 SST

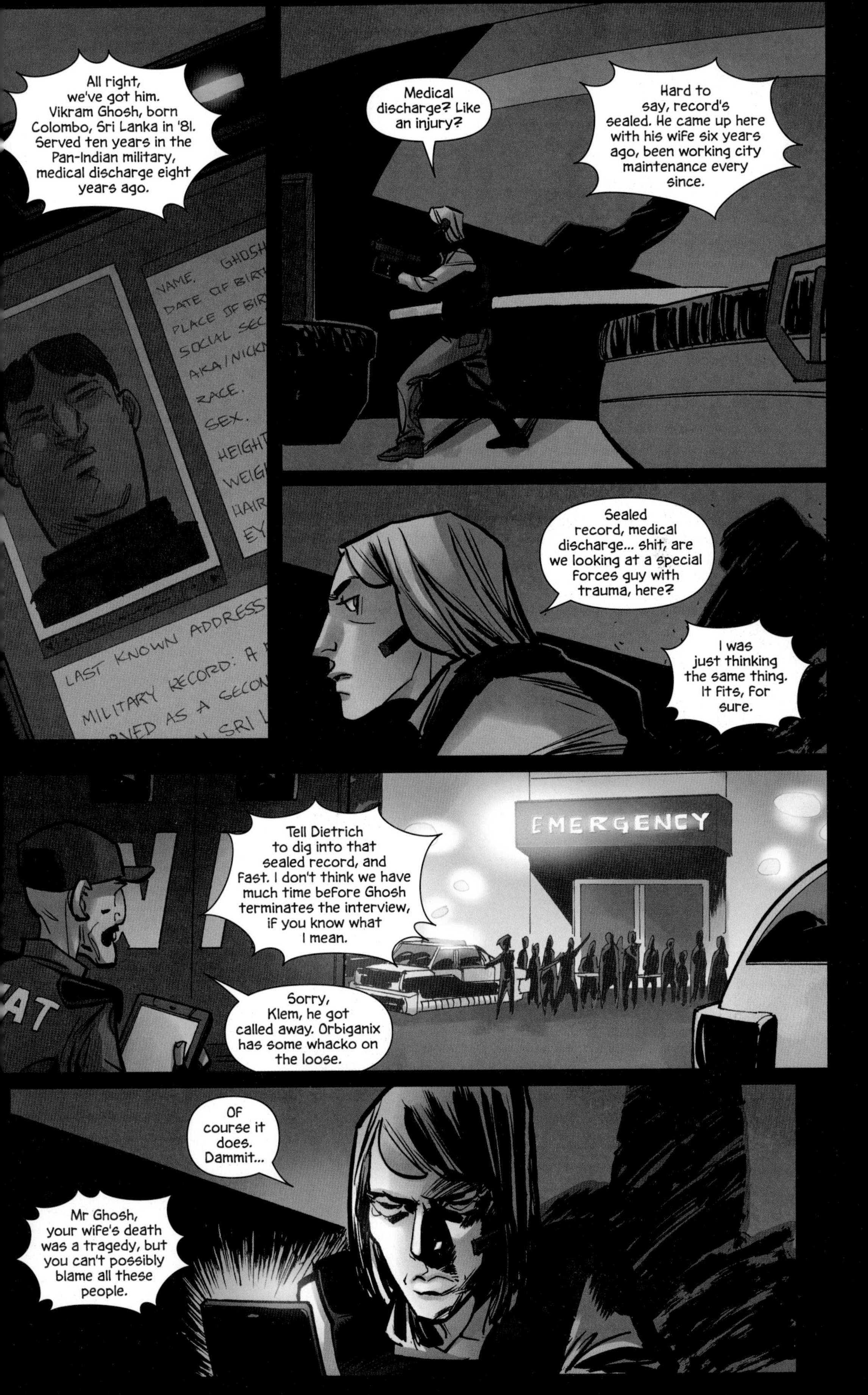
All right, we've got him. Vikram Ghosh, born Colombo, Sri Lanka in '81. Served ten years in the Pan-Indian military, medical discharge eight years ago.
NAME
RACE
SEX
LAST KNOWN ADDRESS
Medical discharge? Like an injury?
Hard to say, record's sealed. He came up here with his wife six years ago, been working city maintenance every since.
Sealed record, medical discharge... shit, are we looking at a special forces guy with trauma, here?
I was just thinking the same thing. It fits, for sure.
EMERGENCY
Tell Dietrich to dig into that sealed record, and fast. I don't think we have much time before Ghosh terminates the interview, if you know what I mean.
Sorry, Klem, he got called away. Orbiganix has some whacko on the loose.
Of course it does. Dammit...
Mr Ghosh, your wife's death was a tragedy, but you can't possibly blame all these people.

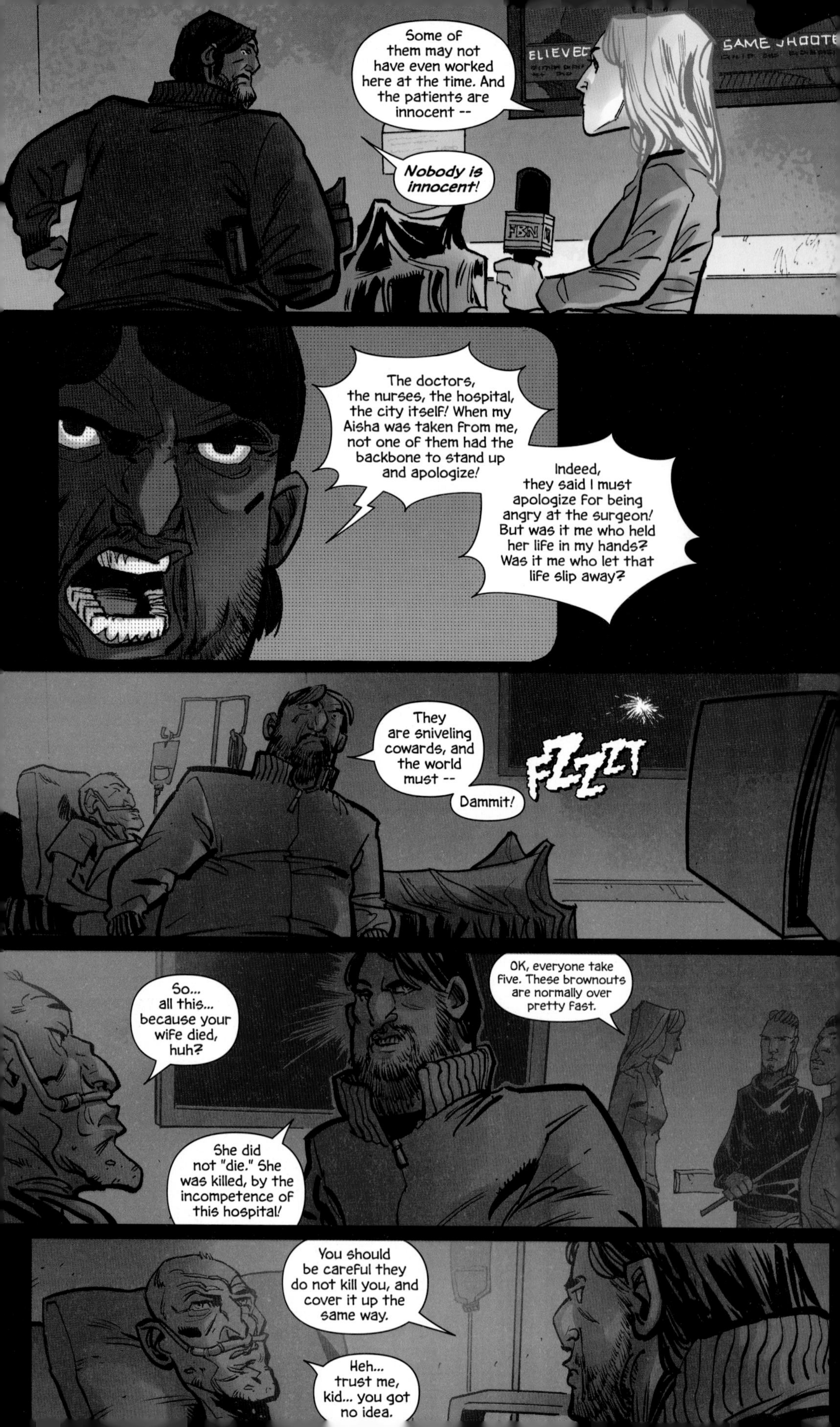
ELIEVED
SAME SHOOTE
Some of them may not have even worked here at the time. And the patients are innocent --
Nobody is innocent!
FBN
The doctors, the nurses, the hospital, the city itself! When my Aisha was taken from me, not one of them had the backbone to stand up and apologize!
Indeed, they said I must apologize for being angry at the surgeon! But was it me who held her life in my hands? Was it me who let that life slip away?
They are sniveling cowards, and the world must --
Dammit!
FZZZT
OK, everyone take five. These brownouts are normally over pretty fast.
So... all this... because your wife died, huh?
She did not "die." She was killed, by the incompetence of this hospital!
You should be careful they do not kill you, and cover it up the same way.
Heh... trust me, kid... you got no idea.

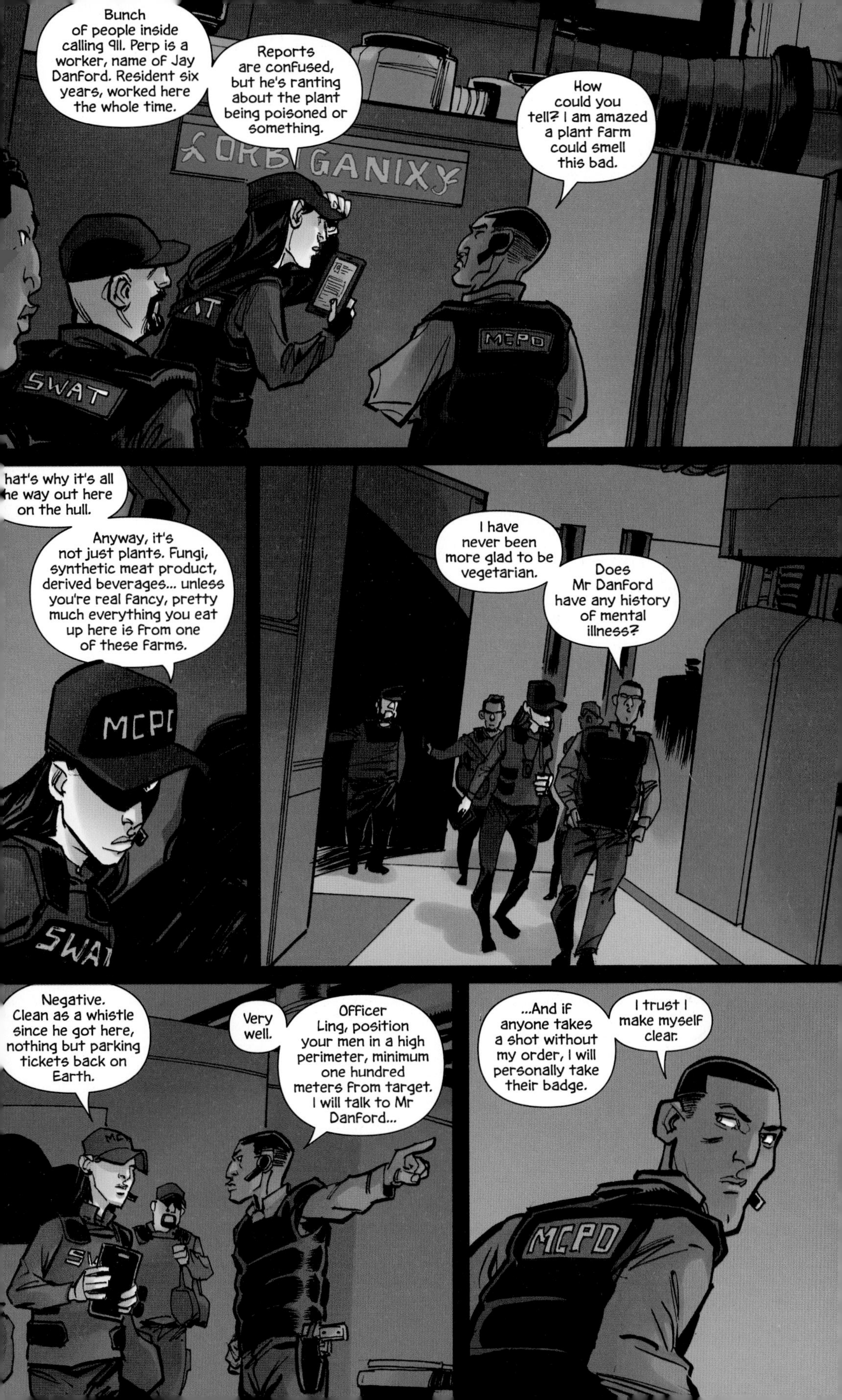
Bunch of people inside calling 911. Perp is a worker, name of Jay Danford. Resident six years, worked here the whole time.
Reports are confused, but he's ranting about the plant being poisoned or something.
ORBGANIX
How could you tell? I am amazed a plant farm could smell this bad.
SWAT
MCPD
hat's why it's all he way out here on the hull.
Anyway, it's not just plants. Fungi, synthetic meat product, derived beverages... unless you're real fancy, pretty much everything you eat up here is from one of these farms.
MCPD
SWAT
I have never been more glad to be vegetarian.
Does Mr Danford have any history of mental illness?
Negative. Clean as a whistle since he got here, nothing but parking tickets back on Earth.
Very well.
Officer Ling, position your men in a high perimeter, minimum one hundred meters from target. I will talk to Mr Danford...
...And if anyone takes a shot without my order, I will personally take their badge.
I trust I make myself clear.
MCPD

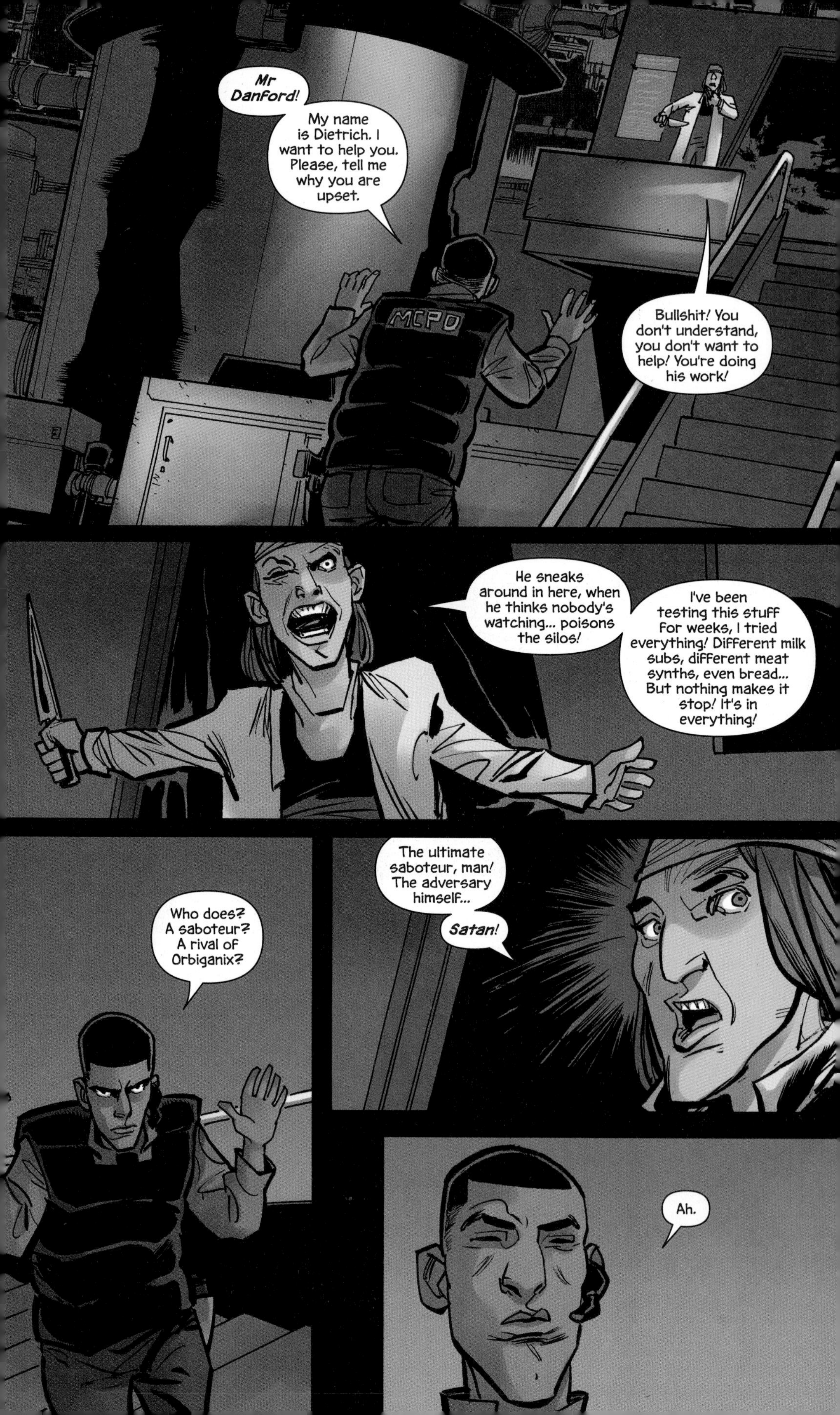
Mr Danford!
My name is Dietrich. I want to help you. Please, tell me why you are upset.
Bullshit! You don't understand, you don't want to help! You're doing his work!
He sneaks around in here, when he thinks nobody's watching... poisons the silos!
I've been testing this stuff for weeks, I tried everything! Different milk subs, different meat synths, even bread... But nothing makes it stop! It's in everything!
Who does? A saboteur? A rival of Orbiganix?
The ultimate saboteur, man! The adversary himself...
Satan!
Ah.

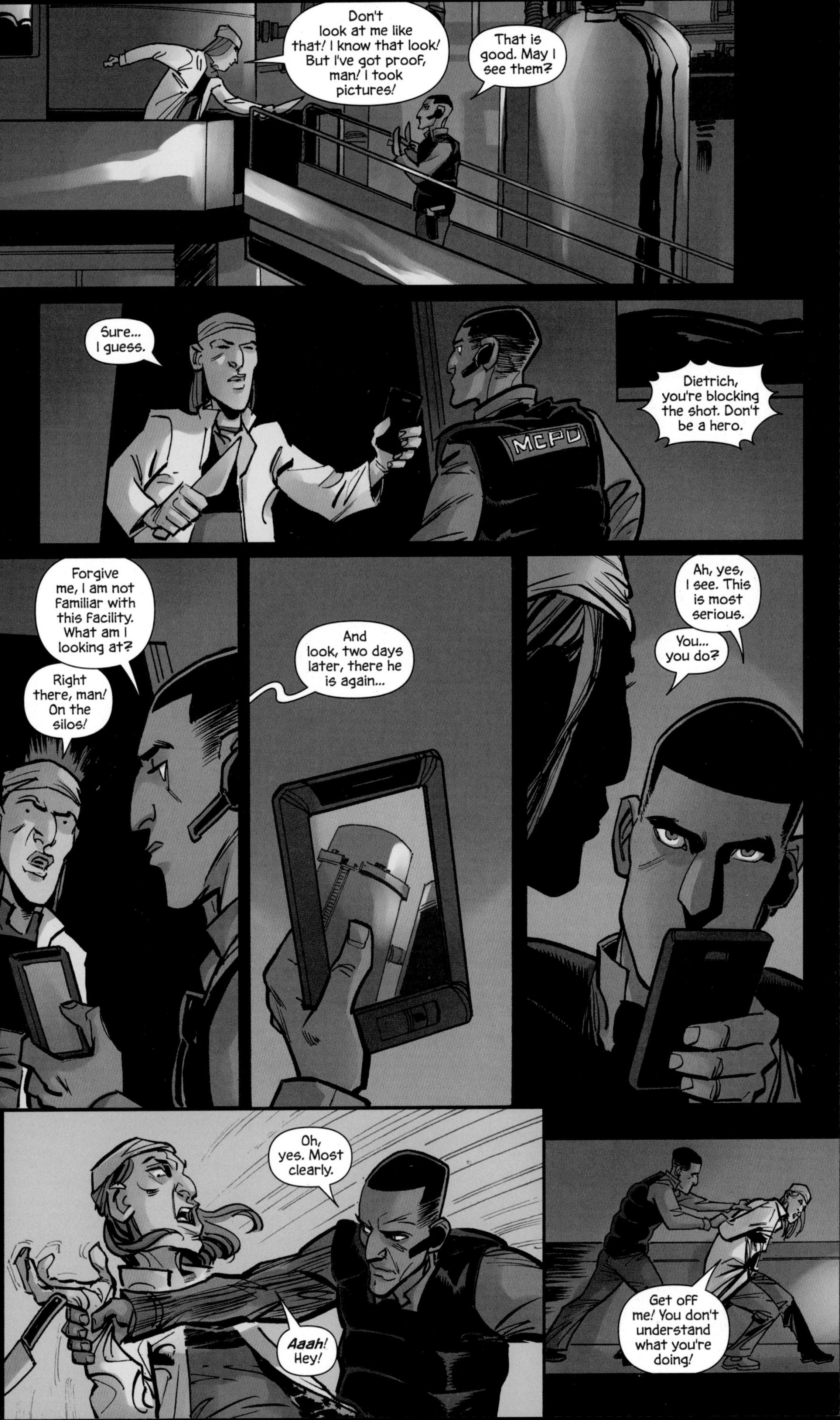
Don't look at me like that! I know that look! But I've got proof, man! I took pictures!
That is good. May I see them?
Sure... I guess.
Dietrich, you're blocking the shot. Don't be a hero.
MCPD
Forgive me, I am not familiar with this facility. What am I looking at?
Right there, man! On the silos!
And look, two days later, there he is again...
Ah, yes, I see. This is most serious.
You... you do?
Oh, yes. Most clearly.
Aaah! Hey!
Get off me! You don't understand what you're doing!

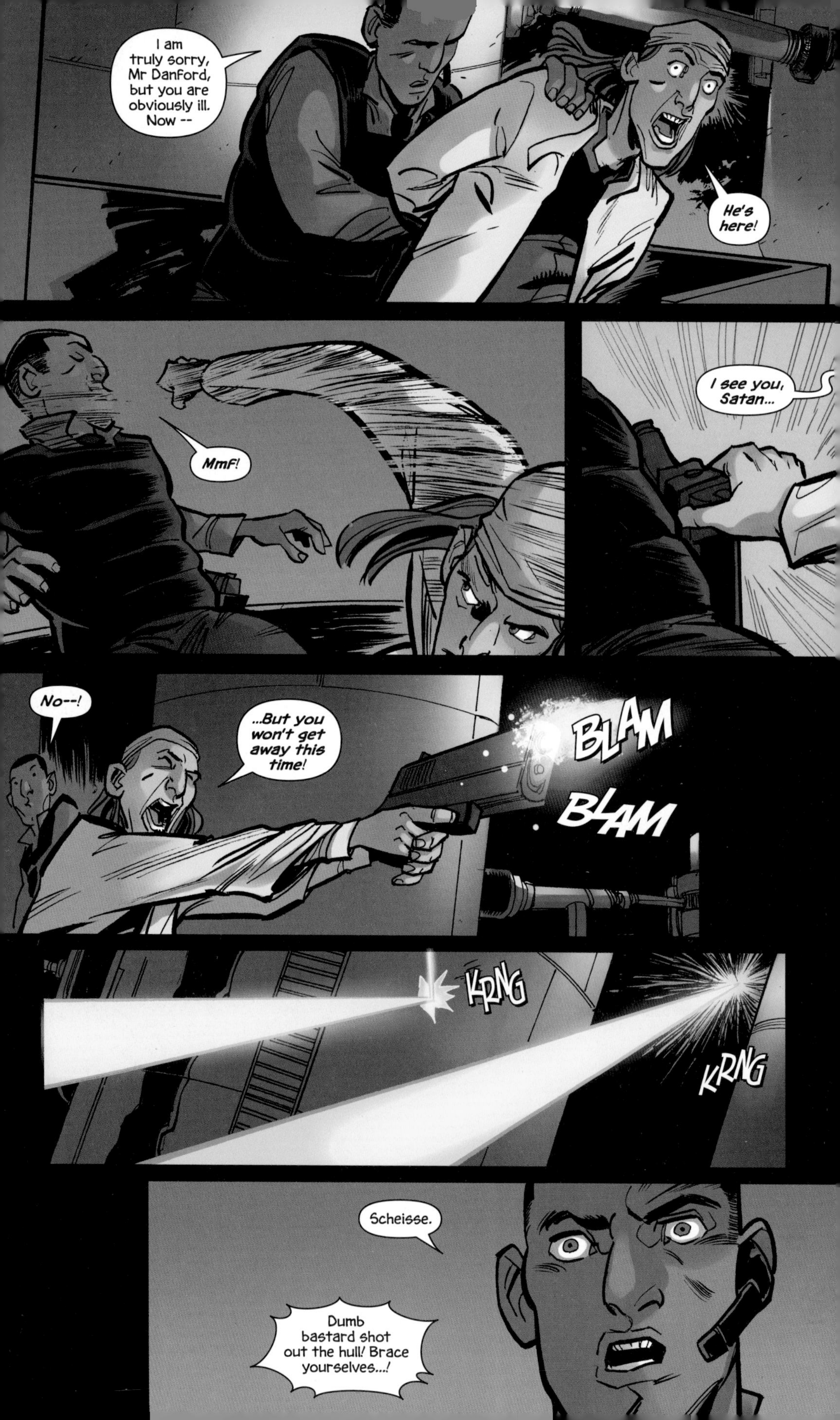

I am truly sorry, Mr Danford, but you are obviously ill. Now --
He's here!
Mmf!
I see you, Satan...
No--!
...But you won't get away this time!
BLAM
BLAM
KRNG
KRNG
Scheisse.
Dumb bastard shot out the hull! Brace yourselves...!

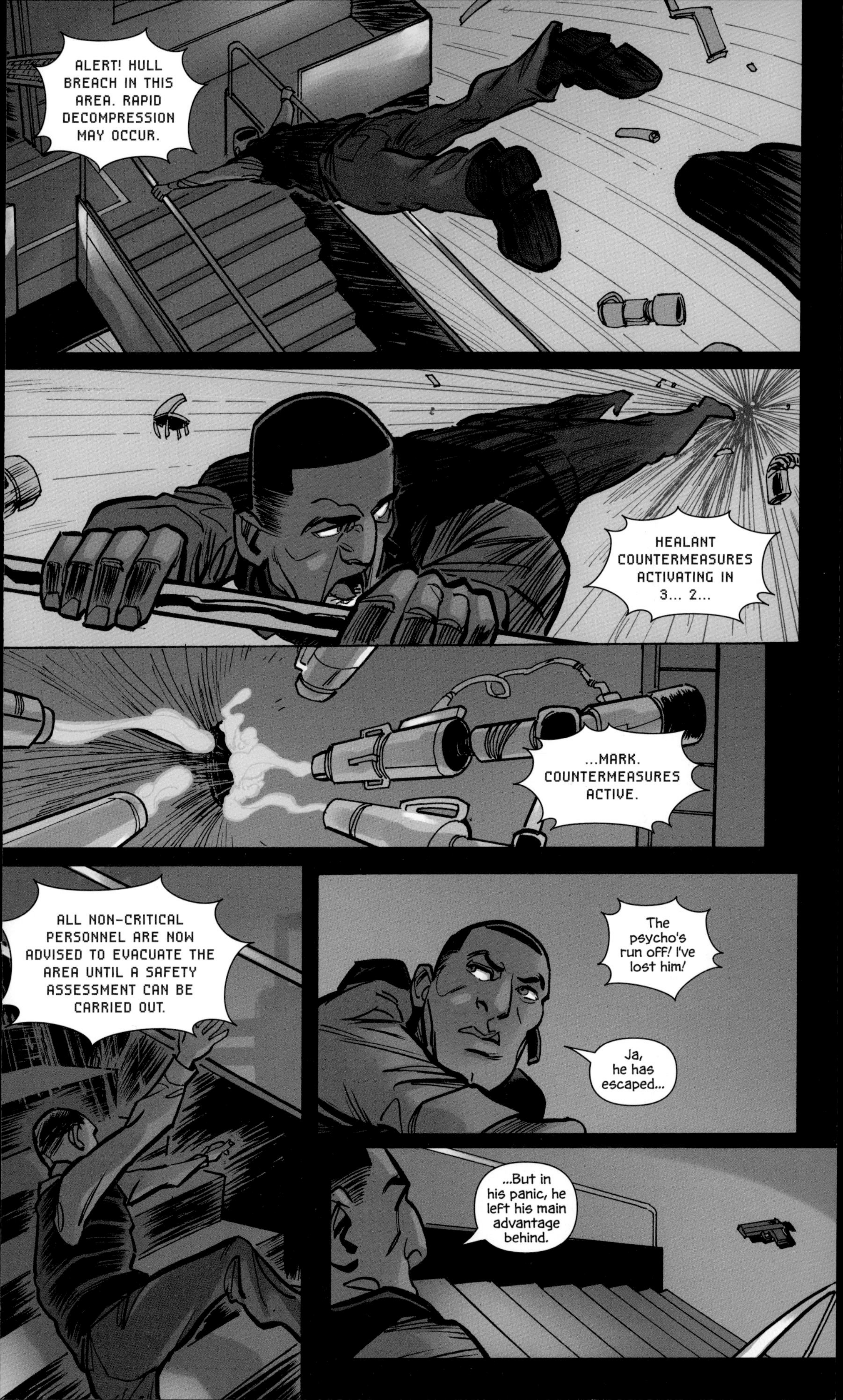
ALERT! HULL BREACH IN THIS AREA. RAPID DECOMPRESSION MAY OCCUR.
HEALANT COUNTERMEASURES ACTIVATING IN 3... 2...
...MARK. COUNTERMEASURES ACTIVE.
ALL NON-CRITICAL PERSONNEL ARE NOW ADVISED TO EVACUATE THE AREA UNTIL A SAFETY ASSESSMENT CAN BE CARRIED OUT.
The psycho's run off! I've lost him!
Ja, he has escaped...
...But in his panic, he left his main advantage behind.

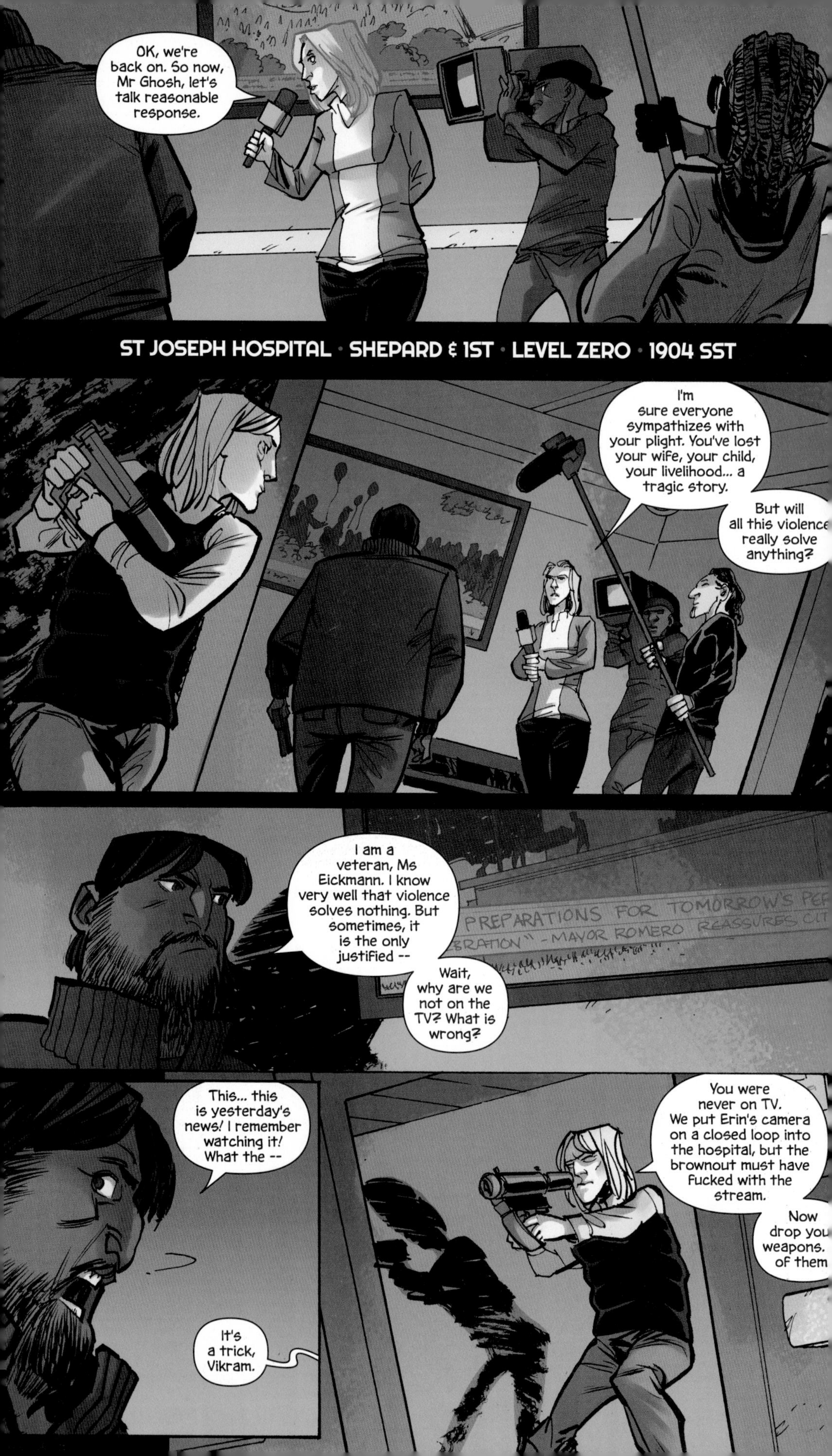
OK, we're back on. So now, Mr Ghosh, let's talk reasonable response.
ST JOSEPH HOSPITAL · SHEPARD & 1ST · LEVEL ZERO · 1904 SST
I'm sure everyone sympathizes with your plight. You've lost your wife, your child, your livelihood... a tragic story.
But will all this violence really solve anything?
I am a veteran, Ms Eickmann. I know very well that violence solves nothing. But sometimes, it is the only justified --
PREPARATIONS FOR TOMORROW'S
" -MAYOR ROMERO
Wait, why are we not on the TV? What is wrong?
This... this is yesterday's news! I remember watching it! What the --
You were never on TV. We put Erin's camera on a closed loop into the hospital, but the brownout must have fucked with the stream.
Now drop you weapons. of them
It's a trick, Vikram.

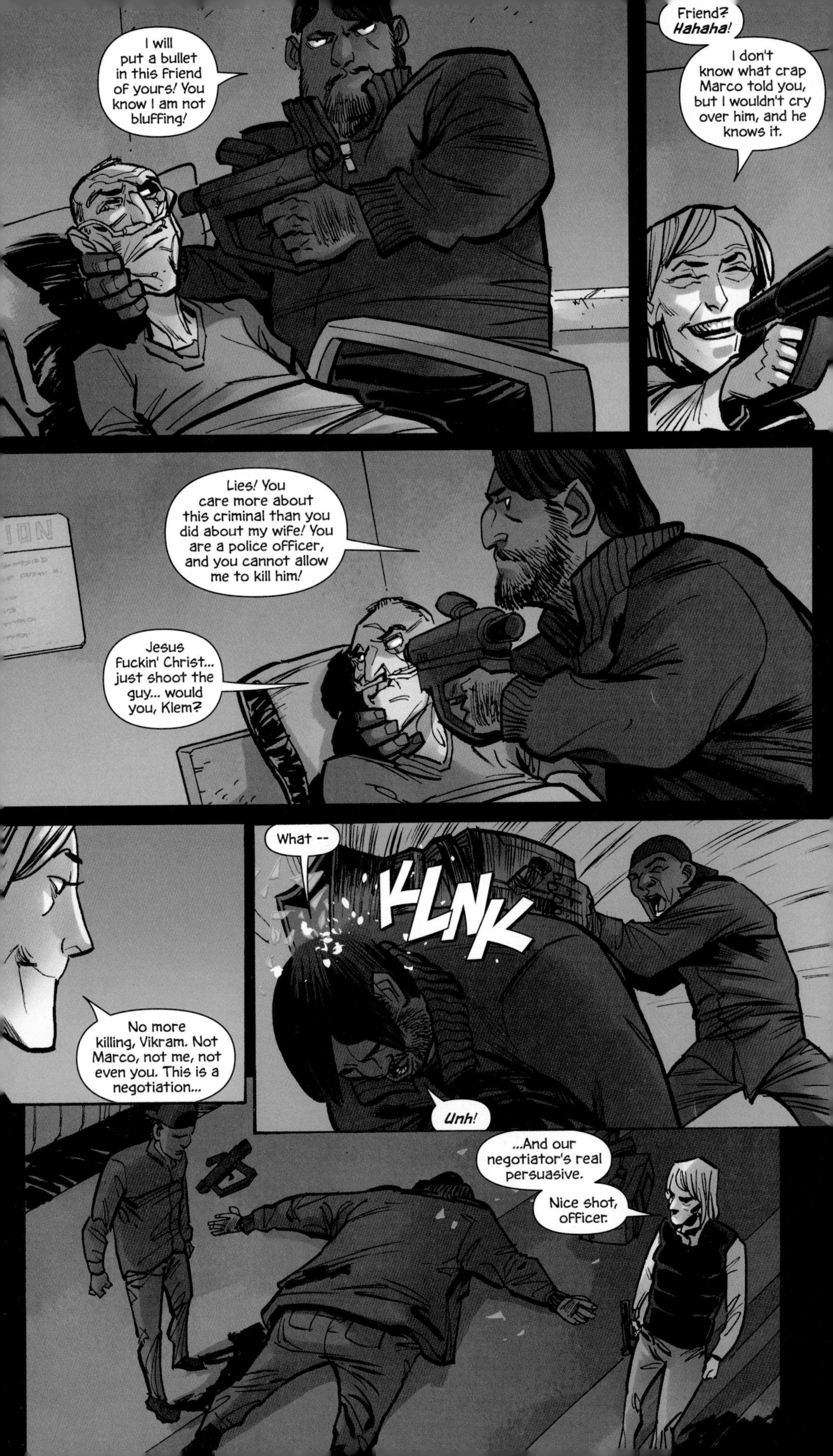

I will put a bullet in this friend of yours! You know I am not bluffing!
Friend? Hahaha!
I don't know what crap Marco told you, but I wouldn't cry over him, and he knows it.
Lies! You care more about this criminal than you did about my wife! You are a police officer, and you cannot allow me to kill him!
Jesus Fuckin' Christ... just shoot the guy... would you, Klem?
No more killing, Vikram. Not Marco, not me, not even you. This is a negotiation...
What --
KLNK
Unh!
...And our negotiator's real persuasive.
Nice shot, officer.

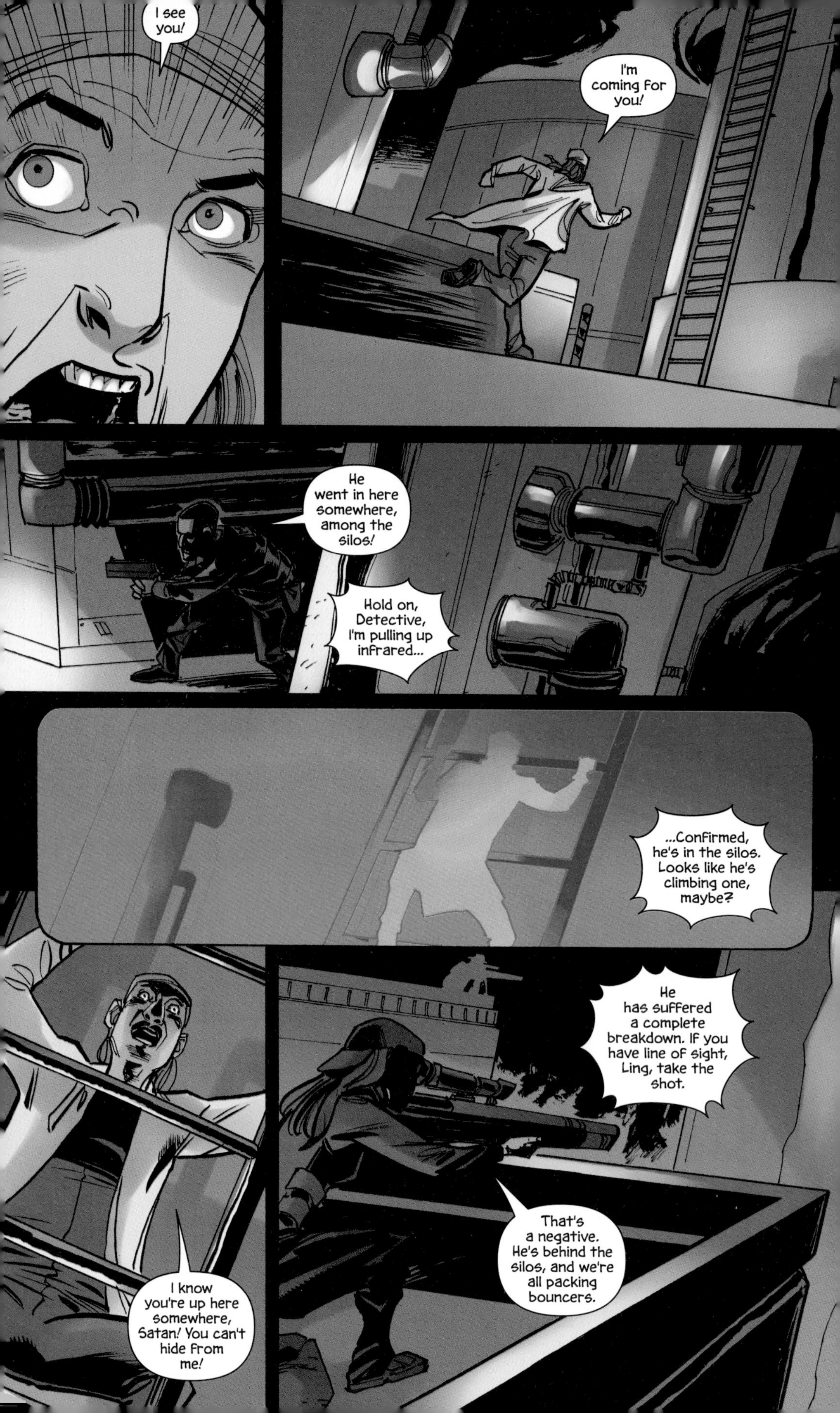
I see you!
I'm coming for you!
He went in here somewhere, among the silos!
Hold on, Detective, I'm pulling up infrared...
...Confirmed, he's in the silos. Looks like he's climbing one, maybe?
He has suffered a complete breakdown. If you have line of sight, Ling, take the shot.
That's a negative. He's behind the silos, and we're all packing bouncers.
I know you're up here somewhere, Satan! You can't hide from me!

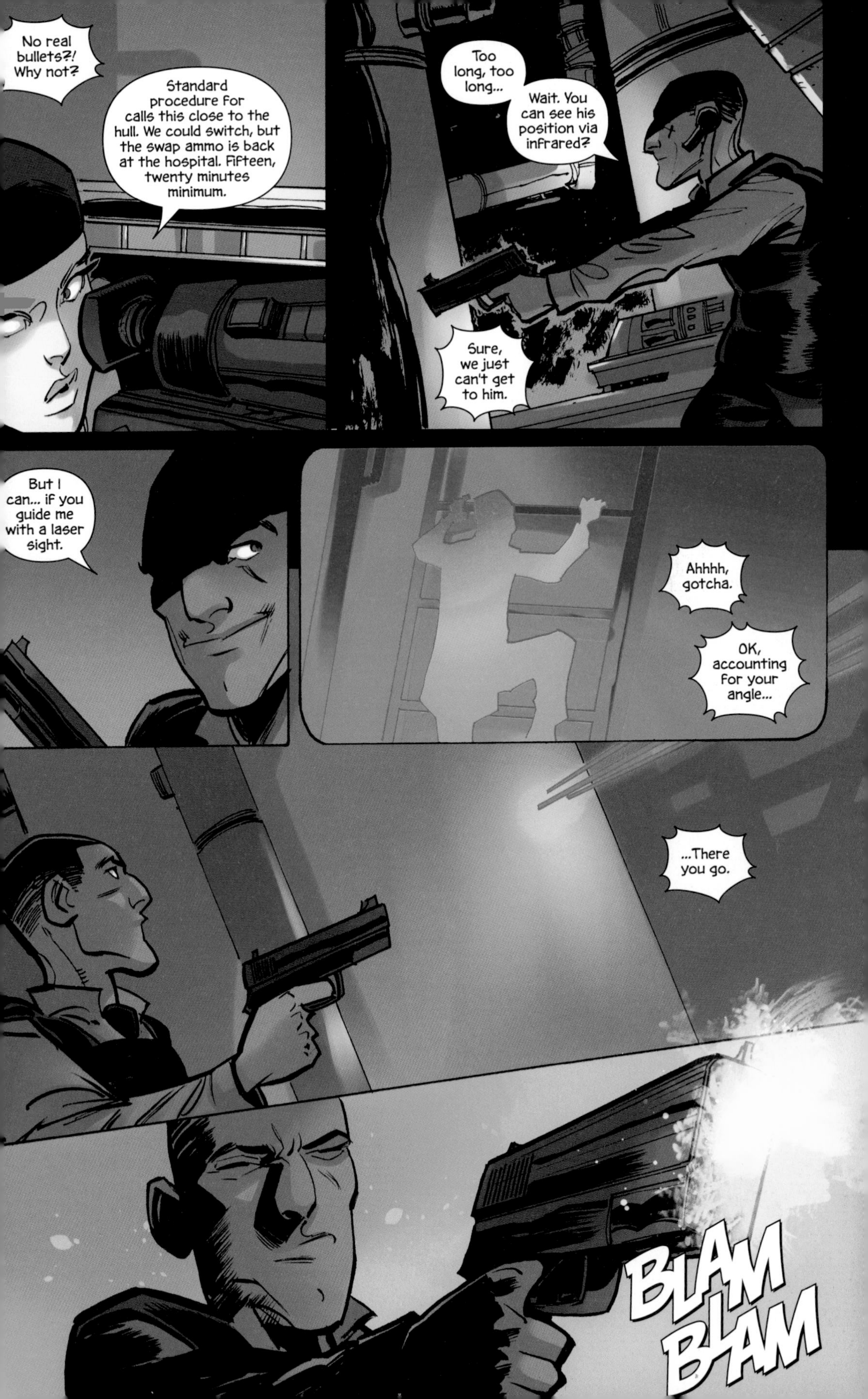
No real bullets?! Why not?
Standard procedure for calls this close to the hull. We could switch, but the swap ammo is back at the hospital. Fifteen, twenty minutes minimum.
Too long, too long...
Wait. You can see his position via infrared?
Sure, we just can't get to him.
But I can... if you guide me with a laser sight.
Ahhhh, gotcha.
OK, accounting for your angle...
...There you go.
BLAM
BLAM

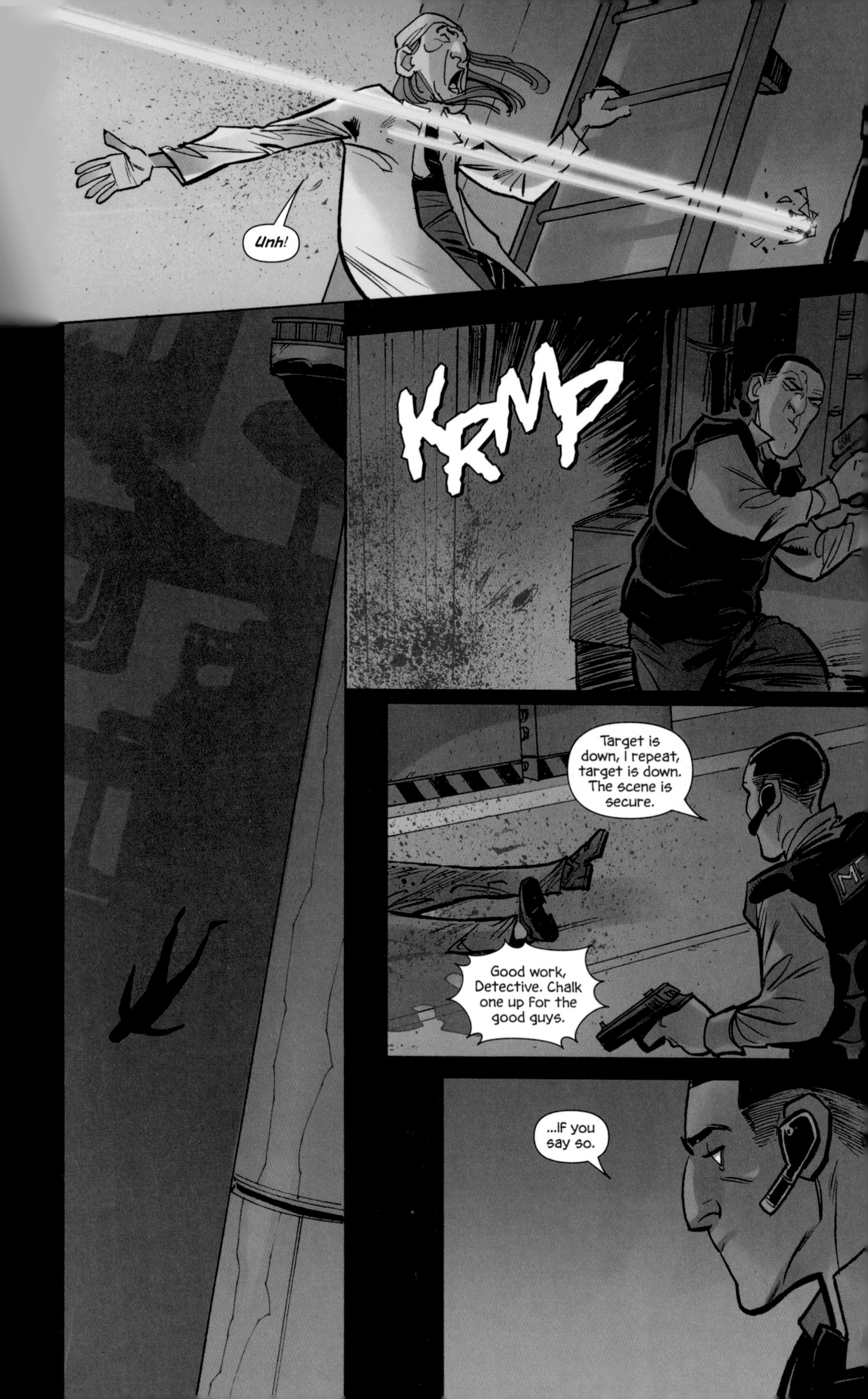
Unh!
KRMP
Target is down, I repeat, target is down. The scene is secure.
Good work, Detective. Chalk one up for the good guys.
...If you say so.

ST JOSEPH HOSPITAL · SHEPARD & 1ST · LEVEL ZERO · 1916 SST

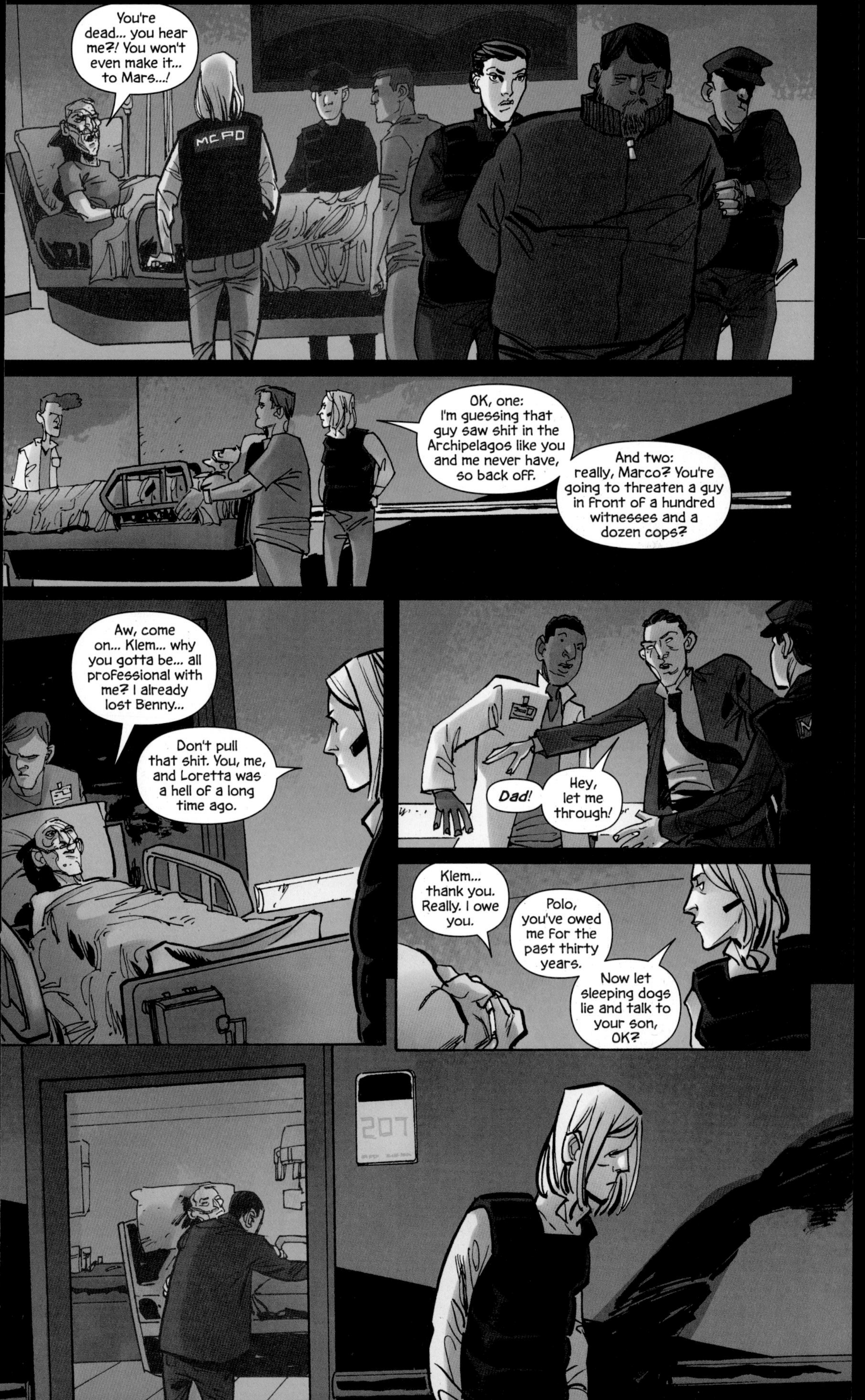
You're dead... you hear me?! You won't even make it... to Mars...!
OK, one: I'm guessing that guy saw shit in the Archipelagos like you and me never have, so back off.
And two: really, Marco? You're going to threaten a guy in front of a hundred witnesses and a dozen cops?
Aw, come on... Klem... why you gotta be... all professional with me? I already lost Benny...
Don't pull that shit. You, me, and Loretta was a hell of a long time ago.
Dad!
Hey, let me through!
Klem... thank you. Really. I owe you.
Polo, you've owed me for the past thirty years.
Now let sleeping dogs lie and talk to your son, OK?

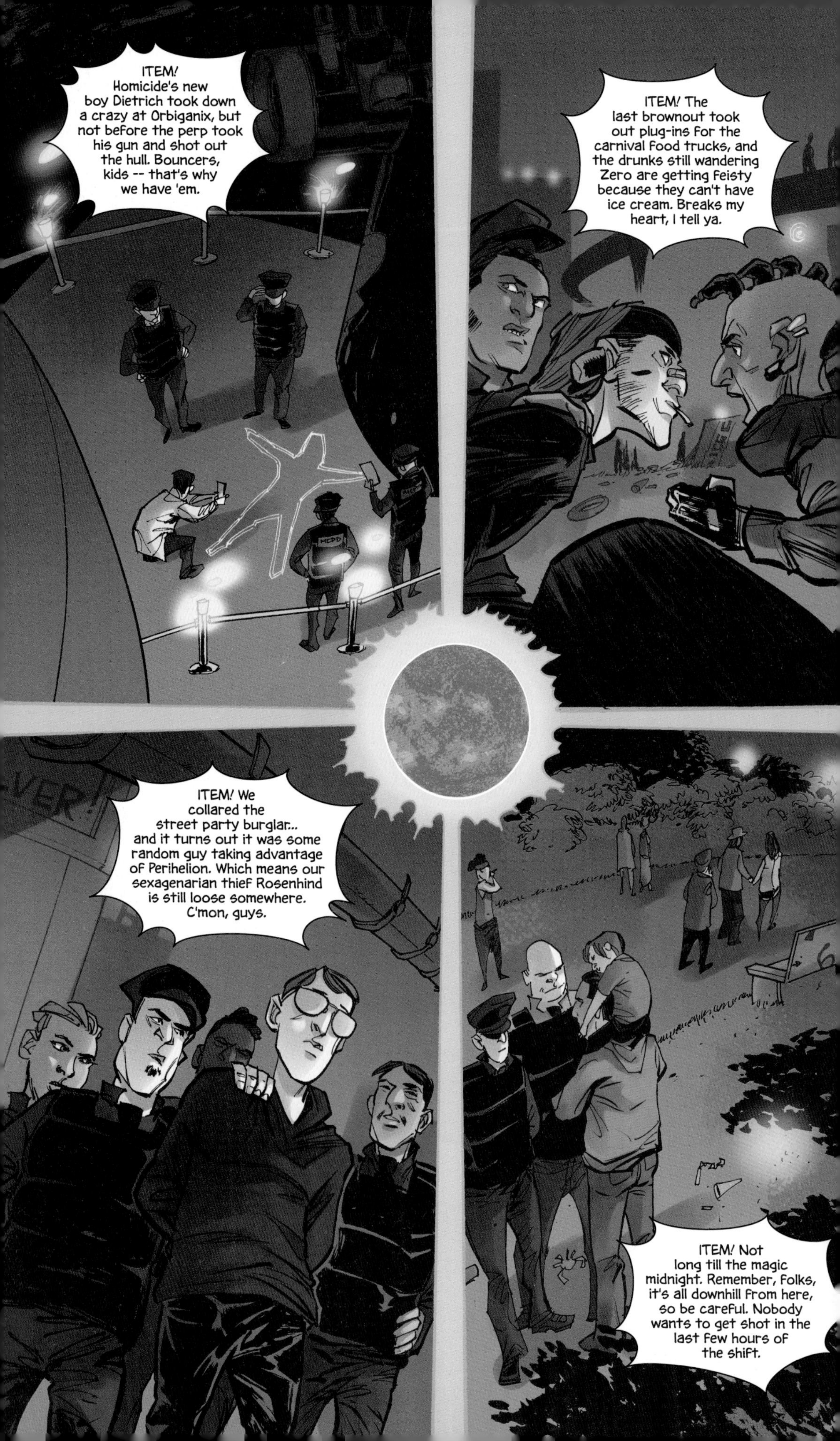
ITEM! Homicide's new boy Dietrich took down a crazy at Orbiganix, but not before the perp took his gun and shot out the hull. Bouncers, kids -- that's why we have 'em.
ITEM! The last brownout took out plug-ins for the carnival food trucks, and the drunks still wandering Zero are getting feisty because they can't have ice cream. Breaks my heart, I tell ya.
ITEM! We collared the street party burglar... and it turns out it was some random guy taking advantage of Perihelion. Which means our sexagenarian thief Rosenhind is still loose somewhere. C'mon, guys.
ITEM! Not long till the magic midnight. Remember, folks, it's all downhill from here, so be careful. Nobody wants to get shot in the last few hours of the shift.

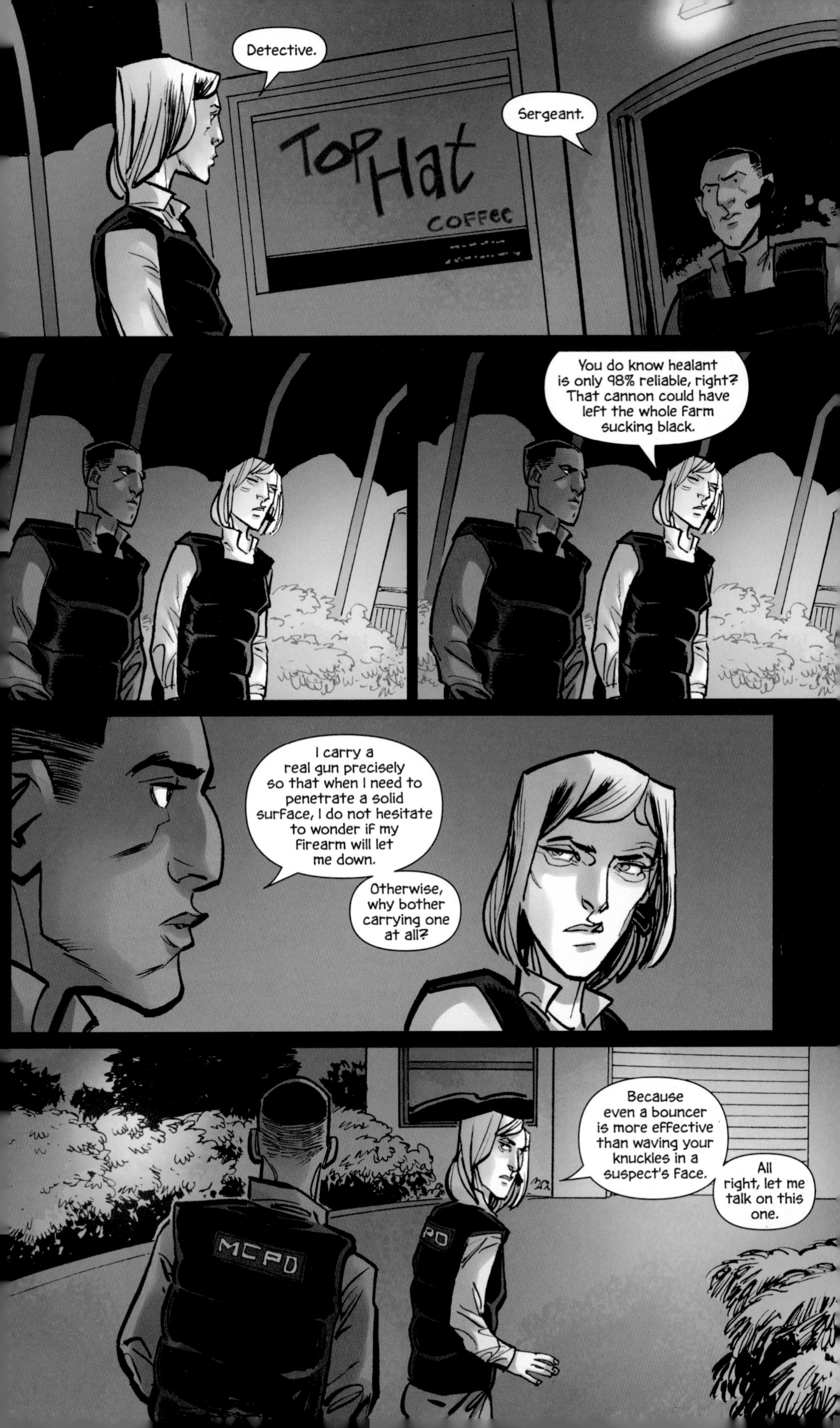

Detective.
Sergeant.
Top Hat
coffee
You do know healant is only 98% reliable, right? That cannon could have left the whole farm sucking black.
I carry a real gun precisely so that when I need to penetrate a solid surface, I do not hesitate to wonder if my firearm will let me down.
Otherwise, why bother carrying one at all?
MCPD
PD
Because even a bouncer is more effective than waving your knuckles in a suspect's face.
All right, let me talk on this one.

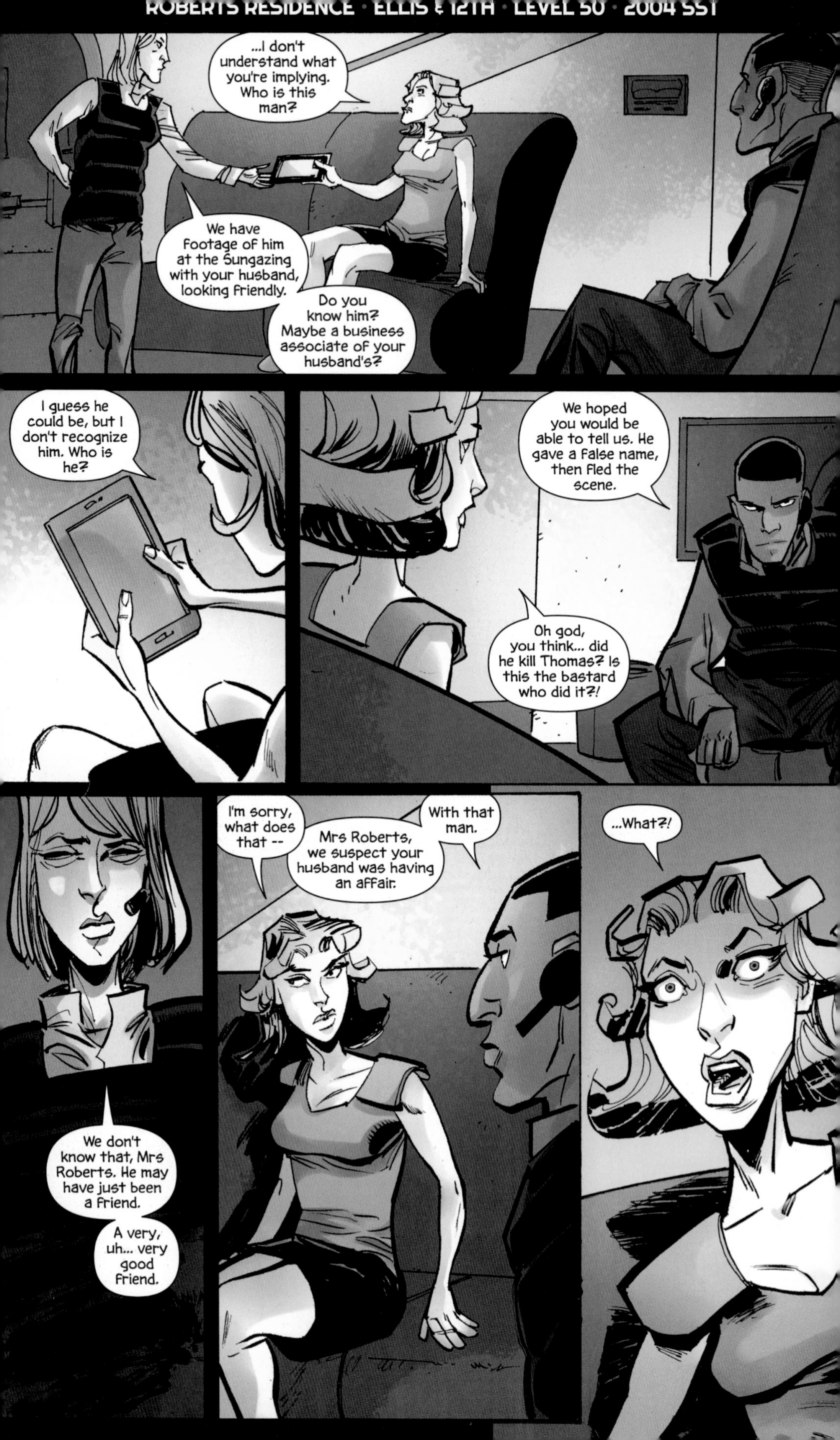

ROBERTS RESIDENCE · ELLIS & 12TH · LEVEL 50 · 2004 SST
...I don't understand what you're implying. Who is this man?
We have footage of him at the Sungazing with your husband, looking friendly.
Do you know him? Maybe a business associate of your husband's?
I guess he could be, but I don't recognize him. Who is he?
We hoped you would be able to tell us. He gave a false name, then fled the scene.
Oh god, you think... did he kill Thomas? Is this the bastard who did it?!
We don't know that, Mrs Roberts. He may have just been a friend.
A very, uh... very good friend.
I'm sorry, what does that --
Mrs Roberts, we suspect your husband was having an affair.
With that man.
...What?!

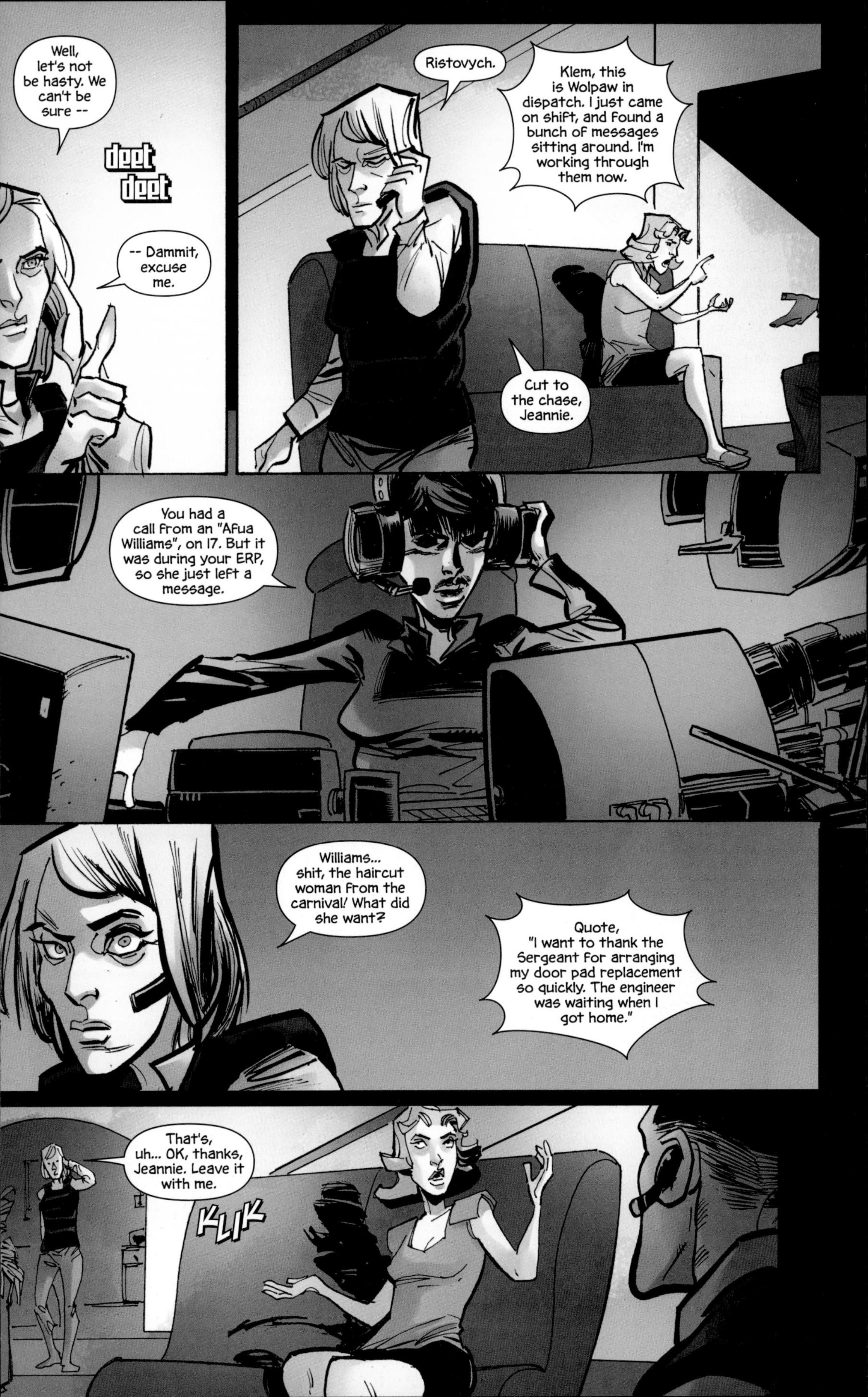
Well, let's not be hasty. We can't be sure --
deet deet
-- Dammit, excuse me.
Ristovych.
Klem, this is Wolpaw in dispatch. I just came on shift, and found a bunch of messages sitting around. I'm working through them now.
Cut to the chase, Jeannie.
You had a call from an "Afua Williams", on 17. But it was during your ERP, so she just left a message.
Williams... shit, the haircut woman from the carnival! What did she want?
Quote, "I want to thank the Sergeant for arranging my door pad replacement so quickly. The engineer was waiting when I got home."
That's, uh... OK, thanks, Jeannie. Leave it with me.
KLIK

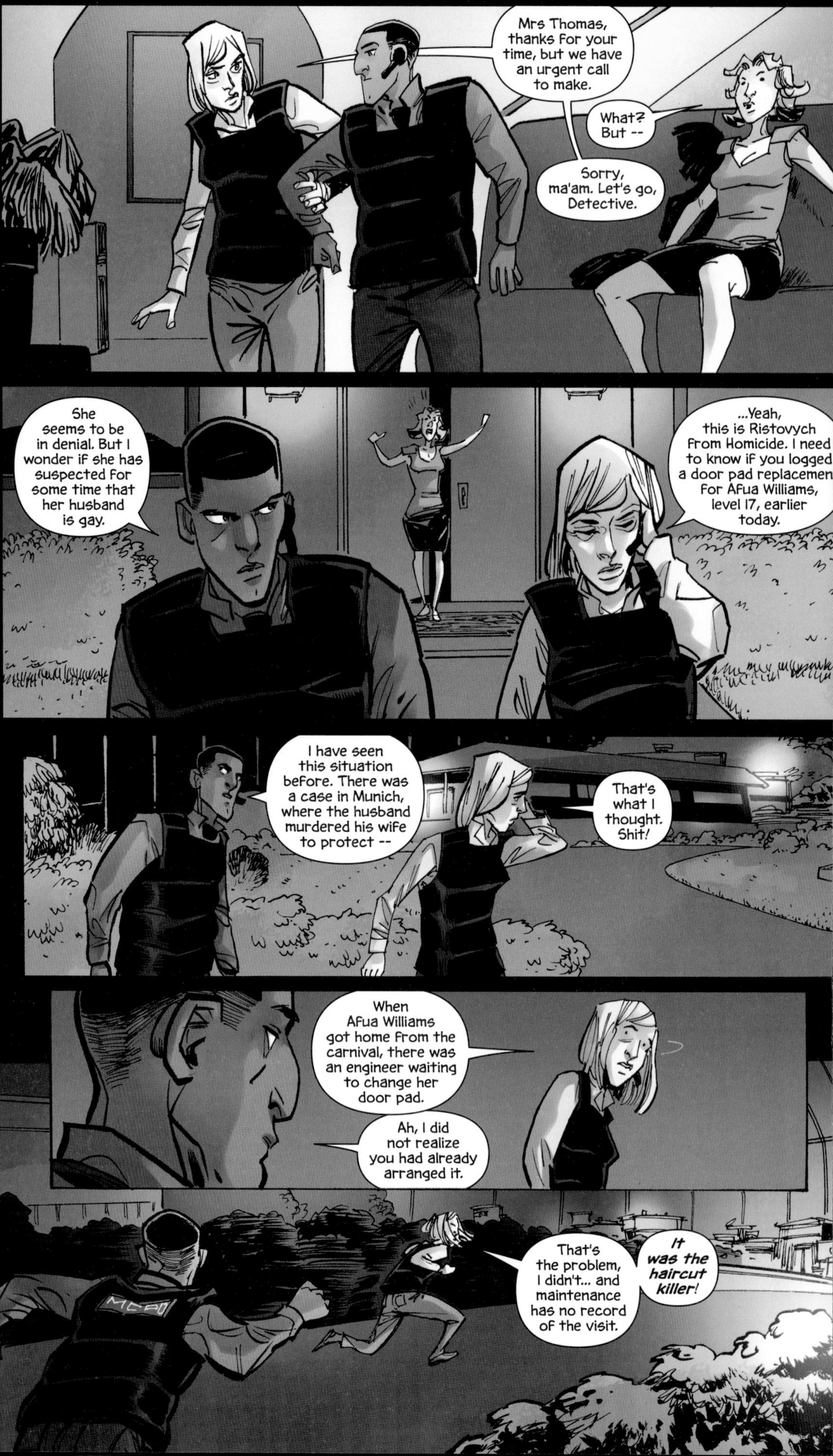
Mrs Thomas, thanks for your time, but we have an urgent call to make.
What? But --
Sorry, ma'am. Let's go, Detective.
She seems to be in denial. But I wonder if she has suspected for some time that her husband is gay.
...Yeah, this is Ristovych from Homicide. I need to know if you logged a door pad replacemen for Afua Williams, level 17, earlier today.
I have seen this situation before. There was a case in Munich, where the husband murdered his wife to protect --
That's what I thought. Shit!
When Afua Williams got home from the carnival, there was an engineer waiting to change her door pad.
Ah, I did not realize you had already arranged it.
That's the problem, I didn't... and maintenance has no record of the visit.
It was the haircut killer!
MCPD

PART 6

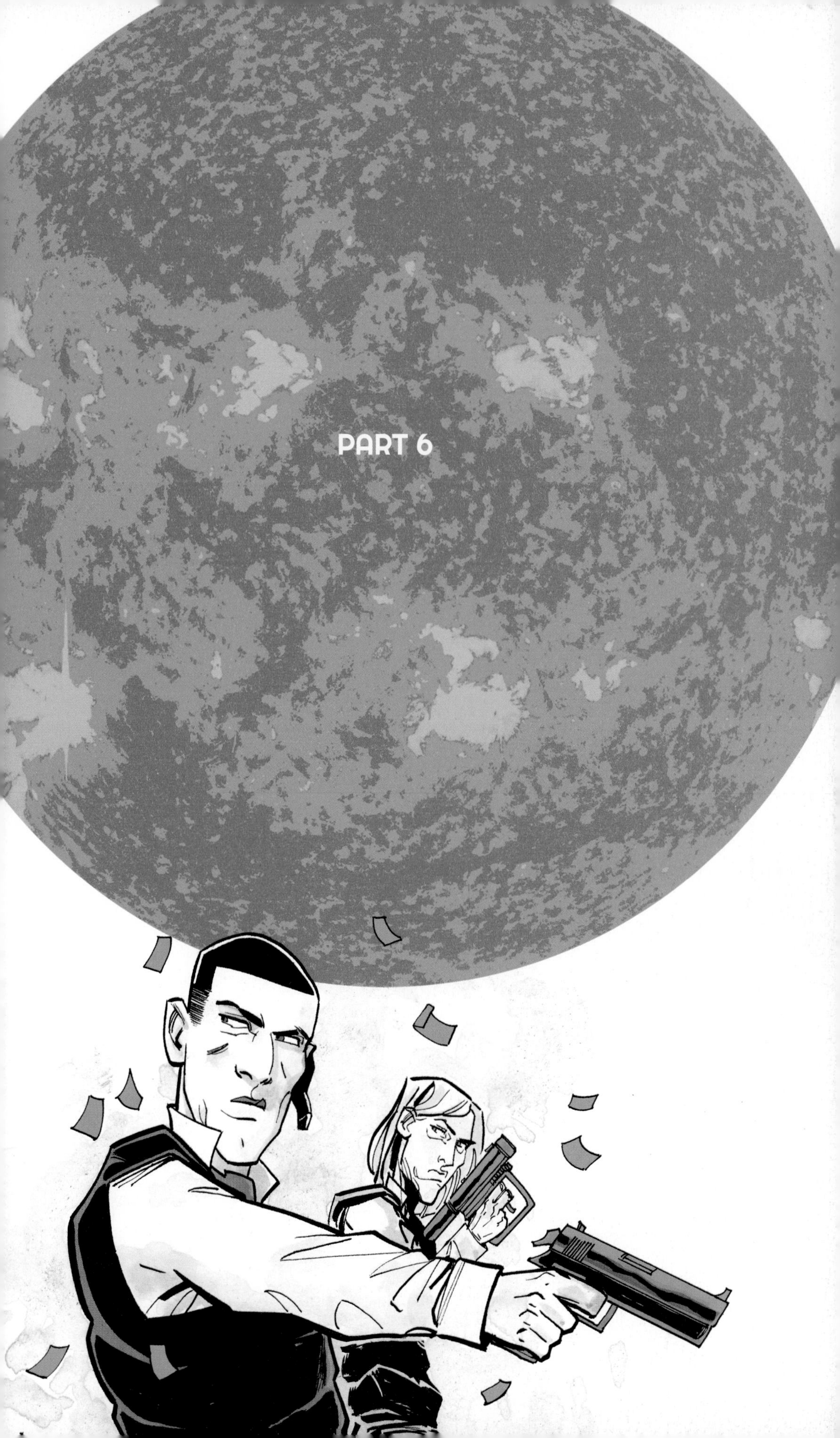

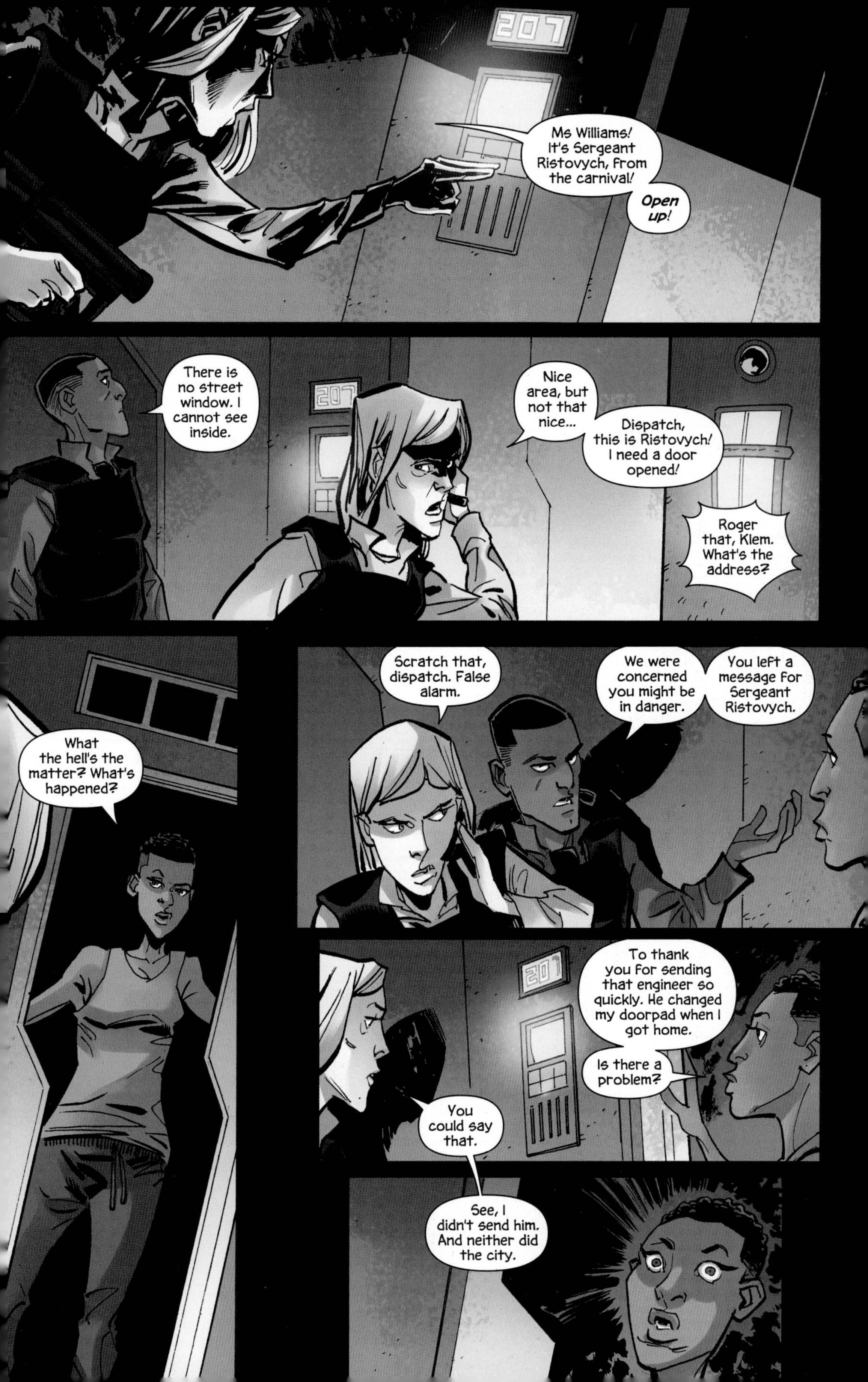
207
Ms Williams! It's Sergeant Ristovych, from the carnival!
Open up!
There is no street window. I cannot see inside.
207
Nice area, but not that nice...
Dispatch, this is Ristovych! I need a door opened!
Roger that, Klem. What's the address?
What the hell's the matter? What's happened?
Scratch that, dispatch. False alarm.
We were concerned you might be in danger.
You left a message for Sergeant Ristovych.
207
To thank you for sending that engineer so quickly. He changed my doorpad when I got home.
Is there a problem?
You could say that.
See, I didn't send him. And neither did the city.

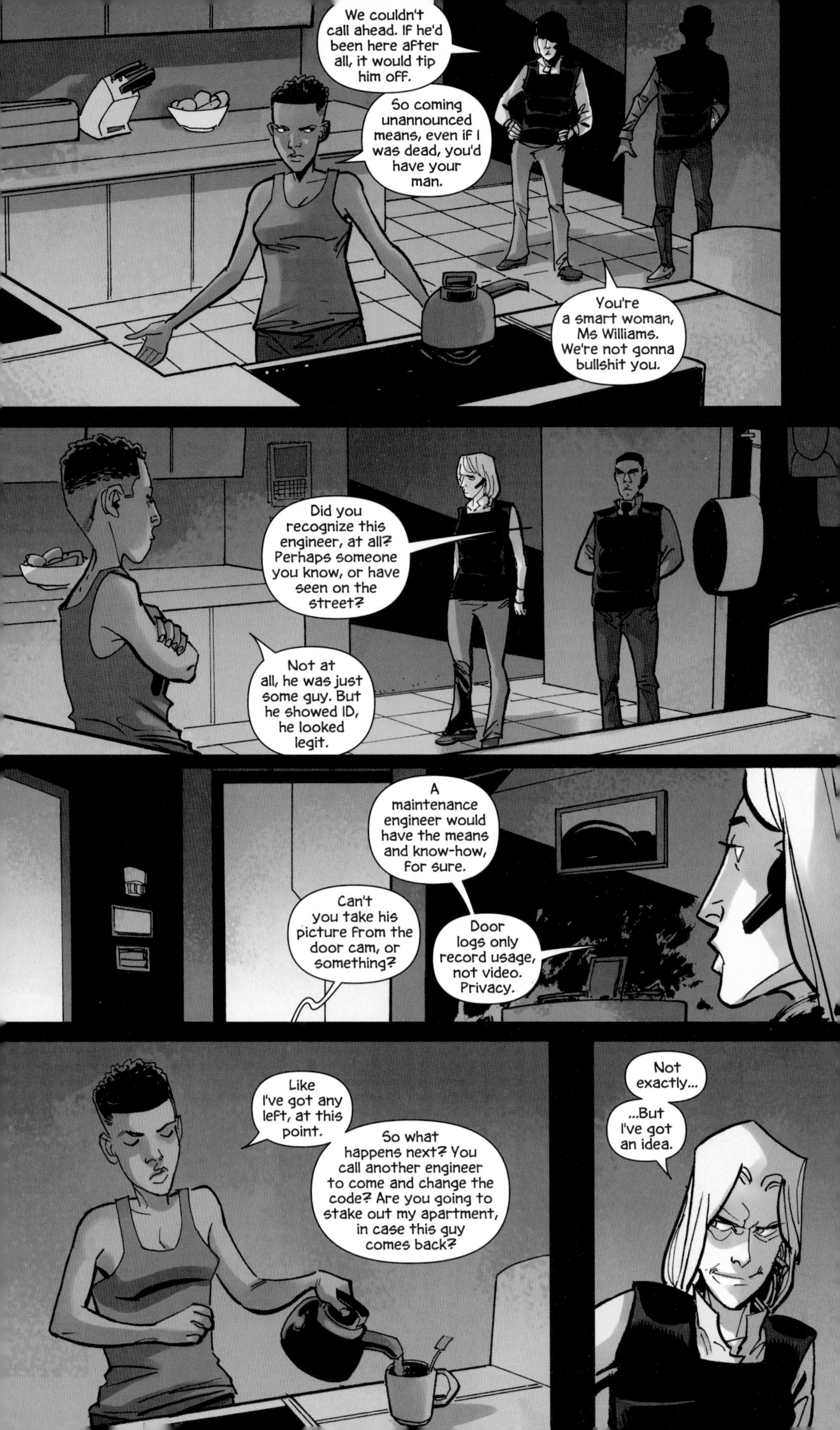
We couldn't call ahead. If he'd been here after all, it would tip him off.
So coming unannounced means, even if I was dead, you'd have your man.
You're a smart woman, Ms Williams. We're not gonna bullshit you.
Did you recognize this engineer, at all? Perhaps someone you know, or have seen on the street?
Not at all, he was just some guy. But he showed ID, he looked legit.
A maintenance engineer would have the means and know-how, for sure.
Can't you take his picture from the door cam, or something?
Door logs only record usage, not video. Privacy.
Like I've got any left, at this point.
So what happens next? You call another engineer to come and change the code? Are you going to stake out my apartment, in case this guy comes back?
Not exactly...
...But I've got an idea.

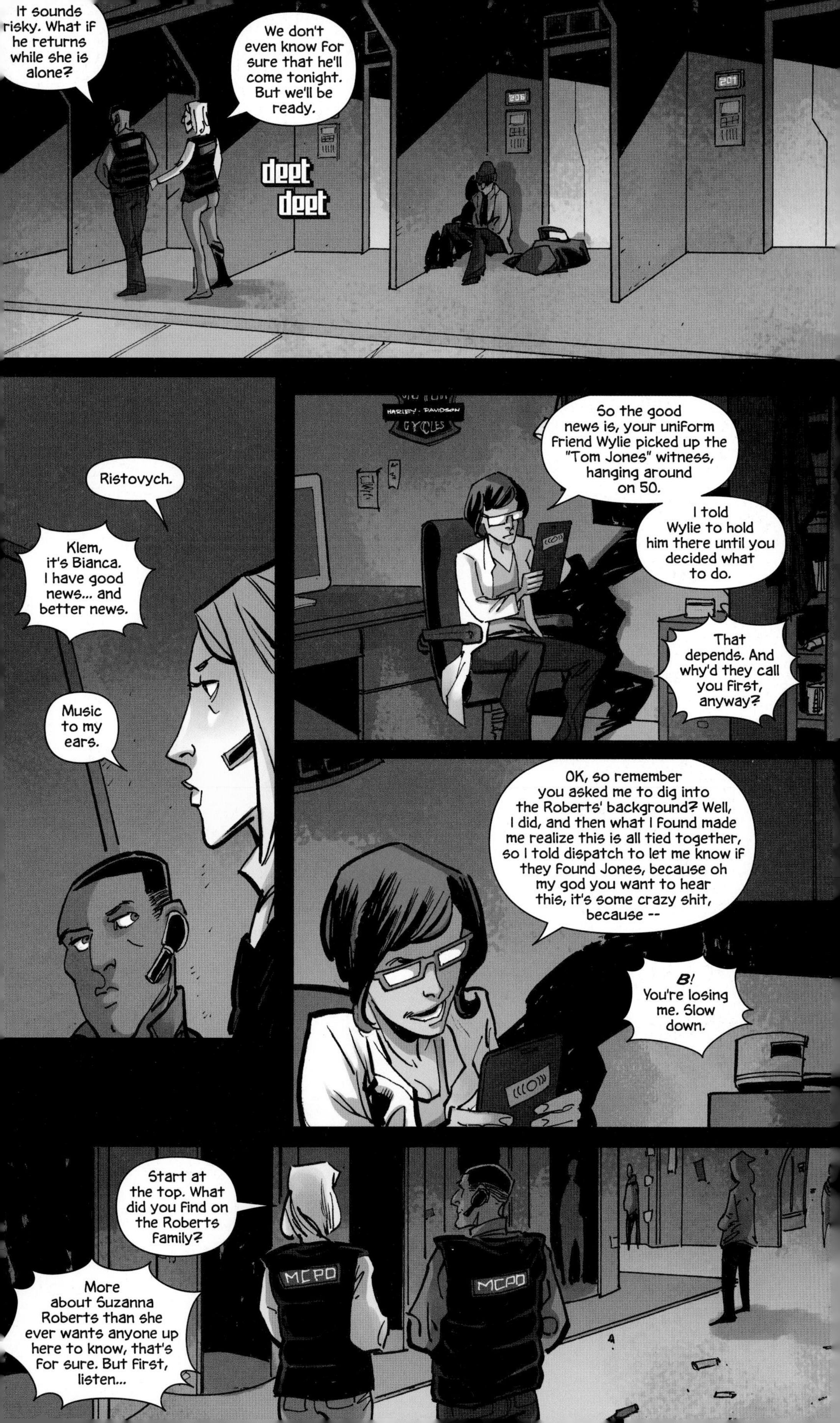

It sounds risky. What if he returns while she is alone?
We don't even know for sure that he'll come tonight. But we'll be ready.
deet deet
Ristovych.
Klem, it's Bianca. I have good news... and better news.
Music to my ears.
So the good news is, your uniform friend Wylie picked up the "Tom Jones" witness, hanging around on 50.
I told Wylie to hold him there until you decided what to do.
That depends. And why'd they call you first, anyway?
OK, so remember you asked me to dig into the Roberts' background? Well, I did, and then what I found made me realize this is all tied together, so I told dispatch to let me know if they found Jones, because oh my god you want to hear this, it's some crazy shit, because --
B! You're losing me. Slow down.
Start at the top. What did you find on the Roberts family?
More about Suzanna Roberts than she ever wants anyone up here to know, that's for sure. But first, listen...

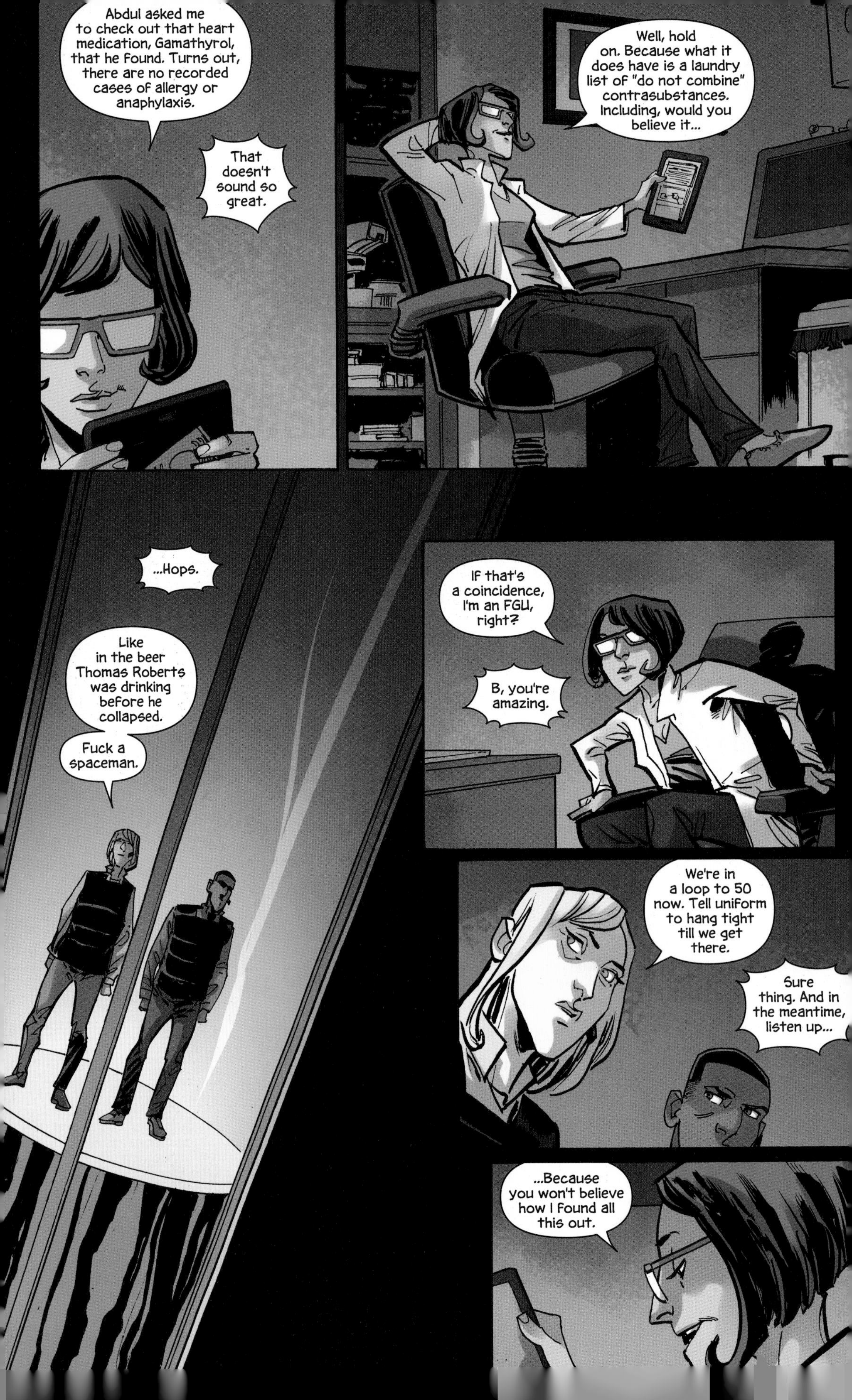
Abdul asked me to check out that heart medication, Gamathyrol, that he found. Turns out, there are no recorded cases of allergy or anaphylaxis.
That doesn't sound so great.
Well, hold on. Because what it does have is a laundry list of "do not combine" contrasubstances. Including, would you believe it...
...Hops.
Like in the beer Thomas Roberts was drinking before he collapsed.
Fuck a spaceman.
If that's a coincidence, I'm an FGU, right?
B, you're amazing.
We're in a loop to 50 now. Tell uniform to hang tight till we get there.
Sure thing. And in the meantime, listen up...
...Because you won't believe how I found all this out.

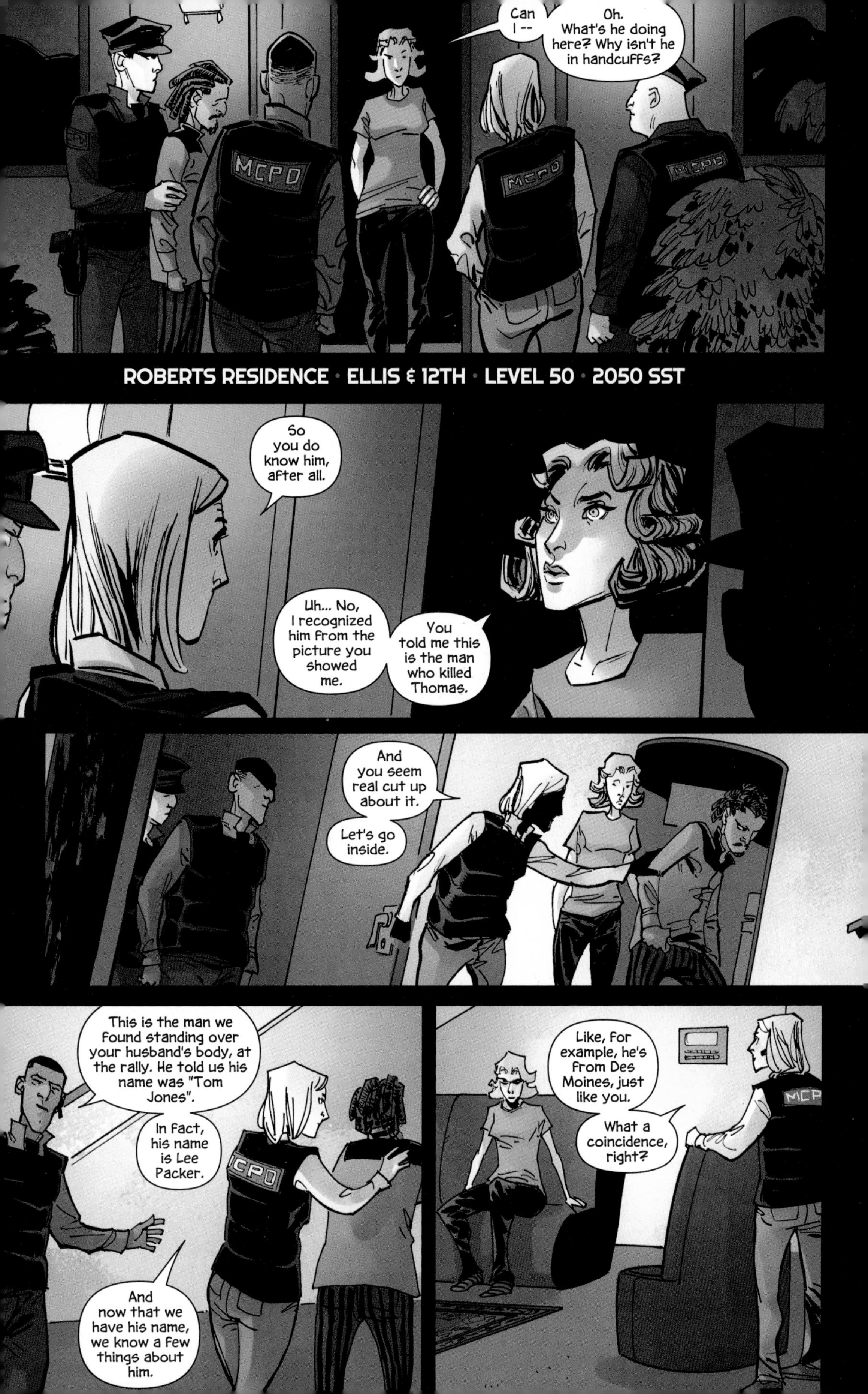
Can I --
Oh. What's he doing here? Why isn't he in handcuffs?
ROBERTS RESIDENCE • ELLIS & 12TH • LEVEL 50 • 2050 SST
So you do know him, after all.
Uh... No, I recognized him from the picture you showed me.
You told me this is the man who killed Thomas.
And you seem real cut up about it.
Let's go inside.
This is the man we found standing over your husband's body, at the rally. He told us his name was "Tom Jones".
In fact, his name is Lee Packer.
And now that we have his name, we know a few things about him.
Like, for example, he's from Des Moines, just like you.
What a coincidence, right?

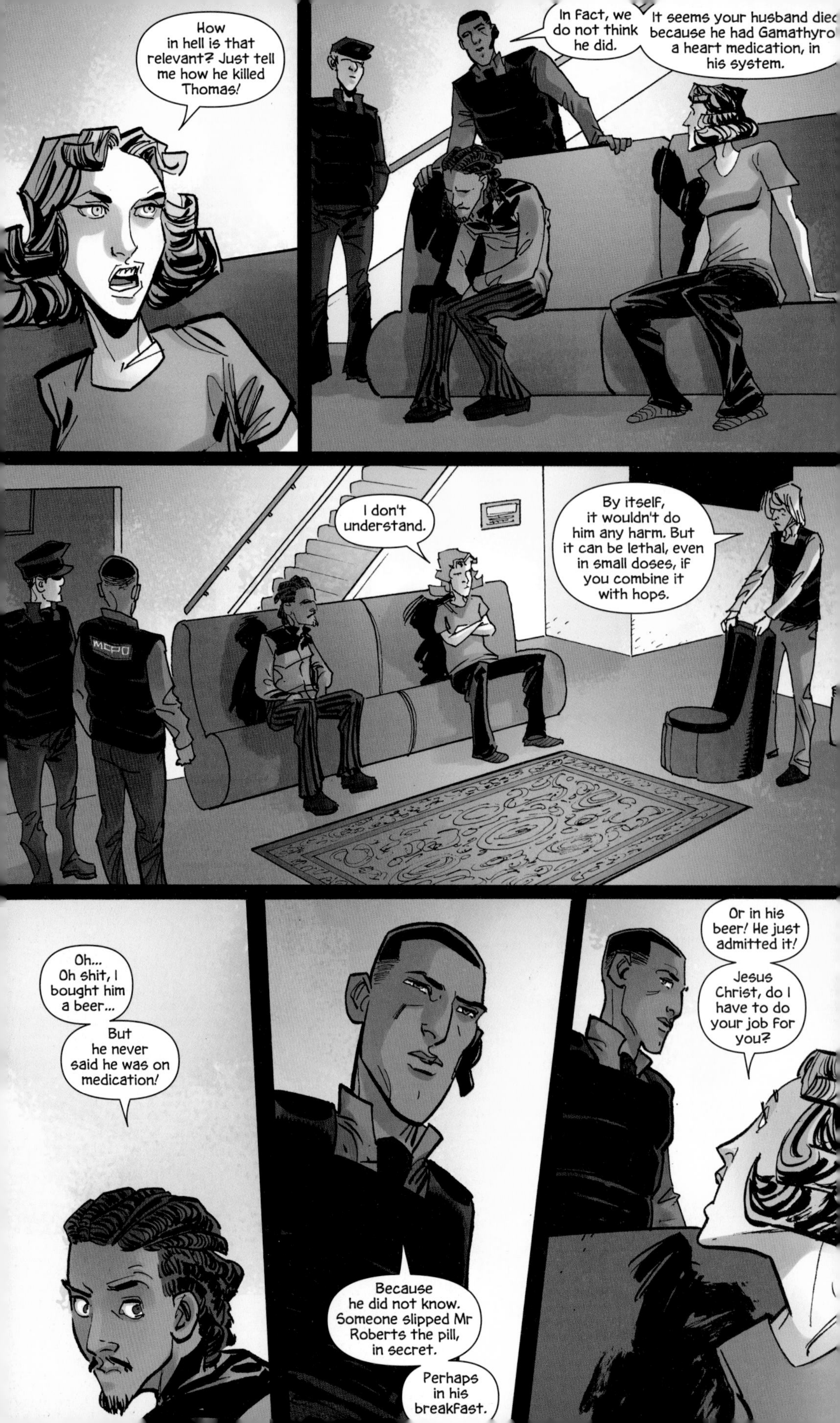
How in hell is that relevant? Just tell me how he killed Thomas!
In fact, we do not think he did.
It seems your husband died because he had Gamathyro a heart medication, in his system.
I don't understand.
By itself, it wouldn't do him any harm. But it can be lethal, even in small doses, if you combine it with hops.
MCPD
Oh... Oh shit, I bought him a beer...
But he never said he was on medication!
Because he did not know. Someone slipped Mr Roberts the pill, in secret.
Perhaps in his breakfast.
Or in his beer! He just admitted it!
Jesus Christ, do I have to do your job for you?

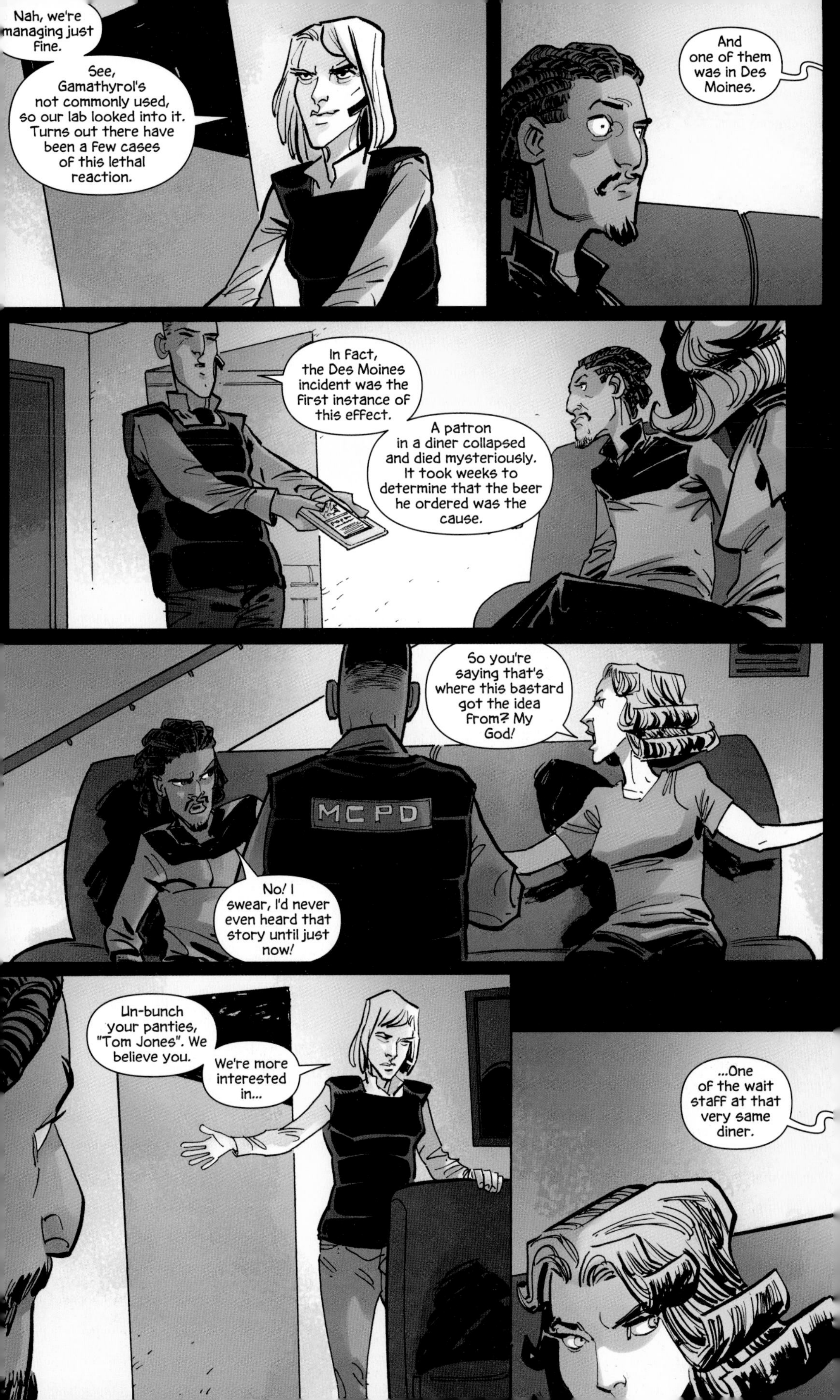
Nah, we're managing just fine.
See, Gamathyrol's not commonly used, so our lab looked into it. Turns out there have been a few cases of this lethal reaction.
And one of them was in Des Moines.
In fact, the Des Moines incident was the first instance of this effect.
A patron in a diner collapsed and died mysteriously. It took weeks to determine that the beer he ordered was the cause.
So you're saying that's where this bastard got the idea from? My God!
MCPD
No! I swear, I'd never even heard that story until just now!
Un-bunch your panties, "Tom Jones". We believe you.
We're more interested in...
...One of the wait staff at that very same diner.

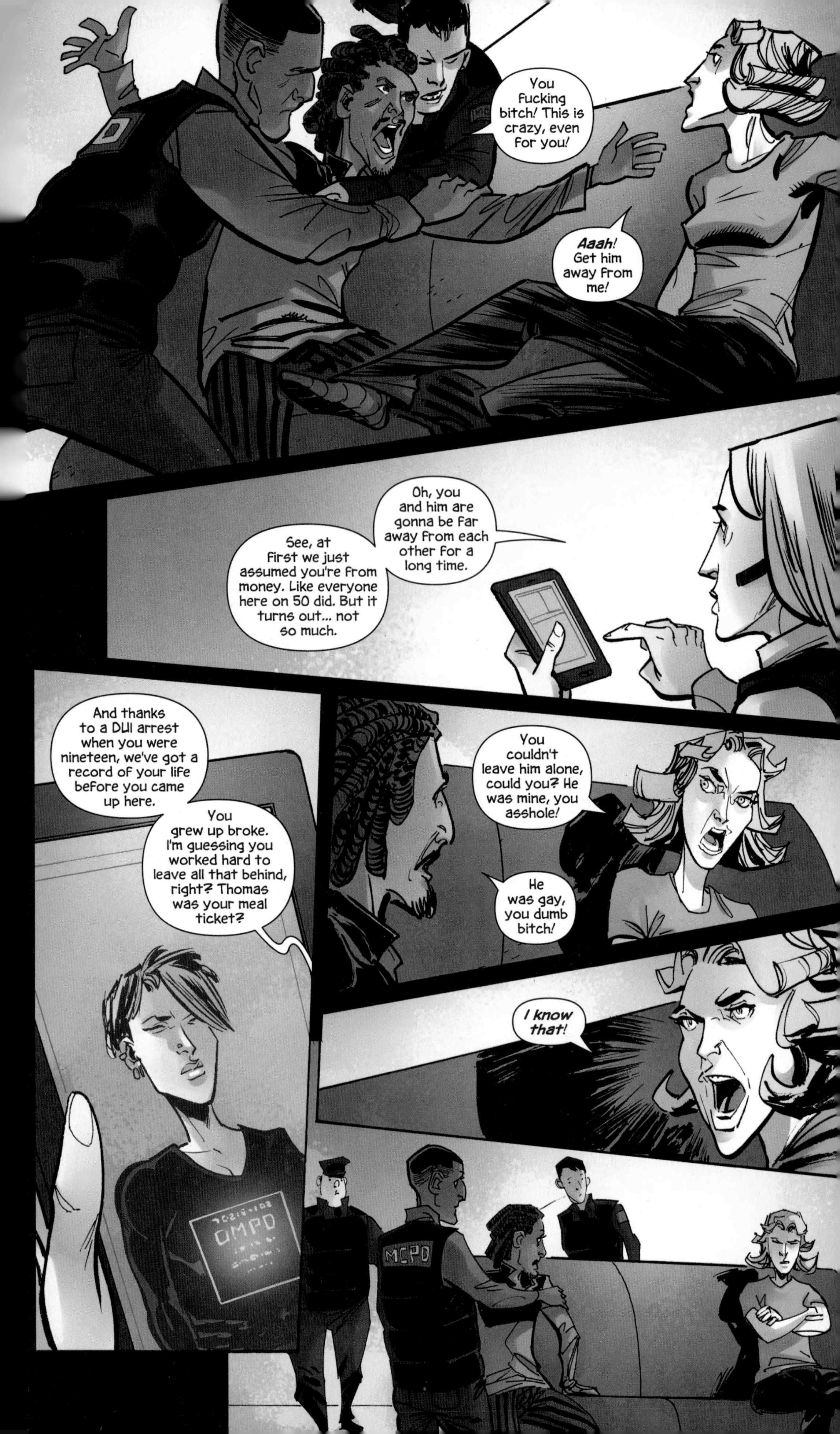
You fucking bitch! This is crazy, even for you!
Aaah! Get him away from me!
Oh, you and him are gonna be far away from each other for a long time.
See, at first we just assumed you're from money. Like everyone here on 50 did. But it turns out... not so much.
And thanks to a DUI arrest when you were nineteen, we've got a record of your life before you came up here.
You grew up broke. I'm guessing you worked hard to leave all that behind, right? Thomas was your meal ticket?
You couldn't leave him alone, could you? He was mine, you asshole!
He was gay, you dumb bitch!
I know that!
MCPD
MCPD

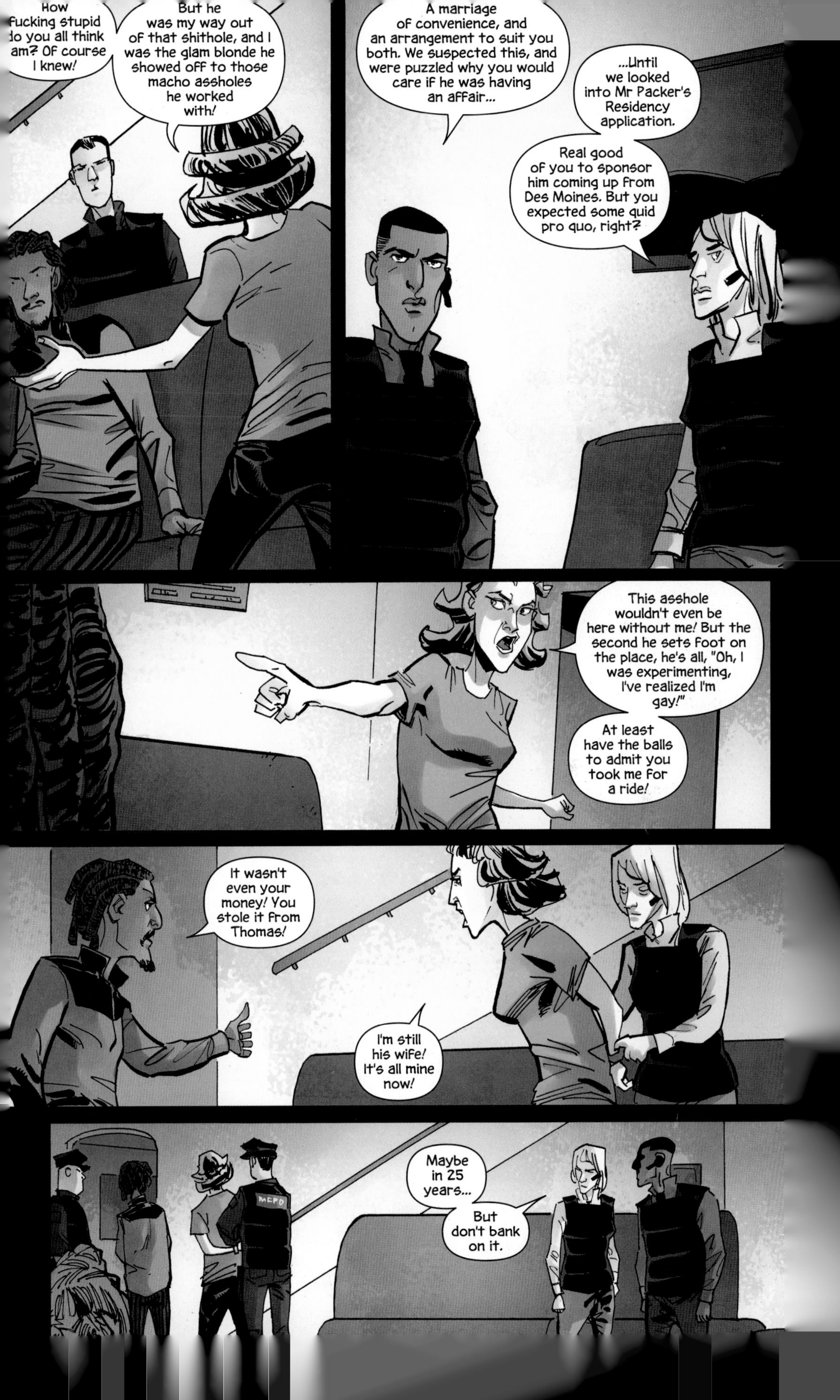
How fucking stupid do you all think I am? Of course I knew!
But he was my way out of that shithole, and I was the glam blonde he showed off to those macho assholes he worked with!
A marriage of convenience, and an arrangement to suit you both. We suspected this, and were puzzled why you would care if he was having an affair...
...Until we looked into Mr Packer's Residency application.
Real good of you to sponsor him coming up from Des Moines. But you expected some quid pro quo, right?
This asshole wouldn't even be here without me! But the second he sets foot on the place, he's all, "Oh, I was experimenting, I've realized I'm gay!"
At least have the balls to admit you took me for a ride!
It wasn't even your money! You stole it from Thomas!
I'm still his wife! It's all mine now!
MCPD
Maybe in 25 years...
But don't bank on it.

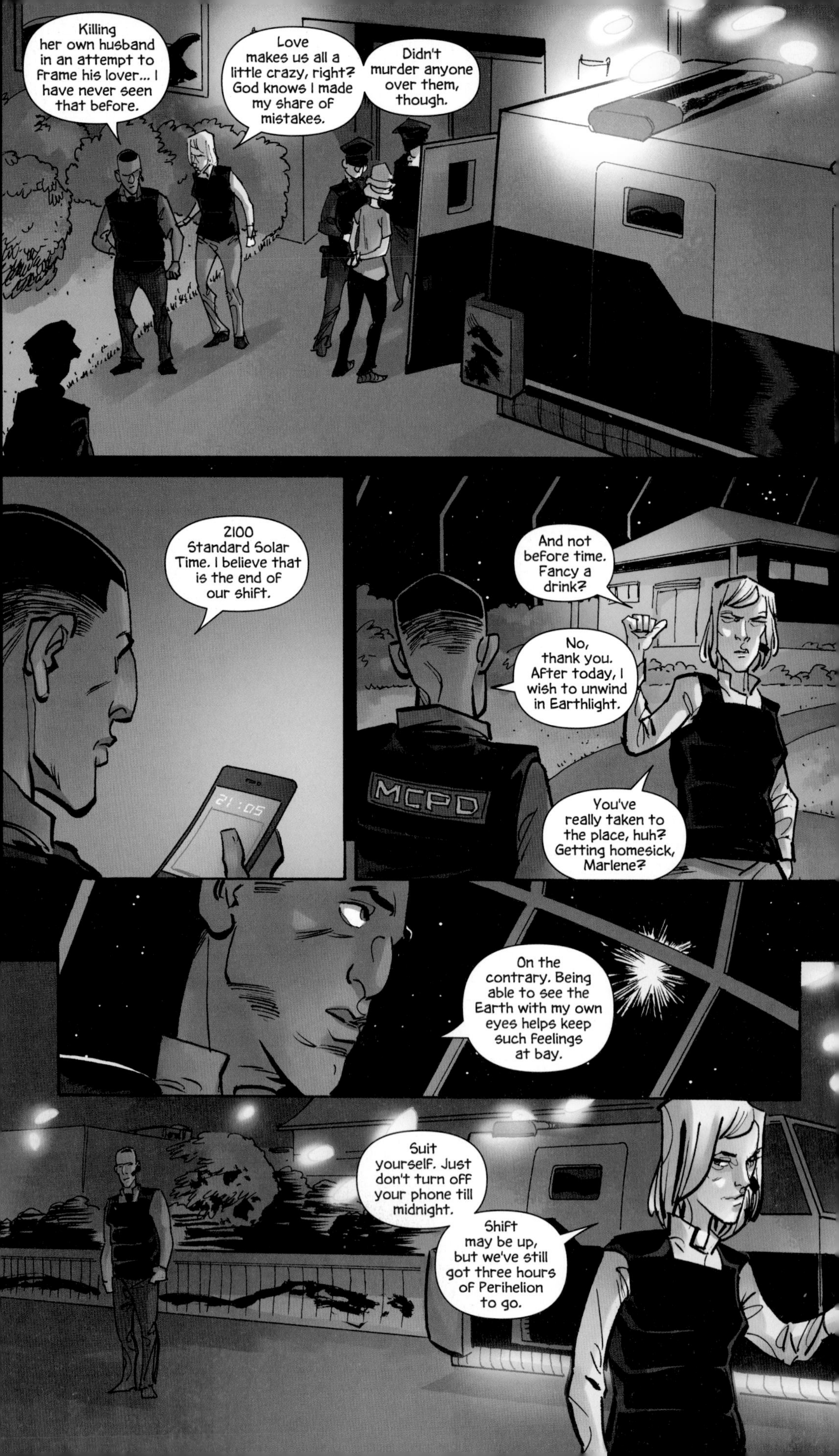
Killing her own husband in an attempt to frame his lover... I have never seen that before.
Love makes us all a little crazy, right? God knows I made my share of mistakes.
Didn't murder anyone over them, though.
2100 Standard Solar Time. I believe that is the end of our shift.
21:05
And not before time. Fancy a drink?
No, thank you. After today, I wish to unwind in Earthlight.
MCPD
You've really taken to the place, huh? Getting homesick, Marlene?
On the contrary. Being able to see the Earth with my own eyes helps keep such feelings at bay.
Suit yourself. Just don't turn off your phone till midnight.
Shift may be up, but we've still got three hours of Perihelion to go.

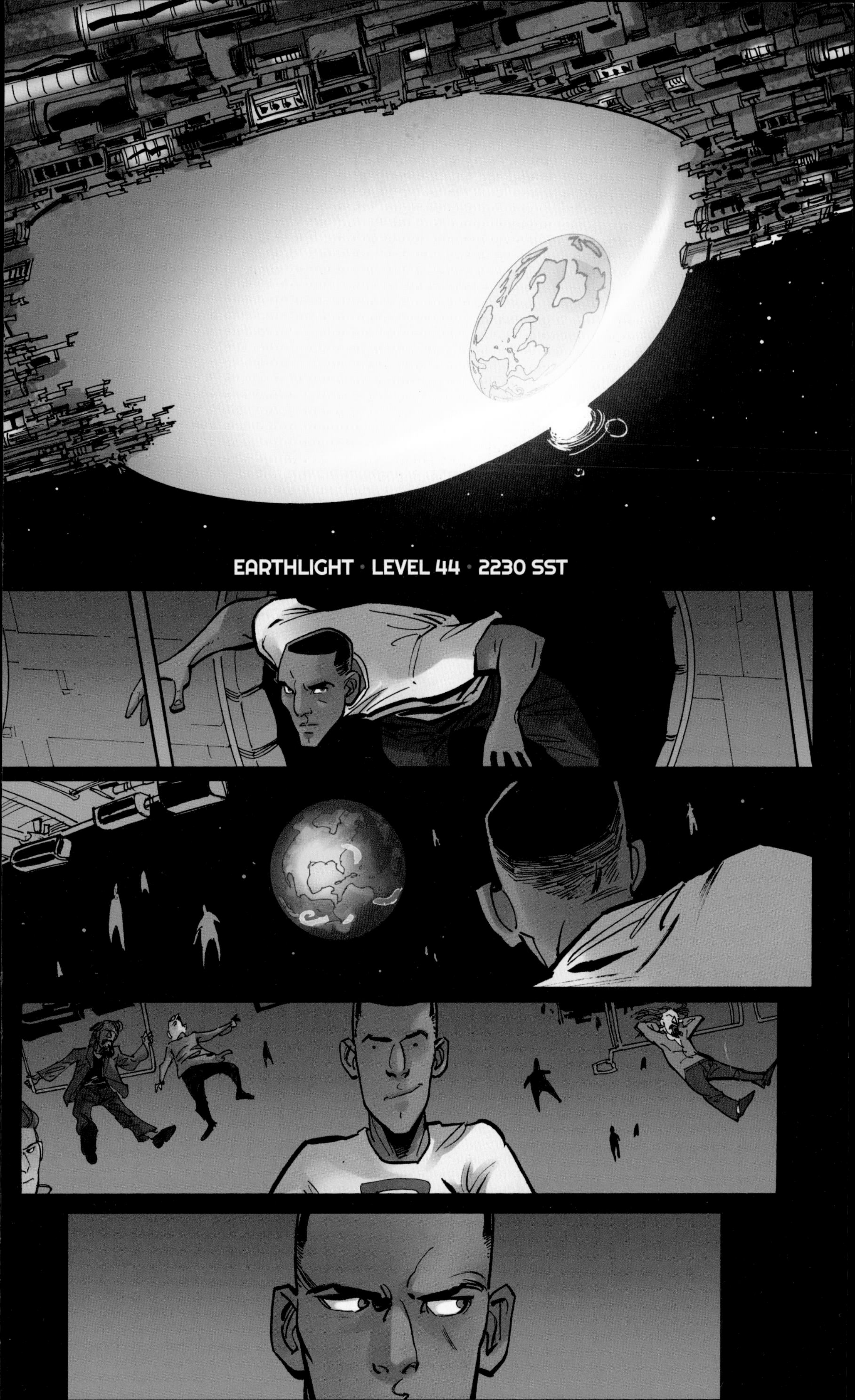
EARTHLIGHT • LEVEL 44 • 2230 SST

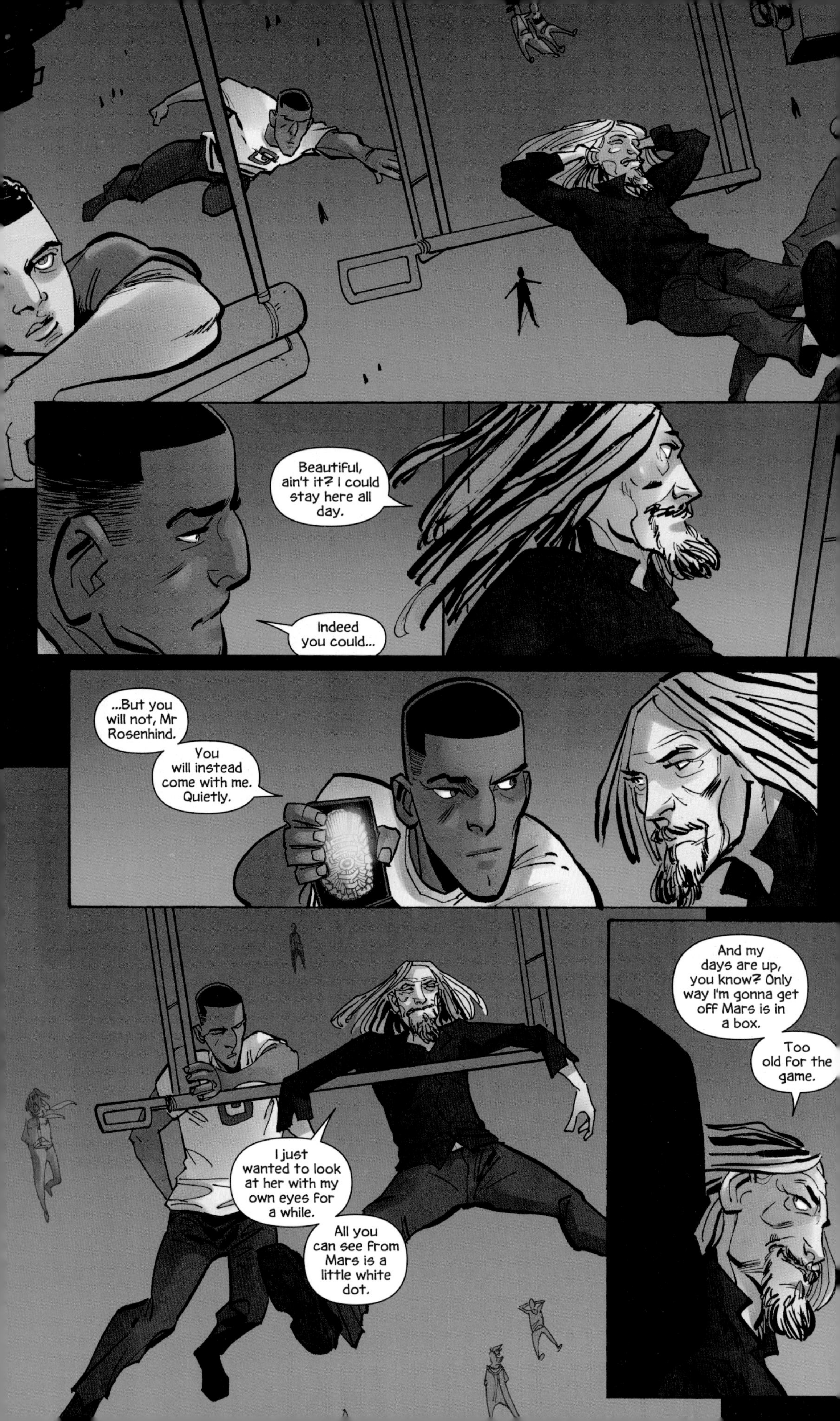
Beautiful, ain't it? I could stay here all day.
Indeed you could...
...But you will not, Mr Rosenhind.
You will instead come with me. Quietly.
I just wanted to look at her with my own eyes for a while.
All you can see from Mars is a little white dot.
And my days are up, you know? Only way I'm gonna get off Mars is in a box.
Too old for the game.

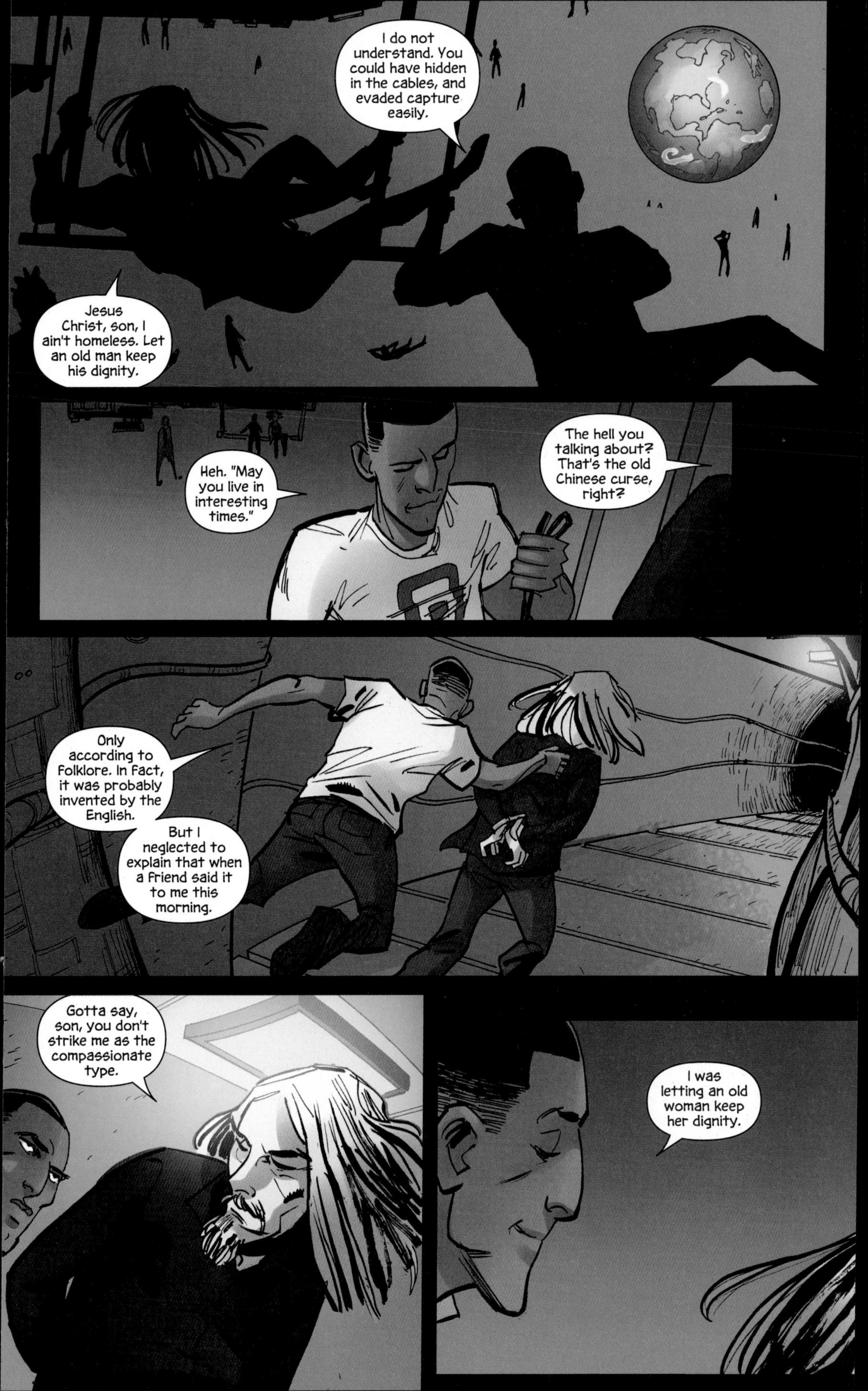
I do not understand. You could have hidden in the cables, and evaded capture easily.
Jesus Christ, son, I ain't homeless. Let an old man keep his dignity.
Heh. "May you live in interesting times."
The hell you talking about? That's the old Chinese curse, right?
Only according to folklore. In fact, it was probably invented by the English.
But I neglected to explain that when a friend said it to me this morning.
Gotta say, son, you don't strike me as the compassionate type.
I was letting an old woman keep her dignity.

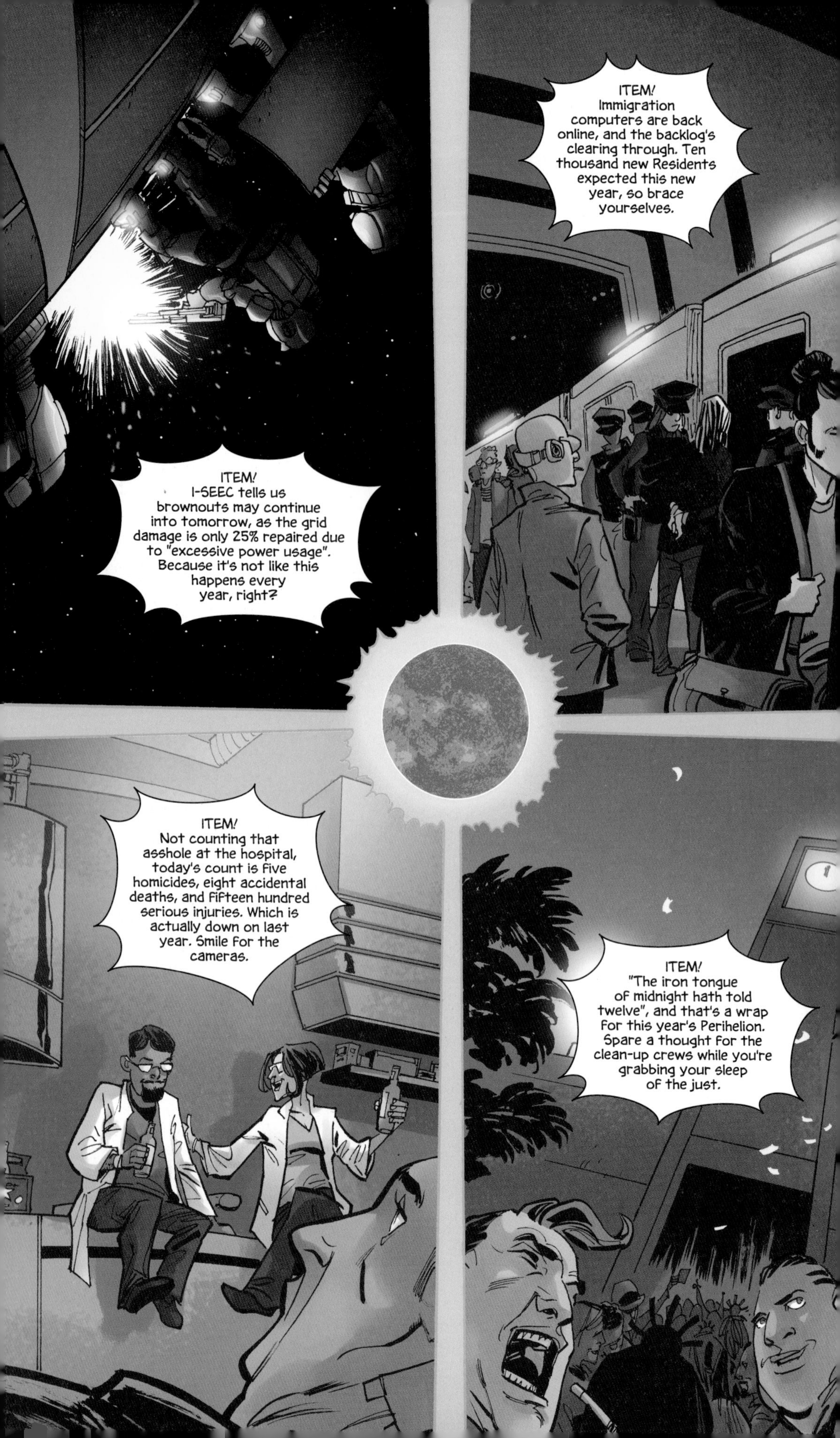
ITEM! Immigration computers are back online, and the backlog's clearing through. Ten thousand new Residents expected this new year, so brace yourselves.
ITEM! I-SEEC tells us brownouts may continue into tomorrow, as the grid damage is only 25% repaired due to "excessive power usage". Because it's not like this happens every year, right?
ITEM! Not counting that asshole at the hospital, today's count is five homicides, eight accidental deaths, and fifteen hundred serious injuries. Which is actually down on last year. Smile for the cameras.
ITEM! "The iron tongue of midnight hath told twelve", and that's a wrap for this year's Perihelion. Spare a thought for the clean-up crews while you're grabbing your sleep of the just.

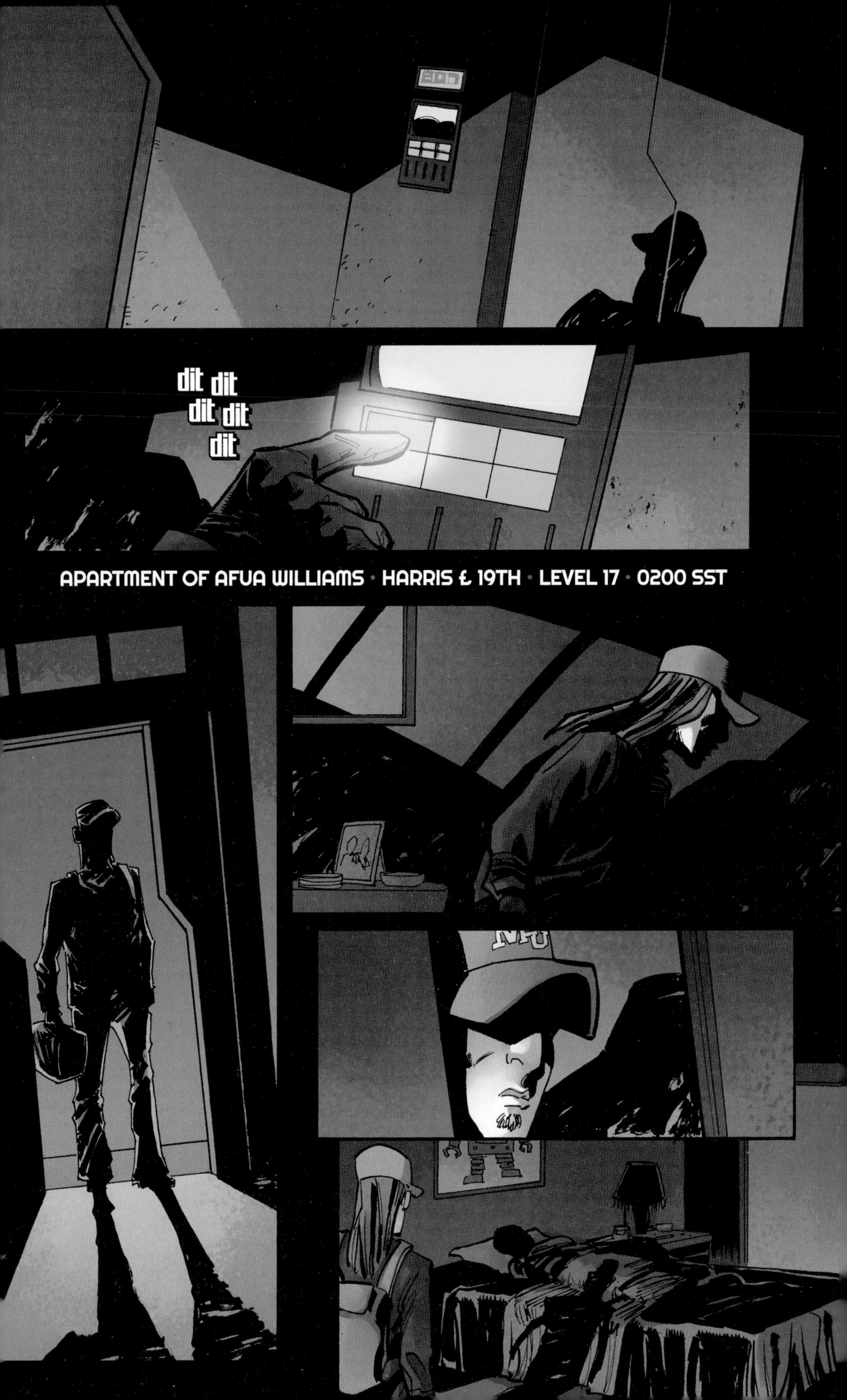
dit dit
dit dit
dit
APARTMENT OF AFUA WILLIAMS • HARRIS & 19TH • LEVEL 17 • 0200 SST

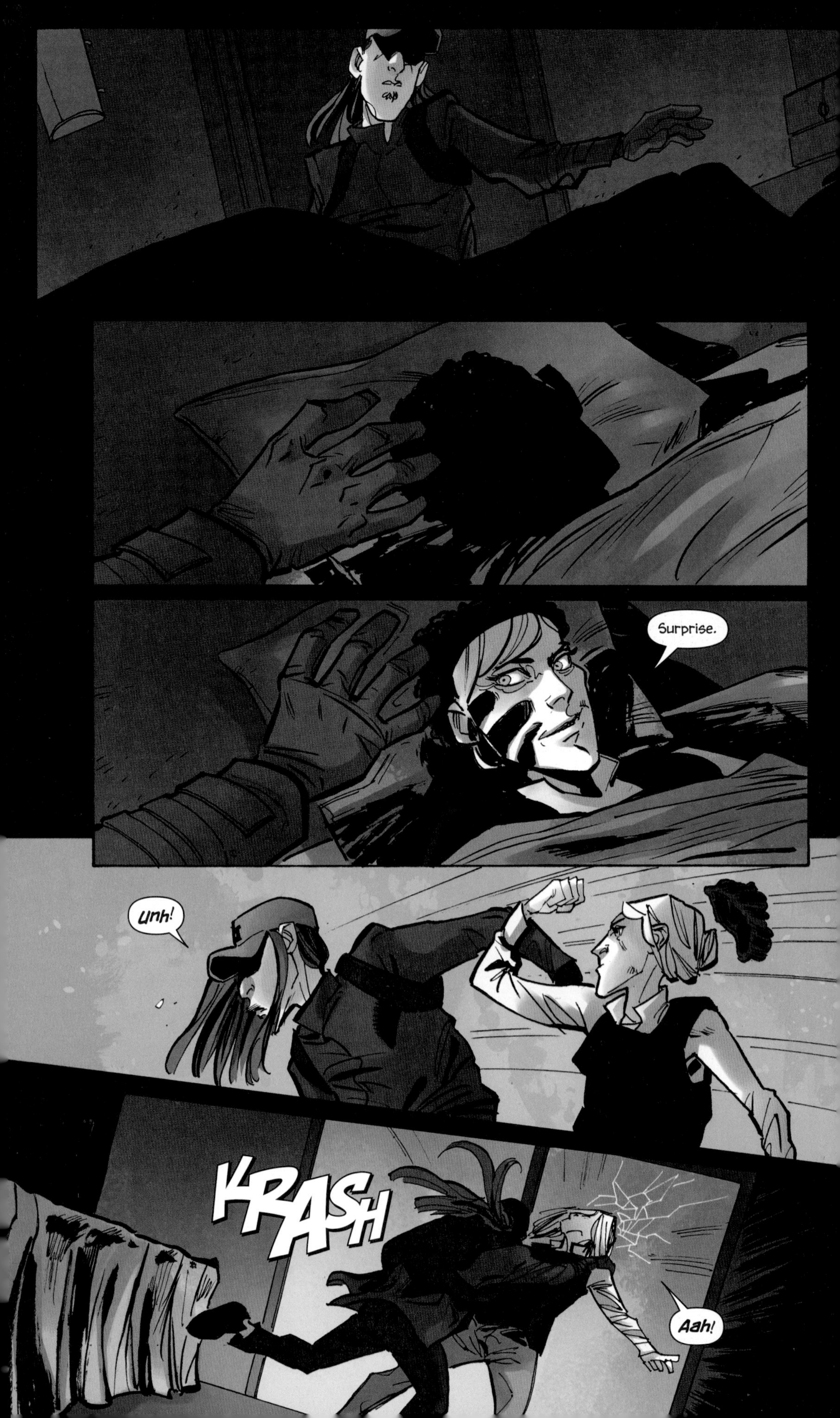
Surprise.
Unh!
KRASH
Aah!

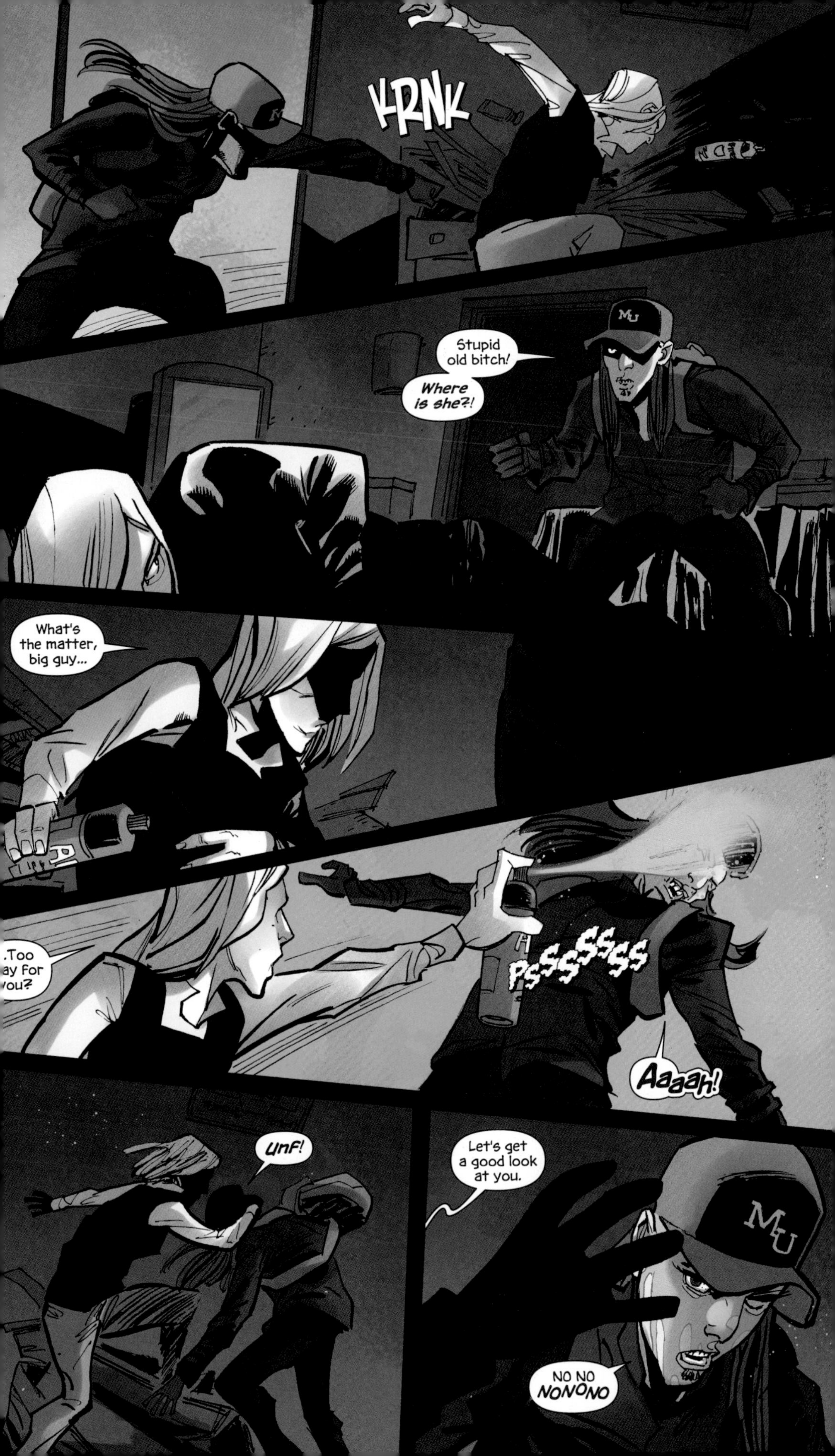
KRNK
Stupid old bitch!
Where is she?!
What's the matter, big guy...
.Too ay for you?
PSSSSSSS
Aaaah!
Unf!
Let's get a good look at you.
NO NO NONONO

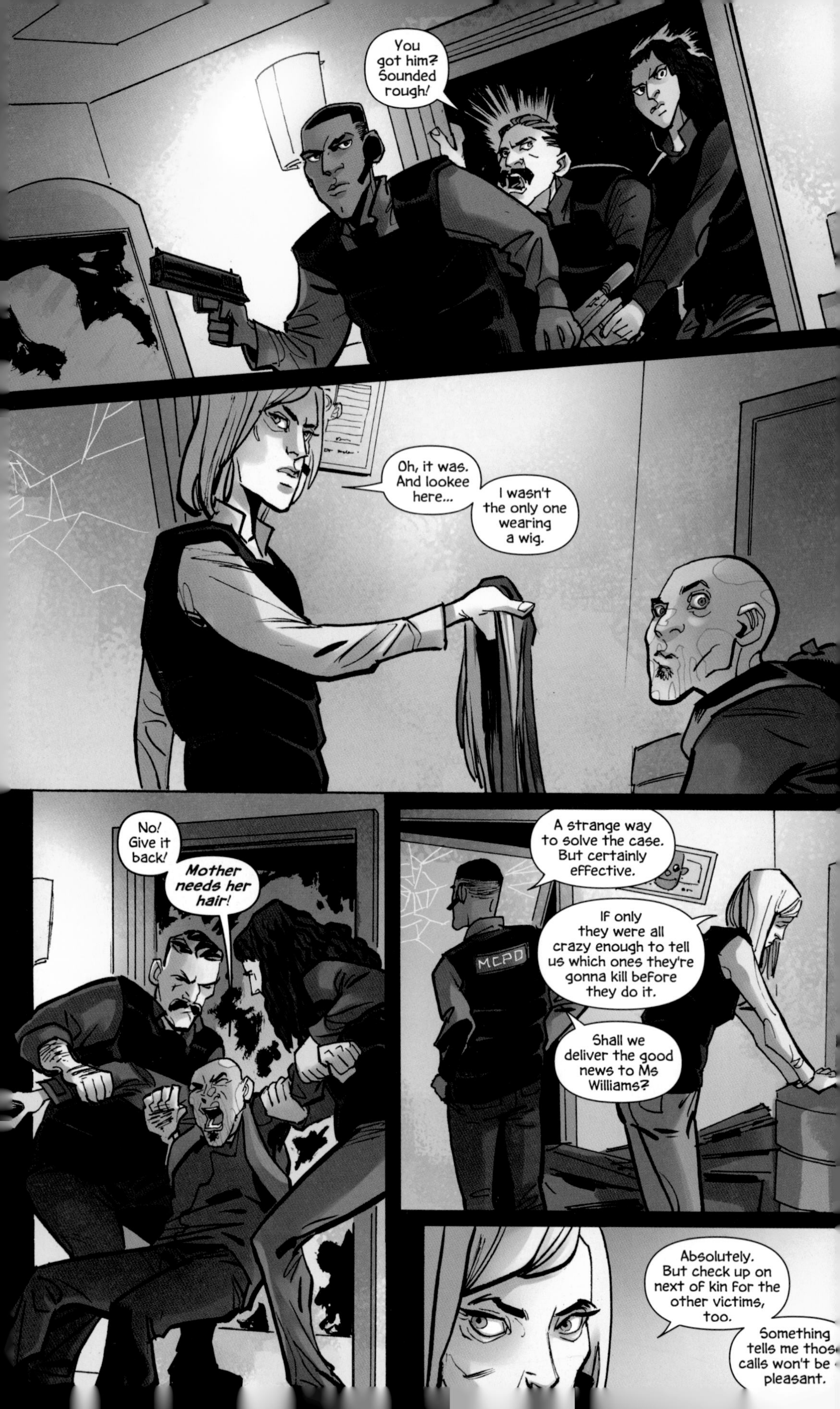
You got him? Sounded rough!
Oh, it was. And lookee here...
I wasn't the only one wearing a wig.
No! Give it back!
Mother needs her hair!
A strange way to solve the case. But certainly effective.
If only they were all crazy enough to tell us which ones they're gonna kill before they do it.
Shall we deliver the good news to Ms Williams?
Absolutely. But check up on next of kin for the other victims, too.
Something tells me those calls won't be pleasant.
MCPD

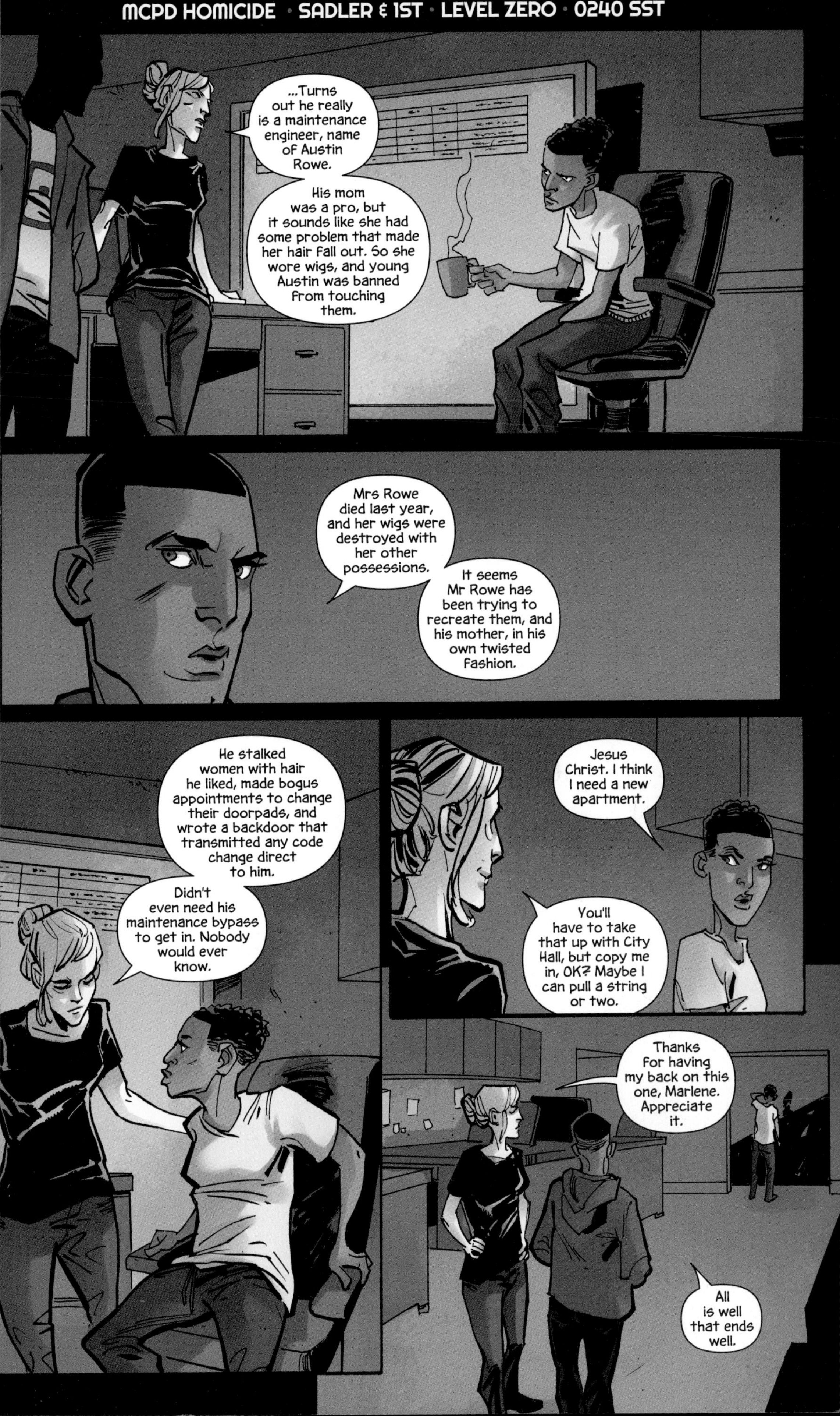
MCPD HOMICIDE · SADLER & 1ST · LEVEL ZERO · 0240 SST
...Turns out he really is a maintenance engineer, name of Austin Rowe.
His mom was a pro, but it sounds like she had some problem that made her hair fall out. So she wore wigs, and young Austin was banned from touching them.
Mrs Rowe died last year, and her wigs were destroyed with her other possessions.
It seems Mr Rowe has been trying to recreate them, and his mother, in his own twisted fashion.
He stalked women with hair he liked, made bogus appointments to change their doorpads, and wrote a backdoor that transmitted any code change direct to him.
Didn't even need his maintenance bypass to get in. Nobody would ever know.
Jesus Christ. I think I need a new apartment.
You'll have to take that up with City Hall, but copy me in, OK? Maybe I can pull a string or two.
Thanks for having my back on this one, Marlene. Appreciate it.
All is well that ends well.

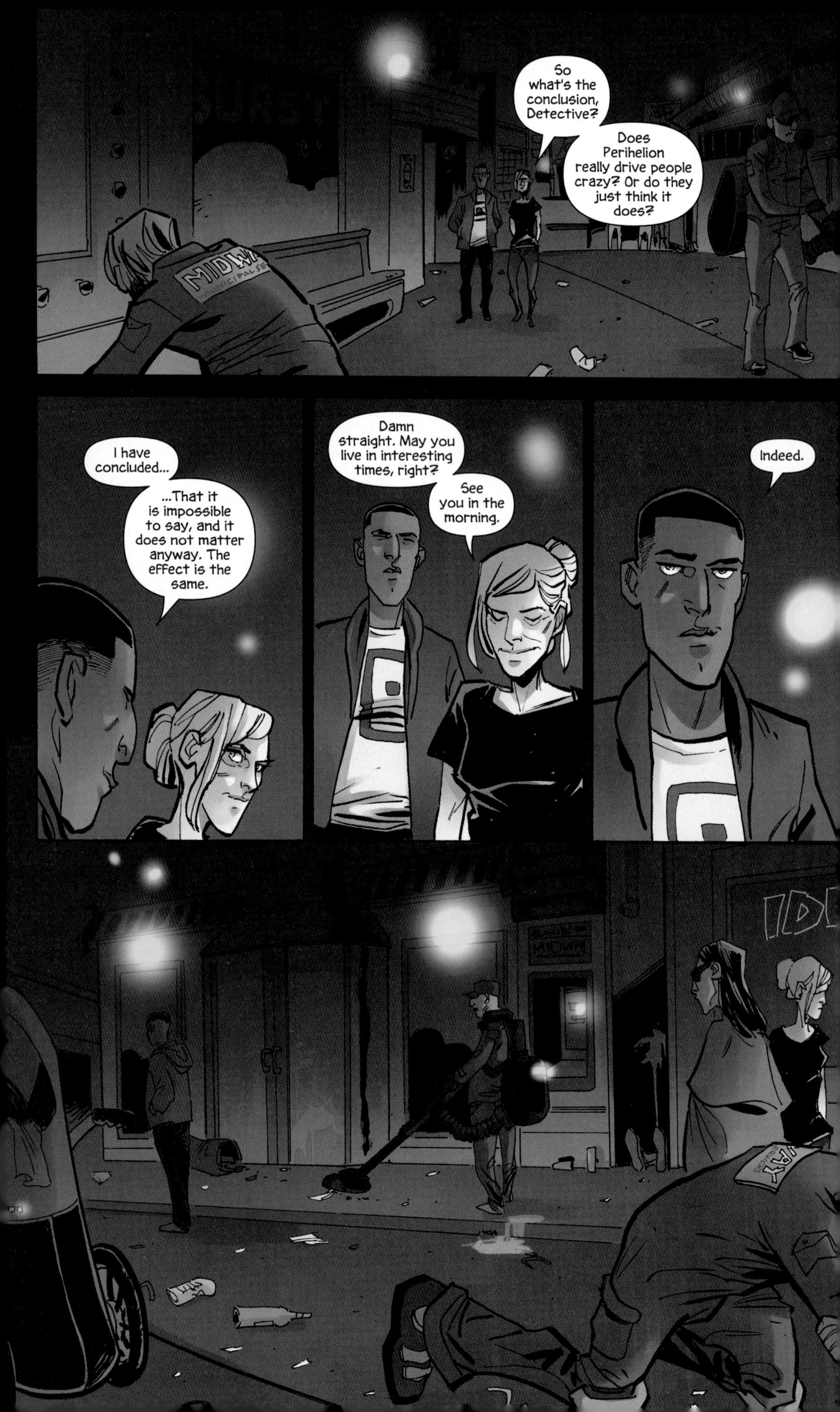
So what's the conclusion, Detective?
Does Perihelion really drive people crazy? Or do they just think it does?
I have concluded...
...That it is impossible to say, and it does not matter anyway. The effect is the same.
Damn straight. May you live in interesting times, right?
See you in the morning.
Indeed.

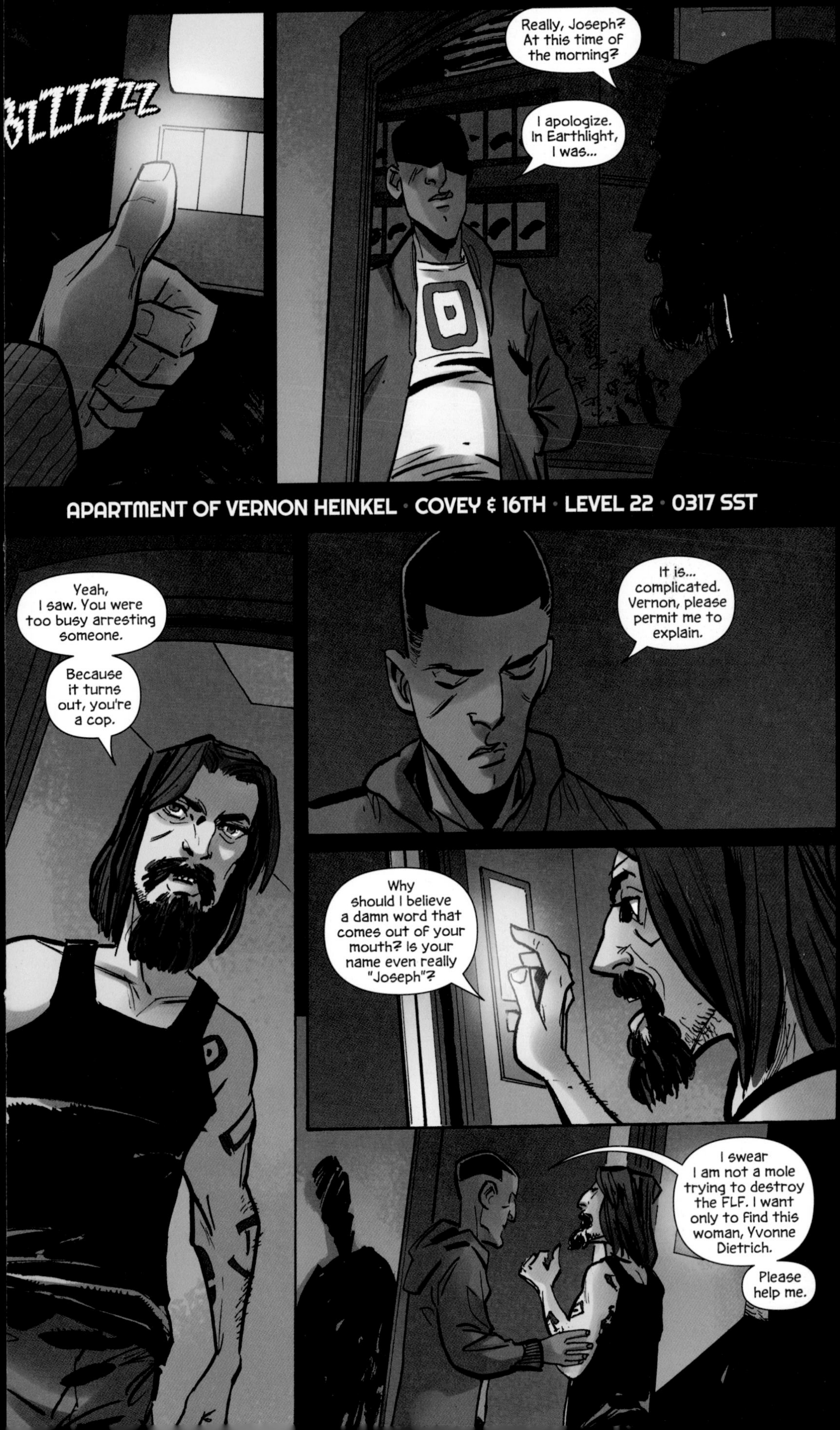
BZZZZzz
Really, Joseph? At this time of the morning?
I apologize. In Earthlight, I was...
APARTMENT OF VERNON HEINKEL • COVEY & 16TH • LEVEL 22 • 0317 SST
Yeah, I saw. You were too busy arresting someone.
Because it turns out, you're a cop.
It is... complicated. Vernon, please permit me to explain.
Why should I believe a damn word that comes out of your mouth? Is your name even really "Joseph"?
I swear I am not a mole trying to destroy the FLF. I want only to find this woman, Yvonne Dietrich.
Please help me.

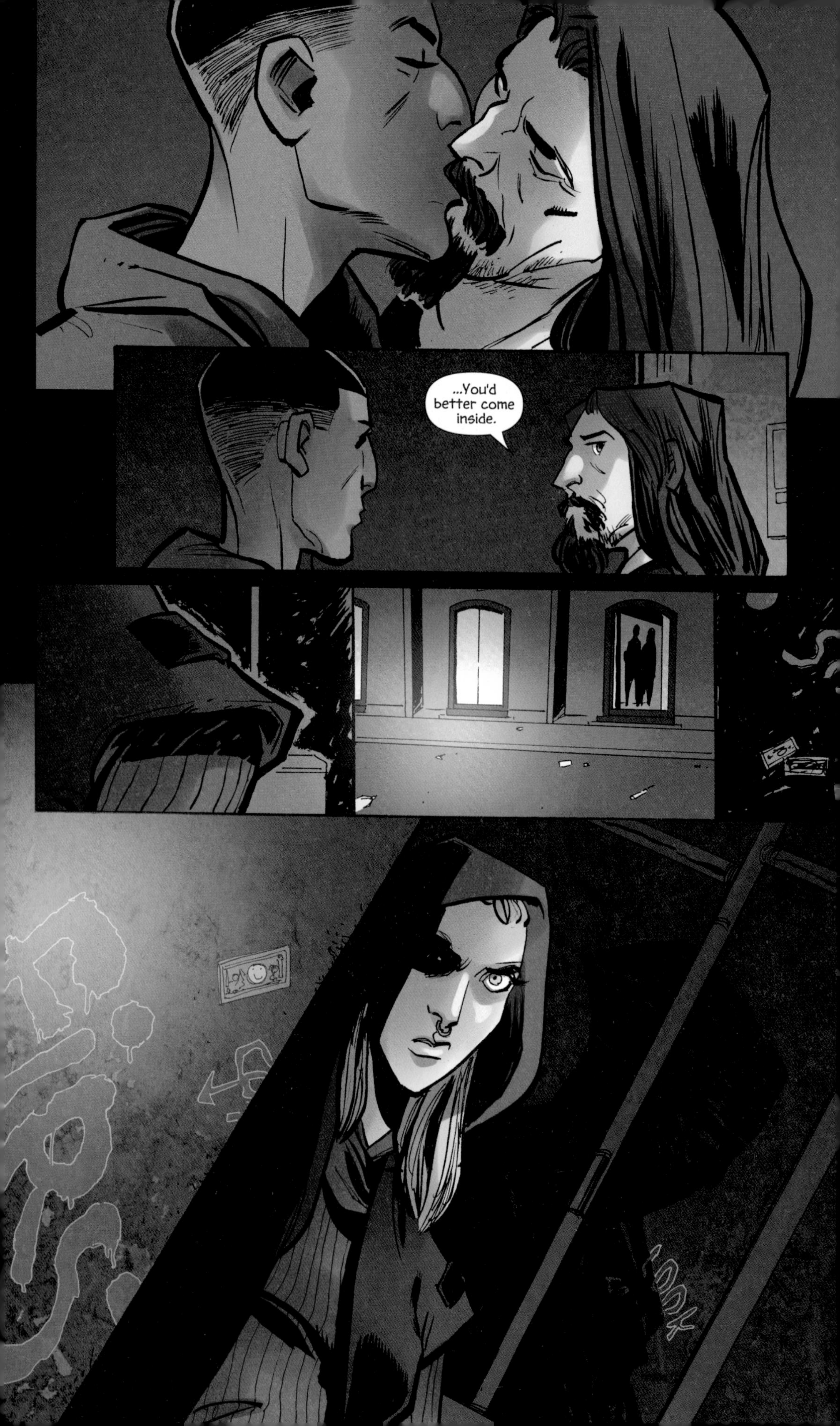
...You'd better come inside.

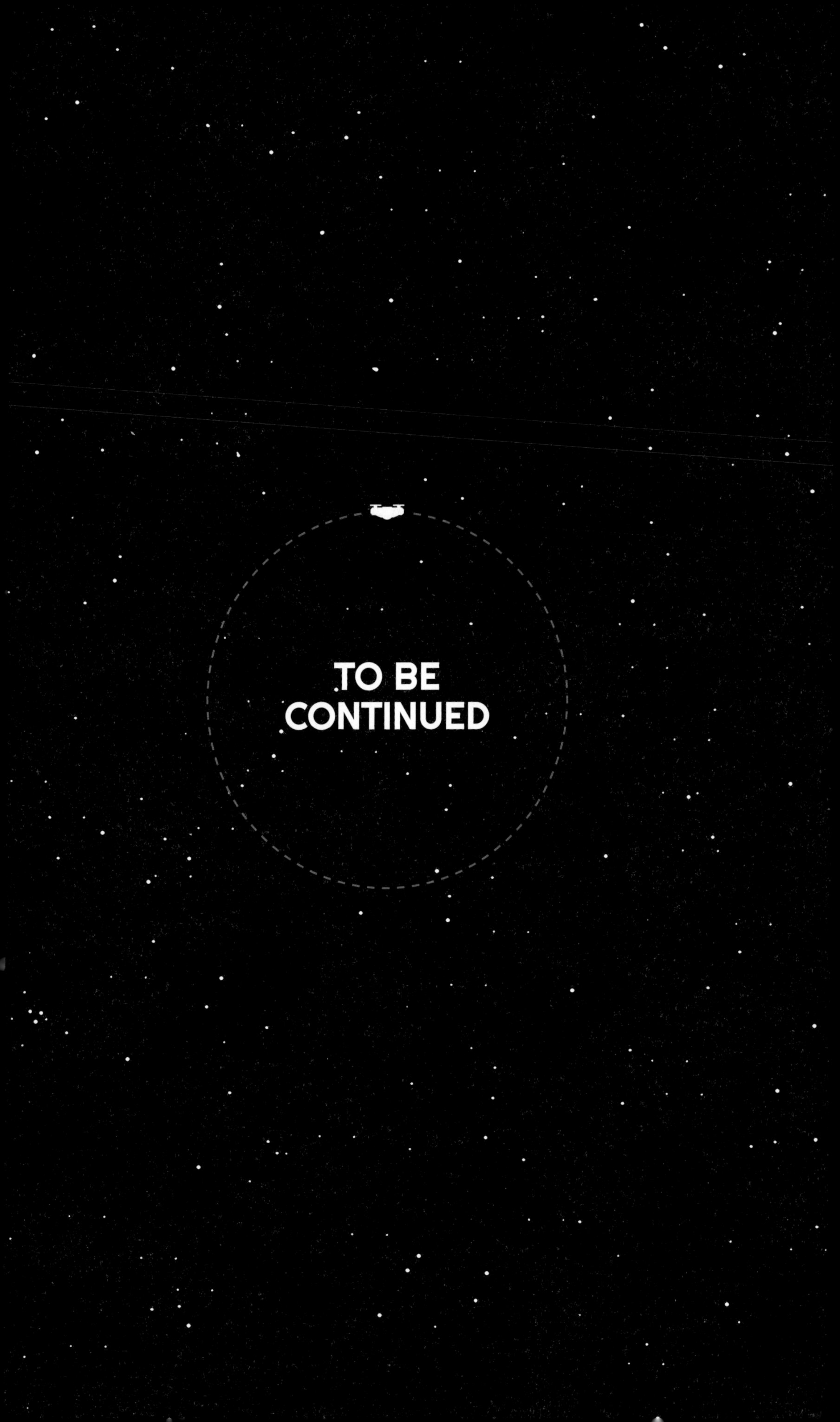
TO BE
CONTINUED

ANTONY JOHNSTON

Antony is an award-winning, *New York Times* bestselling author of graphic novels, videogames, and books, with titles including *Wasteland*, *The Coldest City*, *Codename Baboushka*, *Dead Space*, *Shadow of Mordor*, *ZombiU*, and more. He has adapted books by bestselling novelist Anthony Horowitz, collaborated with comics legend Alan Moore, and reinvented Marvel's flagship character *Wolverine* for manga. His titles have been translated throughout the world, and optioned for film and TV. He lives and works in England.

ANTONYJOHNSTON.COM · @ANTONYJOHNSTON

JUSTIN GREENWOOD

Justin is a Bay Area comic artist best known for his work on creator-owned series like *The Fuse*, *Stumptown*, *Stringers*, *Wasteland*, and *Resurrection*. When not drawing, he can be found running around the East Bay with his wife Melissa and their dual wildlings, tracking down unusual produce and the occasional card game with equal vigor.

JUSTINGREENWOODART.COM · @JKGREENWOOD_ART

SHARI CHANKHAMMA

Shari is an artist living in Thailand. Her own works include *The Sisters' Luck*, *The Clarence Principle*, and *Pavlov's Dream*. Her latest project is *Codename Baboushka*, also written by Antony, and her other colorist work includes *Kill Shakespeare* and *Sheltered*. In her spare time she likes to collect games on Steam with no hope of ever finishing them.

SHARII.COM · @SHARIHES

RYAN FERRIER

Ryan is a Canadian comic book letterer and writer. He has lettered comics for Image, Dark Horse, Oni Press, Black Mask, BOOM! Studios, Monkeybrain, Rosy Press, Ghostface Killah, El Rey Network, and many indie/small press creators. His writing credits include *D4VE*, *Curb Stomp*, *Kennel Block Blues*, *Hot Damn*, and *Sons of Anarchy*.

READCHALLENGER.COM · @RYANWRITER

A TALE FROM

WRITER · IAN MAYOR
ARTIST · MACK CHATER
COLORIST · ABBY RYDER
LETTERER · RYAN FERRIER

*Originally published in one-page instalments as a
back-up story in issues #7-12 of The Fuse.*

IAN MAYOR is the Senior Scriptwriter for Reflections: A Ubisoft Studio, and has written
for *Watch_Dogs*, *Tom Clancy's The Division*, *The Crew*, and *Driver: San Francisco*, as well
as producing narrative content for Lego and Acclaim. He trained in screenwriting and
television production, and has been involved in all aspects of games narrative for 15
years, as well as being an experienced games designer. *Tabloid* is his comics debut.
@IANMAYOR

MACK CHATER is a 20-year veteran of the games industry, and now a full time comic
artist/illustrator. His other work includes a section in Alex de Campi's *Ashes*, a short with
Tom Taylor for IDW's horror anthology *In The Dark*, and *S6X* for 451 Media, with George
Pelecanos (*The Wire*) and Andi Ewington.
MYVELOCITYSINGS.TUMBLR.COM

ABBY RYDER is a children's book illustrator, comic artist, and colorist based in
Manchester, England. She also works in a comic store.
DUMPYLITTLEROBOT.COM

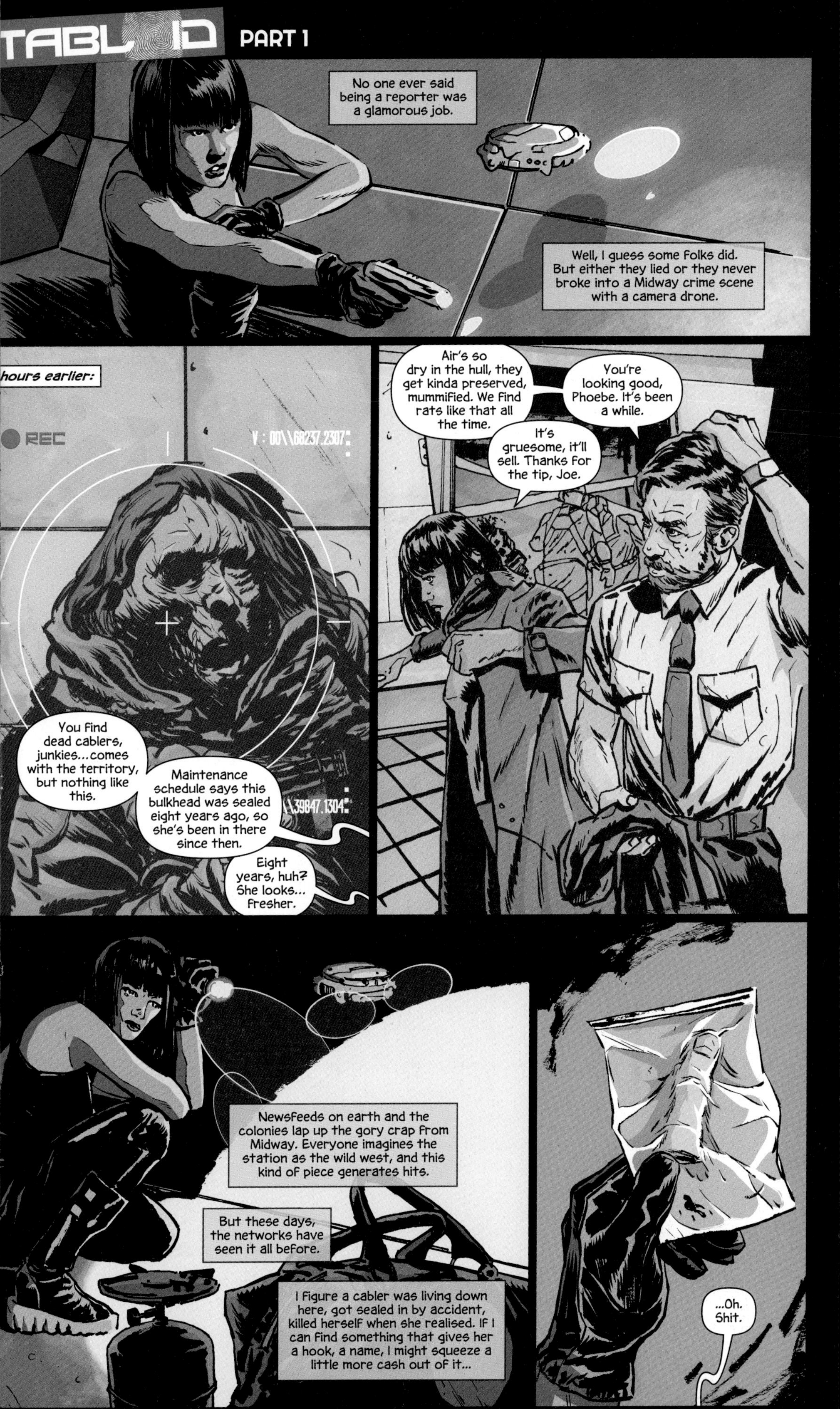

TABLOID PART 1
No one ever said being a reporter was a glamorous job.
Well, I guess some folks did. But either they lied or they never broke into a Midway crime scene with a camera drone.
hours earlier:
REC
V : 00\\68237.2307
You find dead cablers, junkies...comes with the territory, but nothing like this.
Maintenance schedule says this bulkhead was sealed eight years ago, so she's been in there since then.
\\39847.1304
Eight years, huh? She looks... fresher.
Air's so dry in the hull, they get kinda preserved, mummified. We find rats like that all the time.
You're looking good, Phoebe. It's been a while.
It's gruesome, it'll sell. Thanks for the tip, Joe.
Newsfeeds on earth and the colonies lap up the gory crap from Midway. Everyone imagines the station as the wild west, and this kind of piece generates hits.
But these days, the networks have seen it all before.
I figure a cabler was living down here, got sealed in by accident, killed herself when she realised. If I can find something that gives her a hook, a name, I might squeeze a little more cash out of it...
...Oh. Shit.

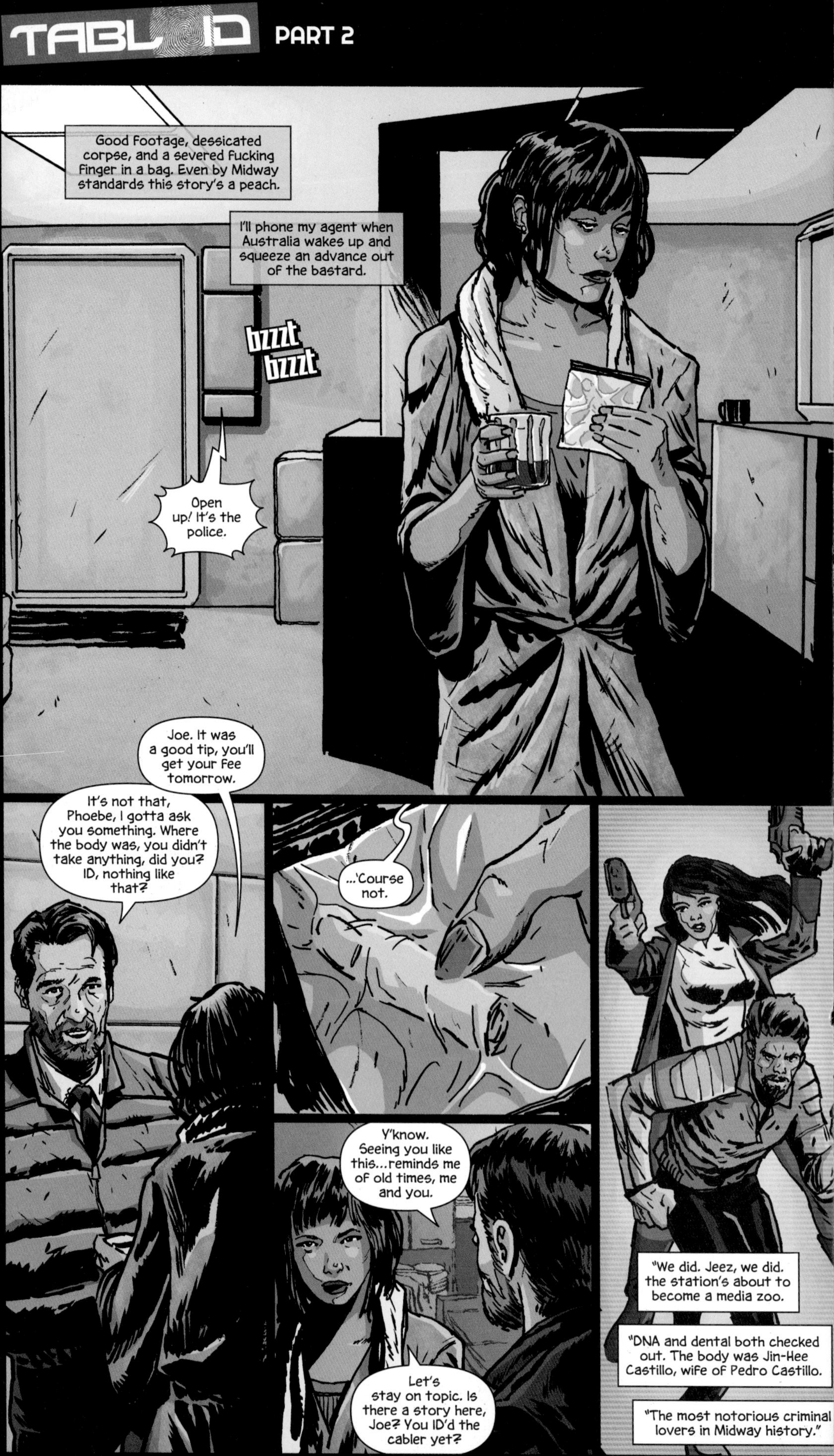
TABLOID PART 2
Good Footage, dessicated corpse, and a severed fucking finger in a bag. Even by Midway standards this story's a peach.
I'll phone my agent when Australia wakes up and squeeze an advance out of the bastard.
bzzzt bzzzt
Open up! It's the police.
Joe. It was a good tip, you'll get your fee tomorrow.
It's not that, Phoebe, I gotta ask you something. Where the body was, you didn't take anything, did you? ID, nothing like that?
...'Course not.
Y'know. Seeing you like this...reminds me of old times, me and you.
Let's stay on topic. Is there a story here, Joe? You ID'd the cabler yet?
"We did. Jeez, we did. the station's about to become a media zoo.
"DNA and dental both checked out. The body was Jin-Hee Castillo, wife of Pedro Castillo.
"The most notorious criminal lovers in Midway history."

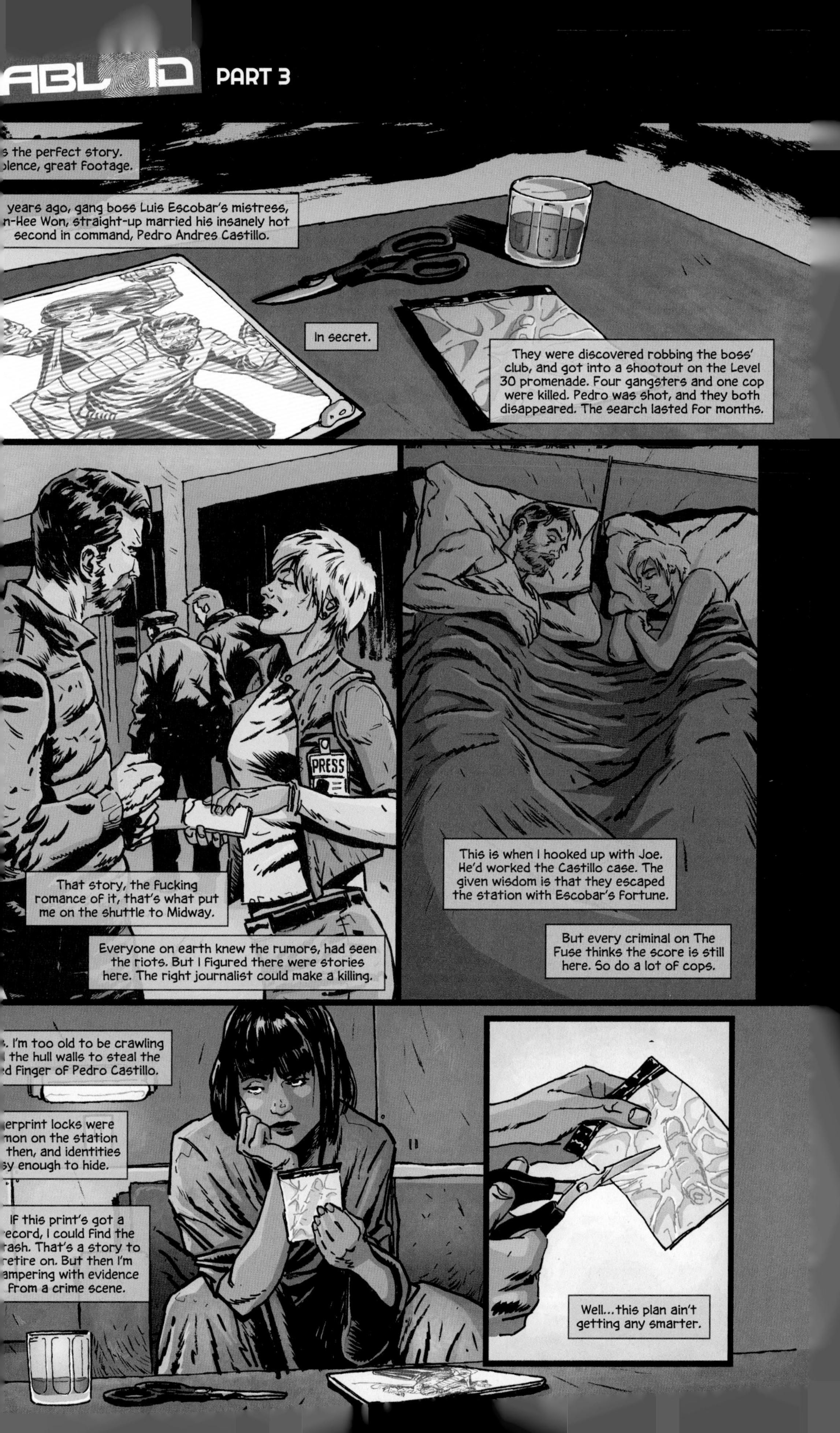

ABL ID PART 3
s the perfect story. plence, great footage.
years ago, gang boss Luis Escobar's mistress, n-Hee Won, straight-up married his insanely hot second in command, Pedro Andres Castillo.
In secret.
They were discovered robbing the boss' club, and got into a shootout on the Level 30 promenade. Four gangsters and one cop were killed. Pedro was shot, and they both disappeared. The search lasted for months.
That story, the fucking romance of it, that's what put me on the shuttle to Midway.
Everyone on earth knew the rumors, had seen the riots. But I figured there were stories here. The right journalist could make a killing.
PRESS
This is when I hooked up with Joe. He'd worked the Castillo case. The given wisdom is that they escaped the station with Escobar's fortune.
But every criminal on The Fuse thinks the score is still here. So do a lot of cops.
. I'm too old to be crawling the hull walls to steal the d finger of Pedro Castillo.
erprint locks were mon on the station then, and identities sy enough to hide.
If this print's got a ecord, I could find the ash. That's a story to retire on. But then I'm ampering with evidence from a crime scene.
Well...this plan ain't getting any smarter.

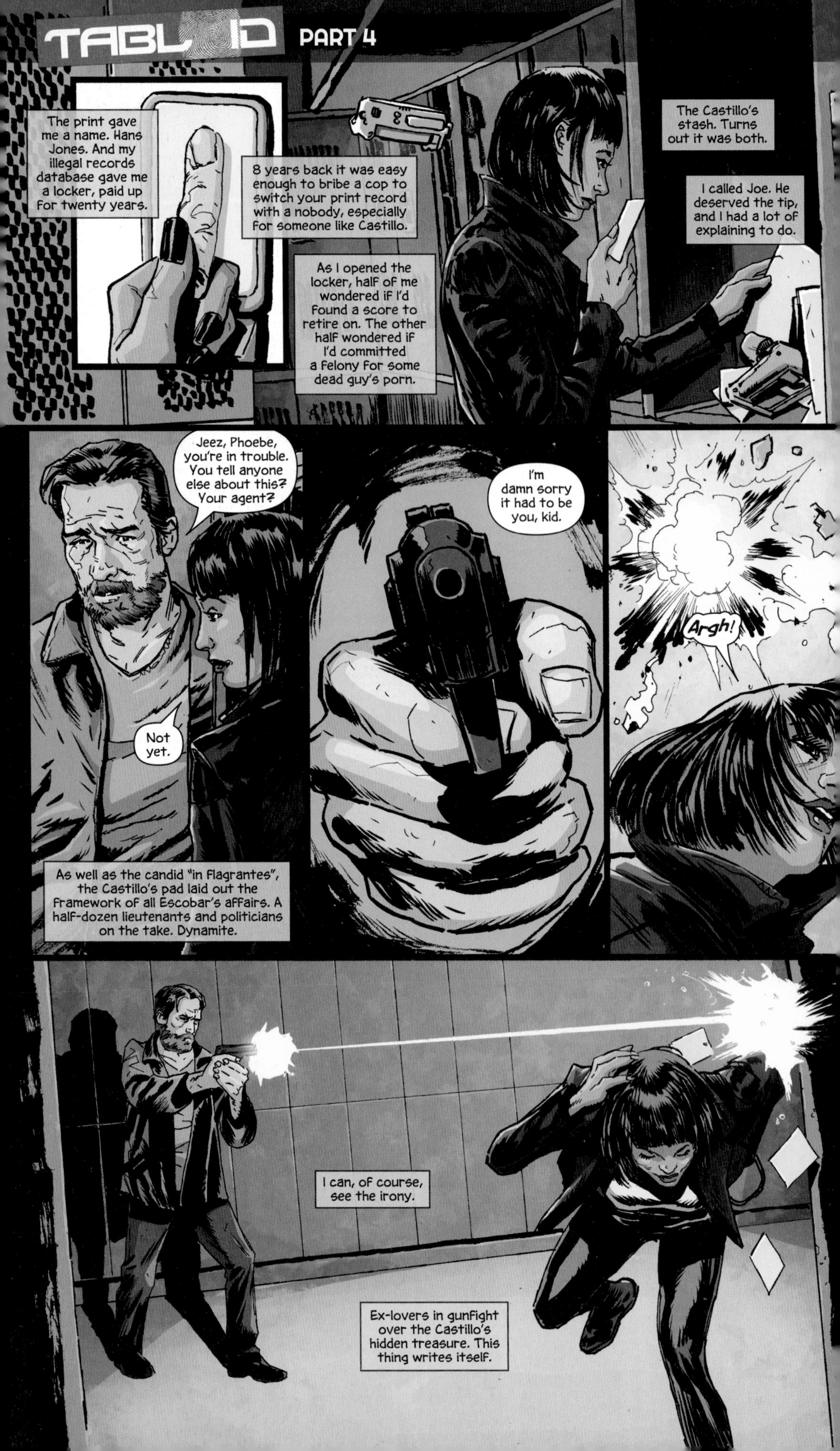
TABLOID PART 4
The print gave me a name. Hans Jones. And my illegal records database gave me a locker, paid up for twenty years.
8 years back it was easy enough to bribe a cop to switch your print record with a nobody, especially for someone like Castillo.
As I opened the locker, half of me wondered if I'd found a score to retire on. The other half wondered if I'd committed a felony for some dead guy's porn.
The Castillo's stash. Turns out it was both.
I called Joe. He deserved the tip, and I had a lot of explaining to do.
Jeez, Phoebe, you're in trouble. You tell anyone else about this? Your agent?
Not yet.
As well as the candid "in Flagrantes", the Castillo's pad laid out the framework of all Escobar's affairs. A half-dozen lieutenants and politicians on the take. Dynamite.
I'm damn sorry it had to be you, kid.
Argh!
I can, of course, see the irony.
Ex-lovers in gunfight over the Castillo's hidden treasure. This thing writes itself.

TABLOID PART 5

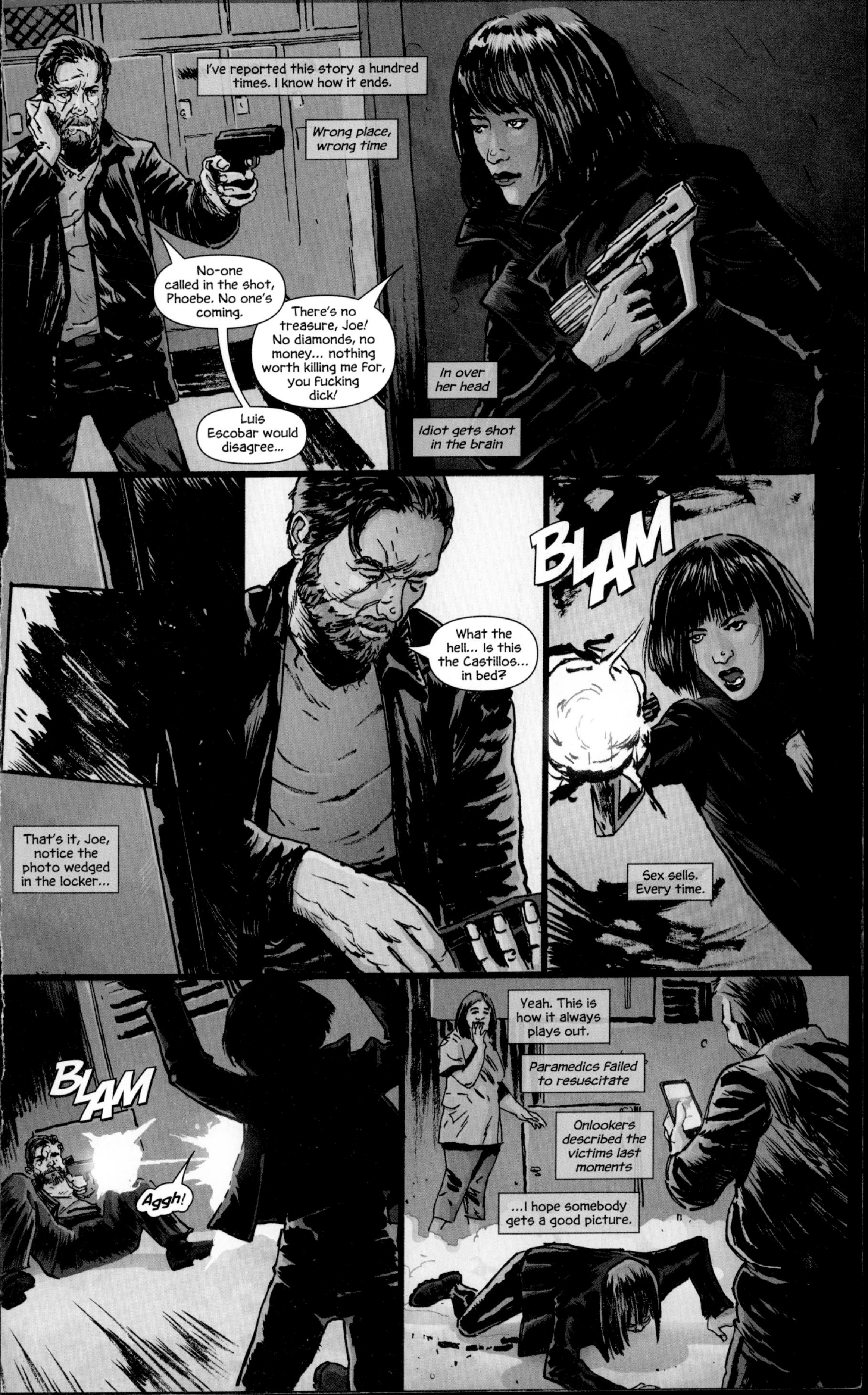

I've reported this story a hundred times. I know how it ends.
Wrong place, wrong time
No-one called in the shot, Phoebe. No one's coming.
There's no treasure, Joe! No diamonds, no money... nothing worth killing me for, you fucking dick!
Luis Escobar would disagree...
In over her head
Idiot gets shot in the brain
What the hell... Is this the Castillos... in bed?
That's it, Joe, notice the photo wedged in the locker...
BLAM
Sex sells. Every time.
BLAM
Aggh!
Yeah. This is how it always plays out.
Paramedics failed to resuscitate
Onlookers described the victims last moments
...I hope somebody gets a good picture.

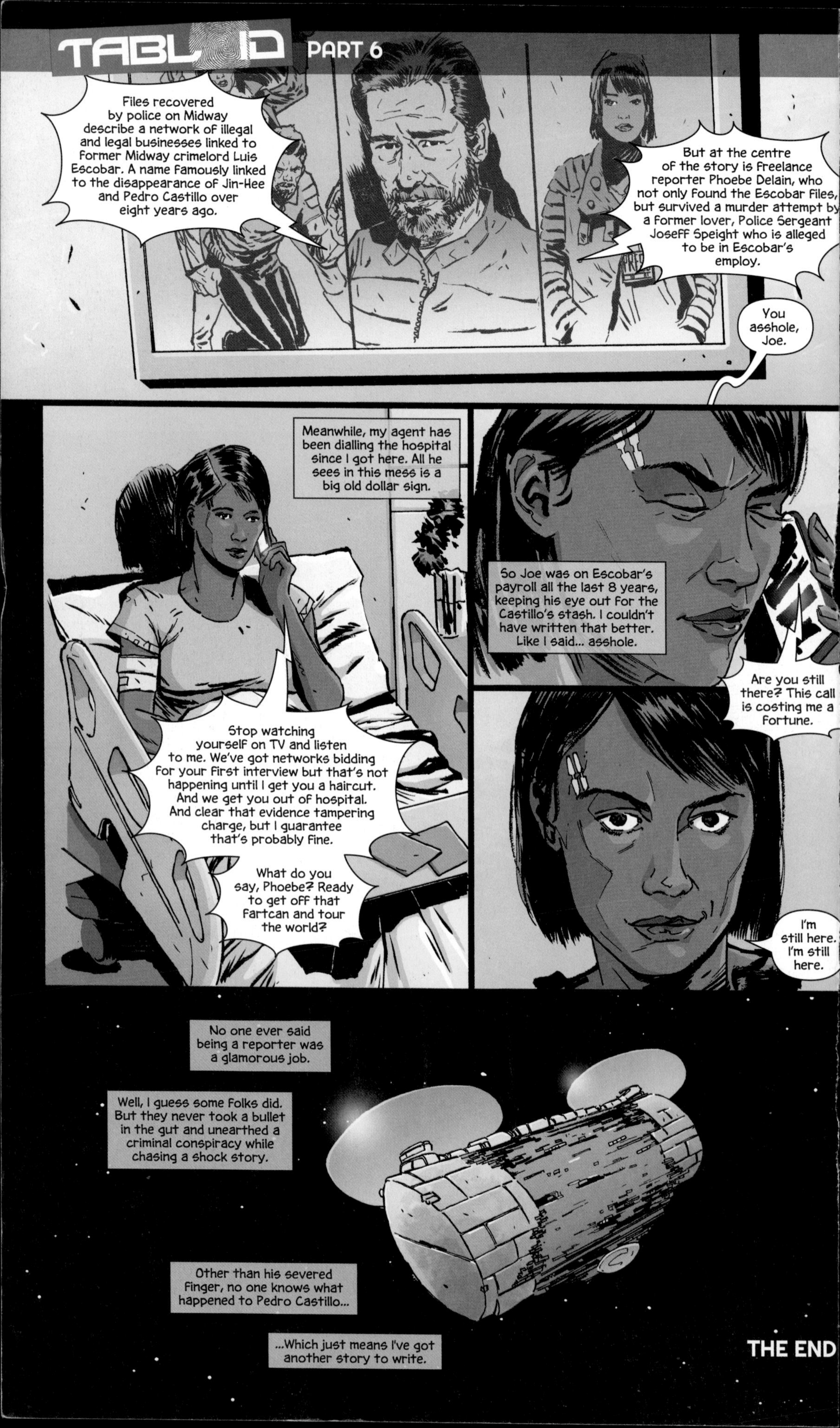
TABLOID PART 6
Files recovered by police on Midway describe a network of illegal and legal businesses linked to former Midway crimelord Luis Escobar. A name famously linked to the disappearance of Jin-Hee and Pedro Castillo over eight years ago.
But at the centre of the story is freelance reporter Phoebe Delain, who not only found the Escobar Files, but survived a murder attempt by a former lover, Police Sergeant Joseff Speight who is alleged to be in Escobar's employ.
You asshole, Joe.
Meanwhile, my agent has been dialling the hospital since I got here. All he sees in this mess is a big old dollar sign.
Stop watching yourself on TV and listen to me. We've got networks bidding for your first interview but that's not happening until I get you a haircut. And we get you out of hospital. And clear that evidence tampering charge, but I guarantee that's probably fine.
What do you say, Phoebe? Ready to get off that fartcan and tour the world?
So Joe was on Escobar's payroll all the last 8 years, keeping his eye out for the Castillo's stash. I couldn't have written that better. Like I said... asshole.
Are you still there? This call is costing me a fortune.
I'm still here. I'm still here.
No one ever said being a reporter was a glamorous job.
Well, I guess some folks did. But they never took a bullet in the gut and unearthed a criminal conspiracy while chasing a shock story.
Other than his severed finger, no one knows what happened to Pedro Castillo...
...Which just means I've got another story to write.
THE END

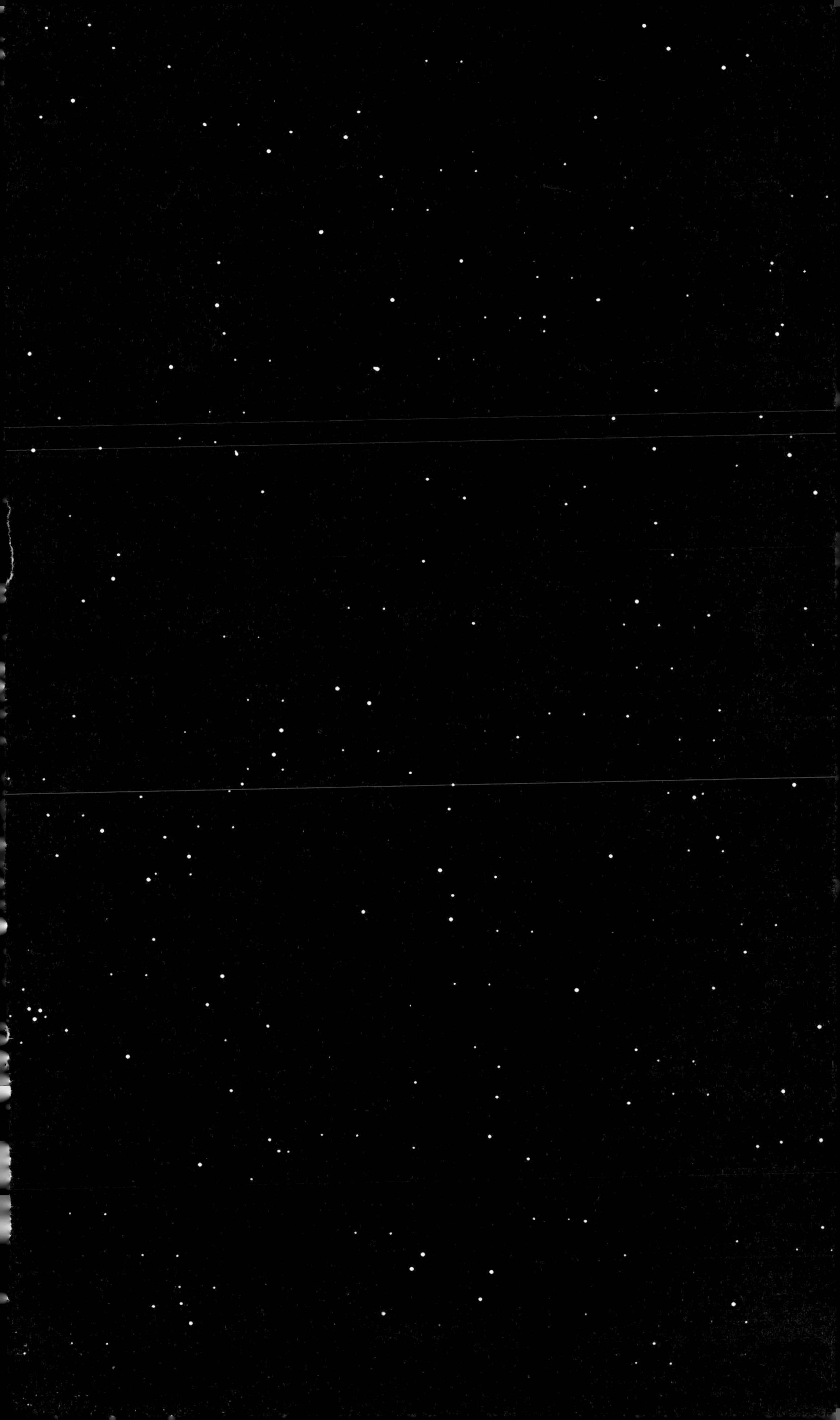